The Shaping of Turkey in the British Imagination, 1776–1923

David S. Katz

The Shaping of Turkey in the British Imagination, 1776–1923

palgrave
macmillan

David S. Katz
Department of History
Tel Aviv University
Tel Aviv, Israel

ISBN 978-3-319-82256-3   ISBN 978-3-319-41060-9   (eBook)
DOI 10.1007/978-3-319-41060-9

Cover illustration: © The Art Archive / Alamy Stock Photo

Printed on acid-free paper

This Palgrave Macmillan imprint is published by Springer Nature
The registered company is Springer International Publishing AG Switzerland

In memory of Kevin Sharpe (1949–2011)

ACKNOWLEDGEMENTS

How does an historian of early modern English religious and intellectual history come to write a book about Turkey? When asked that question over the past few years, I would reply by saying that I wrote three books about Jews in England, followed by three books about Christians in England, so maybe this is the first of a trilogy about Muslims. The real truth is that I finally followed the advice that I give to students who come to study history, already armed with a foreign language that they learned at home. Many of them flee from their kitchen Russian and begin to study, say, French. I tell them to improve their existing skills to a higher level first, instead of ending up with two poorly made tools.

Responding to a remark I made years ago about Turkish history in a faculty seminar, one of my colleagues joked that "David has Turkish from home". By marrying the professor of Ottoman history, I had to learn Turkish, or be condemned to sitting smiling in the corner during our frequent visits to Istanbul and extended trips around Turkey. I soon noticed that little had been written about the shaping of Turkey in the British imagination during the 'long early modern period', between the Renaissance and the moment when Science became a separate discipline at the end of the nineteenth century, a key defining feature of the modern world. More scholarship had been published about British perceptions of Turkey in the sixteenth and seventeenth centuries, but there wasn't much about the later period. What had been published was mostly written without the benefit of Turkish, without which it is impossible to understand the numerous references in the texts to people, places, and culture in the Ottoman Empire. It was clear that there were a number of books about

Turkey that everyone reading English read from Gibbon onwards, and the picture presented therein was largely favourable, despite British classical education and philhellenism.

This research was begun while a Senior Fellow at the Research Center for Anatolian Civilizations of Koç University in Istanbul. I would like to thank Scott Redford (now of SOAS, and then Director of the Center) for his help and friendship during my time there, and the members of staff, especially the then-librarian Duygu Kızılaslan, and the then-administrator Esra Erol. Mr Ömer Koç was kind enough to give me the run of his incredible and extensive private library, a treasure store of unique materials. Many return visits to RCAC enabled me to complete the research and the writing, none of which would have been possible without the daily lunches at Fıccın, the local Ossetian restaurant.

A good portion of the reading was done while Visiting Professor at Boğaziçi University in 2011. The intellectual enthusiasm of my colleagues Edhem Eldem and Selim Deringil was both pleasurable and encouraging. The final draft was completed at the History Department of Princeton University, while a Visiting Fellow during the academic year 2014–2015. For this opportunity I thank Tony Grafton, William C. Jordan, and David Dobkin. The warm welcome that I received from everyone there (and the enormous office, lent by David Bell) formed a pleasant background while rewriting text and checking sources. So many new friends were made that year that I restrain myself from making a list. The Princeton History Department will remain for me a model of scholarship, dedication, and most of all, collegiality, that I hadn't thought really existed in academia.

Parts of the book were test run in public lectures at various institutions: Koç University (Istanbul), the American Research Institute in Turkey (Istanbul), Collège de France—CNRS—EHESS (Paris), University of St Andrews (Scotland), Orient-Institut (Istanbul), Bahçeşehir University (Istanbul), University of Mississippi (Oxford), Princeton University, University of Washington (Seattle), and the British Institute at Ankara. I should like to thank my hosts at these institutions—Tony Greenwood, the late Gilles Veinstein, Rob Bartlett, Chandrika Kaul, Richard Wittmann, Enver Yücel, Nicolas Trépanier, Max Weiss, Reşat Kasaba, and Stephen Mitchell—whose hospitality made each of these occasions both productive and enjoyable.

This book is dedicated to the memory of Kevin Sharpe (1949–2011), whose connection with Turkey stretched no further than Tommy Cooper imitations. Kevin was the hardest working, and hardest playing, historian that I ever met. Our friendship began when we were in our early twenties, grubbing away in the Upper Reading Room of the Bodleian Library in Oxford, both of us pupils of Hugh Trevor-Roper (not yet Lord Dacre). History was a job for Kevin, and like the working-class lad he was, he put in his hours every day, five days a week, resulting in a flood of first-rate, deeply researched books. He made his name with 'revisionist' political history of seventeenth-century England, and by the time he was appointed to his last academic position it was as professor of Renaissance Studies at Queen Mary, University of London. Kevin was a great character, and a warm and loyal friend, greatly missed.

But back to the professor of Ottoman history. My greatest debt is to Professor Amy Singer, *en can dostum ve hayat arkadaşım*, which will come as no surprise to anyone.

CONTENTS

CHAPTER 1

Introduction: 'Bag and Baggage'

On 18 December 1916, President Woodrow Wilson of the United States sent a formal diplomatic communication to all nations involved in the conflict that would become known as World War I, asking for their views on what the future peace might look like. Since the United States was still considering if and when it would enter the war, the answer to Wilson's question was of the highest importance. The Allied governments replied on 11 January 1917: 'The Entente objects of the war are well known', they insisted, and went on to list the points that the 'civilized world knows that they imply'. Among these were 'the enfranchisement of populations subject to the bloody tyranny of the Turks' and 'the expulsion from Europe of the Ottoman Empire, decidedly alien to Western civilization'. The 'civilized world' of the Allies was the European world, based upon cultural foundations that rested on the soil of Rome, and, beneath that, the bedrock of ancient Greece. The Osmanlı Turks, the Ottoman descendants of Ertuğrul and his son, the eponymous Osman Gazi, were invaders who had swept down from somewhere out in central Asia and whose presence had caused nothing but trouble for real Europeans during the past six hundred years. The Ottoman decision to tie their fate to that of the Germans was only further evidence for the Allies of inherent Turkish barbarity. The defeat and surrender of the Ottoman Empire, and the occupation of Istanbul by the Allies in November 1918, offered an opportunity to redraw the map of Europe, partly by restoring some of the shattered glory of Greece and the Byzantine world. With the support

© The Author(s) 2016
D.S. Katz, *The Shaping of Turkey in the British Imagination, 1776–1923*,
DOI 10.1007/978-3-319-41060-9_1

of the British government and the approval of the Allies, Greek forces landed at Smryna on 15 May 1919 and proceeded to gobble up large segments of western Anatolia. Not only was the Ottoman Empire to be expelled from Europe; so too were the progeny of Osman to be driven away from the Mediterranean shores where the 'civilized world' was born. By 9 September 1922, this Allied delusion was in ruins, as the last Greek soldiers clambered on board their ships from the same port city of Smyrna and returned home in utter defeat. A little more than a year later, on 29 October 1923, Mustafa Kemal (Atatürk) (1881–1938) declared the establishment of the Turkish Republic.

When the Allies in 1917 called for 'the expulsion from Europe of the Ottoman Empire' they were simultaneously affirming that Turkey was at that time a part of Europe. When Turkey in 1959 made its first application to become part of the European Economic Community, Ankara was really saying that it wanted to be *readmitted* to Europe. The debate over the renewed inclusion of Turkey in the European Union has been fierce at times, conducted not only at the level of rational discourse, but also against the historical and emotional background of how the Ottoman Empire has been perceived in the West.

This is a book about some of the principal writings that shaped the perception of Turkey for informed readers in Britain, from Edward Gibbon's positing of imperial *Decline and Fall* to the proclamation of the Turkish Republic, illustrating how Turkey has always been a part of the modern British and European experience. Many people have written about Turkey and the Ottoman Empire. But the five celebrated authors discussed here were especially influential in shaping the image of Turkey, helping to balance the philhellenic prejudice that was the natural result of an educational programme based on the study of classical literature. No doubt there were other writers who might have been included, but certainly these five authors have a compelling claim to be among the shapers. These works were enormously influential in that their audience was the political nation, people whose views mattered in Britain, where decisions were taken in that period that had an enormous effect on the modern Near and Middle East. Strictly in terms of political history, the final scenes of the movement for Turkish independence were played out against the background of British strategic and conceptual blundering, so this study is more than an adventure up blind alleys, but rather the re-creation of a vanished mental landscape on which the modern Turkish Republic was built and the present map of Europe was drawn.

This is a study in the history of ideas, specifically the image of Turkey in the mind of what literary critic Stanley Fish called 'the informed or at-home reader' in England who lived (and read) in the long nineteenth century.[1] Fish's work promoted among English speakers the approach of reader-response criticism and reception theory that had developed in Germany following upon the inaugural lecture of Hans Robert Jauss (1921–1997) in April 1967 at the University of Constance, subsequently soon published. Jauss believed in 'a dialogical and at once process-like relationship between work, audience, and new work' and proclaimed 'an aesthetics of reception [*Rezeptionsästhetik*] and influence'. He insisted that we need to be aware of 'the historical sequence of literary works' since we read texts one after another and are therefore inevitably influenced in our reading by what we have read before:

> A corresponding process of the continuous establishing and altering of horizons also determines the relationship of the individual text to the succession of texts that form the genre. The new text evokes for the reader (listener) the horizon of expectations and rules familiar from earlier texts, which are then varied, corrected, altered, or even just reproduced.[2]

To the notion of a 'horizon of expectations' approached by each reader when confronted with a new text, Stanley Fish added the idea of 'interpretive communities' which are 'made up of those who share interpretative strategies not for reading (in the conventional sense) but for writing texts'. Like Jauss, Fish believed that 'these strategies exist prior to the act of reading and therefore determine the shape of what is read rather than, as is usually assumed, the other way around'. The strategies are constantly changing as we approach and crest each succeeding horizon of expectations.[3]

Edward Said argued that, for Europeans and Americans, the Orient was 'a textual universe', that is, 'less a place than a *topos*, a set of references, a congeries of characteristics, that seems to have its origin in a quotation, or a fragment of a text, or a citation from someone's work on the Orient, or some bit of previous imagining, or an amalgam of all these'.[4] No doubt this was true for most people, who had never travelled to Istanbul and parts east and south and formed their views of the (Middle) East from print. But not everything written about that part of the world relied on caricature and borrowed knowledge. There were many writers who went to these places or studied them dispassionately with a mental horizon of expectations which yielded readily when transversed, replaced with images based on what was actually before their eyes. But Said was certainly correct in insisting that ideas (and ideologies) do indeed have real effects, something often forgotten when historians become overwhelmed with material explanations for past events.

Some of the writers discussed here achieved everlasting glory, such as Edward Gibbon (1737–1794). Despite the title, the final three of the six volumes of his *Decline and Fall of the Roman Empire* (1776–1788) actually deal with Asia Minor and the Ottomans and are therefore seldom read or studied today, but they were essential texts at the end of the eighteenth century and long afterwards. Gibbon's tomes were important for another reason: they established in the public mind the trope of 'decline and fall'. Gibbon was not the first to speak in those terms, and there were other writers who chose to contemplate the paradox of great empires declining and falling. But every informed reader in Britain read Gibbon (or at least dipped into his massive volumes) and he set the framework for understanding imperial decay, a model which shaped the way Turkish history was perceived from the late eighteenth century until our own times.

Lord Byron (1788–1824) also provided a prism through which to view Turkey, but in a way that was radically different from Gibbon's. Byron became the symbol of the struggle for Greek independence from the Turks, and his fame was ruthlessly exploited by English philhellenes and Greek exiles in London. As it happened, in reality Byron was not very keen on Greeks. What attracted him to Greece was the romance of the East, and the people in Greece he admired were really Muslim Albanians. When Byron first visited Greece in 1809, the entire area was under Ottoman rule. The Greeks, Turks and Jews in any case were defined primarily by religion rather than by linguistic or ethnic criteria. Like most nineteenth-century British travellers to the East, Byron was quickly disabused of the notion that modern Greeks were anything like the heroes he had read about in classical literature. He and many Victorians were distinctly unhappy until they found more satisfying and authentic experiences when they reached Istanbul.

Benjamin Disraeli (1804–1881) was an ardent admirer of Byron, and made a Grand Tour in the great poet's footsteps over the course of a year in the East (June 1830–July 1831). From London, Disraeli voyaged by way of Gibraltar, Spain and Malta to Albanian Greece (like Byron), visiting many of the same sights. Byron's faithful manservant Giovanni Battista ('Tita') Falcieri (1798–1874), who was with him when he expired at Missolonghi and who brought Byron's body back to England, was even hired by Disraeli and his friends and came with them on their travels. Disraeli, like Byron, had a wonderful time in Istanbul, a life-changing experience. Turkey was followed by Jerusalem and finally Egypt, giving Disraeli a background in reality on which to pin his Oriental fantasies. This Grand Tour to Ottoman lands then became the foundation for Disraeli's life-long pro-Ottoman foreign policy, which also had the effect of introducing racial arguments (including modern antisemitism) into British political discourse.

The key moment in Anglo-Turkish relations came in 1876, the year when W.E. Gladstone (1809–1898) harangued Great Britain in his *Bulgarian Horrors and the Question of the East*. His arch-rival, Disraeli, was merely continuing traditional British foreign policy in supporting an intact Ottoman Empire as a barrier against Russian encroachment and as a more peaceful alternative to carving up the sick man's carcass. But for Disraeli the Ottoman Empire was also part of his beloved East, inhabited by Jewish and Arab Semites whose history and inherent racial characteristics destined them for glory. Although Disraeli managed to set British foreign policy almost until his death, and to look out for Turkey's interests (and Britain's) at the Congress of Berlin (1878), Gladstone returned to office in April 1880 and proceeded to steer the ship of state in an entirely new direction.

Gladstone saw his mission as liberating Christians from the barbarous Ottomans and began the process that evicted Turkey from Europe, no matter how much European land was under Ottoman rule:

Let the Turks now carry away their abuses in the only possible manner, namely by carrying off themselves. Their Zaptiehs and their Mudirs, their Bimbashis and their Yuzbachis, their Kaimakams and their Pashas, one and all, bag and baggage, shall, I hope, clear out from the province they have desolated and profaned. This thorough riddance, this most blessed deliverance, is the only reparation we can make to the memory of those heaps on heaps of dead; to the violated purity alike of matron, of maiden, and of child; to the civilisation which has been affronted and shamed; to the laws of God or, if you like, of Allah; to the moral sense of mankind at large.[5]

The Ottomans, in need of European support, were forced to shift their allegiance to Germany, a change symbolized by the visit to Istanbul of Kaiser Wilhelm II in October 1898. This was a fateful decision that would bear poisoned fruit less than twenty years later in the First World War.

It was in that Great War that John Buchan (1875–1940) had his military moment, serving as an Intelligence Corps major in France. Following on the success of *The Thirty-Nine Steps* (1915), Buchan produced another blockbuster novel called *Greenmantle* (1916), which painted a rather favourable view of Turkey and its people, based in part on Buchan's visit to Istanbul only five years earlier. Together with his popular historical writing, Buchan helped detach Turkey in British public opinion from its alliance with the German enemy in the First World War. At the same time, *Greenmantle* reflects the contemporary British fascination with the Islamic institution of the caliphate, and the fear of a Muslim uprising that might undermine their rule in India. For Buchan, popular literature was the continuation of mobilized history by other means, and he was a pioneer in the use of mass-market non-fiction and historical novels as a subtle means of constructing public opinion.

Buchan was a close personal friend of the celebrated classicist and secret spy-master Gilbert Murray (1866–1957), whose daughter would marry historian Arnold Toynbee (1889–1975). Toynbee made his own year-long Grand Tour to Greece (1911–1912), and like Byron before him, was cured of the English schoolboy fantasy that ancient Greeks lived on in their ancestral homeland. During the Great War, Toynbee, like Buchan, was employed in manufacturing propaganda that would help the British war effort, and in that service he drew up a detailed report, *The Treatment of the Armenians in the Ottoman Empire, 1915–1916*, published in London in 1916. While trying to be as accurate as possible, Toynbee was actually tasked with assembling materials that would help build a case against the Turks. What he left out of his investigation was the puzzle of why Armenians and Turks hated each other.

This was the question on his mind when five years later he took a leave of absence from his post-war position as professor of Byzantine and Modern Greek History and went off to Turkey as the *Manchester Guardian*'s special correspondent covering the Turkish War of Independence. Toynbee spent nearly eight months in Turkey in 1921, not just as a frontline witness to the battles between the Greeks and the Turks, but as an active participant. Indeed, in May and June 1921, he and his wife Rosalind (Murray) personally saved the lives of hundreds of Turkish civilians (including many women and children), huddled on the shore at Yalova on the Sea of Marmara across from Istanbul, trapped by retreating Greek forces who were determined to massacre as many Turks as possible. It was on 17 September 1921 en route to London aboard the *Orient Express* that Toynbee had the idea to write his grand (if misguided) *A Study of History* (1934–1961), twelve volumes inspired by the decline and fall of the Ottoman Empire that he himself had witnessed.

Few people today have a good word for Toynbee, whose *Study* seems now to be a monumental, ramshackle folly of over-systemization. Yet Toynbee's writings helped to reverse the trend that had been put so effectively in place by Gladstone after the death of Disraeli, shifting British public opinion in favour of Turkey once again. Across the Atlantic, Toynbee became America's most celebrated historian in the years immediately after the Second World War, appearing on the cover of *Time* magazine in 1947.

Opinion makers, for better or worse, are those writers who manage to capture the public imagination, satisfying a thirst for general knowledge and a cogent explanation or interpretation of events. Then, as now, academics complained that the circulation of their own works was often limited to a small professional audience. The writings that caught the eye even of the educated public were often parasitic on the books and articles of historians and scholars of every variety. Samuel Huntington's notion of a 'clash of civilizations' infuriated specialists of the Islamic world from Berkeley to Beijing, but this shorthand concept set the agenda for readers of the *New York Review of Books*, the *Times Literary Supplement* and the *New Republic*. The nineteenth century had its own Huntingtons, its own Fukuyamas and *Da Vinci Codes*, books that were in their time inescapable, centrepieces on which was painted a compelling picture for millions of readers.

This book looks carefully at those authors whose writings set the horizon of expectations about Turkey for British readers from 1776 to 1923, and is thus a study in the history of ideas. It is not a social history about publishing and print runs. It is most definitely not a political history of the Ottoman Empire during that period, and is drawn from the British point of view. But it is a great sweep of a story: from Gibbon as standard textbook, through Bryon the pro-Turkish poet, and Disraeli the Romantic novelist of things Eastern, followed by Gladstone's Turkish volte-face, Buchan's *Greenmantle* First World War espionage fantasies, and then *Manchester Guardian* reporter Arnold Toynbee narrating the fight for Turkish independence. Viewed from this long perspective, the contemporary struggle of the Turkish Republic to be given its place in Europe can be seen not only as a demand for readmission, but a recognition that what Gibbon could claim of Constantinople–Istanbul in the late eighteenth century is still valid in the early twenty-first, that it can never 'be despoiled of the incomparable situation which marks her for the metropolis of a great empire; and the genius of the place will ever triumph over the accidents of time and fortune'.[6]

NOTES

1. Stanley E. Fish, 'Interpreting the Variorum', *Critical Inquiry*, 2 (1975–6), 476.
2. Hans Robert Jauss, *Towards an Aesthetic of Reception* (Brighton, 1982), Chap. 1: 'Literary History as a Challenge to Literary Theory'. The title of the original lecture in April 1967 was 'What Is and For What Purpose Does One Study Literary History?' a paraphrase of the title of Friedrich Schiller's inaugural lecture at the University of Jena (1789), substituting the word 'literary' for 'universal'. See also Wolfgang Iser, *Theorie ästhetischer Wirkung* (Munich, 1976), trans. as *The Act of Reading: A Theory of Aesthetic Response* (Baltimore, 1978).
3. Fish, 'Variorum', pp. 465–85, esp. pp. 473–4, 481, 483–4. Cf. idem, 'Literature in the Reader: Affective Stylistics', *New Literary History*, 2 (1970–1), 123–62, esp. pp. 126–7, 140. On p. 145, Fish explains that 'the reader is the informed reader'.
4. Edward Said, *Orientalism* (London, 1978): (Penguin edn, Harmondsworth, 1985), p. 177. Many scholars have applied Said's paradigm to Byron, including Said's nephew Saree Makdisi, *Romantic Imperialism* (Cambridge, 1998), esp. Chap. 6. Among the angrier ones are Mohammed Sharafuddin, *Islam and Romantic Orientalism: Literary Encounters with the Orient* (London, 1994); Seyed Mohammad Marandi, 'The Oriental World of Lord Byron and the Orientalism of Literary Scholars', *Critique*, 15 (2006), 317–37; G.K. Rishmawi, 'The Muslim East in Byron's Don Juan', *Papers on Lang. & Lit.*, 35 (1999), 227–43; Shahin Kuli Khan Khattak, *Islam and the Victorians: Nineteenth-Century Perceptions of Muslim Practices and Beliefs* (London, 2008).
5. W.E. Gladstone, *Bulgarian Horrors and the Question of the East* (London, 1876), p. 31.
6. Edward Gibbon, *The History of the Decline and Fall of the Roman Empire*, ed. David Womersley (Penguin edn, London, 1994), iii. 969–70 (Chap. 68).

CHAPTER 2

Edward Gibbon's Eastern Question (1776–1788)

The first volume of *The Decline and Fall of the Roman Empire* by Edward Gibbon (1737–1794) was published in 1776, concluding with the infamous chapters fifteen and sixteen which were extraordinarily critical of the early Church. It took Gibbon five years to produce his next two volumes, which appeared together in 1781, carrying the story up until the fall of the Roman Empire in the West during the fifth century. Afterwards, the 'majesty of Rome was faintly represented by the princes of Constantinople,' he explained, 'the feeble and imaginary successors of Augustus. Yet they continued to reign over the East, from the Danube to the Nile and Tigris'. While perhaps not as noble as their Western counterparts, Gibbon hoped that 'the history of the *Greek* emperors may still afford a long series of instructive lessons, and interesting revolutions.'[1]

Gibbon was well aware that there really was no such thing as a 'Byzantine Empire'. The inhabitants of Constantinople thought they were living in the Roman Empire. It might be severely truncated and they all spoke Greek rather than Latin, but their emperor was indeed the successor of Augustus in a very real and legally binding sense. The Roman Empire fell only in 1453 when the soldiers of Sultan Mehmed II stormed the walls of Constantinople. A thousand years separated that dramatic moment from the year AD 476, when a really feeble Augustus—Romulus Augustus—was deposed from his perch as puppet Western emperor. Gibbon admitted in the sixth and final volume of *Decline and Fall* that the second and third volumes (1781) 'were composed at a time when I entertained the wish, rather than the hope, of concluding my history'.[2]

© The Author(s) 2016
D.S. Katz, *The Shaping of Turkey in the British Imagination, 1776–1923*,
DOI 10.1007/978-3-319-41060-9_2

What was so terrible about the history of the Eastern 'Byzantine' Empire? At the beginning of 1781, Gibbon lent a copy of the second volume to his lukewarm friend Horace Walpole (1717–1797), who told him to his face that it was boring:

> 'Mr Gibbon, I am sorry *you* should have pitched on so disgusting a subject as the Constantinopolitan history. … though you have written the story as well as it could be written, I fear few will have patience to read it.' He coloured; all his round features squeezed themselves into sharp angles; he screwed up his button-mouth and rapping his snuff-box, said, 'It had never been put together before' … —*so well* he meant to add—but gulped it. … Well from that hour to this I have never seen him, though he used to call once or twice a week; nor has sent me the third volume, as he promised. I well knew his vanity, even about his ridiculous face and person, but thought he had too much sense to avow it so palpably.[3]

Eight years later, after Gibbon had completed all his six volumes and the full blast of Byzantine history was in print, Walpole still insisted that in these 'volumes I was a little confounded by his leaping backwards and forwards, and I could not recollect all those *fainéant* emperors of Constantinople, who come again and again, like the same ships in a moving picture. How he could traverse such acres of ill-written histories, even to collect such a great work, astonishes me.'[4] Some historians of Byzantium today speak apologetically about their subject, insisting that despite what we may have been told, those one thousand years actually included a number of gripping moments and stirring events. But even Gibbon regretted that Byzantine history was 'a tedious and uniform tale of weakness and misery'.[5]

Yet the decline and fall of the Eastern Roman Empire was far from boring. From the narrative point of view, volumes four and five build up to the first paragraph of Chap. 64 in the sixth volume, when Gibbon proclaims that

> From the petty quarrels of a city and her suburbs, from the cowardice and discord of the falling Greeks, I shall now ascend to the victorious Turks; whose domestic slavery was ennobled by martial discipline, religious enthusiasm, and the energy of the national character. The rise and progress of the Ottomans, the present sovereigns of Constantinople, are connected with the most important scenes of modern history: but they are founded on a previous knowledge of the great eruption of the Moguls and Tartars; whose rapid conquests may be compared with the primitive convulsions of nature, which have agitated and altered the surface of the globe. I have long

since asserted my claim to introduce the nations, the immediate or remote authors of the fall of the Roman empire; nor can I refuse myself to those events, which, from their uncommon magnitude, will interest a philosophic mind in the history of blood.[6]

When Gibbon thus asserted his claim to introduce the Turks into the history of the Roman Empire, the pinnacle of Western civilization in the set classical curriculum, he also introduced the Turks into Europe and European history. Everyone read Gibbon. By not shrinking from Ottoman history but, 'conscious of his own imperfections', going forward where the narrative took him, Gibbon set Turkey in Britain for educated at-home readers.[7]

I

Edward Gibbon almost became an Orientalist. Even his youthful attraction to the study of history itself was a fortuitous circumstance, as he himself recalled:

My first introduction to the historic scenes, which have since engaged so many years of my life, must be ascribed to an accident. In the summer of 1751 I accompanied my father on a visit to Mr Hoare's in Wiltshire: but I was less delighted with the beauties of Stourhead than with discovering in the library a common book, the continuation of Echard's *Roman History*, which is indeed executed with more skill and taste than the previous work. To me the reigns of the successors of Constantine were absolutely new; and I was immersed in the passage of the Goths over the Danube when the summons of the dinner-bell reluctantly dragged me from my intellectual feast. This transient glance served rather to irritate than to appease my curiosity, and no sooner was I returned to Bath than I procured the second and third volumes of Howel's *History of the World*, which exhibit the Byzantine period on a larger scale.

From the history of Rome to the Byzantines: the next step was obvious:

Mahomet and his Saracens soon fixed my attention: and some instinct of criticism directed me to the genuine sources. Simon Ockley, an original in every sense, first opened my eyes, and I was led from one book to another till I had ranged round the circle of Oriental history. Before I was sixteen I had exhausted all that could be learned in English of the Arabs and Persians, the Tartars and Turks, and the same ardour urged me to guess at the French of d'Herbelot, and to construe the barbarous Latin of Pocock's Abulpharagius. Such vague and multifarious reading could not teach me

to think, to write or to act; and the only principle that darted a ray of light
into the indigested chaos was an early and rational application to the order
of time and place.

'I arrived at Oxford with a stock of erudition that might have puzzled a
doctor, and a degree of ignorance of which a schoolboy would have been
ashamed.'[8]

Gibbon attempted to expand his knowledge of the East once he
was settled at Magdalen College. 'Since the days of Pocock and Hyde,
Oriental learning has always been the pride of Oxford,' he remembered,
'and I once expressed an inclination to study Arabic.' Gibbon's tutor, Dr
Thomas Waldegrave (1721–1784), 'one of the best of the tribe', with
his 'prudence discouraged this childish fancy'. So Gibbon was left without Arabic, or indeed without any other Oriental language, but when he
came to the Turks among 'the immediate or remote authors of the fall of
the Roman empire', he began with the authors whose erudition had first
impressed him while still a boy.[9]

By his own account, then, Gibbon's first history book was 'the
Continuation of Echard's Roman History', which introduced him to the
successors of Constantine and the Goths. Laurance Echard (1672–1730)
was an astonishingly prolific clergyman historian, whose *History of England*
(1707–18) was the first to be written by a single author.[10] Gibbon chanced
upon Echard's survey of *The Roman History*, first published in 1695, and
then in a bewildering number of editions, ultimately in five volumes.
Echard was responsible only for the first two, and indeed in the preface
to volume three, confesses that the subsequent books were produced 'by
one whose person is unknown to me'.[11] Echard cheerfully revised some of
the text, true to his maxim that 'in matters of Plagiary I shall always study
my Reader's profit before my own Reputation'.[12] Revisions to Echard's
volumes are not in synch, and library sets of *The Roman History* often
comprise varying renditions.

As Gibbon recounts, Echard only succeeded to 'irritate rather than to
appease' his curiosity. To learn more about 'the Byzantine period on a larger
scale', Gibbon's next move was to dive into the book by Restoration historian William Howell (1631/2–1683), *An Institution of General History*,
which first appeared in 1661, covering in straight-forward synchronic fashion the history of the world from Creation to Constantine. Howell died
before he could publish the sequel, but his widow had it printed in 1685,
carrying on the story of humankind to include Christianity East and West.[13]

From the Byzantines, it was a natural progression to 'Mahomet and his Saracens'.[14] He writes that 'some instinct of criticism directed me to the genuine sources'. Gibbon had no Arabic, Persian or Turkish, so his guide had to be Simon Ockley (1679–1720), who became his main authority on Islam. Ockley was both cantankerous and colourful. The antiquarian Thomas Hearne recorded that as for Arabic 'Ockley understands the Language tolerably well, & perhaps better than most now in England, but he is somewhat crazed'.[15] As Sir Thomas Adams's Professor of Arabic at Cambridge, Ockley was also eccentric among his colleagues in actually working on his scholarship. Ockley had begun his Oriental studies with Hebrew, but switched to Arabic and the study of Islam after meeting and reading *The True Nature of Imposture Display'd in the Life of Mahomet*, a biography by Humphrey Prideaux (1648–1724), dean of Norwich, published in 1697.[16] Ockley came to a more sympathetic view of Islam, which was made clear in his study of the first three caliphs (632–656 AD), published in 1708 as *The Conquest of Syria*. The continuation of Ockley's Islamic narrative came ten years later when he published *The History of the Saracens* (1718), which moved events forward to the beginning of the eighth century. By Gibbon's day, both volumes had been published together using the title of the second work for the set (1757). Ockley's volumes were clearly aimed at a wider audience, especially those who, not being 'sufficiently acquainted with that Nation, have entertain'd too mean an Opinion of them, looking upon them as meer Barbarians, which mistaken Notion of theirs, has hinder'd all further Enquiry concerning them'. Islamic history was not the most lucrative of academic disciplines in eighteenth-century England, and when volume two of his history was published, Ockley was in fact being held in Cambridge Castle for debt, so he dated the preface from prison. Friends secured his release, but Ockley died two years later and left his family penniless.[17]

As Gibbon explains, before he was sixteen he had plowed through Echard, Howell and Ockley and moved on to the first encyclopaedic source of Oriental studies, the *Bibliothèque orientale* of Barthélémy d'Herbelot (1625–1695), professor of Syriac at the Collège de France. Gibbon would come to rely on this 'agreeable miscellany', although he could never come to 'digest the alphabetical order' of the work, such an arrangement not yet having become the reference work default.[18] D'Herbelot had the patronage of Louis XIV's extraordinary finance minister Jean-Baptiste Colbert (1619–1683), who was fascinated by things Oriental, sponsored such studies and helped acquire books and manuscripts. By a great stroke of luck, one of these manuscripts in the collection was the *Kashf al-Zanun* of Katip Çelebi (1609–1657), the Ottoman scholar who in that prodigious Arabic work listed and described 14,500 books in alphabetical order. Perhaps d'Herbelot concluded that his own work should be arranged in letter order as a tribute to the great Turkish encyclopaedist of Istanbul. In any case, via the French mediation of d'Herbelot, this important Arabic reference tool, indeed the first encyclopedia of Islam, made its way into the mental library of Edward Gibbon. D'Herbelot, like Humphrey Prideaux, argued that Muhammad was an impostor, but unlike many of his fellow Orientalists, d'Herbelot never bothered to visit the Middle East. His encyclopaedia was published posthumously by his friend Antoine Galland (1646–1715), who had spent fifteen years in Istanbul and other parts East, attached to the French embassy, from 1709 finishing up his career as professor of Arabic at the Collège Royal. It was Galland who made the French translation (1704–17) of *The Thousand and One Nights* upon which the others into various European languages was based, and which introduced that medieval classic into the Western corpus of an imagined Orient. 'The Arabian Nights', Gibbon would say, was 'a faithful and amusing picture of the Oriental world.'[19]

When Gibbon sat down to write the latter part of his great work, he also came to rely on the scholarship of Joseph de Guignes (1721–1800), the author of the *Mémoire historique sur l'origine des Huns et des Turcs* (Paris, 1748), which won him fellowship in the Royal Society of London in 1752. De Guignes published a more comprehensive *Histoire générale des Huns, des Mongoles, des Turcs et des autres Tartares occidentaux* which appeared in three volumes (Paris, 1756–58), during which time he took the chair in Syriac at the Collège de France. Gibbon took from 'the laborious History of the Huns, by M. de Guignes' the claim that the Huns of Roman history were also the Xiongnu (Hsiung-nu) in the annals of the Chinese. Even more outlandishly, de Guignes believed that the Chinese were of Egyptian origin, as shown by the relationship between Chinese ideograms and Egyptian hieroglyphs. 'Without those two learned Frenchmen, I should be blind indeed in the Eastern world', wrote Gibbon of d'Herbelot and de Guignes.[20]

Gibbon complains that in his youthful pursuit of knowledge he was forced 'to construe the barbarous Latin of Pocock's Abulpharagius'. In some ways, it is odd that Gibbon should speak so disrespectfully of the great Edward Pococke (1604–1691), whose combined abilities in Arabic, Hebrew, Syriac and Ethiopic were polished beyond compare by five and a half years at Aleppo as chaplain of the Levant Company.[21] Pococke returned to Oxford in 1636 as first professor of Arabic there, bringing with him from Aleppo an Arabic manuscript of the 'History of the Dynasties' by Gregory Bar Hebraeus (1226–1286), the bishop of the Syriac Orthodox Church known also by his original Arabic name of Abūl-Faraj.[22] The language of the original text is Syriac and it was divided into two parts. What scholars now call the *Chronicon Syriacum* is concerned with political history; the *Chronicon Ecclesiasticum* covers religion, and together they deal with events between Creation and Bar Hebraeus's own time. Gibbon as a young man had tried his hand at the *Chronicon Syriacum*, which had been revised and translated into Arabic by Bar Hebraeus himself, and then turned into allegedly 'barbarous Latin' by Edward Pococke as the *Historia Compendiosa Dynastiarum*.[23]

These were the books on the young Gibbon's bibliography, and towards his goal of exhausting 'all that could be learned in English of the Arabs and Persians, the Tartars and Turks', he soon needed to become acquainted with other works, which he described in a long footnote in *Decline and Fall*.[24] Another source used by Gibbon was the first Turkish history written in English, that by Richard Knolles (late 1540s–1610), brought up to date by Paul Rycaut (1629–1700) and printed in London in 1687. Rycaut had already published his own book as well: *The History of the Present State of the Ottoman Empire* (London, 1665), which Gibbon also used. Rycaut was private secretary to the British ambassador to Istanbul, and later himself British consul at Smyrna.[25]

An important authority was London solicitor George Sale (c.1696–1736). Fully occupied with his profession, Sale never left England, but he became involved with the project going on in offices at the Middle Temple occupied by the Society for Promoting Christian Knowledge (SPCK) to produce a New Testament in Arabic, which indeed was published in 1727. Sale seems to have learned his Arabic from the two Syrian Orthodox Christians who worked there. At any rate, Sale was fascinated by Islam, and in 1734 published his own translation into English of the Koran, which became the basis for nearly all other European translations until the nineteenth century.[26] An earlier English Koran made from a French translation had already appeared in 1649.[27] Even more useful for Sale's Koranic research was a Latin Koran produced in Padua in 1698 by Ludovico Marracci (1612–1700), sporting an attack on Islam, described by Gibbon as 'virulent, but learned'.[28] A third translation used by Gibbon was produced by Claude Étienne Savary (1750–1788), heavily based on

Marracci and Sale, topped up with some colloquial Arabic that he had picked up in Egypt. Savary also included a biography of Muhammad.[29]

After all of this reading of what Gibbon called his 'general vouchers', when he came to reflect on Islam itself, his judgement was far more positive than many of his contemporaries: 'More pure than the system of Zoroaster, more liberal than the law of Moses, the religion of Mahomet might seem less inconsistent with reason, than the creed of mystery and superstition, which, in the seventh century, disgraced the simplicity of the gospel.'[30]

II

Edward Gibbon was undoubtedly intrigued by the history of Muslim lands over the centuries since the beginning of Islam, but he was never a scholar entombed in an ivory tower, despite his prodigious work ethic. Gibbon was very active in the South Hampshire militia, first as a captain (with his father as major), even rising to the rank of lieutenant-colonel, until he resigned his commission in 1770. He made the obligatory Continental Grand Tour (1763–1765) in which he renewed his European acquaintances from the five years spent in Lausanne (1753–1758), having been exiled there by his father after a brief flirtation with Roman Catholicism at Oxford. Gibbon spent more time in Lausanne in later life, and his letters show him to be well aware of what was going on in his own time, not just during the life span of the Roman Empire. Indeed, Gibbon wrote about the Turks against the background of momentous changes that were unfolding in the Ottoman Empire at exactly the same time.

'The stages in the decline of Ottoman power and grandeur are well marked by public, international treaties,' posited Bernard Lewis, 'The first was the treaty of Sitvatorok, signed with Austria in November 1606.'[31] It has long been toxically unfashionable to champion the thesis of Ottoman decline, now viewed as being merely an Orientalist variant of the notorious teleological Whig interpretation of history, reading events backwards from a comfortable end-point. That being said, by Gibbon's day a number of barriers had been breached, a succession of 'firsts' had been established in the relationship between the Ottoman Empire and Europe. Indeed, in the Treaty of Sitvatorok between Austria and the Ottomans, the sultan was compelled for the first time to concede the title of 'emperor' to the Habsburg monarch, now equal in status to the sultan and not merely a Viennese king. Two Russo-Turkish wars later, having failed to conquer Vienna (1683), and losing Hungary in the process (1687), in the Treaty of Karlowitz (26 January 1699) between Turkey and the Holy League (Austria, Russia, Poland and Venice), the Ottomans for the first time were forced to cede Muslim territories long under their rule. There were numerous other symptoms of Turkish distress in the early eighteenth century, but from 1747 to 1768 there was peace between the Ottoman Empire and Christian Europe, the longest conflict hiatus in their history.[32]

That this peace came to an end and ushered in another step in perceived Ottoman decline was no fault of the Turks. The Poles, fed up with Russian domination, rose in 1768 and were quickly put back in their place. Polish rebels fled across the border into Turkey by June, pursued by Cossacks. Encouraged by the French, the Ottoman authorities decided to protect the rebel refugees, and by the beginning of October, the Russians and the Turks were at war once again. Their battles this time ranged over the entire Black Sea area, not only on the Balkan side, but also in the Caucasus to the east. Although the Ottoman army was three times the size of the Russian forces, the British helped the Russians by lending officers to their navy, and there were many disaffected Crimean Tartars who longed to overthrown their Turkish masters.

The Russo-Turkish War in its latest incarnation dragged on for nearly six years. A ceasefire came into effect on 30 May 1772, during which Russia, Prussia, and Austria clubbed together to agree on the First Partition of Poland (5 August 1772), punishing the country that started the chain reaction which had led to the current war. After the ceasefire ended ten months later, the Russians managed to cross the Danube by the summer of 1774, which effectively finished the conflict. The resulting Treaty of Küçük Kaynarca was the product of negotiations between the two empires conducted at that place in Bulgaria.[33] The Russians approved the draft as soon as they received it. Abdülhamid I (r. 1774–1789) dragged out the ratification until January 1775, and reading the text it is easy to see why. Russia made many gains, most especially the right to sail merchant ships on the Black Sea, which was no longer to be a Turkish lake. Many of these merchant ships were manned by Greeks flying the Russian flag, and from 1783 the Russians dared to float warships, although of course the Turks would not let them pass through the Bosphorus and the Dardanelles into the Mediterranean. In the same line of thinking, the Crimea was given independence, for a while at least, until Russia simply annexed the territory in 1783.

The loss of the Crimea was a blow to Turkey, as Muslims who had long been under Ottoman rule were no longer political subjects of the sultan. But the sultan had a religious title as well, caliph, and he remained caliph of the Crimean Tartars, as stipulated in Article 3 of the peace treaty. This too was a 'first'. Since the end of the classical Islamic caliphate during the middle ages, each ruler was seen as caliph in his own territory. Now according to this agreement made with a Christian empire, the caliph was defined as a sort of Muslim pope whose writ ran over the faithful who were not in fact his own subjects. As part of this redefinition, the historical legend was invented at this time that the last of the Abbasid caliphs had transferred the caliphate to Ottoman sultan Selim I when the Turks conquered Cairo in 1517 and put an end to Mamluk rule there, turning over the mantle and sword of Muhammad himself.[34]

Russia also made some religious gains, including the right to put up an Orthodox church in Istanbul, which in fact was never built. More importantly, Russia was given some rather vague rights to make representations on behalf of this theoretical church 'and those who serve it'. One might think that Russia was being given an intentionally imprecise and vague mandate to protect Orthodox Christians in the Ottoman Empire. Certainly that is how Russia came to see it, and having acquired by the same treaty the right to station consuls and vice-consuls in the Ottoman Empire, they often sent Greeks to keep an eye on matters both commercial and spiritual. The Russians were forced to return Moldavia and Wallachia to Turkey, but all of these open-ended benefits, and the annexation of the Crimea nine years later, made the Treaty of Küçük Kaynarca seem like a clear win.

The European powers saw the treaty much as Russia did, and were rather concerned. Russia now had a naval presence on the Black Sea and might be tempted to use it against Istanbul one day. Other countries coveted Black Sea privileges as well. Austria was taking no chances, and in September 1774 occupied Bukovina (on the northern frontier of Moldavia, again Ottoman by this time). By May, the Turks had to make the Austrian gains official. If there were any loose threads, they were tied up on 21 March 1779 in the Convention of Aynalıkavak, a restatement of the treaty agreed four years earlier. The key clarifications recognized the religious ties between the Crimean Tartars and their caliph, but warned the sultan as political ruler of the Ottoman Empire not to use religion as an excuse for meddling in Crimean affairs: that was Russia's job.

It was a task that the Russians performed with great enthusiasm. Maria Theresa of Austria died at the end of November 1780, putting an end to the problematic joint rulership of the Holy Roman Empire which she shared with her son Joseph II (r. 1765/1780–1790). But this enlightened and ambitious monarch, now a few months away from forty years of age, was soon allied with another formidable woman, Catherine the Great (1762–1796) of Russia, who had even more far-reaching plans for disposing of the Ottoman Empire. Her idea was to parcel out the Ottoman territory on the Polish model, with everyone taking a piece. At the same time, enough contiguous territory would be left for a resurrected Byzantine Empire to be ruled from Constantinople by her grandson, the Grand Duke Constantine Pavlovich (1779–1831), who meanwhile was only a few years old.

On 8 January 1784, the Ottoman Empire recognized the Russian annexation of the Crimea, but it was clearly not the end of the struggle in the Black Sea region. Three years later, Catherine and Prince Griporii Potemkin (1739–1791) accompanied Joseph II of Austria down the Dnieper River, admiring the 'Potemkin Villages' that had been hastily erected for their benefit. Russia now demanded the surrender of Ottoman Georgia, and not only did Abdülhamid I refuse, but he wanted the Crimea back as well. The Russo-Turkish War of 1787–1792 was the next in the series.

Yet the Russians were not very popular in British commercial circles at that particular moment. In 1786, Britain failed to renew the commercial treaty with Russia signed twenty years before, and learned with horror that the French had taken their place in the arrangement. This was the first ministry of William Pitt the younger (1759–1806), from 26 December 1783 until 17 March 1801, and British fears were intensified when in 1788 the Russians captured the Ottoman fortress of Ochakov after a long siege. The worry was that the Russians could use the fortress to block Polish trade down the Bug and Dniester rivers to the Black Sea and the Mediterranean, and this was too much power for the rising Russian Empire. Indeed, British concerns about Ochakov, and Pitt's obsession with it down to the end of the war, mark an important shift in British attitudes to Russia and a corresponding warmth towards the Ottoman Empire, constantly having to defend herself against these northern aggressors.

England's task was made somewhat easier in April 1789 by the accession of the new sultan, Selim III (r. 1789–1807), who removed himself to the old Ottoman capital of Edirne facing the Balkans and girded for war. As it happened, the British Parliament was much less enthusiastic about getting involved in a war with Russia, especially now that other Western countries were becoming involved, adding the possibility that events might spin out of control. In July 1789, the Ottoman Empire and Sweden signed a treaty. The following year, Prussia signed treaties with both Turkey and Poland, anxious to forestall Austria from attempting to try to gain something or somewhere from Turkey. Even leaving aside the French Revolution, if possible, the death of Joseph II of Austria on 20 February 1790 made that unlikely, but one could never be sure in the unstable diplomatic alignments of the end of the eighteenth century. Great Britain since 13 August 1788 was part of a Triple Alliance with Prussia and the Dutch Republic, which signaled the end of British diplomatic isolation and a willingness to play a larger role on the international stage.

A claim might be made that in being deeply troubled by Russian aggression on the Black Sea, William Pitt the younger was the first prime minister to grasp that the Middle East was critical for British interests, especially with regard to land routes to India. The final disappearance of Poland in 1795, wiped off the map of Europe by diplomatic negotiation, looked to make Russia even more of a menace. Be that as it may, Pitt's pro-Ottoman foreign policy was very odd, since Britain and the Muscovy Company had legitimate financial interests in keeping the peace with Russia, and few people understood how the gains of a new foreign policy alignment could possibly outweigh the losses.

Pitt's support of the Ottomans and enmity towards the Russians during the latest incarnation of their conflict came to the test in the Ochakov Crisis of March 1791. Ever worried about that fortress remaining in Russian hands, Pitt joined up with Prussia in issuing an ultimatum to Catherine demanding that she return it to the Turks and generally turn back the clock to 1788 when the current hostilities had just begun, or face the avenging wrath of the Triple Alliance. Pitt himself drafted the threatening letter, and the next day (28 March 1791), Parliament met to discuss a naval augmentation that would be required to defend the Ottoman Empire against the Russians. The debate in the House of Commons was intense. One MP noted that the Black Sea is 'a sea in which, of all the seas of the globe, not a single British ship ever appears'.[35] Charles James Fox insisted that Russia was 'a power whom we could neither attack, nor be attacked by; and this was the power against whom we were going to war'.[36] Edmund Burke spoke against Pitt's ultimatum, and saw no reason that Britain should go to war to defend 'Turkish savages'. Pitt replied briefly, citing Montesquieu regarding the importance of the Ottoman Empire in and to Europe, and won the vote, 228:135. The following day, the motion came before the House of Lords, where Viscount Stormont reminded those present that Turkey was 'a state with which we had the least to do of any on the face of the globe' and that Britain's interests lay with supporting Russia. Pitt won anyway, 97:34.

But it was clear that there was very substantial opposition to a pro-Turkish anti-Russian foreign policy if it meant putting British men and ships in harm's way, so Pitt was forced to back down and withdraw his ultimatum, allowing Catherine to keep Ochakov unopposed. It was a humiliation for Pitt, who admitted 'with tears in his eyes, that it was the greatest mortification he had ever experienced'. Foreign Secretary Lord Grenville (1759–1834) was forced to resign. It was subsequent to these events that in 1793 the Ottoman Empire opened its first permanent legation in Europe, with ambassador to England Yusuf Aga Effendi.[37]

III

From 1768 to 1792, then, European foreign affairs were dominated by the spectacle of epic conflict between the rising Russian and the struggling Ottoman empires. British policy towards both of these empires was unstable, and much of the toing and froing was played out in Parliament, one of whose members was Edward Gibbon. Gibbon's letters show him alert to developments in the Russo-Turkish sphere of influence. On 26 May 1772, a bit more than two months before the first partition of Poland, he wrote to his close friend John Baker Holroyd (later first Earl of Sheffield) (1735–1821) expressing his views.[38] After the signing of the Treaty of Küçük Kaynarca, Gibbon wrote again to Holroyd noting that the 'victory of the Russians is real but not decisive'.[39] Gibbon was much taken with General Pyotr Rumyantsev (1725–1796), who had played such an important part in the Russo-Turkish War of 1768–1774, and expressed his admiration in yet another letter to Holroyd:

What think you of the Turks and Russians? Romanzow is a great Man. He wrote an account of his amazing success to [Aleksei Semenovich] Mouskin Pouskin [Russian ambassador to London, 1769–1778] here, and declared his intention of retiring as soon as he had conducted the army home; desiring that Pouskin would send him the best plan he could procure of an English Gentleman's farm. In his answer Pouskin promised to get it, but added that at the same time he should send the Empress *a plan of Blenheim* a handsome Compliment, I think.[40]

As it happened, it was just at this moment that Gibbon began negotiating with publishers Strahan and Cadell regarding a contract for a proposed history of the decline and fall of the Roman Empire. Gibbon had published a number of more modest works before, but now he had found direction and his life's project. As Gibbon himself recalled, these were the years when he was beginning 'to methodize the form, and to collect the substance of my Roman decay, of whose limits and extent I had yet a very inadequate notion.'[41] The press began its work with the manuscript in June 1775. The first volume of *Decline and Fall* appeared on 17 February 1776, which ends with his notorious chapters fifteen and sixteen on the history of the early Christian church.

Alas, Gibbon lost his seat in Parliament in September 1780 when his patron there commanded the voters to transfer their votes to the Opposition, but Gibbon used his unwanted leisure to write volumes two and three, which were published together on 1 March 1781. Gibbon now stood before an academic challenge of a new kind. Having published three well-received volumes of his *History*, Gibbon already knew how to conduct his research, how to organize and master his material, and to produce arresting literary prose. But he was now leaving his intellectual comfort zone and embarking on a journey to the Eastern Roman ('Byzantine') Empire and those who brought about its defeat, the Ottoman Turks. Gibbon began the second half of his project by not writing. He took a year off to read the Greek sources and the great Orientalists of his youth who could open even a small window into the history of the Ottoman Empire.

Thanks to the efforts of Lord North, Gibbon was back in the House of Commons in June 1781, this time as member for Lymington. Nevertheless, he kept on working, and by 1783 he had almost finished the fourth volume, which carries his story up to the seventh century, with incursions up to the seventeenth century to take in the future history of Ethiopian Christianity. Gibbon always felt as much at home in Lausanne as in London, so he made the calculation that rather than being underpaid and pathetic in England he could live rather better abroad. On 1 September 1783, he left London en route to the grand house of a friend in Lausanne and made his home there.

The last three volumes, half of the entire work, were completed while he was in Lausanne, and in his famous recollection, he noted that it 'was on the day or rather the night of the 27th June 1787, between the hours of eleven and twelve, that I wrote the last lines of the last page in a summer-house in my garden'.[42] Gibbon brought the manuscript himself to London in August 1787, and the last three volumes of *Decline and Fall* were published on 8 May 1788, Gibbon's fifty-first birthday. By the end of July 1788, Gibbon was back in Lausanne, but he stayed in touch with British politics. Indeed, he even advised his old friend Lord Sheffield on 18 May 1791 in the aftermath of the Ochakov Crisis: 'Pray do not go to War with Russia: it is very foolish. I am quite angry with Pitt.'[43] Gibbon returned to England in April 1793, dying in London on 16 January 1794 after a botched operation on his scrotum with a dirty scalpel.

IV

'In the midst of these obscure calamities, Europe felt the shock of a revolution, which first revealed to the world the name and nation of the Turks.' Thus Gibbon, in the forty-second chapter of the fourth volume of *Decline and Fall*, which he probably wrote sometime in 1781. Unlike many of the forgotten tribes and peoples who inhabit the latter part of his book, the Turks were destined for great things, and Gibbon brought them on stage with flourishing signs of coming imperial greatness. 'Like Romulus, the founder of that martial people was suckled by a she-wolf, who afterwards made him the father of a numerous progeny' he noted.[44] The Turks, the Ottomans, and Islam in general bulk large by the fifth volume of *Decline and Fall* (Chap. 50), Gibbon having 'pursuing above six hundred years the fleeting Cæsars of Constantinople and Germany'. 'As in this and the following chapter I shall display much Arabic learning,' he warned, but 'I must profess my total ignorance of the Oriental tongues, and my gratitude to the learned interpreters, who have transfused their science into the Latin, French, and English languages. Their collections, versions, and histories, I shall occasionally notice.'[45] Gibbon devotes Chap. 52 to an inquiry in which he seeks to 'unfold the events that rescued our ancestors of Britain, and our neighbours of Gaul from the civil and religious yoke of the Koran; that protected the majesty of Rome, and delayed the servitude of Constantinople'. Gibbon immediately describes the first siege of Constantinople (AD 674–678), after the Battle of Yarmouk (AD 636) that ended Byzantine rule in Syria, and recounts how 'the naval forces of the Saracens passed through the unguarded channel of the Hellespont, which even now, under the feeble and disorderly government of the Turks, is maintained as the natural bulwark of the capital.'

In this same Chap. 52, Gibbon delivers one of his most famous quotations, musing on the fateful Battle of Tours (AD 732) in which Charles

Martel, the grandfather of Charlemagne, arrested the advance of Islam in the West, followed by the final retreat of the Muslims over the Pyrenees (AD 759):

> A victorious line of march had been prolonged above a thousand miles from the rock of Gibraltar to the banks of the Loire; the repetition of an equal space would have carried the Saracens to the confines of Poland and the Highlands of Scotland: the Rhine is not more impassable than the Nile or Euphrates, and the Arabian fleet might have sailed without a naval combat into the mouth of the Thames. Perhaps the interpretation of the Koran would now be taught in the schools of Oxford, and her pulpits might demonstrate to a circumcised people the sanctity and truth of the revelation of Mahomet.[46]

In Chap. 55, Gibbon turns his attention to eastern Europe, beginning with the Bulgarians, closely followed by the Hungarians. '*Magiar* is the national and oriental denomination of the Hungarians;' Gibbon explains, 'but, among the tribes of Scythia, they are distinguished by the Greeks under the proper and peculiar name of *Turks*, as the descendants of that mighty people who had conquered and reigned from China to the Volga.' Not content with the usual discussions about the migrations of nomads, in a footnote Gibbon weighs in on this new thorny philological issue of whether Hungarian is part of the Finnish language family or is related to Turkish. He studied 'several comparative tables' and admits that the 'affinity is indeed striking, but the lists are short, the words are purposely chosen'. On the whole, Gibbon inclined towards a connection between Hungarian and Finnish, but ruled that the question was still obscure.[47]

Gibbon then moved on to the Russians, fully aware that anything he had to say about their contacts with the Turks had great contemporary relevance:

> In a period of one hundred and ninety years, the Russians made four attempts to plunder the treasures of Constantinople: the event was various, but the motive, the means, and the object, were the same in these naval expeditions. The Russian traders had seen the magnificence and tasted the luxury of the city of the Cæsars. A marvellous tale, and a scanty supply, excited the desires of their savage countrymen: they envied the gifts of nature which their climate denied; they coveted the works of art which they were too lazy to imitate and too indigent to purchase: the Varangian princes unfurled the banners of piratical adventure, and their bravest soldiers were

drawn from the nations that dwelt in the northern isles of the ocean. The image of their naval armaments was revived in the last century, in the fleets of the Cosacks, which issued from the Borysthenes, to navigate the same seas for a similar purpose.

Nine centuries separated these invasions from the birth of Christ; the same time span again until Gibbon's own day when the immutable Russian character once again was seen to wreak havoc in the eastern Mediterranean. In many instances, Gibbon points out in a footnote, 'we may read old Russians, for modern Cosacks'.[48]

Gibbon chides the Byzantines for their failure to deal with the Russian problem back in the ninth century: 'Had the Greek emperors been endowed with foresight to discern, and vigour to prevent, perhaps they might have sealed with a maritime force the mouth of the Borysthenes [Dnieper River].' Thanks to their 'indolence', the shores of the Black Sea were exposed to Russian attacks: 'but as long as the capital was respected, the sufferings of a distant province escaped the notice both of the prince and the historian.' Eventually, the storm 'burst on the Bosphorus of Thrace; a streight of fifteen miles, in which the rude vessels of the Russian might have been stopped and destroyed by a more skilful adversary'. The Russians eventually withdrew from the port of Constantinople in the face of bad weather, but they kept trying to take the city, and would continue to do so until the twentieth century.[49] Most importantly, Gibbon warns,

> In our own time, a Russian armament, instead of sailing from the Borysthenes, has circumnavigated the continent of Europe; and the Turkish capital has been threatened by a squadron of strong and lofty ships of war, each of which, with its naval science and thundering artillery, could have sunk or scattered an hundred canoes such as those of their ancestors. Perhaps the present generation may yet behold the accomplishment of the prediction, of a rare prediction, of which the style is unambiguous and the date unquestionable.[50]

These distant events of the ninth and tenth centuries had direct contemporary relevance.

Like modern historians, Gibbon lacks any real evidence regarding the Islamization of the Turks. All he can say is that 'the whole body of the Turkish nation embraced with fervour and sincerity the religion of Mahomet.' Other barbarians followed suit, and Gibbon is impressed that although Christians did indeed make converts in places where they ruled, 'the triumph of the Koran is more pure and meritorious, as it was not assisted by any visible splendour of worship which might allure the Pagans by some resemblance of idolatry'.[51]

The Battle of Manzikert (26 August 1071) was one of the most decisive moments in Byzantine history, and even if scholars have more recently often tried to wean us away from the concept of decisive moments, there is no escaping the importance of what happened on that summer's day in eastern Anatolia.[52] Gibbon, as usual, did not shrink from its dramatic potential, but he remained skeptical of writing its history only from stand-point of Byzantine historians: 'Is it ignorance, or jealousy, or truth?' From any perspective, Gibbon reminded his readers, 'in this fatal day the Asiatic provinces of Rome were irretrievably sacrificed'.[53] The progress of the battle as described by Gibbon little differs from what we read in modern historians, including the famous exchange between the captive Byzantine emperor and the Turkish sultan Alp Arslan, who ultimately agrees to ransom the fallen ruler back to his ungrateful subjects. Romanos IV Diogenes the defeated was soon deposed and blinded, dying of his wounds shortly thereafter. Alp Arslan for his part 'was satisfied with the trophies of his victory, and the spoils of Anatolia, from Antioch to the Black Sea.' Gibbon is also careful to remind his readers that victory at Manzikert did not mean that hordes of Turks came pouring into a defenceless Byzantium, for the 'sultan disdained to pursue the fugitive Greeks; but he meditated the more glorious conquest of Turkestan, the original seat of the house of Seljuk', where he was assassinated in his own royal tent by a rebel captive. 'Alp Arslan possessed the virtues of a Turk and a Musulman', Gibbon judged.[54]

As was often the case, Gibbon reminds the reader that, while undeniably interesting, all of this Turkish history was also directly relevant to the grand theme of his book:

> Since the first conquests of the caliphs, the establishment of the Turks in Anatolia or Asia Minor was the most deplorable loss which the church and empire had sustained. By the propagation of the Moslem faith, Soliman deserved the name of *Gazi*, a holy champion; and his new kingdoms, of the Romans, or of *Roum*, was added to the tables of Oriental geography. It is described as extending from the Euphrates to Constantinople, from the Black Sea to the confines of Syria.

But the importance of this Turkification of Anatolia was much more than merely military, political and geographical. Everything was changing in what had been a huge hinterland of the Eastern Roman Empire, which in a quantitative sense had already fallen, even if Constantinople would remain in Imperial hands for another four hundred years:

> The unity of God, and the mission of Mahomet, were preached in the moschs; the Arabian learning was taught in the schools; the Cadhis judged according to the law of the Koran; the Turkish manners and language prevailed in the cities; and Turkman camps were scattered over the plains and mountains of Anatolia. On the hard conditions of tribute and servitude, the Greek Christians might enjoy the exercise of their religion; but their most holy churches were profaned; their priests and bishops were insulted; they were compelled to suffer the triumph of the *Pagans,* and the apostasy of their brethren; many thousand children were marked by the knife of circumcision; and many thousand captives were devoted to the service or the pleasures of their masters.

But the Turkish threat to the remnant of Rome was clearly perceived on the spot, and Emperor Alexius I Comnenus 'trembled behind the walls of his capital.' Indeed, Gibbon writes, the emperor's 'plaintive epistles were dispersed over Europe, to excite the compassion of the Latins, and to paint the danger, the weakness, and the riches, of the city of Constantine.'[55]

'But the most interesting conquest of the Seljukian Turks, was that of Jerusalem,' Gibbon wrote in amusing understatement, 'which soon became the theatre of nations.' Gibbon gives the dates of Selçuk rule in Jerusalem as 1076–1096: 'After the defeat of the Romans, the tranquillity of the Fatimite caliphs was invaded by the Turks.' As had been the case in Anatolia, a Selçuk beylik grew up in the Holy Land, known as the Artuqids (Artuklu Beyliği) after their eponymous Turkman founder: the 'Oriental Christians and the Latin pilgrims deplored a revolution, which, instead of the regular government and old alliance of the caliphs, imposed on their necks the iron yoke of the strangers of the North.' The Turkish sultan 'had adopted in some degree the arts and manners of Persia; but the body of the Turkish nation, and more especially the pastoral tribes, still breathed the fierceness of the desert'. Tales of indignities suffered by Christians at the hands of the Turks in Jerusalem 'excited the millions of the West to march under the standard of the cross to the relief of the holy land'. The Turks had inadvertently sparked one of the defining moments in history, the Crusades: 'a new spirit had arisen of religious chivalry and papal dominion: a nerve was touched of exquisite feeling; and the sensation vibrated to the heart of Europe.' And with that, Gibbon concluded the fifth and penultimate volume of *Decline and Fall.*[56]

The first six chapters of the sixth volume (Chaps. 58–63) are about the Crusades and their impact on the Byzantine Empire.[57] As we might have expected, Gibbon is sceptical about the entire mission of the Crusades, 'the desperate adventure of possessing or recovering a tomb-stone two thousand miles from their country.'[58] It was certainly true that by 1096, 'the victorious arms of the Turks presented a real and urgent apprehension of these losses. They had subdued in less than thirty years the kingdoms of Asia, as far as Jerusalem and the Hellespont; and the Greek empire tottered on the verge of destruction.' At the same time, an irrational and unjustified fear of Islam in general and Turks in particular took hold of Europe:

> A pernicious tenet has been imputed to the Mahometans, the duty of *extir-pating* all other religions by the sword. This charge of ignorance and bigotry is refuted by the Koran, by the history of the Musulman conquerors, and by their public and legal toleration of the Christian worship. But it cannot be denied, that the Oriental churches are depressed under their iron yoke; that, in peace and war, they assert a divine and indefeasible claim of universal empire; and that, in their orthodox creed, the unbelieving nations are continually threatened with the loss of religion or liberty.

In any case, rational argument had little place in the fanaticism of those years, and 'arguments glance aside from the leaden shield of superstition'.[59] Gibbon declines to write a detailed history of the Crusades, which are important to his story only insofar as they helped to bring about the decline and fall of the Byzantine Empire. 'However splendid it may seem,' Gibbon sighs, 'a regular story of the crusades would exhibit the perpetual return of the same causes and effects; and the frequent attempts for the defence or recovery of the Holy Land, would appear so many faint and unsuccessful copies of the original.'[60]

Having dealt with the Crusades in a general sense, in Chap. 60 Gibbon zeroes in more closely on Constantinople, beginning with the religious crisis of the ninth century that divided Latin Catholics and Greek Orthodox: 'the schism of Constantinople, by alienating her most useful allies and provoking her most dangerous enemies, has precipitated the decline and fall of the Roman empire in the East.' But the focus of Gibbon's attention is the Fourth Crusade of 1204, when the Latins were diverted from their mission of rescuing the Holy Sepulchre to conquer and occupy Constantinople until 1261. 'By the recent invasion', Gibbon observes, 'the Greeks were awakened from a dream of nine centuries; from the vain presumption that the capital of the Roman empire was impregnable to foreign arms'. In the long run, 'the knowledge that Constantinople *might* be taken, was of more avail than the local precautions which that knowledge had inspired for its defence'. Yet the greatest damage was cultural, irreparable:

> Of the writings of antiquity, many that still existed in the twelfth century are now lost. But the pilgrims were not solicitous to save or transport the volumes of an unknown tongue: the perishable substance of paper or parchment can only be preserved by the multiplicity of copies; the literature of the Greeks had almost centered in the metropolis; and, without computing the extent of our loss, we may drop a tear over the libraries that have perished in the triple fire of Constantinople.

In a moment, Gibbon laments, 'the soul of genius evaporated in smoke'.[61]

This lack of intellectual curiosity puzzled Gibbon, who found it hard to understand how the Latin invaders of Constantinople could look upon 'with careless indifference the literature of the Greeks and Arabians'. Although some Eastern knowledge of a minor nature may have rubbed off on merchants, soldiers, and even physicians, nevertheless

> the commerce of the Orientals had not diffused the study and knowledge of their languages in the schools of Europe. If a similar principle of religion repulsed the idiom of the Koran, it should have excited their patience and curiosity to understand the original text of the Gospel; and the same grammar would have unfolded the sense of Plato and the beauties of Homer. Yet in a reign of sixty years the Latins of Constantinople disdained the speech and learning of their subjects; and the manuscripts were the only treasures which the natives might enjoy without rapine or envy. Aristotle was indeed the oracle of the Western universities; but it was a barbarous Aristotle; and, instead of ascending to the fountain-head, his Latin votaries humbly accepted a corrupt and remote version from the Jews and Moors of Andalusia.

The Renaissance of the early thirteenth century that never happened bothered Gibbon, who was not shy about counter-factual speculation.[62]

One of the greatest virtues of this sixth and final volume of *Decline and Fall* is the way in which Gibbon integrates Byzantine and Turkish history, not only in interweaved chapters emphasizing one or the other, but as we have seen, within an individual chapter as need applies. This fraternization has seldom been the case since Gibbon, not only because of the question of languages, but also because of very divergent historiographical traditions, not to mention national and political proclivities. Gibbon's next chapter (64) brings him back to the Muslims, whose history so fascinated him. 'So flexible is the title of my History', he confessed in his memoirs, 'that the final era might be fixed at my own choice; and I long hesitated whether I should be content with the three volumes, the fall of the Western Empire, which fulfilled my first engagement with the public'.[63] The hero of this chapter in any case is Temujin, otherwise known as Genghis Khan (1162?-1227), ruler of the Mongol Empire.

Some of what Gibbon writes is mere polemic:

> But it is the religion of Zingis [Khan] that best deserves our wonder and applause. The Catholic inquisitors of Europe, who defended nonsense by cruelty, might have been confounded by the example of a Barbarian, who anticipated the lessons of philosophy, and established by his laws a system of pure theism and perfect toleration. His first and only article of faith was the existence of one God, the author of all good; who fills by his presence the heavens and earth, which he has created by his power.

In a curious footnote to this excerpt, Gibbon suggests that

> A singular conformity may be found between the religious laws of Zingis Khan and of Mr. Locke (Constitutions of Carolina, in his works, vol. iv. p. 535, 4th edition, 1777).

Gibbon's narrative is dramatic if somewhat overenthusiastic about a subject that is important yet somewhat tangential to his theme. 'I shall not enumerate the crowd of sultans, emirs, and atabeks, whom he trampled into dust', he writes of Genghis Khan:

> Since the invasion of the Arabs in the eighth century, Europe had never been exposed to a similar calamity; and if the disciples of Mahomet would have oppressed her religion and liberty, it might be apprehended that the shepherds of Scythia would extinguish her cities, her arts, and all the institutions of civil society.

Clearly, trends of such magnitude were not without contemporary relevance.[64] 'In this shipwreck of nations, some surprise may be excited by the escape of the Roman empire', Gibbon smiles, pointing out that the Byzantines were indeed pressed 'by the shepherds of Scythia; and had the Tartars undertaken the siege, Constantinople must have yielded to the fate of Pekin, Samarcand, and Bagdad.' But a series of fortuitous circumstances diverted the Tartars from that prize, the Byzantine capital was spared, and 'the decline of the Mogols gave a free scope to the rise and progress of the OTTOMAN EMPIRE.'[65]

Gibbon's account of the origins of the Ottomans is conventional, but for most of his readers it was the first time that they had heard the tale, and the authority and popularity of his volumes ensured that his telling would remain paradigmatic. Although we stand at a distance of more than two centuries from Gibbon, our ability to correct his narrative has hardly changed. As Professor Colin Imber confessed, the 'best thing that a modern historian can do is to admit frankly that the earliest history of the Ottomans is a black hole. Any attempt to fill this hole will result simply in the creation of more fables.'[66] Gibbon writes that after the retreat of the Mongols, there were 'many Turkman hords that had attached themselves to the sultan's fortune.' Among their minor leaders was a certain Ertuğrul, who established his camp in a place called Söğüd, fathered a boy whom we know as Osman, 'and if we describe that pastoral chief as a shepherd and a robber, we must separate from those characters all idea of ignominy and baseness.' Gibbon continues:

> Othman possessed, and perhaps surpassed, the ordinary virtues of a soldier; and the circumstances of time and place were propitious to his independence and success. The Seljukian dynasty was no more; and the distance and decline of the Mogul khans soon enfranchised him from the control of a superior. He was situate on the verge of the Greek empire: the Koran sanctified his *gazi*, or holy war, against the infidels; and their political errors unlocked the passes of mount Olympus, and invited him to descend into the plains of Bithynia.[67]

These followers of Osman would be known to Western history as the Ottomans.

The date of Osman's first invasion into the territory of Nicomedia (modern İzmit) was recorded precisely as 27 July 1299, 'and the singular accuracy of the date seems to disclose some foresight of the rapid and destructive growth of the monster.' Osman's forces grew in strength and in size as 'his hereditary troops were multiplied in each campaign by the accession of captives and volunteers.' Finally, in 1326, the city of Bursa was captured by the Ottomans, not by Osman himself who died just at that moment, but by his son Orhan (r. 1326–1362), who established his capital there as Ottoman sultan. 'From the conquest of Prusa', Gibbon writes, 'we may date the true æra of the Ottoman empire.' Indeed, Osman and five of his successors are buried in Bursa, the first Ottoman capital.[68]

The Byzantine Empire was powerless to stop the relentless expansion of the Ottomans because it was fatally crippled in the middle of the fourteenth century by civil war, which had been the subject of Gibbon's Chap. 63. But he could not resist repeating his outrage that in return for Ottoman military support, John VI Cantacuzenos's daughter 'Theodora was delivered to her barbarous lord' Orhan in 'the marriage of a Christian princess with a sectary of Mahomet'. Later on, as Greek emperor, Cantacuzenos and Orhan had a lovely outing with their families at Üsküdar (Scutari) on the Asian side, and Theodora was allowed to spend some days with her mother in Constantinople. Orhan's support was only temporary, and he switched sides when it was convenient.[69]

Even more fateful in the long run was the introduction of Turks into Europe. Gibbon had already lamented this process in the previous chapter, when in the course of Cantacuzenos's withdrawal to Thrace, 'a body of ten thousand Turks had been detached to the assistance of the empress Anne'. But 'these calamities were of a transient nature' and once it was all over, 'at the conclusion of the civil and foreign wars, Europe was completely evacuated by the Moslems of Asia.' The situation ten years later in 1354 was completely different, for

> It was in his last quarrel with his pupil that Cantacuzene inflicted the deep and deadly wound, which could never be healed by his successors, and which is poorly expiated by his theological dialogues against the prophet Mahomet. Ignorant of their own history, the modern Turks confound their first and their final passage of the Hellespont, and describe the son of Orchan as a nocturnal robber, who, with eighty companions, explores by stratagem a hostile and unknown shore. Soliman, at the head of ten thousand horse, was transported in the vessels, and entertained as the friend, of the Greek emperor. In the civil wars of Romania, he performed some service and perpetrated more mischief; but the Chersonesus was insensibly filled with a Turkish colony; and the Byzantine court solicited in vain the restitution of the fortresses of Thrace.

In the end, 'Gallipoli, the key of the Hellespont, was rebuilt and repeopled' by Turks.[70]

Gibbon keeps up the dramatic tension, focussing on the circle closing in on Constantinople. Orhan's successor was his son Murat I (r. 1362–1389), who had the honour of capturing the city of Adrianople (Edirne), well into the European side (and today at the point where Turkey, Greece and Bulgaria meet):

> By the pale and fainting light of the Byzantine annals, we can discern, that he subdued without resistance the whole province of Romania or Thrace, from the Hellespont to Mount Hæmus, and the verge of the capital; and that Adrianople was chosen for the royal seat of his government and religion in Europe. Constantinople, whose decline is almost coeval with her foundation, had often, in the lapse of a thousand years, been assaulted by the Barbarians of the East and West; but never till this fatal hour had the Greeks been surrounded, both in Asia and Europe, by the arms of the same hostile monarchy. Yet the prudence or generosity of Amurath postponed for a while this easy conquest

The attention of Murat I was directed towards Europe, in the conquest of the Balkans, where many young boys were forcibly drafted into the sultan's army, becoming 'new soldiers' (*yeniçeriler*), 'Janissaries':

> Such was the origin of these haughty troops, the terror of the nations, and sometimes of the sultans themselves. Their valour has declined, their discipline is relaxed, and their tumultuary array is incapable of contending with the order and weapons of modern tactics; but at the time of their institution, they possessed a decisive superiority in war; since a regular body of infantry, in constant exercise and pay, was not maintained by any of the princes of Christendom.[71]

The dissolution of the Janissaries was still long in the future, and it was not until 1826 that Sultan Mahmud II (r. 1808–1839) put an end to a military system that had become archaic and counter-productive. Murat I conquered Sofia in 1385, and four years later (1389) defeated the Christian armies at Kosovo, which signalled the submission of Bulgaria to the Turks for 500 years. As Gibbon tells the story, Murat I met his untimely end when 'a Servian solidier started from the crowd of dead bodies' and the sultan 'was pierced to the belly with a mortal wound.'[72] Others say the Serbian was a deserter who was introduced into the sultan's tent promising information. Either way, like Alp Arslan three centuries before, Murat I perished by assassination at close quarters.

After dispatching Murat I, Gibbon backtracks a bit and recounts the almost operatic story of the joint rebellion in the spring of 1373 of Andronicus IV Palaeologus (the son of Byzantine emperor John V) and Savci Çelebi (the son of Ottoman sultan Murat I) as 'the two youths conspired against the authority and lives of their parents'. Gibbon writes that they 'had formed, at Adrianople, an intimate and guilty friendship'. John V had the previous year formally become the vassal of Murat I, so desperate was he to ward off the Turks, and thus he really had no choice but to follow the sultan's example and to order the customary blinding of his son (and just to be sure, his three-year-old grandson, the future John VII): 'But the operation was so mildly, or so unskilfully, performed, that the one retained the sight of an eye, and the other was afflicted only with the infirmity of squinting.' The further adventures of the son and grandson are recounted by Gibbon, but the spectacle of Byzantine–Ottoman cooperation even in rebellion made for a wonderful story.[73]

Murat I was succeeded by his son Beyazit I, surnamed 'Yıldırım', 'lightning', who 'though he strenuously laboured for the propagation of the law, he invaded, with impartial ambition, the Christian and Mahometan princes of Europe and Asia'.[74] Thankfully, Gibbon recounts,

His progress was checked, not by the miraculous interposition of the apostle, not by a crusade of the Christian powers, but by a long and painful fit of the gout. The disorders of the moral, are sometimes corrected by those of the physical, world; and an acrimonious humour falling on a single fibre of one man, may prevent or suspend the misery of nations.

Nevertheless, the position of the Byzantines was dire:

The Roman world was now contracted to a corner of Thrace, between the Propontis and the Black Sea, about fifty miles in length and thirty in breadth; a space of ground not more extensive than the lesser principalities of Germany or Italy, if the remains of Constantinople had not still represented the wealth and populousness of a kingdom.

Beyazit I besieged Constantinople from 1394 to 1402, but he had other ambitions as well and battles to fight in Bulgaria and the Balkans, including an important victory at Nicopolis (Nikopol) on 25 September 1396, against the combined forces of Philip the Bold of Burgundy and Sigismund of Hungary. Meanwhile, the sultan built the Anadolu Hisarı, a fortress on

the Asian side of the Bosphorus at its most narrow point, in preparation
for the coming invasion:

> Against such an enemy, prayers and resistance were alike unavailing; and the
> savage would have devoured his prey, if, in the fatal moment, he had not
> been overthrown by another savage stronger than himself. By the victory
> of Timour or Tamerlane, the fall of Constantinople was delayed about fifty
> years; and this important, though accidental, service may justly introduce
> the life and character of the Mogul conqueror.

As if his story were not grand enough, Gibbon was now back in central
Asia, whose dim history was so fascinating to him.[75]

'The conquest and monarchy of the world was the first object of the
ambition of TIMOUR', Gibbon writes at the beginning of Chap. 65,
'To live in the memory and esteem of future ages was the second wish
of his magnanimous spirit.' Timur, Timurlenk, Tamerlane (1336–1405),
was the last of the great nomadic leaders, who began with a small territory near Samarkand and by the end of the fourteenth century had built a
confederation of tributary entities that reached to Anatolia as 'he obtained
the merit of the *gazie*, or holy war'. Once he had conquered Sebasteia
(Sivas) and Melitene (Malatya), his territory was beginning to overlap with
areas under Ottoman rule, forcing the local leaders to choose which leader
would get their protection money. It was endlessly repeated local conflict
that compelled Beyazit I to take action against this last invader from central Asia:

> Between two jealous and haughty neighbours, the motives of quarrel will
> seldom be wanting. The Mogul and Ottoman conquests now touched each
> other in the neighbourhood of Erzerum, and the Euphrates; nor had the
> doubtful limit been ascertained by time and treaty. Each of these ambi-
> tious monarchs might accuse his rival of violating his territory; of threaten-
> ing his vassals; and protecting his rebels; and, by the name of rebels, each
> understood the fugitive princes, whose kingdoms he had usurped, and
> whose life or liberty he implacably pursued. The resemblance of character
> was still more dangerous than the opposition of interest; and in their victori-
> ous career, Timour was impatient of an equal, and Bajazet was ignorant of
> a superior.

Nevertheless, there was some mutual respect, Gibbon suggests. After the
conquest and destruction of Sivas in 1400,

As a Musulman he seemed to respect the pious occupation of Bajazet, who was still engaged in the blockade of Constantinople; and after this salutary lesson, the Mogul conqueror checked his pursuit, and turned aside to the invasion of Syria and Egypt. In these transactions, the Ottoman prince, by the Orientals, and even by Timour, is styled the *Kaissar of Roum*, the Cæsar of the Romans: a title which, by a small anticipation, might be given to a monarch who possessed the provinces, and threatened the city, of the successors of Constantine.

But this was merely a reprieve to the fall of the Eastern Roman Empire, and Gibbon's narrative pushes on to its predetermined end.[76]

On 28 July 1402, at Ankara, there took place 'a memorable battle, which has immortalised the glory of Timour and the shame of Bajazet'. The Ottomans defeated, Timur 'dispersed on all sides the ministers of rapine and destruction'. The Battle of Ankara was of particular interest to Gibbon because it gave him the opportunity to indulge in a little set piece of erudition about Turkish history. 'The *iron cage* in which Bajazet was imprisoned by Tamerlane' he concludes in apparent reference to Christopher Marlowe's *Tamburlaine the Great* (1587), 'so long and so often repeated as a moral lesson, is now rejected as a fable by the modern writers, who smile at the vulgar credulity.' Indeed, Beyazit's condition of imprisonment at Akşehir was further embellished over time, and one still reads of how he was fed with scraps and used as Timur's footstool, while his wife Zabina became a servant, indignities which finally drove the proud sultan insane and led him to bash his head against the iron bars until he died, although others claim that the cause of death was poison concealed in a ring which oddly enough he was allowed to keep even in confinement.[77]

Gibbon was unwilling to accept or to reject the story until he had examined the evidence. 'The scepticism of Voltaire', he noted, 'is ready on this, as on every occasion, to reject a popular tale, and to diminish the magnitude of vice and virtue; and on most occasions his incredulity is reasonable.'[78] But on this weighty matter, one needed to keep an open mind as 'the harsh and ignominious treatment of Bajazet is attested by a chain of witnesses, some of whom shall be produced in the order of their time and country'. Produce them he does, bringing together over several pages five important groups of evidence regarding the iron cage. His last collection 'is that of the Turkish annals, which have been consulted or transcribed by Leunclavius, Pocock, and Cantemir' who 'unanimously deplore the captivity of the iron cage', but Gibbon is inclined to explain the Turkish support for the tale by 'national historians, who cannot stigmatize the Tartar without uncovering the shame of their king and country.' At the end of his investigation, Gibbon is willing to concede the iron cage, but 'not as a wanton insult, but as a rigorous precaution' after an escape attempt involving a tunnel under the captive's tent was foiled. Beyazit's death while in Timur's captivity was an accident, but it 'might, without injustice, be ascribed to the severity of Timour':[79]

> Asia was in the hands of Timour; his armies were invincible, his ambition was boundless, and his zeal might aspire to conquer and convert the Christian kingdoms of the West, which already trembled at his name. He touched the utmost verge of the land; but an insuperable, though narrow, sea rolled between the two continents of Europe and Asia; and the lord of so many *tomans*, or myriads, of horse, was not master of a single galley. The two passages of the Bosphorus and Hellespont, of Constantinople and Gallipoli, were possessed, the one by the Christians, the other by the Turks. On this great occasion, they forgot the difference of religion to act with union and firmness in the common cause: the double straits were guarded with ships and fortifications; and they separately withheld the transports, which Timour demanded of either nation, under the pretence of attacking their enemy. At the same time, they soothed his pride with tributary gifts and suppliant embassies, and prudently tempted him to retreat with the honours of victory.

Timur had his heart set on China, thinking that the 'torrents which he had shed of Musulman blood could be expiated only by an equal destruction of the infidels'. Timur stayed a year in Asia Minor after his victory at Ankara and in late 1403 returned to Samarkand 'where he was expected by the angel of death.'[80]

Timur's successors were unable to keep his empire together, and the Ottomans were understandably only too glad to see them go:

> The massy trunk was bent to the ground, but no sooner did the hurricane pass away, than it again rose with fresh vigour and more lively vegetation. When Timour, in every sense, had evacuated Anatolia, he left the cities without a palace, a treasure, or a king. The open country was overspread with hords of shepherds and robbers of Tartar or Turkman origin; the recent conquests of Bajazet were restored to the emirs, one of whom, in base revenge, demolished his sepulchre; and his five sons were eager, by civil discord, to consume the remnant of their patrimony.

After a certain amount of warfare and carnage, Beyazit I's son Mehmed I emerged victorious and ruled as sultan from 1413 to 1421. 'In these conflicts, the wisest Turks, and indeed the body of the nation, were strongly attached to the unity of the empire;' Gibbon explains,

> Their efforts might have instructed the Christian powers; and had they occupied with a confederate fleet, the streights of Gallipoli, the Ottomans, at least in Europe, must have been speedily annihilated. But the schism of the West, and the factions and wars of France and England, diverted the Latins from this generous enterprise: they enjoyed the present respite, without a thought of futurity; and were often tempted by a momentary interest, to serve the common enemy of their religion.

Byzantium's reprieve was not due to any material help from Christendom: Timur 'followed the impulse of ambition; and the deliverance of Constantinople was the accidental consequence.'[81]

Gibbon concludes Chap. 65 with an extraordinary hymn of praise for the Ottomans and for the Turkish nation, made even more outstanding if we always keep in mind that the Ottoman Empire was not only still a powerful force in the late eighteenth century, but very much a topic of discussion in an age which so emphasized national character and moral virtues. Gibbon begins by noting that in 'the establishment and restoration of the Turkish empire, the first merit must doubtless be assigned to the personal qualities of the sultans; since, in human life, the most important scenes will depend on the character of a single actor'. After this clear statement of his philosophy of history, Gibbon notes that 'except in a single instance' the first nine reigns of the Ottoman sultans, a period of two and a half centuries, were occupied 'by a rare series of warlike and active princes'. These Ottoman rulers did not grow up in 'the slothful luxury of the seraglio' but instead these 'heirs of royalty were educated in the council and the field' and entrusted with great responsibility from an early age, which 'must have essentially contributed to the discipline and vigour of the monarchy'. Furthermore, Gibbon explains, the Ottomans can claim no glorious patrimony, neither in the Islamic ancestral hierarchy nor from the Tartar khans, since their supposed familial connection with 'the house of Zingis, appears to be founded in flattery rather than in truth'. But the strong characters of these sultans made all the difference: 'Their origin is obscure; but their sacred and indefeasible right, which no time can erase and no violence can infringe, was soon and unalterably implanted in the minds of their subjects' and 'the Ottoman succession has been confirmed by the practice of five centuries, and is now incorporated with the vital principle of the Turkish nation'. Gibbon continues his analysis by denying a genetic base to 'the spirit and constitution of that nation':

> The primitive subjects of Othman were the four hundred families of wandering Turkmans, who had followed his ancestors from the Oxus to the Sangar; and the plains of Anatolia are still covered with the white and black tents of their rustic brethren. But this original drop was dissolved in the mass of voluntary and vanquished subjects, who, under the name of Turks, are united by the common ties of religion, language, and manners. In the cities, from Erzeroum to Belgrade, that national appellation is common to all the Moslems

Although he had been critical of the Janissaries in Chap. 64, now he is full of admiration for them, which being 'a servile class, an artificial people, was raised by the discipline of education to obey, to conquer, and to command.' Taken from 'the hardy and warlike natives of Europe', the Balkans and Thrace 'became the perpetual seminary of the Turkish army'. Raised even to the ranks of ministers and generals, they were ultimately 'without parents and without heirs, dependent on the hand which had raised them from the dust, and which, on the slightest displeasure, could break in pieces these statues of glass, as they are aptly termed by the Turkish proverb.' In an eerie precursor of Jacob Burckhardt's famous passage about Renaissance individualism, Gibbon emphasizes that 'the *man*, naked and alone, was reduced to the standard of his personal merit'. The Janissaries, for all that they had become by Gibbon's day, an impediment to a better Turkish military, in the context of the fifteenth century, he believed, they compared quite favourably against the ignorance and vices 'which so long contaminated the armies of Europe'.[82]

'In the four last centuries of the Greek emperors, their friendly or hostile aspect towards the pope and the Latins, may be observed as the thermometer of their prosperity or distress; as the scale of the rise and fall of the Barbarian dynasties.'[83] Gibbon thus begins Chap. 66, returning to the Byzantines. In quite understandable panic over the siege of Constantinople by Beyazit I, and still unaware that Timur and the Mongols were on their way from Central Asia and would soon foil Turkish military plans, Manuel II made a very long pilgrimage to Europe (December 1399–June 1403). He visited Venice, Padua and Milan, moving on to Paris, where he lived in the Louvre for eighteen months. Next stop was London, where he visited Henry IV. Manuel II also toured the Holy Roman Empire, met with the queen of Denmark, and did not neglect Aragon. While Manuel II trolled the West in the vain hope of obtaining substantial military assistance against the Turks, his nephew John [VII] (d. 1408) was left in charge, negotiating a treaty with one of the Ottoman pretenders during their own civil war. Manuel II died in 1425, and his son John VIII Palaeologus (r. 1425–1448) carried on with the same strategy, attending the Council of Ferrara-Florence (1438–1439), even taking along the Patriarch Joseph II, who died in Florence in 1439 and is buried there. Two celebrated Greek scholars also attended: George Scholarius Gennadius (c.1400–1473), who would become the first patriarch after the Turkish conquest; and George Gemistus Plethon (c.1355–1452), in whose honour Cosimo de' Medici founded a Platonic Academy. Finally, on 6 July 1439, in the cathedral of Florence, the Orthodox representatives conceded papal primacy and fudged a large bit over the *filioque* dispute that had become the symbol of the schism between East and West.

The importance and relevance of the Ottoman siege of Constantinople from the beginning of the fifteenth century on the development and expansion of the Renaissance is not always given sufficient weight in our conventional narrative. Under the influence of Jacob Burckhardt's paradigmatic study of *The Civilization of the Renaissance in Italy* (1860), we tend to begin with the political fragmentation of late medieval Italy, and the resulting desire of its illegitimate leaders to enhance their standing in the eyes of the public by employing another group of self-made individuals, the artists and scholars, to produce work that enhanced the ruler's glory. So too does Gibbon note that 'Italy was divided into many independent states; and at that time, it was the ambition of princes and republics to vie with each other in the encouragement and reward of literature.'[84] But for Gibbon, the Turks can truly be said to be the co-authors of the Italian Renaissance, more by sheer luck than anything else, for it was more than a matter of simply besieging Constantinople until its scholarly elite was propelled towards Florence. 'The arms of the Turks undoubtedly pressed the flight of the muses,' he writes, 'yet we may tremble at the thought, that Greece might have been overwhelmed, with her schools and libraries, before Europe had emerged from the deluge of barbarism; that the seeds of science might have been scattered by the winds, before the Italian soil was prepared for their cultivation'.[85] The scholars of Renaissance Italy recognized that 'the subjects of the Byzantine throne were still possessed of a golden key that could unlock the treasures of antiquity; of a musical and prolific language'.[86] As Greek scholars even more fearful of the Turks than the Roman Catholics began to evacuate Constantinople, previously unknown texts made their way to the West:

> In the shipwreck of the Byzantine libraries, each fugitive seized a fragment of treasure, a copy of some author, who, without his industry, might have perished: the transcripts were multiplied by an assiduous, and sometimes an elegant, pen; and the text was corrected and explained by their own comments, or those of the elder scholiasts.

The effects of this dispersion of knowledge were prodigious:

> After a short succession of foreign teachers, the tide of emigration subsided; but the language of Constantinople was spread beyond the Alps; and the natives of France, Germany, and England, imparted to their country the sacred fire which they had kindled in the schools of Florence and Rome.

Looking in the long term at the hopeless and degrading attempts of the Byzantines to convince the rest of Christendom to do more than just pray for their rescue, Gibbon concluded that.

> The journies of three emperors were unavailing for their temporal, or perhaps their spiritual, salvation; but they were productive of a beneficial consequence; the revival of the Greek learning in Italy, from whence it was propagated to the last nations of the West and North.

These pages on the Italian Renaissance were much more than a digression for Gibbon, but were indeed a reflection of the unintended consequences of yet another Turkish influence on European history.[87]

The fall of Constantinople was now inevitable, unless Christendom made a collective decision to come to the rescue of the Byzantine Empire:

> But the spirit of the crusades had expired; and the coldness of the Franks was not less unreasonable than their headlong passion. In the eleventh century, a fanatic monk could precipitate Europe on Asia for the recovery of the holy sepulchre; but in the fifteenth, the most pressing motives of religion and policy were insufficient to unite the Latins in the defence of Christendom.

There was still time: 'if the fleets of the West could occupy at the same moment the streights of the Hellespont, the Ottoman monarchy would be dissevered and destroyed.'[88]

Although not the last section of his six volumes, Chap. 68 is the climax, the Ottoman conquest of Constantinople on 29 May 1453 and the final, irrevocable fall of the remaining eastern part of the Roman Empire, the Byzantine. Even more than the notorious fifteenth and sixteenth chapters of the first volume, this chapter is gripping, even inspiring, in its depiction of the final days and hours of the Byzantine Empire. Gibbon clearly admires Mehmed II, but is not above making an unsourced claim 'that the noblest of the captive youth were often dishonoured by his unnatural lust', although he does admit that with 'Voltaire, I laugh at the foolish story of a slave purposely beheaded, to instruct the painter in the action of the muscles' in the process of getting his royal portrait done by Gentile Bellini (c.1429–1507).[89]

'Before I enter on the siege of Constantinople', Gibbon notes, 'I shall observe, that except the short hints of Cantemir and Leunclavius, I have not been able to obtain any Turkish account of this conquest'. As a result, 'I must therefore depend on the Greeks, whose prejudices, in some degree, are subdued by their distress.' Gibbon uses the standard Greek sources but takes 'leave to disregard' the 'hearsay relations' of 'the distant Latins'.[90] Gibbon tells the whole dramatic story, beginning with the building of the Rumeli Hisarı on the European shore of the Bosphorus, a fortress directly opposite the one built by Beyazit I half a century earlier, just before the Mongol invasion dramatically changed Ottoman priorities. The passage of the Bosphorus was now under Turkish control, and a Venetian ship that tried to run the blockade without paying tribute was sunk by cannon fire, the surviving sailors being put to death:

> While Mahomet threatened the capital of the East, the Greek emperor implored with fervent prayers the assistance of earth and heaven. But the invisible powers were deaf to his supplications; and Christendom beheld with indifference the fall of Constantinople, while she derived at least some promise of supply from the jealous and temporal policy of the sultan of Egypt. Some states were too weak, and others too remote; by some the danger was considered as imaginary, by others as inevitable: the Western princes were involved in their endless and domestic quarrels; and the Roman pontiff was exasperated by the falsehood or obstinacy of the Greeks. Instead of employing in their favour the arms and treasures of Italy, Nicholas the fifth had foretold their approaching ruin; and his honour was engaged in the accomplishment of his prophecy. Perhaps he was softened by the last extremity of their distress; but his compassion was tardy; his efforts were faint and unavailing; and Constantinople had fallen, before the squadrons of Genoa and Venice could sail from their harbours.[91]

Meanwhile, back in Constantinople, the last Byzantine emperor Constantine XI Dragases (r. 1448–1453) made a desperate attempt to spur European leaders into sending help, using yet again the well-worn strategy of agreeing to religious union with the Roman Catholic on their terms. On 12 December 1452, in the great church of Hagia Sophia, the Union of Florence from 1439 was reaffirmed, in the presence of the emperor and the papal delegate Cardinal Isidore, a Greek as well but now himself a high-ranking Roman Catholic churchman. Isidore was caught up in Constantinople at the conquest, but managed to escape 'from Galata in a plebian habit', possibly having been bought and sold as a slave in the interim.[92] Gennadius, who had been in Florence in 1439, retired to his cell at the Church of the Pantocrator (soon to become the mosque known as Zeyrek Camii), coming out only at the conquest. So too does Gibbon quote the remark of 'the first minister of the empire' Lucas Notaras 'that he had rather behold in Constantinople the turban of Mahomet, than the pope's tiara or a cardinal's hat.'[93] Gibbon had no love for the Byzantines, and admits that the 'nation was indeed pusillanimous and base; but the last Constantine deserves the name of an hero', despite having fudged his faith.[94] 'Amidst the deserts of Anatolia and the rocks of Palestine,' bewails Gibbon yet again,

> the millions of the crusades had buried themselves in a voluntary and inevitable grave; but the situation of the Imperial city was strong against her enemies, and accessible to her friends; and a rational and moderate armament of the marine states might have saved the relics of the Roman name, and maintained a Christian fortress in the heart of the Ottoman empire.[95]

Sultan Mehmed II left his capital of Edirne on 23 March 1453, a week before his twenty-first birthday, and arrived himself at the walls of Constantinople a fortnight later. The bombardment of the city began the next day, 6 April 1453, targeting the Civil Gate of St Romanus, which would become known as the Top Kapı, 'the cannon gate'. The dramatic story of the siege of Constantinople is well-told by Gibbon, especially the part about the procession of boats dragged up the very steep valley to what is today's Taksim Square, and then down to the Golden Horn, coming out behind the chain that the Byzantines had stretched across the harbour. 'The real importance of this operation was magnified by the consternation and confidence which it inspired:' Gibbon explains, 'but the notorious, unquestionable, fact was displayed before the eyes, and is recorded by the pens, of the two nations'.[96]

The final hours of the Roman Empire are told with the emotional effect that we would expect from Gibbon, yet throughout he retains his critical judgement, even while his narrative is in full flow:

> But in the uniform and odious pictures of a general assault, all is blood, and horror, and confusion; nor shall I strive, at the distance of three centuries and a thousand miles, to delineate a scene, of which there could be no spectators, and of which the actors themselves were incapable of forming any just or adequate idea.[97]

On 29 May 1453, after a siege of fifty-three days, Constantinople fell to the Turks. 'Her empire only had been subverted by the Latins:' Gibbon asserts, 'her religion was trampled in the dust by the Moslem conquerors.'[98]

The destruction of so many Byzantine treasures pains Gibbon deeply, as it had done two and a half centuries before when he described the Crusaders rampaging through Constantinople in 1204.[99] A philosopher, he notes,

> will more seriously deplore the loss of the Byzantine libraries, which were destroyed or scattered in the general confusion: one hundred and twenty thousand manuscripts are said to have disappeared ... We may reflect with pleasure that an inestimable portion of our classic treasures was safely deposited in Italy; and that the mechanics of a German town had invented an art which derides the havock of time and barbarism.[100]

Mehmed II paraded down Constantinople's main street from the Civil Gate of St Romanus down to the Hagia Sophia.

> From St. Sophia he proceeded to the august, but desolate, mansion of an hundred successors of the great Constantine; but which in a few hours had been stripped of the pomp of royalty. A melancholy reflection on the vicissitudes of human greatness, forced itself on his mind; and he repeated an elegant distich of Persian poetry: "The spider has wove his web in the Imperial palace; and the owl hath sung her watch-song on the towers of Afrasiab."

For all his jibes about the inadequacies of Dimitrie Cantemir, Cantemir was Gibbon's source for this wonderful phrase, which entered English literary consciousness and remained there as a quotation not often used but never entirely forgotten. 'This distich, which Cantemir gives in the original,' Gibbon admits, 'derives new beauties from the application.'[101]

The Hagia Sophia was now a mosque, the 'Aya Sofya Camii'. The holiest icon in Byzantium, the Virgin Hodegetria, said to have been painted by Saint Luke himself, was destroyed when the Turks overran the Church of St Saviour in Chora, situated almost underneath the point where the city walls were breached. On 21 June 1453, Mehmed II and his court returned to Edirne, awaiting the repair and rebuilding of suitable palaces for his stay in Constantinople, while 'the hippodrome streamed with the blood of his noblest captives.' In the end,

> Constantinople had been left naked and desolate, without a prince or a people. But she could not be despoiled of the incomparable situation which marks her for the metropolis of a great empire; and the genius of the place will ever triumph over the accidents of time and fortune. Boursa and Adrianople, the ancient seats of the Ottomans, sunk into provincial towns; and Mahomet the second established his own residence, and that of his successors, on the same commanding spot which had been chosen by Constantine.

With more than a subtle reference to his own time, Gibbon reminds us that at Istanbul, 'the *grand signor* (as he has been emphatically named by the Italians) appears to reign over Europe and Asia; but his person on the shores of the Bosphorus may not always be secure from the insults of a hostile navy.' Whether this navy would be Russian or English was a key question in the late eighteenth century.[102]

'The importance of Constantinople was felt and magnified in its loss' Gibbon writes:

> Had every breast glowed with the same ardour; had the union of the Christians corresponded with their bravery; had every country, from Sweden to Naples, supplied a just proportion of cavalry and infantry, of men and money, it is indeed probable that Constantinople would have been delivered, and that the Turks might have been chased beyond the Hellespont or the Euphrates.[103]

'As I am now taking an everlasting farewell of the Greek empire,' Gibbon begins the last footnote of Chap. 68, 'I shall briefly mention the great collection of Byzantine writers, whose names and testimonies have been successively repeated in this work.' And so he does, ending this glorious chapter of his splendid book.[104]

V

In the first ages of the decline and fall of the Roman empire, our eye is invariably fixed on the royal city, which had given laws to the fairest portion of the globe. We contemplate her fortunes, at first with admiration, at length with pity, always with attention; and when that attention is diverted from the Capitol to the provinces, they are considered as so many branches which have been successively severed from the Imperial trunk. The foundation of a second Rome, on the shores of the Bosphorus, has compelled the historian to follow the successors of Constantine; and our curiosity has been tempted to visit the most remote countries of Europe and Asia, to explore the causes and the authors of the long decay of the Byzantine monarchy.[105]

With that, Gibbon begins his Chap. 69, which with Chaps. 70 and 71 completes his six volumes. 'Nor shall I dismiss the present work', he explains, 'till I have reviewed the state and revolutions of the ROMAN CITY, which acquiesced under the absolute dominion of the popes about the same time that Constantinople was enslaved by the Turkish arms.'[106] His aim is to carry the history of Rome at least until the middle of the fifteenth century, catching up the history of the West after having so dramatically disposed of the East. Almost apologetically, Gibbon appends a footnote of advice: 'The reader has been so long absent from Rome, that I would advise him to recollect or review the xlix[th] chapter, in the vth volume of this History.'[107]

The final chapter (71) of *Decline and Fall* is a time for summing up. 'In the preceding volumes of this History, I have described the triumph of barbarism and religion;' writes Gibbon as he looks back over his six volumes, 'and I can only resume, in a few words, their real or imaginary connection with the ruin of ancient Rome.' The weight was rather on the second triumph than the first, since the 'shepherds of Scythia and Germany', he argues, were not really the problem: 'From these innocent Barbarians, the reproach may be transferred to the Catholics of Rome.'[108] When Christians did the conquering the first thing they did was to demolish all traces of their pagan predecessors:

> But if the forms of ancient architecture were disregarded by a people insensible of their use and beauty, the plentiful materials were applied to every call of necessity or superstition; till the fairest columns of the Ionic and Corinthian orders, the richest marbles of Paros and Numidia, were

degraded, perhaps to the support of a convent or a stable. The daily havock which is perpetrated by the Turks in the cities of Greece and Asia, may afford a melancholy example; and in the gradual destruction of the monuments of Rome, Sixtus the fifth may alone be excused for employing the stones of the Septizonium in the glorious edifice of St. Peter's.

Gibbon notes sardonically that even a 'fragment, a ruin, howsoever mangled or profaned, may be viewed with pleasure and regret', but so many of the ancient structures were totally destroyed by the Christians, and the marble burnt to lime in order to make cement.[109]

> The historian may applaud the importance and variety of his subject; but, while he is conscious of his own imperfections, he must often accuse the deficiency of his materials. It was among the ruins of the Capitol, that I first conceived the idea of a work which has amused and exercised near twenty years of my life, and which, however inadequate to my own wishes, I finally deliver to the curiosity and candour of the Public.
> LAUSANNE,
> *June 27*, 1787.[110]

VI

> Diligence and accuracy are the only merits which an historical writer may ascribe to himself; if any merit indeed can be assumed from the performance of an indispensable duty. I may therefore be allowed to say, that I have carefully examined all of the original materials that could illustrate the subject which I had undertaken to treat.[111]

Not for the first time, Gibbon was being unnecessarily modest. Modern scholars are in agreement that in regard to facts and narrative, Gibbon usually gets it right. In perhaps the most extraordinary demonstration of Gibbon's prescience, one only has to look at the way in which he pondered the *gazi* thesis, a century and a half *avant la lettre*.

From 4 to 6 May 1937, the great Austrian Ottomanist Paul Wittek (1894–1978) gave a series of lectures at the University of London, published the following year.[112] Here he expounded his favourite thesis, that the early Ottomans were not an ethnic tribe, but rather a group of *gazi*s, unrelated warriors who came together to fight for Islam against the Byzantine Christians. Wittek argued that since the genealogies proclaimed by the Ottomans were fictitious, therefore it was incorrect to believe Ottoman historical traditions that explained their own origins as a Turkish tribe that migrated from Central Asia under pressure from the Mongols until they reached Anatolia and settled there. Wittek's personality and power in the field of Ottoman studies until his death ensured that his '*gazi* thesis' remained the party line, tinkered with but never wholly abandoned.[113]

Gibbon was fully acquainted with the *gazi* figure, ruling that Suleiman ibn Kutulmış (r. 1077–1086) 'deserved the name of *Gazi*, a holy champion'.[114] As for Osman, the founder of the Ottomans, 'the Koran sanctified his *gazi*, or holy war, against the infidels'.[115] Gibbon judged that Timur (Tamerlane) 'obtained the merit of the *gazie*, or holy war'.[116] But Gibbon had studied the Scythian hordes, and looked at them with the keen eye of a modern anthropologist: nomad tribes, he wrote,

> preserve, with conscious pride, the inestimable treasure of their genealogy; and whatever distinctions of rank may have been introduced, by the unequal distribution of pastoral wealth, they mutually respect themselves, and each other, as the descendants of the first founder of the tribe. The custom, which still prevails, of adopting the bravest, and most faithful, of the captives, may countenance the very probable suspicion, that this extensive consanguinity is, in a great measure, legal and fictitious. But the useful prejudice, which has obtained the sanction of time and opinion, produces the effects of truth[117]

Gibbon's anthropology was based on a contemporary event which gave him an eighteenth-century insight into an eleventh-century tribal movement, namely the migration

> of the black Calmucks, who remained about a century under the protection of Russia; and who have since returned to their native seats on the frontiers of the Chinese empire. The march, and the return, of those wandering Tartars, whose united camp consists of fifty thousand tents or families, illustrate the distant emigrations of the ancient Huns.

To those whose interests did not stray to central Asia, Gibbon helpfully footnotes his remarks, recording that this 'great transmigration of 300,000 Calmucks, or Torgouts, happened in the year 1771.'[118] He also used a wealth of sources from ancient times onwards in order to understand the 'pastoral manners', diet, habitations, 'exercises', and government, of nomads in general.[119] Even without the benefits of modern anthropology, Gibbon had a deep insight into what it meant to be part of a nomadic tribe. Gibbon would have enjoyed the '*gazi* thesis' of Paul Wittek, which even now maintains a ghostly presence among Ottoman historians, for whom *The Decline and Fall of the Roman Empire* is not on any urgent bibliography.

Gibbon put Turkey on the table in British culture, not only because he was a great writer but because he was usually right, even in extraordinary contexts, such as his invention of the *gazi* thesis before it was pronounced as orthodoxy. A huge portion of his great work is devoted to Turkish history, since Gibbon understood that it was impossible to understand his world without knowing about the history of the Turks. English men and women read Gibbon because they were weaned on Classics, and once having read him, it was impossible to look at Turkey as a blank page.

NOTES

1. Edward Gibbon, *The History of the Decline and Fall of the Roman Empire*, ed. David Womersley (Penguin edn, London, 1994), ii. 507 (Chap. 38).
2. Ibid., iii. 791 n. 1 (Chap. 64).
3. Horace Walpole to William Mason, 27 Jan. 1781, from Berkeley Square: Horace Walpole, *Correspondence*, ed. W.S. Lewis *et al.* (New Haven, 1937–83), 29:95–99 esp. pp. 98–9.
4. Walpole to Lady Ossory, from Berkeley Square, 10 Feb. 1789: 34: 38–41, esp. pp. 39–40.
5. Gibbon, *Decline and Fall*, ed. Womersley, iii. 23 (Chap. 48). Cf. Steven Runciman, 'Gibbon and Byzantium', *Dædalus*, 105 (1976), 103–10, esp. pp. 106–7 for the general disparagement of Byzantine history by many of Gibbon's contemporaries. According to Runciman, Gibbon himself was so critical that the 'splendor of his style and the wit of his satire killed Byzantine studies for nearly a century.' (p. 109).
6. Gibbon, *Decline and Fall*, ed. Womersley, iii. 791 (Chap. 64).
7. 'Gibbon's influence on the Western perception of the Prophet, Islam, and their place in history was enormous': Bernard Lewis, 'Gibbon on Muhammad', *Dædalus*, 105 (1976), 89–101, esp. p. 100.
8. Edward Gibbon, *Memoirs of My Life*, ed. Betty Radice (Penguin edn, Harmondsworth, 1984), pp. 72–3.

9. Ibid., pp. 81, 82.
10. Deborah Stephan, 'Laurence Echard – Whig Historian', *Hist.Jnl*, 32 (1989), 843–866; Ronald T. Riley, 'The Forgotten Historian: Laurence Echard and the First History of the Roman Republic', *Ancient Society*, 27 (1996), 277–315.
11. G.F.R. Barker, 'Laurence Echard', *Dict.Nat.Biog.* (1885–1900).
12. Laurence Echard, *A General Ecclesiastical History* (London, 1702), preface: quoted in R.T. Ridley, 'Echard, Laurence (1672-1730)', *Oxford Dict.Nat.Biog.* (2004–12).
13. D.R. Woolf, 'Howell, William (1631/2–1683)', *Oxford Dict.Nat. Biog.*
14. Generally on Islamic studies in Gibbon's time, see Dorothy Vaughan, *Europe and the Turk* (Liverpool, 1954); Johann W. Fück [Fueck], *Die Arabischen Studien in Europe bis in den Anfang des 20. Jahrhunderts* (Leipzig, 1955); G.E. von Grunebaum, 'Islam: the Problem of Changing Perspective', in *The Transformation of the Roman World: Gibbon's Problem after Two Centuries*, ed. Lynn White, Jr. (Berkeley & Los Angeles, 1966), Chap. 5; G.J. Toomer, *Eastern Wisedome and Learning: the Study of Arabic in Seventeenth-Century England* (Oxford, 1996); Nabil Matar, *Islam in Britain 1558–1685* (Cambridge, 1998); idem, *Turks, Moors and Englishmen in the Age of Discovery* (New York, 1999); David Womersley, *Gibbon and the 'Watchmen of the Holy City'* (Oxford, 2002), Chap. 4: '"Enthusiasm and Imposture": Gibbon and Mahomet'; Robert Irwin, *For Lust of Knowing: The Orientalists and their Enemies* (London, 2006).
15. Thomas Hearne, *Remarks and Collections*, vol. iii, ed. C.E. Doble (Oxford, 1889), p. 286.
16. Humphrey Prideaux, *The True Nature of Imposture Fully Display'd in the Life of Mahomet* (3rd edn, London, 1698). Gibbon also had available to him a more sympathetic *La Vie de Mahomed* (Amsterdam, 1731) [repr. from London edn of 1730], by Henri, comte de Boulainvilliers (1658–1722), where Islam is described as being refreshingly undogmatic, unmystical, and tolerant. Gibbon was critical of both biographies: 'the adverse wish of finding an impostor or an hero, has too often corrupted the learning of the doctor and the ingenuity of the count.': Gibbon, *Decline and Fall*, ed. Womersley, iii. 190 n. 111 (Chap. 50). Gibbon was more impressed with 'the best and most authentic of our guides', Jean/John Gagnier

(c.1670–1740), the French-born Orientalist who came to Oxford and in 1723 published an Arabic edition (with Latin translation and notes) of the life of Muhammad written in the fourteenth century by Abu'l-Fida (1273–1331), which he used as the basis for a two-volume study of *La Vie de Mahomet* (Amsterdam, 1732), authoritative until the middle of the nineteenth century, when Gustav Weil (1808–89) published *Mohammed der Prophet* (Stuttgart, 1843): Gibbon, *Decline and Fall*, ed. Womersley, iii. 190 n. 111 (Chap. 50).

17. Simon Ockley also published *The History of the Present Jews, Throughout the World* (London, 1707), an English translation from the Italian of Leone Modena (1571–1648), *Historia de gli riti hebraici* (Paris, 1637), which Modena republished in Venice the following year in a revised and slightly sanitized version. The book had already appeared in an English translation by Edmund Chilmead (1610–54) as *the History of the Rites, Customs, and Manner of Life, of the Present Jews, Throughout the World* (London, 1650). For more on Ockley, see P.M. Holt, 'Ockley, Simon (*bap.* 1679, d. 1720), *Oxford Dict.Nat.Biog*; A. J. Arberry, 'The Pioneer Simon Ockley', in his *Oriental Essays* (London, 1960), pp. 11–47.

18. Gibbon, *Decline and Fall*, ed. Womersley, iii. 238 n. 15 (Chap. 51). See also Nicholas Dew, *Orientalism in Louis XIV's France* (Oxford, 2009); and idem, 'The Order of Oriental Knowledge: the Making of d'Herbelot's *Bibliothèque orientale*', in *Debating World Literature*, ed. Chrisopher Prendergast (London, 2004), pp. 233–252.

19. Gibbon, *Decline and Fall*, ed. Womersley, iii. 316 n. 199 (Chap. 51). Another useful source would have been Sir James Porter, *Observations on the Religion, Law, Government, and Manners, of the Turks* (Dublin, 1768). Porter (1710–76) served as ambassador at Constantinople (1746–62). His grandson Sir George Larpent produced a memoir with additional writings as *Turkey; its History and Progress* (London, 1854). Hugh Trevor-Roper judged Porter to be the 'ablest English writer on Turkish affairs': Hugh Trevor-Roper, 'Dimitrie Cantemir's *Ottoman History* and its Reception in England', *Revue roumaine d'histoire*, 24 (1985), 51–66: repr. in his *History and the Enlightenment* (New Haven, 2010), Chap. 4 (pp. 54–70, 284–6), esp. p. 66. The great philologist Sir William Jones (1746–94), 'A Prefatory Discourse to An Essay on the History of the Turks', in his *Memoirs*, ed. Lord Teignmouth (2nd edn, London, 1806), Appx B [pp. 491–513] refers to Porter as 'so judicious a writer'

(p. 498). 'My Turkish History will go to the press on Monday', Jones wrote in a letter dated 16 Jan. 1772, 'Lord Radnor has given me leave, in the most flattering terms, to inscribe it to him.' (Jones to Mr. Hawkins, from Westminster: ibid., p. 106). Jones was angling in 1771 for the post of British ambassador to Turkey: ibid., pp. 101–2. 'Whether the Turkish History, which Mr. Jones mentions as ready for the press, was ever finished,' Lord Teignmouth notes in his capacity as editor of the memoirs, 'I am not informed; part of the original manuscript still remains; the introduction to it was printed, but not published, and will form a number in the Appendix.' (ibid., p 106). The introduction appears as Appx B [pp. 491–513], but although Teignmouth appears to have seen some of the text of Jones's Turkish history, the manuscript has since been lost.

20. Gibbon, *Decline and Fall*, ed. Womersley, iii. 541 n. 41 (Chap. 57).
21. The Levant Company was chartered in 1581 in order to establish 'factories' (trading centres) in the Ottoman Empire. Its members, the 'Turkey merchants', made their headquarters in Aleppo, and there were other branches in Istanbul, Smyrna and Alexandria, dealing mostly with cotton imports and some silk. Its monopoly was abolished in 1754, and the Levant Company itself was dissolved in 1825. See A.C. Wood, *A History of the Levant Company* (Oxford, 1935); and M. Epstein, *The Early History of the Levant Company* (New York, 1908).
22. He was from Malatya, now in Turkey, more specifically from a village called 'Ebra nearby, but his father was apparently Jewish as well, giving rise to the name by which he is known.
23. For modern editions of the *Chronicon Syriacum*, see *Gregorii Barhebraei Chronicon Syriacum*, ed. Paul Bedjan (Paris, 1890) in Latin; and *The Chronicle of Gregory Abû'l Faraj*, ed. E.A. Wallis Budge (London, 1932) in English. For a modern edition of the *Chronicon Ecclesiasticum*, see *Gregorii Barhebraei Chronicon Ecclesiasticum*, ed Joannes B. Abbeloos & Thomas J. Lamy (Leuven, 1872–7), in Latin with the original Syriac in parallel columns.
24. Gibbon, *Decline and Fall*, ed. Womersley, iii. 190 n. 111 (Chap. 50). 'By the end of the nineteenth century Gibbon's texts had largely been replaced by critical editions – though one would be hard pressed to find an occasion on which any conclusion drawn by him was vitiated by a false reading in a text, and Gibbon made more use

than most modern scholars of the great commentaries of seventeenth- and eighteenth-century editors, some of them unsurpassed to this day.': John Matthews, 'Gibbon and the later Roman Empire: causes and circumstances', in *Edward Gibbon and Empire*, ed. Rosamond McKitterick & Roland Quinault (Cambridge, 1997), Chap. 1, esp. p. 26.

25. See Sonia Anderson, *An English Consul in Turkey: Paul Rycaut at Smyrna, 1667–1678* (Oxford, 1989); Linda T. Darling, 'Ottoman Politics through British Eyes: Paul Rycaut's *The Present State of the Ottoman Empire*', *Jnl World Hist.*, 5 (1994), 71–97.

26. George Sale, *The Koran, Commonly called The Alcoran of Mohammed, Translated into English immediately from the Original Arabic* (London, 1734), including 'A Preliminary Discourse' rather unsympathetic to Islam. Sale's translation remained the standard English version until the publication of John Rodwell (1808–1900), *The Koran* (London, 1861), which was also printed in 'Everyman's Library' (1909) with an introduction by George Margoliouth (1853–1924). The next English Koran was that of E.H. Palmer (1840–82), published in two volumes in 1880, as part of the fifty-volume series of 'Sacred Books of the East', produced by Friedrich Max Müller (1823–1900). Bernard Lewis describes Sale as 'the first English Arabist of any consequence who was not a clergyman, and one of the first in Europe': Lewis, 'Gibbon', p. 91. Cf. A.J. Arberry, 'The Linguist: Edward Henry Palmer', in his *Oriental Essays*, pp. 122–59.

27. [Alexander Ross], *The Alcoran of Mahomet* (London, 1649): Ross was originally from Aberdeen, but was later a Royalist clergyman living in the south of England: David Allan, 'Ross, Alexander (1591–1654)', *Oxford Dict.Nat.Biog.* Ross notes on the title page that his book is 'Translated out of *Arabique* into *French*, By The *Sieur Du Ryer*, Lord of *Malezair*, and Resident for the King of *France*, at *Alexandria*. And newly Englished, for the satisfaction of all that desire to look into the *Turkish* vanities.' Ross helpfully provides at the beginning of the book in four pages 'A Summary of the Religion of The Turks.' The original French text was published by André du Ryer as *L'Alcoran de Mahomet* (Paris, 1647); he also produced a *Grammaire turque* in 1630.

28. Ludovico Marracci, *Alcorani textus* (Padua, 1698); Gibbon, *Decline and Fall*, ed. Womersley, iii. 189 n. 110 (Chap. 50).

29. [Claude Etienne] Savary, *Le Coran; traduit de l'Arabe, accompagné de notes, et précédé d'un abrégé de la vie de Mahomet* (Paris, 1783).

30. Gibbon, *Decline and Fall*, ed. Womersley, iii. 190 n. 111 (Chap. 50); iii. 316 (Chap. 51).

31. Bernard Lewis, *The Emergence of Modern Turkey* (3rd edn, Oxford, 2002) [1st pub. 1961], p. 36.

32. See generally the still very useful narrative in M.S. Anderson, *The Eastern Question 1774–1923* (London, 1966).

33. See generally M.S. Anderson, 'Great Britain and the Russo-Turkish War of 1768–74', *Eng.Hist.Rev.*, 69 (1954), 39–58; Roderic H. Davison, '"Russian Skill and Turkish Imbecility": the Treaty of Kuchuk Kainardji Reconsidered', *Slavic Rev.*, 35 (1976), 463–483.

34. P.M. Holt, 'Some Observations on the 'Abbāsid Caliphate of Cairo', *Bull.S.O.A.S.*, 47 (1984), 501–507: 'The legend that the Caliph al-Mutawakkil III formally transferred the caliphate to Selim the Grim on the overthrow of the Mamlūk sultanate has long been recognized as a fabrication.'

35. Allan Cunningham, 'The Oczakov Debate', *Middle Eastern Studies*, 1 (1965), 209–37, esp. p. 228.

36. J.W. Derry, *Charles James Fox* (London, 1972), p. 285; Langford, p. 203.

37. Four years later, in 1797, an Ottoman legation was opened in Paris as well. There is an engraving of 1797 by Mather Brown (1761–1831) of 'His Majesty and the Officers of State Receiving the Turkish Ambassador and Suite': Victoria and Albert Museum, Prints and Drawings Study Room, Level D, Case 112, Shelf 6.

38. *The Letters of Edward Gibbon*, ed. J.E. Norton (New York, 1956), i. 318–9 (letter #184).

39. Ibid., ii. 24 (letter #257).

40. Ibid., ii. 28 (letter #260).

41. Gibbon, *Memoirs*, ed. Radice, p. 151.

42. Ibid., p. 169.

43. Edward Gibbon, *Miscellaneous Works*, ed. Lord Sheffield (Dublin, 1796), i. 220.

44. Gibbon, *Decline and Fall*, ed. Womersley, ii. 694 (Chap. 42). Cf. Peter B. Golden, *An Introduction to the History of the Turkic Peoples* (Wiesbaden, 1992), pp. 115–20. A popular digestion of Golden's old-school ethnolinguistic erudition can be found in Carter Vaughn Findley, *The Turks in World History* (Oxford, 2005), Chap. 1.

45. Gibbon, *Decline and Fall*, ed. Womersley, iii. 151 and n. 1 (Chap. 50). More modern sources might include: John F. Haldon, *Byzantium in the Seventh Century* (rev. edn, Cambridge, 1990); Warren Treadgold, *A History of the Byzantine State and Society* (Stanford, 1997); Nadia Maria El-Cheikh, *Byzantium Viewed by the Arabs* (Cambridge, USA, 2004); Walter E. Kaegi, 'Confronting Islam: Emperors versus Caliphs (641-c.850)', in *The Cambridge History of the Byzantine Empire c.500–1492*, ed. Jonathan Shepard (Cambridge, 2008), pp. 365–394; James Howard-Johnston, *Witness to a World Crisis: Historians and Histories of the Middle East in the Seventh Century* (Cambridge, 2010).

46. Gibbon, *Decline and Fall*, ed. Womersley, iii. 336 and n. 30 (Chap. 52).

47. Ibid., iii. 447 and n. 22 (Chap. 55).

48. Ibid., iii. 460 and n. 58 (Chap. 55).

49. Ibid., iii. 461 (Chap. 55).

50. Ibid., iii. 462–3 and 463 n. 66 (Chap. 55).

51. Ibid., iii. 531 (Chap. 57).

52. The town of Malazgirt is located today in the Turkish province of Muş; the site of the battle is to the south-east, towards Lake Van. For modern historical accounts, see: Carole Hillenbrand, *Turkish Myth and Muslim Symbol: The Battle of Manzikert* (Edinburgh, 2007); D.A. Korobeinikov, 'Raiders and Neighbours: The Turks (1040–1304)', in *The Cambridge History of the Byzantine Empire c.500–1492*, ed. Jonathan Shepard (Cambridge, 2008), Chap. 19 (pp. 692–727), esp. pp. 701–704.

53. Gibbon, *Decline and Fall*, ed. Womersley, iii. 537 n. 34, 538 (Chap. 57).

54. Ibid., iii. 540–1 (Chap. 57).

55. Ibid., iii. 546–8 (Chap. 57).

56. Ibid., iii. 548, 553–4 (Chap. 57).

57. Ibid., iii. 559–60 (Chap. 58).

58. Ibid., iii. 624 (Chap. 59). Gibbon also criticizes, in a footnote, 'the Mohammedan writers, who are dry and sulky on the subject of the first crusade': ibid., iii. 590 n. 80 (Chap. 58).

59. Ibid., iii. 564 (Chap. 58).

60. Ibid., iii. 615–18 (Chap. 59).

61. Ibid., iii. 655, 685, 690, 697 (Chap. 60).

62. Ibid., iii. 726–7 (Chap. 61).

63. Gibbon, *Memoirs*, ed. Radice, p. 164. Cf. the postscript to the preface of volume iii (1781): 'The entire History, which is now published, of the Decline and Fall of the Roman Empire in the West, abundantly discharges my engagements with the Public.': Gibbon, *Decline and Fall*, ed. Womersley, i. 3. In a famous footnote, already quoted, Gibbon erects a useful signpost to the development of his great project: 'The reader is invited to review the chapters of the second and third volumes; the manners of pastoral nations, the conquests of Attila and the Huns, which were composed at a time when I entertained the wish, rather than the hope, of concluding my history.': ibid., iii. 791 n. 1 (Chap. 64).

64. Ibid., iii. 793, 793 n. 6, 800, 803 (Chap. 64). See J.G.A. Pocock, 'Gibbon and the Idol Fo: Chinese and Christian History in the Enlightenment', in *Sceptics, Millenarians and Jews*, ed. David S. Katz & Jonathan I. Israel (Leiden, 1990), 15–34. Generally, on everything connected with Gibbon and his influence, see J.G.A. Pocock, *Barbarism and Religion* (Cambridge, 1999–2015), 6 vols.

65. Gibbon, *Decline and Fall*, ed. Womersley, iii. 807–9 (Chap. 64).

66. Colin Imber, 'The Legend of Osman Gazi', in *The Ottoman Emirate (1300–1389)*, ed. Elizabeth Zachariadou (Rethymnon, 1993), pp. 67–75, esp. p. 75.

67. Gibbon, *Decline and Fall*, ed. Womersley, iii. 809–10 (Chap. 64). Bithynia was the area from about Nicaea (İznik) to the Black Sea, the border between the Byzantine Empire and the territory controlled by the Turks.

68. Ibid., iii. 810–11 (Chap. 64).

69. Ibid., iii. 814–15 (Chap. 64). Cf. Anthony Bryer, 'Greek Historians on the Turks: the Case of the First Byzantine-Ottoman Marriage', in *The Writing of History in the Middle Ages, Essays Presented to Richard William Southern* (Oxford, 1981), pp. 471–93, repr. in his *Peoples and Settlement in Anatolia and the Caucasus, 800–1900* (London, 1988), Chap. 4.

70. Gibbon, *Decline and Fall*, ed. Womersley, iii. 815–16 (Chap. 64).

71. Ibid., iii. 816–17 (Chap. 64).

72. Ibid., iii. 818 (Chap. 64).

73. Ibid., iii. 823 (Chap. 64).

74. 'The surname of Ilderim, or lightning, is an example that the conquerors and poets of every age have *felt* the truth of a system which

derives the sublime from the principle of terror.': ibid., iii. 818 and n. 56 (Chap. 64).

75. Ibid., iii. 820, 823, 825 (Chap. 64).
76. Ibid., iii. 826, 831, 835, 837 (Chap. 65).
77. Ibid., iii. 841–3 (Chap. 65).
78. Gibbon's citation for Voltaire is *Essai sur l'histoire générale*, c.88. See generally G.-H. Bousquet, 'Voltaire et l'Islâm', *Studia Islamica*, 28 (1968), 109–26; Djavad Hadidi, *Voltaire et l'Islam* (Paris, 1974); Magdy Gabriel Badir, *Voltaire et l'Islam* (Banbury, 1974).
79. Gibbon also concedes that Timour had 'a design of leading his royal captive in triumph to Samarcand.': Gibbon, *Decline and Fall*, ed. Womersley, iii. 844–7 (Chap. 65). Leunclavius is Johann Loewenklau (c.1533–1593), who produced one of the first works of Turkish history that used primary sources, *Historiae Musulmanae Turcorum* (Frankfurt, 1591). He also published a few years earlier another work to which Gibbon refers, the *Annales sultanorum Othmanidarum* (Frankfurt, 1588), translated from Turkish to German by Johann Gaudier (Spiegel). Dimitrie Cantemir (1673–1723) was the last native prince of Moldavia, a tributary of the Ottoman Empire, and indeed he lived in Istanbul from the age of fifteen, even after his nominal succession as prince in 1693. He gained actual power in 1710, but immediately joined up with Peter the Great (r. 1682–1725) in the Russo-Turkish War of 1710–11. The defeat of Russia forced him to remain there until his death a dozen years later. Dimitrie Cantemir was a prolific Enlightenment man of letters, and wrote on many subjects, including history, religion and music. For Gibbon, the key work was Cantemir's *The History of the Growth and Decay of the Othman Empire*, published in London in 1734–5, thanks to the efforts of his son Antioh Cantemir (1708–1744), who was Russian envoy to Britain (1732–8), before moving on to the same position in Paris, where he became friends with Voltaire, Montesquieu and other contemporary intellectuals. The original Latin manuscript was lost, so the English translation was the one used by Gibbon and everyone else, made by Nicholas Tindal (1687–1774), vicar of Great Waltham, Essex. There were further editions: French (1743), German (1745), and an English reprint in 1756. See Trevor-Roper, 'Dimitrie Cantemir's *Ottoman History*'.
80. Gibbon, *Decline and Fall*, ed. Womersley, iii. 847–50 (Chap. 65).

81. Ibid., iii. 853, 855–7 (Chap. 65). In one of his triple-edged foot-notes, Gibbon amplifies his comments about Timor by slamming 'our ingenious Sir William Temple (his works, vol. iii. p. 349, 350. octavo edition), that lover of exotic virtue. After the conquest of Russia, &c. and the passage of the Danube, his Tartar hero relieves, visits, admires, and refuses the city of Constantine. His flattering pencil deviates in every line from the truth of history: yet his pleasing fictions are more excusable than the gross errors of Cantemir.': ibid., iii. 856–7 n. 79 (Chap. 65).

82. Ibid., iii. 859–62 (Chap. 65).

83. Ibid., iii. 864 (Chap. 66).

84. Ibid., iii. 906 (Chap. 66).

85. Ibid., iii. 896 (Chap. 66).

86. Ibid., iii. 894 (Chap. 66).

87. Ibid., iii. 894, 904–5, 907 (Chap. 66).

88. Ibid., iii. 910, 916 n. 13, 917–18, 919 (Chap. 67).

89. Ibid., iii. 934, 935 n. 7, 936 (Chap. 68).

90. Ibid., iii. 937 n. 11 (Chap. 68).

91. Ibid., iii. 944–5 (Chap. 68).

92. Ibid., iii. 965 (Chap. 68).

93. Ibid., iii. 949 (Chap. 68). Lucas Notarus had his wish, and at the conquest was the most important Byzantine official taken prisoner.

94. Ibid., iii. 950 (Chap. 68).

95. Ibid., iii. 955 (Chap. 68).

96. Ibid., iii. 956 (Chap. 68).

97. Ibid., iii. 961 (Chap. 68).

98. Ibid., iii. 963 (Chap. 68). Gibbon here appends a note that the contemporary Greek humanist Demetrius 'Chalcocondyles most absurdly supposes that Constantinople was sacked by the Asiatics in revenge for the ancient calamities of Troy; and the grammarians of the xv th century are happy to melt down the uncouth appellation of Turks, into the more classical name of *Teucri*.': Gibbon, *Decline and Fall*, ed. Womersley, iii. 963 n.63 (Chap. 68). Cf. Steven Runciman, 'Teucri and Turci' in *Medieval and Middle Eastern Studies in Honor of Aziz Suryal Atiya*, ed. Sami A. Hanna (Leiden, 1972), pp. 344–8.

99. Gibbon does, however, wrongly place the blame on Mehmed II for personally smashing off the head of one of the three serpents on the twisted column in the Hippodrome 'as a trial of his strength': Gibbon, *Decline and Fall*, ed. Womersley, iii. 967–8 (Chap. 68). In

fact, it was a drunken Polish nobleman in Gibbon's own time who did the terrible deed. Earlier, Gibbon claimed that the 'beauty of the Hippodrome has been long since defaced by the rude hands of the Turkish conquerors: but, under the similar appellation of Atmeidan, it still serves as a place of exercise for their horses', and explained in a footnote that 'Mahomet the Second broke the under-jaw of one of the serpents with a stroke of his battle-axe.': ibid., i. 597 & n. 48 (Chap. 17). The headless statue is still on display in the Hippodrome in Istanbul.

100. Ibid., iii. 967 (Chap. 68).
101. Ibid., iii. 968 and n. 77 (Chap. 68). For more on the 'spider' quotation, see Anthony Bryer, 'Gibbon and the later Byzantine Empires', in *Gibbon*, ed. McKitterick & Quinault, Chap. 5, esp. p. 110 n. 33.
102. Gibbon, *Decline and Fall*, ed. Womersley, iii. 969–70 (Chap. 68).
103. Ibid., iii. 974–5 (Chap. 68).
104. Ibid., iii. 976–7 n. 97 (Chap. 68).
105. Ibid., iii. 978 (Chap. 69).
106. Ibid., iii. 979 (Chap. 69).
107. Ibid., iii. 979 n. 2 (Chap. 69).
108. Ibid., iii. 1068–9 (Chap. 71).
109. Ibid., iii. 1072 (Chap. 71).
110. Ibid., iii. 1085 (Chap. 71).
111. 'Advertisement' to 1st vol.: ibid., i. 5.
112. Paul Wittek, *The Rise of the Ottoman Empire* (London, 1938), repr. with translations of other work by Wittek and a critical introduction (pp. 1–27) by Colin Heywood (London, 2012). For more on Wittek, see Colin Heywood, 'Wittek and the Austrian Tradition', *Jnl.Roy.Asiatic Soc.*, 120 (1988), 7–25; idem, '"Boundless Dreams of the Levant": Paul Wittek, the George-*Kreis*, and the Writing of Ottoman History', *Jnl.Roy.Asiatic Soc.Gr. Brit. & Ireland*, 1 (1989), 32–50; idem, 'A Subterranean History: Paul Wittek (1894–1978) and the Early Ottoman State', *Die Welt des Islams*, new ser., 38 (1998), 386–405. Cf. idem, 'Between Historical Myth and 'Mythohistory': the Limits of Ottoman History', *Byz. & Mod. Greek Stud.*, 12 (1988), 315–45: these articles are repr. in his *Writing Ottoman History* (Variorum edn, Farnham, 2002). See also Colin Imber, 'Paul Wittek's "De la défaite d'Ankara à la prise de Constantinople"', *Osmanlı Araştırmaları*, 5 (1986), 65–81; idem, 'The Ottoman Dynastic Myth', *Turcica*, 19 (1987), 7–27; idem,

The Ottoman Empire, 1300–1481 (Istanbul, 1990); idem, 'What Does *Ghazi* Actually Mean?', in *The Balance of Truth: Essays in Honour of Professor Geoffrey Lewis*, ed. Çiğdem Balım-Harding & Colin Imber (Istanbul, 2000), pp. 165–78. Cf. Stanford J. Shaw, 'In Memoriam: Professor Paul Wittek, 1894–1978', *Intl.Jnl.Mid.East Stud.*, 10 (1979), 139–41.

113. The most detailed examination came from Rudi Paul Linder, 'Nomadism, Horses and Huns', *Past and Present*, 92 (1981), 3–19; idem, 'What Was a Nomadic Tribe?', *Comp.Stud.Soc.Hist.*, 24 (1982), 689–711; idem, 'Stimulus and Justification in Early Ottoman History', *Greek Orthodox Theological Rev.*, 27 (1982), 207–24; idem, *Nomads and Ottomans in Medieval Anatolia* (Bloomington, 1983). Linder used modern anthropological studies to show that nomadic tribes were and are based on self-identification and that a close blood or familial relation is not necessary in order to join, despite the fact that nomads often fabricate genealogies for social cohesion. See also Peter Heather, 'The Huns and the End of the Roman Empire in Western Europe', *Eng.Hist.Rev.*, 110 (1995), 4–41.

114. Gibbon, *Decline and Fall*, ed. Womersley, iii. 546 (Chap. 57).

115. Ibid., iii. 809–10 (Chap. 64).

116. Ibid., iii. 831 (Chap. 65).

117. Ibid., i. 1031 (Chap. 26).

118. Ibid., i. 1041–2 and n. 51 (Chap. 26).

119. Ibid., i. 1025–32 (Chap. 26).

CHAPTER 3

Lord Byron, Turkophile and His Grand Tour to the East (1809–1811)

Many towns in Greece have a Vyronis Street, in honour of the romantic English lord who came to free Hellas from the Ottoman yoke. Nearly all Greeks would be surprised to learn that Lord Byron (1788–1824) much preferred the company of Turks, and Muslims in general, over Greeks. As a matter of fact, he was rather duped into joining the struggle of the Greek diaspora to foist independence and political unity on their homeland, and regretted having come the moment he set foot in Greece in 1824. Byron regretted his voyage even more when he took ill three months later and died at Missolonghi shortly thereafter. It was such a waste, really, because Byron never got the chance to fire a single shot for Greek liberation, and the motley collection of mercenary Albanians whose military service he had purchased with his own money instantly moved on to other patrons who were rather more alive. That Lord Byron should be remembered as the beautiful young English hero who gave his life to liberate Greece is an irony that would have amused him most of all.[1]

I

George Gordon Byron was born on 22 January 1788 in London, and at the age of ten the future poet became the sixth Baron Byron of Rochdale. Lord Byron spent four years at Harrow (1801–1805), and in October 1805 matriculated at Trinity College, Cambridge. Byron took his seat in the House of Lords in 1809, but like very many others of his class

© The Author(s) 2016
D.S. Katz, *The Shaping of Turkey in the British Imagination, 1776–1923,*
DOI 10.1007/978-3-319-41060-9_3

and education, was soon making plans to travel on the obligatory Grand Tour.[2] Byron left for the port of Falmouth on 20 June 1809, in the company of his life-long (and even posthumous) friend John Cam Hobhouse (1786–1869), created Baron Broughton in 1851. He 'is ye. oldest—indeed—ye. only friend I have', Byron wrote years later.[3] It is probably inevitable that Hobhouse is usually seen as Byron's Boswell, or even as his Sancho Panza, but it might be more accurate to see Hobhouse as Byron's straight-man, whose very seriousness allowed his noble friend the freedom to be extravagant. Nearly a year later, deep in the midst of his journey to the East, Byron could content himself in a letter to England with a barebones list of his doings and an excuse that 'Hobhouse will one day inform you of all our adventures, were I to attempt the recital, neither *my* paper nor *your* patience would hold during the operation.'[4] Indeed, Hobhouse's published account of their epic journey,[5] and the unpublished diaries on which it is based,[6] provide us with essential testimony towards appreciating Byron's Grand Tour to the East and the indelible effect that it had on his life and work, and the image of Turkey in England.

When one thinks of an English gentleman's Grand Tour, a pilgrim's map of France, Germany and Italy normally rises before one's eyes. But in the summer of 1809, Napoleon was busy conquering Europe, and a young man's study holiday abroad had to be planned accordingly. The Mediterranean seemed like a better place to begin than anywhere further north, with an option to travel to the East.[7] The *Princess Elizabeth* sailed from Falmouth on 2 July 1809, bound for Lisbon, with Byron and Hobhouse on board. They did Portugal in a fortnight, and on 20 July 1809 they crossed the Tagus River by boat and galloped through Spain on horseback.

Reading Hobhouse's diary and his published account of the Iberian part of their journey, the pattern of the Byron Road Show begins to take shape. There is a good deal of touring, especially taking in historic buildings such as monasteries and convents. They like to get in as much riding as possible, staying at local inns or places that they hire for the night or a few days. There is much dining with other Englishmen, especially those on diplomatic or other official business. They attend a bullfight, see a comedy, and drop in at a sort of burlesque house. But they also tour battle areas. Despite Byron's constant flippancy in his letters home during their travels, it is clear that his first encounter with the effects and detritus of war made a deep impression, and found its reflection in *Childe Harold's Pilgrimage*, Byron's poetic expression of his Grand Tour.

By the end of their month in Portugal and Spain it was clearly time to penetrate more deeply into the Mediterranean. The frigate *Hyperion* sailed from Cadiz to Gibraltar on 3 August 1809, and our two young heroes were on board. They landed the following day, and spent over three weeks on the Rock, where Byron entertained himself by frequenting the library of the English garrison. On 27 August 1809, they boarded the *Townshend* packet bound for Malta. It was only a four-day sail and should have gone smoothly, but when they arrived in Malta in the early afternoon of 31 August 1809, the Maltese shore batteries did not feel inclined to honour the young and unknown English lord with a salute, so they refused to disembark and slept aboard ship instead in order to advertise their displeasure.

The English governor of Malta, Sir Alexander Ball (1756?–1809) tried to make it up to them by extending an invitation to lunch the next day, advising them to proceed to Smyrna without undue delay. Later on, they dined with the English civil and military commander, Major-General Hildebrand Oakes (1754–1822), who advised them to forget about Smyrna and go straight on to Istanbul. Either way, the message Byron and Hobhouse got from both of these senior English local representatives was that if their destination was the Ottoman Empire, they might as well get on with it.

It was at their lodgings that they met Spiridion Foresti (1752–1822) and his son Georgios Foresti. The father had formerly served the British at Zante as their vice-consul (1783–1789) and consul (1789–1797 and 1799) and then at Corfu as resident minister (1799–1807). Since August 1807, Spiridion Foresti was in Malta, and would return to Zante as resident minister in 1810 (until 1814). His son Georgios would be appointed British consul at Ioannina in 1815. The Forestis latched on to Byron and Hobhouse, regaling them with local gossip and tales of Maltese society, offering to show them around and introduce them to amusing people. They were as good as their word, and the very next day, Spiridion presented Byron to the lovely Constance Spencer Smith (1785–1829), the twenty-four-year-old daughter of the Austrian ambassador at Istanbul. The young woman herself was the wife of an Englishman, sometime Minister Plenipotentiary to the Porte. Byron was entranced and quickly developed, as he later confessed, 'a passion for a married woman at Malta'.[8] Over the next fortnight, they spent much time together, a situation which was apparently mutually agreeable.

Spiridion Foresti was pleased to be included in Byron's secret adventure, and gradually began topping up his Malta stories with compelling tales about Tepedelenli Ali Paşa (1750?–1822), the strongman in Ioannina over in southern Albania (or rather Epirus in western Greece) who had been appointed by the Ottomans to serve as *derbendler başbuğu* there, a sort of local governor. He would also become *mutasarrıf* of Trikala (Tirhala) to the East from about 1812, when he was at the height of his power. Ali Paşa was already in 1809 a rather famous old rogue, more of a savage noble than a noble savage. He had carved out for himself a vicious dictatorship in Epirus, where from his capital at Ioannina he managed to subdue almost the entire Greek mainland, all the while walking a tightrope between full independence and fealty to the sultan, who had recognized the reality of his power and co-opted him as Ottoman man on the spot.[9]

Foresti assured Byron and Hobhouse that a visit to Ali Paşa's court could be easily arranged. This was exactly the kind of authentic experience that the two young Englishmen craved, and all thoughts of pushing on to the end of the Mediterranean were shoved aside. On 19 September 1809, having said his goodbyes to Constance and his other new friends, Byron and the faithful Hobhouse boarded the brig-of-war *Spider*, whose mission it was to convey a fleet of British merchant ships from Malta to Patras and Preveza. Seven days later, on 26 September 1809, Byron and Hobhouse set foot in Greece for the first time. They finally disembarked at Preveza on 29 September 1809, wearing their regimental uniforms:

> Now Harold felt himself at length alone,
> And bade to Christian tongues a long adieu:
> Now he adventured on a shore unknown,
> Which all admire, but many dread to view[10]:

Despite what Lord Byron's swooning fans wished to believe, Childe Harold was merely a fictional character whose shadowy pilgrimage followed his creator's actual journey. The real Byron was jolly, witty and rather funny, and had the virtuous Hobhouse to tease, so very unlike the dour and depressive Childe Harold, who travelled quite alone. But even so, when Byron landed in Epirus, now part of what we think of as definitely Greece but in 1809 usually referred to as part of Albania, he must have felt himself to have crossed some kind of invisible border. Byron well knew

Gibbon's famous description of the place in which he now found himself: 'A country in sight of Italy is less known than the wilds of America.'[11] Or as Byron's alter ego Childe Harold put it:

> Land of Albania! let me bend mine eyes
> On thee, thou rugged nurse of savage men!
> The cross descends, thy minarets arise,
> And the pale crescent sparkles in the glen[12]

II

Tepedelenli Ali Paşa was not a nice man. After a dangerous but romantic early life spent in general pillage and brigandage in the area of his native Albanian town of Tepedelen (Tepelenë in the local parlance), Ali in 1787 was officially recognized by his Ottoman rulers as strongman-in-charge, thus beginning a thirty-five year domination of virtually all of mainland Greece, and except for the last two years, under the aegis of the sultan himself. He became more widely known in Europe as a result of his campaign from 1792 to subdue the Souliotes, the Greek-speaking Albanians who lived in the Souli mountains of Epirus in western Greece. It took Ali over ten years to defeat them, and in 1803 the Souliotes were graciously allowed to keep their lives if they left their homes and removed to the port town of Parga or the Ionian Islands off the coast. Many Souliotes apparently chose to stay behind despite the threat of Ali's vengeance. All of Europe would be appalled by the story of the Souliote women who threw their children and then themselves into a mountain gorge rather than leave their ancestral homes. The scene both tragic and arresting was immortalized almost twenty-five years later in a painting by the French academic painter Ary Scheffer (1795–1858) that still hangs in the Louvre.[13]

Ali's ambitions turned rather more international on 17 October 1797, the day that the Treaty of Campo Formio was signed, and the Venetian Republic passed into history as it was transferred into Austrian hands. The Ionian Islands, however, were given to the French. Since the Fourth Crusade (1204), those seven strategically important islands off the west coast of Greece had mostly been Venetian colonies, and had continuously belonged to Venice for the past 300 years (1499–1797). Even when the Turks conquered the Peloponnese in 1715, they let the Venetians keep their islands. The Venetians also remained in possession of the so-called Ionian dependencies, the four towns on the mainland which were the continental points of the supply lifelines that made existence on the islands viable: Butrinto, Parga, Preveza and Vonitza. Ali Paşa coveted those towns, in order to make his control of the mainland more complete, and international instability in the Mediterranean seemed to bring that dream closer.

At the beginning of August 1798 in the Battle of the Nile (Aboukir Bay), Admiral Horatio Nelson (1758–1805) dealt a lethal blow to French ambitions in the eastern Mediterranean. Sultan Selim III (r. 1789–1807, d. 1808) and Czar Paul (r. 1796–1801) thereupon clubbed together to take the Ionian Islands away from the French and rule them as a team, an ambition achieved when Corfu finally fell in March 1799. But once the French were gone, Ali Paşa seized the moment and occupied the mainland town of Preveza, famously adorning the main square with a pyramid of severed heads. He also managed to grab Vonitza and Butrinto, although Parga resisted, being protected by French soldiers still within, and the aforementioned Souliotes without. Ali Paşa also sent 12,000 troops to conquer Corfu, but the Russians beat him to the punch and told him to go home.

To Ali Paşa's disappointment, on 21 March 1800 the Septinsular Republic was established, itself surviving only seven years, although he of course could not have predicted its swift demise. The new state enjoyed Russian protection and was guaranteed by an Ottoman treaty signed in Istanbul. Ali Paşa was entirely ignored, which is really all he could expect. But a year is a long time in international politics, and a year and two days after the birth of the new republic, Czar Paul was assassinated, and his son the Czar Alexander I (r. 1801–1825) failed to see the point of such a distant foreign adventure and ordered the troops home. He soon changed his mind, and by the following August (1802) Russian support for the Septinsular Republic was once again official government policy. From 1803, the Russians alone were effectively the sole occupiers of the Ionian Islands.

Venetians, French, Turks and even Russians: everyone seems to have had a piece of the Ionian Islands at one point or another during the late eighteenth and early nineteenth century, apart from the British, who were supposed to be such a formidable colonial power. This lacuna was painful to the British, who indeed were keen to insinuate themselves into this area of shifting loyalties and transitory ownership. The British ambassador to the Sublime Porte from 1803 to 1804 was William Drummond (1770?–1828), and he must have been intrigued to receive a message from Ali Paşa (1803), requesting that a British emissary be sent out to his Albanian court. When Drummond's man William Hamilton (1777–1859) got there, it was to convey promises of support for Ali Paşa from the government and people of Great Britain. This pro-Paşa policy was continued by the next British ambassador, Charles Arbuthnot (1767–1850), who even dispatched a proper consul-general to Ioannina to represent His Majesty's Government. He was David Richard Morier (1784–1877), who had been born in Smyrna only twenty years earlier. Young as he was, he was nevertheless the son of Isaac Morier (1750–1817), the consul-general to the Turkey Company in Istanbul, and would himself have a long and distinguished diplomatic career.[14] From 1804 to 1805, David Morier's presence at Ali Paşa's court showed the world that at least the British took him seriously as a figure (if not quite an independent ruler) on the world stage.

If the British thought that Ali Paşa was now in their pocket, they were about to become better acquainted with the man and his character. On 2 December 1805, Napoleon's victory over the Austrians at the Battle of Austerlitz gave Dalmatia to the French. In no time at all, French troops turned up along the northern border of Ali Paşa's territory. The limit of his authority was now an international border, and on the other side were the French, the traditional enemies of his new best friends the British. No less than their rivals across the English Channel, the French recognized how useful Ali Paşa might be in future Mediterranean matters, and understood the demands of a dictator's fragile ego. What Ali Paşa wanted first of all was a French resident consul-general to match his English envoys. Napoleon sent him François Charles Hugues Laurent Pouqueville (1770–1838), whose scholarly writings on Albania and environs would be an important source for Byron, as much as he criticized him and found out his errors of fact.[15]

From Ali Paşa's purely functional point of view, the French were beginning to look like an increasingly good bet. Russian-Turkish co-operation came to an end in 1806, and the two empires spent the next six years engaged in sporadic warfare. Ali Paşa's son Veli (for a change under express orders from Istanbul) captured three of the four Ionian dependencies of Vonitza, Preveza and Butrinto, although once again Parga held out, calling in Russian forces from Corfu. In January 1807, the British even bombarded Istanbul as part of the same conflict. There was peace on some of the fronts by the Treaty of Tilsit (7–9 July 1807), by which the Ionian Islands reverted to the French, although the Turks remained in control of the mainland dependencies, apart from exceptional Parga, where the French were allowed to stay.

As a loyal Ottoman official, Ali Paşa could hardly agitate for the removal of his own masters from the coastal towns that he had long coveted. On the other hand, the French claim to the Ionian Islands was based on nothing more than international agreement, which was the most fickle sort of personal relationship even by Mediterranean standards. The British understood his predicament and tried to keep Ali Paşa sweet. The British ambassador to the Sublime Porte from 1809 was Robert Adair (1763–1855), whose chargé d'affaires during the Napoleonic Wars (when the ambassador was absent) was young Stratford Canning (1786–1880), the Foreign Secretary's nephew, who would become one of the most central figures in Britain's Eastern Question. Adair and Canning together cobbled a treaty between Great Britain and the Ottoman Empire, which was signed in January 1809. Adair wrote to Ali Paşa on 9 April 1809, reassuring him of Britain's friendship and support.

By this time, relations with Ali Paşa had been much enhanced. On 21 October 1808, Foreign Secretary George Canning (1770–1827) took the crucial step of appointing a special envoy to Ioannina (until 1810), the topographer William Martin Leake (1777–1860), the English answer to M. Pouqueville. Leake was already a well-known figure, and would become even more famous.[16] In 1799 he had been sent to Istanbul to teach the Ottoman army about the latest artillery equipment. Leake had even already had the pleasure of meeting Ali Paşa in 1807, having been sent to persuade him at a secret rendezvous on a beach north of Preveza that should the Ottoman Empire lose more European territories, he should seize the moment and declare Albanian independence. If he did that, and refused the blandishments of the Russians and the French, then the British navy would support him. Leake was the Englishman in residence at Ioannina, and as we shall see, was on hand to greet Byron and Hobhouse when they came to town.

III

This, then, was the complicated political situation which was unknown to young Lord Byron and his faithful companion Hobhouse when they sailed on 19 September 1809, bound for the 'Land of Albania! where Iskander rose'.[17] It was thanks to his new friend, the well-connected Spiridion Foresti, that Byron was in Albanian Epirus at all, having been diverted by his spirit of adventure from his original plan of sailing to Arabic lands, Turkish Anatolia, or Istanbul itself. It was all Albania now. What Byron and

Hobhouse would learn only later was that when Spiridion was not carousing with the two Englishmen or spinning his tales of Ali Paşa, 'wrong but wromantic', he was packing his trunk for a secret sea voyage.

On 22 September 1809, a mere three days after Byron and Hobhouse left Malta on the *Spider*, a rather larger party set sail. It was an English expeditionary force of 1,857 men led by Major-General Sir John Oswald (1771–1840), whose special advisor on board was none other than Spiridion Foresti. Their mission was to conquer the Ionian Islands for Britain, taking them from the French in a surprise attack. In other words, as Byron and Hobhouse blithely proceeded northwards from the coast on the way to an audience with Ali Paşa, a dictator famous for capricious cruelty, their countrymen and hosts of the previous week were in the process of frustrating this Albanian's chief desire.

They spent their first full day ashore (30 September 1809) riding out to the ruins of Nicopolis (Nikópoli) to the north of Preveza. The following morning, Byron and Hobhouse sailed to Salora and began their journey by land to Ali Paşa's court. They carried a lot of gear: seven trunks, three beds (but only two wooden bedsteads, to keep them away from insects), four English saddles with bridles, and a canteen. The third bed was for Byron's servant, William Fletcher. The rest of the party had to shift for themselves, consisting of two soldiers for bodyguards and a dragoman (translator) named George. Transport was provided by a team of ten horses.

As they rode northwards, and unbeknownst to Byron and Hobhouse, their progress was shadowed by the British expeditionary force as it gathered up the Ionian Islands. On 2 October 1809, the British conquered Zante; Byron and Hobhouse were put off by the rain that day and stayed indoors with their soldier bodyguards. The next day they arrived at Arta, and the following morning slept at an inn halfway along the road to Ioannina. The day after that (5 October 1809), the British conquered Cefalonia, and our heroes arrived at Ioannina, Ali Paşa's seat, although the great man was awaiting them still further north at Tepedelen in Albania.

As yet oblivious to the dicey predicament in which they found themselves, Byron and Hobhouse were having the time of their young lives. They were proud and keenly aware that they were well off the beaten track, and were defying Gibbon's dictum regarding unknown Albania. This was a real adventure, and being children of the Romantic period, they paid especial attention to Nature and her beauties. 'Just before we left the banks of the river to the eastward' of Arta, recorded Hobhouse, 'we passed on our left hand a fine cedar, and the largest plane tree I have ever seen, except that so celebrated at Vostizza, in the Morea.'[18] The next day, arriving at Ioannina on 5 October 1809, their attention was arrested by another tree, or more particularly by the sight of a criminal's severed arm hanging from it *pour encourager les autres*.

Ali Paşa's capital was a surprise for the two travellers. 'The existence of such a city as Ioannina seems, till very lately, to have been almost unknown,' Hobhouse explained, 'and yet, I should suppose it, after Salonika and Adrianople, to be the most considerable place in European Turkey. It has never been my good fortune to meet with a notice of it in any book of an early date, except once in the ponderous history of Knolles.'[19] Even if the Orient was for Westerners a 'textual universe' as has been claimed, Planet Ioannina was not a known world.[20] Uncharted territory was exactly where Byron wanted to be, and the fact that its ruler was a cruel and possibly evil *paşa* right out of Arabian Nights made the moment even more delicious.

Their first stop both out of courtesy and practicality was the residence of William Martin Leake, the official representative of the British government at Ioannina. Sadly, he was not At Home, despite having received advance word of the approach of an English lord and his companion. Leake did, however, take the trouble to find living quarters for them at the house of an Italian-speaking Greek.[21] Leake may have snubbed our travellers, perhaps aware that the last thing he needed at this crucial moment in Anglo-Albanian relations was a couple of loose cannons smashing up the deck of British diplomacy. Ali Paşa himself, however, far from being vexed at having been kept out of the loop despite mutual attestations of loyalty and devotion with the British, was the very soul of hospitality. As soon as Byron and Hobhouse were safely installed in their quarters, they were called upon by the Greek primate of Ioannina and by Ali Paşa's secretary, a certain Spiridion Colovo.[22] Hobhouse confessed that he:

> was quite overwhelmed with the many fine things said by the Secretary, who spoke French; he told me, that his Highness had been aware of our intention to visit Ioannina; that he had ordered every thing to be prepared for our reception; that he was sorry to be obliged to leave his capital, to finish a little war (*une petite guerre*) in which he was engaged, but that he begged we would follow him; and lastly, that an escort was provided for that purpose, to be ready at our command...we were not a little surprised, especially when we learnt that all our provisions were to be daily furnished to us from the Vizier's palace.[23]

The next day (6 October 1809), when the elusive Mr Leake finally called and presumably brought his young visitors up to speed about their country's warlike activities in Ali Paşa's backyard, he found them very much at ease about their situation. Even Leake's faintly hostile demeanour failed to dampen their moods, as they 'Tried on Albanese dresses as fine as pheasants.'[24]

After a return courtesy visit to the unfriendly Mr Leake the following day (7 October 1809), Byron and Hobhouse walked up to Ali Paşa's palace for an appointment with Muhtar Ali, his ten-year-old grandson. As this building no longer exists, Hobhouse's description is particularly important[25]:

> The palace had one long, well-floored, open gallery, with wainscots painted in much the same style as our tea-boards. In one compartment was a tawdry representation of Constantinople, a favourite subject, and one which we recognised in almost every painted house in Turkey. We saw several rooms, not only handsomely, but very comfortably fitted up, especially those which, we were informed were the winter apartments. The coverings of the sofas were of richly-wrought silk; the floors were spread with the best Turkey carpets: and if the windows, which were large and deep, and of clear Venetian glass, had been furnished with curtains, there would have been nothing wanting to complete the elegance of the chambers. Except that one of the rooms was furnished with a marble recess, containing a bath and fountain, the whole palace seemed fitted up in the same style, which is easily accounted for, by the circumstance, that in Turkey there are no rooms set apart for sleeping, but all are indiscriminately used for that purpose, as each chamber contains a closet or cupboard, in which are deposited the mats or quilts, that constitute the whole of the bed of the Orientals.[26]

Clearly, Ali Paşa's palace lived up to their exotic expectations, but this fact did not prevent them from actually seeing what lay before their eyes.

Byron and Hobhouse were not in a hurry to leave Ioannina, despite the fact that their fearsome, if generous, host was awaiting their arrival at Tepedelen a few days' journey to the north. They spent the next day (8 October 1809) riding out in the area, visiting the Procurator of the city, and finally, dining with unpleasant Mr Leake.[27] It being Ramadan, they observed the spectacle of the rush to food at sunset. On the same day that Byron and Hobhouse were enjoying themselves with the locals of Ioannina, the British were conquering Ithaca, which fell to Major Richard Church (1784–1873) and the Corsican Rangers.

Byron and Hobhouse also began to understand the complicated position of ethnic and religious minorities in Greece, and in the Ottoman Empire in general. Hobhouse tried to sort out the situation for his readers:

> The Christians of Ioannina, though inhabiting a part of Albania, and governed by Albanian masters, call themselves Greeks, as do the inhabitants of Arta, Prevesa, and even of many villages higher up in the country: They neither wear the Albanian dress, nor speak the Albanian language, and they partake also in every particular of the manners and customs of the Greeks of the Morea, Roumelia, and the other Christian parts of Turkey in Europe and Asia. As, however, the appellation *Romæos*, or Roman, (once so proud a title, but now the badge of bondage) is a religious, not a national distinction, and means a Christian of the Greek church, and as many of the Albanians are of that persuasion, and denominated accordingly, it is difficult to avoid confusion, in giving to the various people of the country their common names. To prevent, however, any mistake, I shall always use the words Greek and Albanian, with a reference, not to the religion, but to the language and nation of the persons, whom I may have occasion to mention. At the same time, I shall indulge myself in the opposite license, of putting the word Turk as a religious denomination, which, though an undoubted vulgarism, is prevalent amongst the Greeks of the Levant, and does not, as far as I could see, give that offence to the Mahometans, of which I have somewhere read.[28]

Hobhouse is not Byron, but Byron was no less curious about these issues. Less than a fortnight in so-called Greece, and Byron had already learned that it might never be clear which Greeks needed to be liberated.

Two more days were spent in pleasant Ioannina, although their last was marred by pouring rain which drove them to spend it all inside. Still, they did manage to have their first experience of a *hamam*, a Turkish bath, which unsurprisingly turned out to be 'full of Turks, this being Ramadan'. Their bravery disappeared once their clothes came off, however, and they declined to hazard the central area to be properly scrubbed. Finally, on 11 October 1809, they departed Ioannina in the early afternoon under a rainstorm. The journey to Tepedelen was by Ali Paşa's invitation, and the road was safe only because he made it so, emphasized by the armed escort that he provided for the young Englishmen.

The first stage of the journey was short, only to the neighbouring village of Zitsa, to the north-west of Ioannina, where they stayed overnight at the monastery. Part of the attraction of this next part of the trip was that (according to Byron), no Englishman apart from the unromantic William Leake had ever penetrated beyond the capital, and of course, where no Englishman had gone, civilization had not truly penetrated.[29] Zitsa was (and is) a splendid place, and for Byron and Hobhouse it seemed as if they had stumbled upon an undiscovered spot of sacred beauty. Even pedantic Hobhouse was almost moved to poetry:

> A little above the village, which is itself on the steep side of a hill, there is a green eminence crowned with a grove of oak trees, that has been chosen, like almost every other beautiful spot in these parts of the world, for the site of a monastery. Immediately under the monastery, there is a large well-built house of the Vizier's, but there is no one who would not pass by the palace, were it ten times more splendid, to reach the neighbouring grove. Perhaps there is not in the world a more romantic prospect than that which is viewed from the summit of the hill.[30]

Byron himself devoted five stanzas of *Childe Harold's Pilgrimage* to the glories of 'Monastic Zitza', emphasizing in classic Romantic fashion its lonely and majestic natural beauty: 'here men are few,/Scanty the hamlet, rare the lonely cot'.[31] In keeping with the poem's structure as partly an anthropological travel narrative, Byron also added a footnote giving precise directions on how to find this little paradise. 'The situation is perhaps the finest in Greece,' he asserts, and 'I am almost inclined to add the approach to Constantinople'.[32] Byron had no way of knowing that the day he visited Zitsa Monastery (12 October 1809), the British conquered Cerigo. If Byron and Hobhouse had understood that Ali Paşa's international diplomacy was unravelling and leaving him with nothing, they might have been more apprehensive about making a pleasant pilgrimage to the court of a man famous for his cruelty and impatient with having his plans thwarted.

Tearing themselves away from Zitsa, our heroes left the village bright and early on 13 October 1809 and continued on their way north. It took Byron and Hobhouse a further week of travel to reach their destination, arriving in Tepedelen on Thursday, 19 October 1809, as their 'Journey was much prolonged by the torrents that had fallen from the mountains & intersected the roads.' Byron wrote to his mother a month later that, 'I shall never forget the singular scene on entering Tepaleen at five in the afternoon as the Sun was going down', and he meant it. Even more revealing, Byron was not embarrassed to tell her that his first view of Tepedelen 'brought to my recollection (with some change of *dress* however) Scott's description of Branksome Castle in his lay, & the feudal system'.[33] Needless to say, Byron's impressions upon entering Tepedelen found full poetic expression in *Childe Harold's Pilgrimage*, spread over eleven stanzas.[34] Hobhouse also saw Tepedelen as a window into Europe's past. 'The court at Tepellenè,' he wrote, 'presented us, at our first entrance, with a sight something like what we might have, perhaps, beheld some hundred years ago in the castle-yard of a great Feudal Lord.'[35]

The next day in the early afternoon (20 October 1809), Byron and Hobhouse finally had the opportunity

> To greet Albania's chief, whose dread command
> Is lawless law; for with a bloody hand
> He sways a nation, turbulent and bold:

More than a little pedantic, Byron would add a completely superfluous footnote in *Childe Harold's Pilgrimage* explaining that by Albania's chief he meant the 'celebrated Ali Pacha. Of this extraordinary man there is an incorrect account in Pouqueville's Travels.' The young Byron, of course, knew better than the famous French diplomat and geographer when it came to summing up the life, works, and character of one of the most notorious men in the Ottoman Empire. As his later creation Don Juan would explain, 'what's travel,/Unless it teaches one to quote and cavil?'[36]

Hobhouse recounted at length this first audience with Ali Paşa, and their passage in the palace over rubbish and through some shabby rooms, accompanied by their dragoman and secretary Colvo, who had deliberately dressed down rather than giving his master the impression that he was being overpaid. Ali Paşa greeted the young Englishmen while standing, which they understood to be a subtle compliment:

> The Vizier was a short man, about five feet five inches in height, and very fat, though not particularly corpulent. He had a very pleasing face, fair and round, with blue quick eyes, not at all settled into a Turkish gravity. His beard was long and white, and such a one as any other Turk would have been proud of; though he, who was more taken up with his guests than himself, did not continue looking at it, nor smelling and stroking it, as is usually the custom of his countrymen, to fill up the pauses of conversation. He was not very magnificently dressed, except that his high turban, composed of many small rolls, seemed of fine gold muslin, and his attaghan, or long dagger, was studded with brilliants. He was mightily civil; and said he considered us as his children.

Apart from observing the furnishings, Hobhouse also paid note to other details, such as the fact that Ali Paşa was prone to laughing aloud, 'which is very uncommon in a man of consequence: I never saw another instance of it in Turkey'. He also eschewed crowding himself with numerous courtiers, preferring the company of four or five young Albanians, whose main task was to make sure that the host and his guests were well-supplied with fresh pipes, coffee and sweetmeats. Hobhouse may not have been as flamboyant as Byron, but he was clever, as the following observation makes clear:

> There are no common topics of discourse between a Turkish Vizier and a traveller, which can discover the abilities of either party, especially as these conversations are always in the form of question and answer. However, a Frank may think his Turk above the common run, if his host does not put any very foolish interrogatories to him, and Ali did not ask us any questions that betrayed his ignorance. His liveliness and ease gave us very favourable impressions of his natural capacity.[37]

In many ways, this was rather an astute remark.

For Byron, as usual, it was all about him. Recounting this first meeting with Ali Paşa in a long letter to his mother, Byron neglected to mention Hobhouse's presence at all, attributing the aforementioned gracious hospitality to the fact that Ali Paşa 'had heard that an Englishman of rank was in his dominions'. Byron seems already to be rehearsing the role of that yet unborn lone pilgrim Childe Harold who would soon be making his solitary way across untracked and wild Albania. Byron did not forget to tell mother that he was presented wearing a full uniform including 'a very magnificent sabre', and also noted the fact that Ali Paşa received them standing, and bade him be seated next to him. Communicating through the Latin of his physician, Ali Paşa asked Byron the purpose of his visit to Albania, and recounted that according to Leake the young lord 'was of a great family, & desired his respects to my mother':

> He said he was certain I was a man of birth because I had small ears, curling hair, and little white hands, and expressed himself pleased with my appearance & garb. He told me to consider him as a father whilst I was in Turkey, & said he looked on me as his son. Indeed he treated me like a child, sending me almonds & sugared sherbet, fruit & sweetmeats 20 times a day.—He begged me to visit him often, and at night when he was more at leisure—I then after coffee & pipes retired for the first time. I saw him thrice afterwards.—It is singular that the Turks who have no heriditary [sic] dignities & few great families except the Sultan's pay so much respect to birth, for I found my pedigree more regarded than even my title.[38]

Ali Paşa himself Byron described as '60 years old, very fat & not tall, but with a fine face, light blue eyes & a white beard, his manner is very kind & at the same time he possesses that dignity which I find universal amongst the Turks.' Nevertheless, Byron had few illusions about the man and his deeds:

> He has the appearance of any thing but his real character, for he is a remorse-less tyrant, guilty of the most horrible cruelties, very brave & so good a gen-eral, that they call him the Mahometan Buonaparte.—Napoleon has twice offered to make him King of Epirus, but he prefers the English interest & abhors the French as he himself told me, he is of so much consequence that he is much courted by both, the Albanians being the most warlike subjects of the Sultan, though Ali is only nominally dependent on the Porte. He has been a mighty warrior, but is as barbarous as he is successful, roasting rebels &c. &c.—Bonaparte sent him a snuff box with his picture[;] he said the snuffbox was very well, but the picture he could excuse, as he neither liked *it* nor the *original*.

Ali Paşa continued his anti-French theme with his British guests when they met again the following evening (21 October 1809) in a more elegantly furnished apartment. 'Our next conversations were of war & travelling, politics & England', Lord Byron remembered.[39] During this interview, Hobhouse recounted, Ali Paşa

> congratulated us upon the news, which had arrived a fortnight before, of the surrender of Xante, Cefalonia, Ithaca, and Cerigo, to the British Squadron: he said, he was happy to have the English for his neighbours; that he was sure they would not serve him as the Russians and French had done, in pro-tecting his runaway robbers; that he had always been a friend to our Nation, even during our war with Turkey, and had been instrumental in bringing about the Peace.

Byron and Hobhouse assured their host that the illustrious name of Ali Paşa was well-known in England and indeed he was 'a very common sub-ject of conversation in our country'. Ali Paşa in turn continued to rubbish Napoleon, showing the young gentlemen that the emperor's gift to him of a rifle was so paltry that it had to be decently ornamented before it could be put on display even in a backwater like Tepedelen.[40]

Byron and Hobhouse were students of antiquity, so Ali Paşa ordered some horses so that his guests could ride out to see an old wall nearby, which they did the following day. In the evening, they called on Ali Paşa for the third and last time, to say farewell. On being informed that Byron and Hobhouse were intending to travel overland to the south via Trikala, Ali Paşa warned them that this 'part of the country was infested by large bands of robbers', so it was probably a better idea to head for the coast and proceed directly by sea to the Morea, where his son Veli was *paşa* and could be at their service. After a detailed examination of the route, and a few macabre jokes later, 'we withdrew, and took our last leave of this singular man'.[41]

Once again, it is Hobhouse who helps to flesh out the narrative with some interesting anthropological observations. Regarding Ali Paşa himself, Hobhouse testifies,

> Besides his native tongue, he talks Greek fluently, but of the Turkish language he knows very little; and, like Justin and Theodoric, the contemporary lords of the Eastern and Western Empires, has raised himself to his present power, without perhaps knowing the letters of any alphabet.[42]

As for the rest of those he met in Tepedelen,

> There are very few of them who cannot speak Greek, and, as their own is not a written language, a great many write and read that tongue. These are very proud of their acquirements, and so far from thinking it necessary to conceal their education, display their learning as ostentatiously as their valour. Were an Albanian to sit for his picture, he would wish to be drawn, like the admirable Creichton, with a sword in one hand and a book in the other. The Turkish language is known but to very few, even of the Mahometans amongst them. Of the Albanian language, there is collected for your inspection, almost the first specimen ever put to paper. The basis of it is said to be Sclavonian, mixed with a variety of other tongues, of which the Turkish is most predominant, though the modern Greek, the Italian, the French, and even words that sound like English, have a share in the composition of this strange medley. The infinite seems to be formed by the syllable *ti*.[43]

Hobhouse took his Eastern Grand Tour seriously, and never missed a chance to demonstrate some old-fashioned erudition, preferably philological in nature. Byron, for his part, was more impressed with what he observed about the Albanian attitude to women:

> They are perhaps the most beautiful race in point of countenance in the world, their women are sometimes handsome also, but they are treated like slaves, *beaten* & in short complete beasts of burthen, they plough, dig &

sow, I found them carrying wood & actually repairing the highways, the men are all soldiers, & war & the chase their sole occupations, the women are the labourers, which after all is no great hardship in so delightful a climate[44]

Hardly anything, it seems, could dampen Byron's enthusiasm for the new world that he saw in Albania.

The next day, 23 October 1809, Lord Byron and his friend Hobhouse departed from Tepedelen, knowing full well that their chats with the infamous Ali Paşa could provide them with a lifetime of dining out. That night they slept en route, and the next at Delvináki in the same house that had sheltered them on the trip north. Another night at the monastery in enchanting Zitsa, and on 26 October 1809 they rode once again into Ioannina and stayed another week. 'We passed our time at Ioannina, both before and after our visit to Tepellenè, most agreeably;' Hobhouse wrote, '—a sail upon the lake, a ride into the country, or a stroll through the Bazars and Bizestein, occupied our mornings, and our evenings were passed at home in the conversation of our host, or abroad in visits to the principal people of the town.'[45]

Byron always liked to paint his friend as a somewhat humourless pedant, and certainly Hobhouse was unable to enjoy his visit to a traditional *karagöz* performance, the Turkish answer to 'Punch and Judy':

An evening or two before our departure from Ioannina, we went to see the only advance which the Turks have made towards scenic representations. This was a puppet show, conducted by a Jew who visits this place during the Ramazan, with his card performers. The show, a sort of ombre Chinoise, was fitted up in a corner of a very dirty coffee-house which was full of spectators, mostly young boys. The admittance, was two paras for a cup of coffee, and two or three more of those small pieces of money put into a plate handed round after the performance. The hero of the piece was a kind of punch, called Cara-keus, who had, as a traveller has well-expressed it, the equipage of the God of Gardens, supported by a string from his neck. The next in dignity was a droll, called Codja-Haivat, the Sancho of Cara-keus; a man and a woman were the remaining figures, except that the catastrophe of the drama was brought about by the appearance of the Devil himself in his proper person. The dialogue, which was all in Turkish, and supported in different tones by the Jew, I did not understand; it caused loud and frequent bursts of laughter from the audience; but the action, which was perfectly intelligible, was too horribly gross to be described. If you have ever seen the morrice-dancing in some counties of England, you may have a faint idea of it. If the character of a nation, as has been said, can be well appreciated by a view of the amusements in which they delight, this puppet-show would place the Turks very low in the estimation of any observer. They have none, we were informed, of a more decent kind.[46]

In the diary upon which the published version of his travels is based, Hobhouse elaborated upon the 'horribly gross' part of the performance, noting that the hero of the pantomime was a

personage with an immense head and body tapering to the waist of a wasp, and from the regions of his breeches proceeded an enormous yard, supported by a piece of visible string from his neck, which he seemed to wear *par excellence*, none of the other characters having this engine displayed... One of the most admired passages in the play was where the above important character held a soliloquy addressed to the appendage alluded to, which he then snubbed most soundly with his fist, which was a prelude to the devil descending and removing this engine from before and affixing it to his posteriors. To bed at twelve.

'Nothing could be more beastly,' Hobhouse thought, 'but Lord Byron tells me that he has seen puppet-shows in England as bad, and that the morris dances in Nottinghamshire are worse.'[47]

Byron and Hobhouse also had the pleasure of visiting Mahmout Paşa, Ali Paşa's little grandchild, being Veli's eldest son. Byron was impressed by his 'asking whether my fellow-traveller and myself were in the upper or lower House of Parliament', noting that 'this question from a boy of ten years old proved that his education had not been neglected'.[48] Hobhouse, on the other hand, painted a rather more sad and poignant picture of Mahmout and his little brother.[49]

Something clicked for Byron and Hobhouse during these last days in October 1809, as they returned to Ioannina after visiting Ali Paşa, coming back to a town that they had already made their own, in the manner of tourists everywhere. At this point in Hobhouse's published narrative, he was inspired to deliver a paean about the glories of Albania:

There are now not a few inducements which may probably cause many intelligent travellers of our own country to visit Ioannina, and Albania; and from their investigation the world will doubtless be informed of many interesting particulars before unknown. The vicinity of the islands now in our possession, the peaceable state of the country under the government of Ali, the good correspondence that prince maintains with the English, and the wish of exploring regions so long involved in complete obscurity, and, as it were, lost out of the map of Europe, will aid and prompt their enquiries, and we shall soon be as well informed with respect to the people and country of Albania, as we have been for some time on the head of Greece and other provinces of Turkey. Ioannina itself affords a safe and agreeable residence to travellers. The Greeks are of the better sort, and well instructed in the manners and languages of Christendom[50]

Byron, for his part, was inspired in a completely different direction. 'Byron is writing a long poem in the Spenserian stanza,' wrote Hobhouse in his diary entry for 31 October 1809, 'and I am collecting Davies' jokes, reading the Arabian nights in Greek Romaïque—most barbarous Italianisms.'[51] Indeed, on the cover of the original manuscript of *Childe Harold's Pilgrimage*, the following words are inscribed: 'Byron—Ioannina in Albania Begun Oct. 31, 1809 Concluded Canto 2nd March 28, 1810. Byron'. Never mind that Harold began his life as 'Childe Burun': the Byronic hero was born in Ioannina, with consequences not only for Lord Byron himself, but for European literature forever after.

After this agreeable and fateful week, Byron and Hobhouse finally left Ioannina an hour after noon on 3 November 1809, heading south. By sunset the next day they made Arta, and the day after that they arrived at Salora. Taking seriously what Ali Paşa had told them about highwaymen—and who would know better than the chief highwayman himself—they accepted their Albanian host's offer of an armed vessel to take them from Preveza to Patras, and set sail on 8 November 1809. Unfortunately, the crew consisted of incompetents, and nearly sank the boat, barely making it to shore the next day not far from Parga, which was a French port. Our heroes feared for the worst, thinking of their Cornish countrymen who famously scanned the horizon for shipwrecks and potential shipwrecks in hope of loot and plunder. Needless to say, this exciting adventure made its way into Childe Harold's life as well:

LXVII.
It chanced that adverse winds once drove his bark
Full on the coast of Suli's shaggy shore,
When all around was desolate and dark;
To land was perilous, to sojourn more;
Yet for awhile the mariners forbore,
Dubious to trust where treachery might lurk:

At length they ventured forth, though doubting sore
That those who loathe alike the Frank and Turk
Might once again renew their ancient butcher-work.

LXVIII.
Vain fear! the Suliotes stretched the welcome hand,
Led them o'er rocks and past the dangerous swamp,
Kinder than polished slaves, though not so bland,
And piled the hearth, and wrung their garments damp,
And filled the bowl, and trimmed the cheerful lamp,
And spread their fare: though homely, all they had:
Such conduct bears Philanthropy's rare stamp -
To rest the weary and to soothe the sad,
Doth lesson happier men, and shames at least the bad.[52]

Shortly after the following noon (10 November 1809), they were on the road again, arriving back at Preveza by sunset, lodging in the house of the English consul.

Not having learned their lesson, Byron and Hobhouse sailed out from Preveza on 13 November 1809 with the very same incompetent captain as before, arriving the next day after a windless voyage where 'long Utraikey forms its circling cove'.[53] That night, they had a marvellous, Romantic, and formative experience, which like their visit to Ali Paşa's court was another moment when it seemed as if their whole Eastern Grand Tour was worth it. Hobhouse, as usual, tells the facts:

In the evening the gates were secured, and preparations were made for feeding our Albanians. A goat was killed, and roasted whole, and four fires were kindled in the yard, round which the soldiers seated themselves in parties. After eating and drinking, the greater part of them assembled round the largest of the fires, and, whilst ourselves and the elders of the party were seated on the ground, danced round the blaze to their own songs, in the manner before described, but with astonishing energy. All their songs were relations of some robbing exploits. One of them, which detained them more than an hour, began thus—"When we set out from Parga, there were sixty of us;" then came the burden of the verse,
   " Robbers all at Parga!
   " Robbers all at Parga!"
... and as they roared out this stave, they whirled round the fire, dropped, and rebounded from their knees, and again whirled round, as the chorus was again repeated. The rippling of the waves upon the pebbly margin where we were seated, filled up the pauses of the song with a milder, and

not more monotonous music. The night was very dark, but by the flashes of the fires we caught a glimpse of the woods, the rocks, and the lake, which, together with the wild appearance of the dancers, presented us with a scene that would have made a fine picture in the hands of such an artist as the author of the Mysteries of Udolpho. As we were acquainted with the character of the Albanians, it did not at all diminish our pleasure to know, that every one of our guard had been robbers, and some of them a very short time before. The most respectable and best mannered Bolu-bashee with us, had been, four years past, a very formidable one, having had the command of two hundred upon the mountains behind Lepanto, but he had submitted with his men, and was now in the service of Ali. It was eleven o'clock before we had retired to our room, at which time the Albanians, wrapping themselves up in their capotes, went to sleep round the fires.[54]

Byron as Childe Harold incorporated this stupendous evening wholesale into his *Pilgrimage*, devoting stanzas 69–72 of the second canto (the last stanza including the Albanian song as an excursus), with footnotes, to 'the pirates of Parga that dwell by the waves'. The captain's shipwreck was not quite forgiven, however, and now that they had securely disembarked in Utraique, they decided to stick to land, robbers or otherwise, and make their way through the passes down south, guarded by ten Albanian soldiers from the local militia. They reached Missolonghi on 20 November 1809, the mosquito-infested backwater where Byron would die less than fifteen years later.

Byron and Hobhouse spent four months in Greece, visiting Delphi, Thebes, and especially Athens. But it was Istanbul that called them, and they asked for and obtained a travelling firman through Robert Adair, the British ambassador there. When on 4 March 1810 the captain of the British sloop-of-war *Pylades* offered them a place on his boat bound for Smyrna, they eagerly accepted and were under sail within twenty-four hours, arriving at their destination on 7 March 1810. Albania and Greece were certainly part of the Ottoman Empire, but this was Turkey, where it was true even more than in Epirus that as the 'cross descends, thy minarets arise'.

IV

A month in Smyrna might seem like a long time, but it was a good base from which to explore Anatolia. Byron and Hobhouse were the guests of Francis Werry (1745–1832), the British consul-general. Hobhouse was especially pleased at their accommodations: 'Surprised at the excellence of Werry's house—a long, narrow house, like the gallery and chambers of an inn. It has no breadth, but everything is English and comfortable.'[55] They spent a lot of time there, apart from a three-day jaunt to Ephesus and Selçuk. On 28 March 1810, Byron finished the second canto of *Childe Harold's Pilgrimage*, which when published almost exactly two years later, would make his name.

Istanbul was their goal, and while they were in Smyrna, a few developments had made their reception more assured. The British conquered Santa Maura (Lefkada), the island off the coast near Preveza, not without casualties, on 22 March 1810. The next day, Ambassador Adair asked the Turks if he might suggest to Russia that the Danubian Principalities of Moldavia and Wallachia stay under Ottoman control, and that in compensation, the British would give the Russians 'a portion of that superflux of Colonial Establishments which the War has thrown into His Majesty's Hands'. The Turkish reaction to this British generosity made Adair such a local hero that he decided to leave on a high and thereupon quit his post.[56] Byron and Hobhouse left Smyrna on 11 April 1810 aboard the frigate *Salsette* commanded by Captain Walter Bathurst (1764–1827), who was en route to Istanbul with orders to pick up Ambassador Adair and bring him home.[57] Byron told Hobhouse that Mrs. Werry was so sorry to see him go that she 'actually cut off a lock of his hair. I saw her cry at parting,' Hobhouse testified, looking 'pretty well at fifty-six years at least.'[58]

The hop from Smyrna to Istanbul turned out to be a long trip, as they were detained for a fortnight by unhelpful winds 'Waiting for his Sublimity's firman,/The most imperative of sovereign spells', absolutely necessary to enter the Straits.[59] But there was a bright side to the delay, since there was nothing to stop Byron and Hobhouse from taking a small boat to shore in order to visit the site of Troy, or rather a nearby site to the south-east called Pınarbaşı, which had been mis-identified as Troy by Jean Baptiste Le Chevalier (1752–1836).[60] Doubts about everything to do with Troy had already been planted in Byron's mind, but in entirely the wrong direction, by Jacob Bryant (1715–1804), the British mythographer.[61] Byron was very cross about this, and wrote years later that

I have stood upon that plain daily, for more than a month, in 1810; and, if any thing diminished my pleasure, it was that the blackguard Bryant had impugned its veracity. It is true I read 'Homer Travestied' (the first twelve books), because Hobhouse and others bored me with their learned localities, and I love quizzing. But I still venerated the grand original as the truth of history (in the material *facts*) and of *place*. Otherwise, it would have given me no delight. Who will persuade me, when I reclined upon a mighty tomb, that it did not contain a hero?—its very magnitude proved this. Men do not labour over the ignoble and petty dead—and why should not the dead be Homer's dead?[62]

But they were in Turkey now, not ancient Greece, and the contrast was sometimes stark:

> Troops of untended horses; here and there,
> Some little hamlets, with new names uncouth;
> Some shepherds (unlike Paris), led to stare
> A moment at the European youth
> Whom to the spot their school-boy feelings bear;
> A Turk, with beads in hand, and pipe in mouth,
> Extremely taken with his own religion,
> Are what I found there—but the devil a Phrygian.[63]

(Phrygia was much further to the east, where Ankara is located, but never mind.)

Visiting the (supposed) site of Troy was a thrill, but the contrary winds off the Dardanelles brought with them another unexpected adventure, which became an essential part of the entire Byron myth and industry: his pioneering swim across the Hellespont. How pioneering we shall never know. Perhaps swimming across the Dardanelles was the sort of pointless labour that no Turk ever dreamed of attempting. Maybe Byron really was the first person to cross the Straits under his own steam. For him, it was all about rehearsing Greek mythology and recreating Leander's nightly swim from Abydos on the Asian side, to his love Hero, a priestess of Aphrodite who lived in a tower in Sestos on the European shore. She would place a light in her tower to guide him as he swam in the dark, but one dark and stormy night the light went out, and Leander was drowned. Hero looked down and saw his dead body washing up on the shore, and overcome by despair, she jumped down from her tower to perish with him in the waves. It was a great story, made even greater by the knowledge that it was also here in 480 BC that the Persian king Xerxes built a bridge of boats to carry his army across to fight the Greeks. Alexander the Great in 334 BC successfully completed the same crossing, in reverse.[64] Leander, Xerxes, Alexander the Great, and now Byron, twenty-two years old and a very strong swimmer, the water being the one place where his deformed foot did not impede his forward progress.

In the early evening of 16 April 1810, Byron made his first attempt at the crossing from Asia to Europe, accompanied by one of the sailors, Lieutenant William Ekenhead (d. 1810), Sherpa Tenzing to Byron's Edmund Hillary. 'Lord Byron and Mr. Ekenhead got into the water some way above the castle to swim over,' Hobhouse noted in his diary, 'but were obliged to give up from the excessive coldness of the water in an hour, having been carried down by the strength of the current a mile and a half, at least, below the castles, and being about half over.'[65] Byron's own explanation was that he 'failed owing to the North wind and the wonderful rapidity of the tide'.[66]

The firman for entering the Straits arrived on the last day of April, so the *Salsette* could actually enter the Dardanelles.[67] Maybe this was a good omen, so Byron and his companion Ekenhead tried again, this time attempting Leander's return voyage, from the European side to the Asian shore: 'they were determined to make another attempt in warmer weather,' Hobhouse explained,

> and accordingly on the third of May following, at a little past ten in the morning, having left the frigate at her anchorage below the Asiatic castle, they got into the water nearly a mile and a half above Chelit-Bawri, at a point of land forming the western bank of the deep bay or inlet in which stands the town of Maito, on the site of the ancient Madytus. I did not accompany them in the boat, but watched their progress from the frigate. They swam upwards as before, but not for so long a time, and in less than half an hour came floating down the current close to the ship. They then swam strongly to get within the bay behind the castle, and soon succeeding, reached the still water, and landed about a mile and a half below our anchorage. Lord Byron was one hour and ten minutes in the water, his companion, Mr. Ekenhead, five minutes less.[68]

When they finally got to Istanbul, Byron made a note in Hobhouse's diary with his own hand to commemorate this amazing feat:

> P.S. Constantinople The whole distance E. and myself swum was more than 4 miles the current very strong and cold, some large fish near us when half across, we were not fatigued but a little chilled. did it with little difficulty may 26th 1810. Byron.[69]

Ovid tells us that Leander was also aware of his aquatic companions, and told Hero that 'The bending dolphins are now conscious of our tender loves; nor are the fishes of the sea strangers to my flame.'[70] Byron could never resist a chance to display his erudition, and Hobhouse admits in his diary that when Byron and Ekenhead were swimming across the Hellespont, he had 'Ovid's *Hero to Leander* open before me'.[71]

Byron never stopped talking about his epic swim, and even when he was being self-consciously ironic, the pride was always there. He wrote a poem about it, dated 9 May 1810, 'Written After Swimming from Sestos To Abydos'. Even the possibility that his Sherpa beat him to the summit failed to quench his enthusiasm, due in part perhaps to the fact that Ekenhead never survived 1810: after the *Salsette* got back to Malta, Ekenhead was promoted to captain, got drunk, and fell over a bridge to his death. Byron inserted his temporary friend into the English literary canon by including him in his great last poem *Don Juan*:

> A better swimmer you could scarce see ever,
> He could, perhaps, have pass'd the Hellespont,
> As once (a feat on which ourselves we prided)
> Leander, Mr. Ekenhead, and I did.[72]

He boasted to his friend Henry Drury that this 'morning I swam from Sestos to Abydos, the immediate distance is not above a mile but the current renders it hazardous, so much so, that I doubt whether Leander's conjugal powers must not have been exhausted in his passage to Paradise'.[73] To Francis Hodgson a couple of days later he also wrote of his epic swim, and informed his mother that 'when we were at anchor in the Dardanelles, swimming from Sestos to Abydos, in imitation of Monsieur Leander whose story you no doubt know too well for me to add any thing on the subject except that I crossed the Hellespont without so good a motive for the undertaking'.[74] To his solicitor John Hanson, Byron reported that he 'swam from Sestos to Abydos in the Dardanelles, any of your classical men (Hargreaves or Charles) will explain the meaning of the last performance and the old story connected with it'.[75] There were others who were graced with Byron's endless retelling of his cross-channel swim.[76] One hopes slightly with self-irony, he wrote yet again to his mother noting that 'I believe I mentioned to you in my last that my only notable exploit lately, has been swimming from Sestos to Abydos on the 3d. of this month, in humble imitation of *Leander* of amorous memory, although I had no *Hero* to receive me on the other shore of the Hellespont.'[77] Finally, having exhausted this joke, he wrote once again to Francis Hodgson at the beginning of July 1810, saying that

I shall begin by telling you, having only told it you twice before, that I swam from Sestos to Abydos. I do this that you may be impressed with proper respect for me, the performer; for I plume myself on this achievement more than I could possibly do on any kind of glory, political, poetical, or rhetorical. Having told you this I will tell you nothing more, because it would be cruel to curtail Cam's narrative, which, by-the-bye, you must not believe till confirmed by me, the eye-witness. I promise myself much pleasure from contradicting the greatest part of it.[78]

Be that as it may, it was a great story, and an impressive accomplishment. For many people, Byron's aquatic crossing is one of the few memorable facts about his eventful life.

But it was not all a joke, even for Byron. He and his friend were about to enter the heart of the Islamic world, the third segment of their Grand Tour to the mysterious East. Albania and Greece were for them, as for the many others who came before and afterwards, a sort of liminal zone between Europe and the East, a place where one might find a cross as well as a crescent. But it was also wild, and off the beaten track, and the young Byron was not immune to its savage charms, even if in his letters he was unable to keep his tone serious for more than a clause or two. As he explained to his friend Henry Drury while still on board loitering outside the Dardanelles, ten days before arriving in Istanbul:

Albania indeed I have seen more of than any Englishman (but a Mr. Leake) for it is a country rarely visited from the savage character of the natives, though abounding in more natural beauties than the classical regions of Greece, which however are still eminently beautiful…I see not much difference between ourselves & the Turks, save that we have foreskins and they none, that they have long dresses and we short, and that we talk much and they little.—In England the vices in fashion are whoring & drinking, in Turkey, Sodomy & smoking, we prefer a girl and a bottle, they a pipe and pathic.

Having actually visited the place, for Byron, then, Albania was part of Greece and was inhabited by Turks, who are not so different even from Englishmen, the epitome of the human race. At the same time, Byron wrote, 'I like the Greeks, who are plausible rascals, with all the Turkish vices without their courage.—However some are brave and all are beautiful, very much resembling the busts of Alcibiades, the women not quite so handsome.' Greeks, then, were not quite as wonderful as the Turks, but not bad to look at.[79]

On 13 May 1810, the *Salsette* arrived at Istanbul, anchoring near Sarayburnu ('Seraglio Point'), on which stands Topkapı Palace, still then the official residence of the sultan. When the minarets of the Sultan Ahmet 'Blue' Mosque and the Ayasofya (Hagia Sophia) came into view, Hobhouse thought they were 'arranged much in the same order, and having the same appearance, as the distant turrets of King's College Chapel at Cambridge'.[80] Immediately upon landing, Byron and Hobhouse were conveyed by boat to Tophane a little way up the Bosphorus: 'We had not much less than a mile to ride, the whole way on an ascent, before we came to our inn. This was situated at the corner of the main street of Pera, where four ways meet; all of which were not less mean and dirty than the lanes of Wapping.'[81] As Hobhouse explained, 'A fire which had burnt down nearly the half of Pera, rendered it difficult to procure lodgings; but in three days we were settled at a house in the main street, and immediately opposite to a small convent of nuns, and a lane leading to Frantzoos-Seraï, the mansion-house of the French embassy.'[82]

Their first destination was the English embassy, located only a few minutes away, to call on Robert Adair, the ambassador. He offered the two young gentleman apartments within, but they declined, preferring to stay where they were, although Hobhouse thought that the building itself was 'very superb, of stone', with large rooms and suites of apartments, but damp.[83] Byron and Hobhouse did accept the offer of a Janissary to serve as dragoman and were happy to dine at the English palace as often as they could. Hobhouse was not very taken with Adair, who appeared to him to be 'very pale and weak, dark eyes, but an ugly man, mild manners'. Adair told Hobhouse that he knew his father, and generally gave the impression that he 'Detests the Turks'. His colleague Stratford Canning made a better impression, being a 'pleasing young man with a vulgar voice'.[84]

Canning also liked his visitors, and noted in his unpublished (and now lost) memoirs that

> By the *Salsette* two young travellers, both of distinguished merit, and one of world-wide renown, appeared within our horizon. Lord Byron and his friend Mr. Hobhouse, afterwards Lord Broughton, were the luminaries in question. They formed together a most interesting addition to our society. I had already seen the poet at a cricket match between the boys of Eton and those of Harrow; we had both played in the respective elevens, and I had not forgotten the impression then made upon me by Lord Byron's appearance in his flannel jacket with bat over his shoulder. The pleasure of making his acquaintance was reserved for me in the land of 'the citron and

vine'. He was then engaged, as I learnt afterwards, in the composition of his *Childe Harold*. His *Poems of a Minor* were already eclipsed by the success of his tilt against the *Edinburgh Review*. We took several rides together, and I still retain a most agreeable recollection of his good nature and varied conversation.[85]

Byron also 'praises him much'.[86]

Now it was time to play the tourist. They climbed the Galata Tower— 147 steps, Hobhouse counted—and admired the view, although they could not locate the supposed seven hills of Istanbul.[87] Having done Pera, they set off a few days later to explore the older part of Istanbul, Constantinople proper, and they were not disappointed. Hobhouse was very impressed, and noted this down in his diary in his role as recording angel:

Walked up burying-ground to the English Palace, and thence home where wrote this very imperfect account of the day's tour, which has left upon me a much more favourable idea of Constantinople than I entertained before. The streets are clean, more regular, wider, and better built than Pera, and the bazaar and buistun are very striking, even to a person acquainted with and accustomed to the wealth and the shops of London. The number of Jews everywhere immense—not insulted. Saw many armed men.[88]

In his published version of his travel book, Hobhouse was even more complimentary:

I consider the present city to be infinitely superior to the metropolis of the Greek Empire in the reigns of the latter Emperors. The streets are, it is true, narrow, and either ill-paved or not at all; but, except in Ballat, the Fanal and the Armenian quarter, they are much cleaner than those of Pera, and, unless compared with the neatness and regularity of an English town, are far from deserving those epithets of disgust and contempt which are usually bestowed upon them by travellers.[89]

This was Hobhouse, not Byron, but as Byron explained, 'why should I say more of these things? ... has not Hobby got a journal?'[90] 'Mr. Hobhouse, our brother author, will narrate, no doubt, all our adventures, if you seriously incline that way.'[91]

Their wonderful stay in Istanbul was marred by only one bizarre incident, which ended more or less happily. On 28 May 1810, Byron and Hobhouse put on their 'gay regimentals', and went over to the English embassy on their way to a scheduled audience at Topkapı Palace with Sultan Mahmud II (r. 1808–1839). Things did not go according to plan, as Stratford Canning wrote later on in his memoirs:

> On the occasion of these audiences an incident took place so amazingly characteristic of our noble bard that I cannot forbear to record it. We had assembled for the first of them in the hall of our so-called palace when Lord Byron arrived in scarlet regimentals topped by a profusely feathered cocked hat, and coming up to me asked what his place, as a peer of the realm, was to be in the procession. I referred him to Mr. Adair, who had not yet left his room, and the upshot of their private interview was that as the Turks ignored all but officials, any amateur, though a peer, must be content to follow in the wake of the Embassy. His lordship thereupon walked away with that look of scornful indignation which so well became his fine imperious features. Next day the ambassador, having consulted the Austrian Internuncio and received a confirmation of his own opinion, wrote to apprize Lord Byron. The reply gave assurance of the fullest satisfaction, and ended with a declaration that the illustrious penitent would, if permitted, attend the next audience in his excellency's train, and humbly follow 'his ox, or his ass, or anything that was his.' In due time he redeemed his pledge by joining the procession as a simple individual, and delighting those who were nearest to him by his well-bred cheerfulness and good-humoured wit.[92]

Hobhouse noted in his diary that Byron 'went away because he would not suffer Mr. Canning to walk before him', and that night boycotted dinner at the English Palace. When Hobhouse got home, he 'found him packing up and going the day after but one to Smyrna'.[93] It was all smoothed out in the end, but Byron's vanity had been wounded, and his Istanbul adventure almost ended there and then.

Instead, the sightseeing went on. The day after the Precedence Crisis, our heroes were to be found once again at the walls of Istanbul, haunting the Eğri Kapı ('Crooked Gate'), where Constantine XI Dragases, the last Byzantine emperor, threw off his insignia and died fighting the Turks in their conquest of Constantinople on 29 May 1453. They even tried to enter the fortress of Yedikule, into whose dungeon foreign ambassadors were traditionally thrown at the outbreak of war, but they were stopped at the gate.[94] The following fortnight, they went back, and from 'thence walked all along the walls, 118 towers, in one hour seventeen minutes'.[95] There was also the Sultan Ahmet 'Blue' Mosque, the Ayasofya (Hagia Sophia), and the

Nuruosmaniye and Süleymaniye mosque complexes to visit. Byron and Hobhouse spent two full months in Istanbul, and there is no doubt that they did the town.

But the ship they came in on was the vessel sent to take Ambassador Robert Adair away, and eventually it was time to leave. Adair had his final audience with Sultan Mahmud II on 10 July 1810, and this time, Byron was there.[96] Byron, Hobhouse and Adair took their collective leaves of Istanbul, and on 17 July 1810, Hobhouse parted from Byron at Keos ('Zea') and returned alone via Malta to England, leaving Byron to go it solo in Greece for another full year until his own return on 14 July 1811. Adair became a Knight Commander of the Order of the Bath (KCB), but received no further diplomatic appointments. Stratford Canning, now British minister plenipotentiary at the Sublime Porte but not yet twenty-four years old, remained in Istanbul, quite alone. By his own admission, the first thing he did was to lock the door to his room and burst into tears.[97]

V

After a year outside of England, of which time nine months was spent in the Ottoman Empire, Lord Byron and John Cam Hobhouse fancied themselves to be rather expert. Byron's additional year by himself in Ottoman Greece was a further opportunity to internalize impressions, but even now, by July 1810, they had firm opinions about the Turks, their history and their culture. In brief, they liked what they saw, not only because it was different, but because things they had seen on their Grand Tour had shattered their preconceptions and received ideas.

Hobhouse was disabused of the notion of inevitable Turkish decline beginning with the later seventeenth century. He would have none of that:

> the powerful states of Europe have, in the opinion of most writers, been prevented from the expulsion of the Ottomans from Europe, only by their interested jealousies and mutual dissensions. Yet although the existence of this barbarian power in the most flourishing regions of Europe, confined on every side by hostile kingdoms, or by an element possessed by Christians, has been for a century regarded as a reproach to all civilised nations, and a standing wonder, it must be acknowledged, that the decline of the Ottoman empire has by no means been so rapid, nor its disgraces so repeated and uninterrupted, as casual observers are apt to believe.[98]

Hobhouse had now come to realize that many of the armchair strategists who had been so sure of Turkish decline had never even been to the East, unlike Lord Byron and himself:

> The justice and wisdom of expelling them from that portion of the con-
> tinent which they have so long possessed, may be discussed by any one
> accustomed to similar speculations; but the question of the facility with
> which this object might be accomplished, is more competently handled by
> those who have studied the character of the Turks on the spot, and have
> enjoyed the advantage of some personal intercourse with their paradoxical
> nation.[99]

Even Europeans who actually manage to get to Istanbul often miss the point:

> The water of the Golden Horn, which flows between the city and the sub-
> urbs, is a line of separation seldom transgressed by the Frank residents; and
> an English stranger, if he waited for the suggestions of his fellow-countrymen
> of the Levant Company, would pass many weeks at Pera without paying
> one visit to Constantinople...it will not be expected that a traveller should
> insinuate himself into any Turkish company, or enjoy any other society than
> that which is to be found at Pera. The Franks have, as it were, engrafted
> themselves on that limb of the capital, and the shoot has many more charac-
> teristics of the exotic than of the parent plant.[100]

In any case, one should not be too hasty in wishing for the disintegration of the Ottoman Empire:

> But even supposing that the partition of Turkey should be amicably settled
> by the Christian powers, it appears to me that the struggle would be pro-
> tracted and sanguinary, and that the Mussulmans, like the volunteers of
> Mecca who attacked the French in Egypt, would to a man quit the defence
> of their country and their religion only with their lives. I say nothing of the
> extreme improbability of any arrangement of contending interests, by which
> they would be left without a friend to defend themselves against the union
> of all Christendom.[101]

The Ottoman Empire looked very different when standing on the shores of the Bosphorus rather than looking out from the banks of the Thames.

Lord Byron was at this stage more taken with the unexpected beauty of the place, and wrote to his mother that

The walls of the Seraglio are like the walls of Newstead Gardens only higher, and much in the same *order*, but the ride by the walls of the city on the land side is beautiful, imagine, four miles of immense triple battlements covered with *Ivy*, surmounted with 218 towers, and on the other side of the road Turkish burying grounds (the loveliest spots on earth) full of enormous cypresses. I have seen the ruins of Athens, of Ephesus, and Delphi, I have traversed great part of Turkey and many other parts of Europe and some of Asia, but I never beheld a work of Nature or Art, which yielded an impression like the prospect on each side, from the Seven Towers to the End of the Golden Horn

Byron liked the Turks as well, as people. 'I have not been disappointed or disgusted,' Byron wrote. 'I have lived with the highest and the lowest, I have been for days in a Pacha's palace, and have passed many a night in a cow-house, and I find the people inoffensive and kind.' As for the Greeks he had met in the Morea and towards Athens, they were 'inferior to the Turks', although (he added with faint praise) 'they are better than the Spaniards, who in their turn excel the Portuguese'.[102]

Be that as it may, Byron spent the next year travelling around Greece, with Athens as his centre. He had the chance to spend a few days with the formidable Lady Hester Stanhope (1776–1839), Chatham's grand-daughter and the niece of the younger Pitt, for whom she kept house until his death in 1806. Lady Hester was just now beginning her eccentric but romantic Eastern period, which would ultimately leave her destitute and dying in a squalid house in the Lebanese hills. When Byron met her, however, she was anything but pathetic.

Although a firman for travel in Syria and Egypt finally arrived for Lord Byron at the end of January 1811, his eyes were already towards home. On 22 April 1811 he sailed from Piraeus aboard the transport ship *Hydra*, which ironically was also carrying the final shipment of Lord Elgin's marbles on the way to England, an act of cultural plunder which Byron attacked so strongly in his poem *The Curse of Minerva*, dated from Athens, 17 March 1811. He arrived in Malta on 30 April 1811, and had further private meetings with Mrs. Spencer Smith. His ship the *Volage* sailed on 2 June 1811, reaching Gibraltar fifteen days later, and on 14 July 1811 Lord Byron stepped ashore at Sheerness, two years and twelve days after leaving Falmouth, promising never to return. He was just in time for his mother's death, which took place on the first of August. Now truly on his own, it was time for Byron to take his place in literary history, riding the crest of a Turkish wave.

VI

One of the first people who sought Byron out in London was Robert Charles Dallas (1782–1826), his distant relation and an aspiring writer who had already published two novels and some poetry. Dallas had heard that Byron had some written work, but when the two met, Byron gave him a satirical piece called *Hints from Horace*. It was not quite what Dallas had hoped, so Byron lent him the manuscript of *Childe Harold's Pilgrimage* to read. After showing it around, Dallas realized that he was sitting on a literary goldmine, especially poignant as Byron had given him the copyright, still believing that it was unseemly for an English lord to make money writing words like a hack journalist. In effect, Dallas became Byron's literary agent, flogging *Childe Harold* to the publishing house run by John Murray II (1778–1843).

Dallas tried to convince Byron that even if he refused payment for his verses, keeping his very name off the poem was downright perverse. Byron explained that 'I much wish to avoid identifying Childe Harold's character with mine, & that in sooth is my second objection to my name on the T[itle] Page.' Byron also wrote to John Murray himself a couple of days later, informing him that 'If you determine on publication, I have some smaller poems (never published) a few notes & a short dissertation on the Literature of the modern Greeks (written at Athens) which will come in at the end of the volume.'[103] 'Must I write more Notes? are there not enough?' Byron complained, as he continued to revise *Childe Harold's Pilgrimage*.[104] He also answered a stream of questions from Hobhouse, who was putting together his own rather more prosaic account of their Eastern Grand Tour.[105] Byron tried to put his literary friend at his ease:

> My thing shall be sent off to you the moment it is finished & before it is with the public; & so far from impeding you I did hope that it would be a stepping stone instead of a stumbling block in your way.—My notes will not be extensive, nor the specimens numerous, nor shall I say one word on the grammar or minutiae of ye. language.—So don't give up an idea on my account and as to contradicting me, you will only do it where I am wrong, & I shall forgive you & so will the World.—Indeed I have assigned in my notes as a reason for saying so little, that *you* have much more to say on the subject.—So don't make me lie in that respect at least.[106]

Fortunately, Hobhouse took Byron at his word and carried on with his project.

The first two cantos of *Childe Harold's Pilgrimage* appeared on 10 March 1812 and ignited a bombshell of success. Byron's close friend, Thomas Moore, who had read his memoirs before they were destroyed, remembered that 'he himself briefly described it in his memoranda—"I awoke one morning and found myself famous."'[107]

VII

'The subject of conversation, of curiosity, of enthusiasm almost, one might say, of the moment is not Spain or Portugal, Warriors or Patriots but Lord Byron!', wrote the duchess of Devonshire to her son in Washington. *Childe Harold's Pilgrimage* 'is on every table, and himself courted, visited, flattered, and praised whenever he appears'.[108] There were undoubtedly many reasons for the overnight success of the poem, including the public persona of its author and the effective branding of these products by the publisher, John Murray. But leaving aside for a moment the praiseworthy qualities of the poetry, what immediately strikes the eye is that the poem comes with footnotes. Indeed, the word 'footnotes' is misleading, since Byron's elucidations were printed not at the bottom of the page but immediately after the stanza to which they refer, often in the very middle of the page. Apart from these notes, there were also three 'papers', being rather longer footnotes that had footnotes themselves, and an 'Additional note' that covered a few more points as yet unexplained. For all the dramatic power of *Childe Harold's Pilgrimage* that had all of fashionable London in a swoon, one could hardly have thought of a better way to interrupt narrative tension. Modern editions of Byron's works usually banish his notes to the back as if they were a mere rhetorical flourish, or a further example of the author's self-indulgent vanity. We need to have a better look at these notes, not only because Byron intended them to be read with the poem itself, but because without them we misunderstand the key role that Byron would play in shaping Anglo-American attitudes about the Ottoman Empire in the early nineteenth century.

'Land of Albania! Let me bend mine eyes'—the line in the second canto that signals the moment when Childe Harold crosses the divide between West and East—inspires in Byron a long footnote. Naturally, Byron begins with the obligatory quotation from Gibbon (slightly garbled) about how Albania (i.e. Epirus) 'within sight of Italy is less known than the interior of America'. Byron, however, was there: 'Circumstances, of little consequence to mention, led Mr. Hobhouse and myself into that country before we visited any other part of the Ottoman dominions,' Byron coyly explains, 'and with the exception of Major Leake, then officially resident at Joannina, no other Englishmen have ever advanced beyond the capital into the interior, as that gentleman very lately assured me.' Byron gives a brief summary testifying to their travels in the lands of the notorious Ali Paşa, and points the interested reader in the direction of Hobhouse's book. Nevertheless, Byron was convinced that 'some few observations are necessary to the text'. For *Childe Harold's Pilgrimage* was not an ordinary poem to be read and enjoyed. Proper understanding went hand in hand with proper enjoyment, and Byron was keen to convey both factual information and (perhaps more significantly) personal impressions derived from essential first-hand on-the-spot observations obtained from having actually made the hazardous and demanding voyage to that exotic spot where no (English)man had gone before (apart from the taciturn Mr Leake).

Unlike many European travellers, Byron could actually see what he saw. Whatever preconceptions he went with before landing ashore in Albanian Epirus, Byron was curious and wide open to new impressions. Nevertheless, his mind was hardly a blank page. He was well-educated, at least in the eighteenth-century classical core curriculum, and used his historical and philological knowledge to help him make sense of what he saw in the East. 'The Arnaouts, or Albanese', he thought, 'struck me forcibly by their resemblance to the Highlanders of Scotland, in dress, figure, and manner of living. Their very mountains seemed Caledonian, with a kinder climate. The kilt, though white; the spare, active form; their dialect, Celtic in its sound, and their hardy habits, all carried me back to Morven.' Although their 'long hair reminds you of the Spartans', it is to the Scots that the Albanians should be compared. Indeed, not the conquered Scots of post-Culloden Britain, but the proud Scots of yore. With the Albanians, Byron found, 'this almost feudal fidelity is frequent amongst them.'[109]

It was not only Byron's childhood memories of Scotland that led him to see it as the archetypical primitive (but virtuous) society and to compare the peripheral society in the northwest with the liminal society in the southeast of Europe. Byron could not help but be influenced by Sir Walter Scott (1771–1832) and his imagined community of rugged Scottish warriors. When Byron exclaimed 'Land of Albania!' he was echoing Scott's 'O Caledonia!' in the *Lay of the Last Minstrel*, published in 1805, only seven years before *Child Harold's Pilgrimage*. Ali Paşa was in many ways an Eastern version of Scott's Roderick Vich Alpine Dhu. If Byron had the real-life opportunity to 'greet Albania's chief, whose dread command/Is lawless law', Scott's readers (including Byron) already knew that once upon a time in Scotland, there was 'No law, but Roderick Dhu's command'.[110]

Before the vision of Albanians in kilts speaking Gaelic under warm and sunny skies brings a smile to our faces, we should remember that Byron in 1812 was just at the brink of the vogue for the so-called 'comparative method' in the style of Auguste Comte (1798–1857). Indeed, it was a very successful theoretical framework, responsible for the first great scientific breakthroughs in the nineteenth century in anatomy, zoology, embryology and philology, so much so that within a short time it was the main procedure for dealing with any scientific problem. Proto-anthropologists collected a wide amount of ethnographic data with only a tenuous connection, assuming the psychic unity of all mankind. Darwinism was itself a product of the comparative method, and once evolution appeared on the intellectual scene thirty-five years after Byron's death, students of world cultures assumed an orderly evolution of the human mind along with the evolution of the human body. So when Byron saw Scotsmen in Ali Paşa's court, in a sense he was ahead of his time in searching for universal patterns in world cultures.

'No nation are so detested and dreaded by their neighbours as the Albanese,' Byron reported, 'the Greeks hardly regard them as Christians, or the Turks as Moslems; and in fact they are a mixture of both, and sometimes neither.'[111] But Byron liked the Albanians anyway, and was rather less enamoured with the Greeks, which is odd, considering his posthumous reputation as a man who died trying to make Greece free. In fact, the idea of a free Greece seemed to him to be completely improbable: 'The Greeks will never be independent: they will never be sovereigns as heretofore, and God forbid they ever should! but they may be subjects without being slaves. Our colonies are not independent, but they are free and industrious, and such may Greece be hereafter.' Byron compared the Greeks in their suffering to the 'Catholics of Ireland and the Jews throughout the world, and such other cudgelled and heterodox people'.[112] He noted that the 'English have at last compassionated their negroes, and under a less big-oted government, may probably one day release their Catholic brethren; but the interposition of foreigners alone can emancipate the Greeks, who, otherwise, appear to have as small a chance of redemption from the Turks, as the Jews have from mankind in general.' Byron did not mince his words:

To talk, as the Greeks themselves do, of their rising again to their pristine superiority, would be ridiculous: as the rest of the world must resume its barbarism, after re-asserting the sovereignty of Greece; but there seems to be no very great obstacle, except in the apathy of the Franks, to their becoming an useful dependency, or even a free state, with a proper guarantee;—under correction, however, be it spoken, for many and well-informed men doubt the practicability even of this.

Byron also gave his assessment about the geopolitical situation (and remember: this is a poem!):

> The Greeks have never lost their hope, though they are now more divided in opinion on the subject of their probable deliverers. Religion recommends the Russians; but they have twice been deceived and abandoned by that power ... The French they dislike; although the subjugation of the rest of Europe will, probably, be attended by the deliverance of continental Greece. The islanders look to the English for succour, as they have very lately possessed themselves of the Ioanian republic, Corfu excepted. But whoever appear with arms in their hands will be welcome; and when that day arrives, Heaven have mercy on the Ottomans; they cannot expect it from the Giaours.

Some speculations regarding former Greek glory grafted onto contemporary politics, Byron thought, 'can have no more effect on their present lot, than the existence of the Incas on the future fortunes of Peru'.[113]

The reader is tempted to dismiss the political acumen of a twenty-four year-old young man, but Byron is keen to banish such uncharitable thoughts by means of a number of source criticisms and philological pyrotechnics that would disarm a modern academic, let alone a subscriber to the *Edinburgh Review* in the early nineteenth century. Byron's corrections and attacks are directed against the usual Orientalist travellers: Thomas Thornton (d. 1814), William Eton (fl. 1798), Pouqueville, and others. His most bizarre display of erudition comes in a footnote to his footnote to the poem, in a long discussion about Turkish participles, blasting both Thornton and Pouqueville, 'who have been guilty between them of sadly clipping the Sultan's Turkish':

> Dr. Pouqueville tells a long story of a Moslem who swallowed corrosive sublimate in such quantities that he acquired the name of '*Suleyman Yeyen*,' i.e. quoth the Doctor, '*Suleyman, the eater of corrosive sublimate.*' 'Aha,' thinks Mr. Thornton, (angry with the Doctor for the fiftieth time,) have I caught you?'—Then, in a note twice the thickness of the Doctor's anecdote, he questions the Doctor's proficiency in the Turkish tongue, and his veracity in his own.—'For,' observes Mr. Thornton (after inflicting on us the tough participle of a Turkish verb), 'it means nothing more than "*Suleyman the eater*,"' and quite cashiers the supplementary '*sublimate.*' Now both are right, and both are wrong. If Mr. Thornton, when he next resides 'fourteen years in the factory,' will consult his Turkish dictionary, or ask any of his Stamboline acquaintance, he will discover that '*Suleyma'n*

yeyen,' put together discreetly, mean the '*Swallower of sublimate*,' without any '*Suleyman*' in the case: '*Suleyma*' signifying '*corrosive sublimate*,' and not being a proper name on this occasion, although it be an orthodox name enough with the addition of *n*. After Mr. Thornton's frequent hints of profound Orientalism, he might have found this out before he sang such pæans over Dr. Pouqueville.[114]

In sum, Byron asserts, 'Mr. Thornton conceives himself to have claims to public confidence from a fourteen years' residence at Pera; perhaps he may on the subject of the Turks, but this can give him no more insight into the real state of Greece and her inhabitants, than as many years spent in Wapping into that of the Western Highlands' of Scotland. Byron, on the other hand, protested that he himself had that very insight into the real state of Greece, especially that part of which he called Albania, and his readers believed him.[115]

But it is in his 'Additional note on the Turks' that we come to the thrust of his argument, and it is not what we would expect. Byron begins by subtly chastising those experts on Turkey who have never even been to the Ottoman Empire. 'The difficulties of travelling in Turkey have been much exaggerated,' he testified, 'or rather have considerably diminished, of late years. The Mussulmans have been beaten into a kind of sullen civility very comfortable to voyagers.' Yet mere presence was not enough to make an expert. 'It is hazardous to say much on the subject of Turks and Turkey;' Byron explained, 'since it is possible to live amongst them twenty years without acquiring information, at least from themselves.' He then goes on to praise Muslim financial honesty (so unlike what is 'uniformly found' with regard to Greeks) and generosity with 'regard to presents'. Byron praises the character of 'the true Turkish provincial Aga, or Moslem country gentleman'. Even the streets are safer in Turkey than 'in countries with greater pretensions to civilization', although for Westerners, 'Regimentals are the best travelling dress.' In general, Byron insists,

> The Ottomans, with all their defects, are not a people to be despised. Equal, at least, to the Spaniards, they are superior to the Portuguese. If it be difficult to pronounce what they are, we can at least say what they are *not*; they are *not* treacherous, they are *not* cowardly, they do *not* burn heretics, they are *not* assassins, nor has an enemy advanced to *their* capital. They are faithful to their sultan till he becomes unfit to govern, and devout to their God without an inquisition. Were they driven from St. Sophia to-morrow, and the French or Russians enthroned in their stead, it would become a question

whether Europe would gain by the exchange. England would certainly be the loser.

Prejudice was to blame, and European ethnocentricism:

> With regard to that ignorance of which they are so generally, and sometimes justly, accused, it may be doubted, always excepting France and England, in what useful points of knowledge they are excelled by other nations. Is it in the common arts of life? In their manufactures? Is a Turkish sabre inferior to a Toledo? or is a Turk worse clothed, or lodged, or fed and taught, than a Spaniard? Are their Pachas worse educated than a Grandee? or an Effendi than a Knight of St. Jago? I think not.

Here Byron brought up again Ali Paşa's clever grandson who knew so much about the English Houses of Parliament. 'It may be doubted if an English boy at that age knows the difference of the Divan from a College of Dervises; but I am very sure a Spaniard does not.' Spain was admitted into the brotherly league of European nations, but more than three hundred years after the *reconquista*, they still lagged behind the Muslims from whom they were supposed to have been liberated. Once again, Byron used a comparison with the Roman Catholics as an essential part of his argument on behalf of the faithful of Islam.[116]

Even leaving aside Byron's learned footnote-to-a-footnote regarding the intricacies of participles in the Turkish language, there is still a good deal of real knowledge lurking below the text of his notes. Where did he get it from? Some clues remain.[117] Byron's old friend Thomas Moore printed a reading list dated by the poet himself as 30 November 1807, when he was still a student at Trinity College, Cambridge.[118] The books about Turkey are in a category by themselves:

> *Turkey.*—I have read Knolles, Sir Paul Rycaut, and Prince Cantemir, besides a more modern history, anonymous. Of the Ottoman History I know every event, from Tangralopi, and afterwards Othman I., to the peace of Passarowitz, in 1718,—the battle of Cutzka, in 1739, and the treaty between Russia and Turkey in 1790.[119]

Arabian and Persian sources also appear:

> *Arabia.*—Mahomet, whose Koran contains most sublime poetical passages, far surpassing European poetry.

Persia.—Ferdousi, author of the Shah Nameh, the Persian Iliad—Sadi, and Hafiz, the immortal Hafiz, the oriental Anacreon. The last is reverenced beyond any bard of ancient or modern times by the Persians, who resort to his tomb near Shiraz, to celebrate his memory. A splendid copy of his works is chained to his monument[120]

Moore also notes that

In the last edition of Mr. D'Israeli's work on "the Literary Character," that gentleman has given some curious marginal notes, which he found written by Lord Byron in a copy of this work that belonged to him. Among them is the following enumeration of the writers that, besides Rycaut, had drawn his attention so early to the East:–

"Knolles, Cantemir, De Tott, Lady M.W. Montagu, Hawkins's Translation from Mignot's History of the Turks, the Arabian Nights, all travels, or histories, or books upon the East I could meet with, I had read, as well as Rycaut, before I was *ten years old*. I think the Arabian Nights first..."[121]

A few months before he died, Moore notes, Byron apparently told the Greek patriot Alexandros Mavrokordatos (1791–1865) at Missolonghi that the 'Turkish History was one of the first books that gave me pleasure when a child; and I believe it had much influence on my subsequent wishes to visit the Levant, and gave perhaps the oriental colouring which is observed in my poetry.'[122]

It would be an egregious case of academic inflation to present the twenty-four-year-old Lord Byron as a learned Orientalist. Indeed, in the middle of correcting proofs the following year, he wrote a frantic note to his publisher John Murray begging him to

Look out in the Encyclopedia article *Mecca* whether it is there or at *Medina* the Prophet is entombed—if at Medina the first lines of my alteration must run –

"Blest—as the call which from Medina's dome
Invites Devotion to the Prophet's tomb
&c.

if at "Mecca" the lines may stand as before.—Page 45. C[ant]o 2d.—Bride of Abydos.

yrs.
B.

You will find this out either by Article—*Mecca—Medina*—or *Mohammed*—I have no book of reference by me.—[123]

Murray had other things to do apart from working as Lord Byron's research assistant, but that did not stop his author from sending a chaser to his original letter: 'Did you look out?' he asked, 'is it *Medina* or *Mecca* that contains the *holy* sepulchre?—do not make me blaspheme by your negligence—I have no book of reference or I would save you the trouble I *blush* as a good Mussulman to have confused the point.'[124] Be that as it may, from the moment that the first two cantos of *Childe Harold's Pilgrimage* were launched upon the London literary public on 10 March 1812, like it or not, Byron was the first person one thought of when hearing the word 'Turkey'; and Turkey was the first place one imagined when the name 'Byron' came up, and it always did.

VIII

Thomas Moore was one of Byron's first biographers, but he had literary ambitions himself, now completely overshadowed by Childe Harold and his creator. I 'have always regretted that you do not give us an *entire* work and not sprinkle yourself in detached pieces', Byron advised his friend,

—beautiful, I allow, and quite *alone* in our language, but still giving us a right to expect a *Shah Nameh* (is that the name?) as well as Gazels. Stick to the East;—the oracle, [Madame de] Staël [(1766–1817)], told me it was the only poetical policy. The North, South, and West, have all been exhausted

Childe Harold's Pilgrimage was a work in the same vein that Byron was proposing that Moore undertake, but, Byron modestly insisted, the 'little I have done in that way is merely a "voice in the wilderness" for you; and, if it has had any success, that also will prove that the public are orientalizing, and pave the path for you'.[125]

'I have been scribbling another poem—as it is called,' Byron wrote to his future wife 'Annabella' Milbanke (1792–1860) on 10 November 1813,

Turkish as before—for I can't empty my head of the East—and horrible enough—though not so somber quite as ye. Giaour (that unpronounceable name) and for the sake of intelligibility it is *not* a fragment.—The scene is on the Hellespont—a favourite sejour of mine—and if you will accept it—I will send you a copy—there are some Mussulman words in it which I inflict upon you[126]

Byron's first four so-called 'Turkish Tales' appeared in 1813 and 1814, partly in response to public demand, but also because of his continued fascination with Turkey. The first was called *The Giaour*, which was published on 5 June 1813, immediately followed by various editions, each of which had new lines added. The word 'giaour', a Turkish word for non-Muslims, had been around for a long time, first appearing in English in one of Hakluyt's sixteenth-century voyage narratives.[127] But 'giaour' was now on everyone's lips, in Byron's dark swashbuckling Turkish yarn.

It was a great story, and depicted Ali Paşa at his cruellest, which of course made the recent visit of Lord Byron a.k.a. Childe Harold ever more daring. Byron gave the background to the poem in one of his copious notes:

> The circumstance to which the above story relates was not very uncommon in Turkey. A few years ago the wife of Muchtar Pacha complained to his father of his son's supposed infidelity; he asked with whom, and she had the barbarity to give in a list of the twelve handsomest women in Yanina. They were seized, fastened up in sacks, and drowned in the lake the same night! … The fate of Phrosine, the fairest of this sacrifice, is the subject of many a Romaic and Arnaout ditty. … I heard it by accident recited by one of the coffee-house story-tellers who abound in the Levant, and sing or recite their narratives.[128]

Kyra Frosine herself was declared a martyr by the Orthodox Church and her supposed burial place at the monastery of Hagion Anargyron at Ioannina a place of pilgrimage. In some versions of the story, she successfully resisted the attempts of her father-in-law Ali Paşa to rape her in the medrese of the Aslan Paşa Camii (mosque). At any rate, Kyra Frosine became in Greece a symbol of resistance to Ottoman oppression.[129] Byron's poem enabled English readers to shiver at Ali Paşa's wickedness, in this the first of his extraordinarily popular Turkish Tales.

The Bride of Abydos followed on 2 December 1813, and then *The Corsair* in February of the following year, and *Lara* in August 1814. John Murray paid Byron £700 for the copyright of *Lara*, being the first time that he had ever accepted money from a publisher for his own use. The last two Turkish Tales, *The Siege of Corinth* and *Parisina* followed in February 1816, just before Byron left England forever, spending the last eight years of his life abroad.

Byron kept telling people that he was displeased with his own supply to the seemingly endless demand for Turkish stories. 'The Bride of Abydos', Byron claimed in a letter to William Gifford, was 'the work of a week, and scribbled "stans pede in uno" (by the bye the only foot I have to stand on)'.[130] To his diary, Byron confided that 'it was written in four nights to distract my dreams from **. Were it not thus, it had never been composed; and had I not done something at that time, I must have gone mad, by eating my own heart,—bitter diet!'[131] The same figure of four days also appears in a letter to Lord Holland: 'the whole of the Bride cost me *four nights*—and you may easily suppose that I can have no great esteem for lines that can be strung as fast as minutes'.[132]

But if Byron was unhappy with the ease of composition and the even greater ease of public acceptance, he took solace in the fact that through his poetry he was able to convey to the public his love of Turkey and her culture. In that same letter to Lord Holland, Byron explained that

> Bride & Giaour—the popularity of which last really surprised—& (you may think it affectation) but certainly did not raise my opinion of the public taste.—My head is full of Oriental names & scenes—and I merely chose that measure as *next* to *prose* to tell a story or describe a place which struck me

Byron bewailed that he was pandering to the fact that 'the public are orientalizing' and that often his story was over the top,

> but it is my story & my *East*—(& here I am venturing with no one to contend against—from having *seen* what my contemporaries must copy from the drawings of others only) that I want to make palpable—and my skull is so crammed from having lived much with them & in their own way (after Hobhouse went home a year before me) with their scenes & manners—that I believe it would lead me to St. Luke's if not disgorged in this manner[133]

So too to his friend Thomas Moore did Byron insist that

> The success of mine is yet problematical; though the public will probably purchase a certain quantity, on the presumption of their own propensity for "the Giaour" and such "horrid mysteries." The only advantage I have is being on the spot; and that merely amounts to saving me the trouble of turning over books, which I had better read again. If *your chamber* was furnished in the same way, you have no need to *go there* to describe – I mean only as to *accuracy*—because I drew it from recollection.[134]

And finally, even to his private diary (admittedly brought to us courtesy of the aforementioned Thomas Moore alone) did Byron confess that

> The Bride of Abydos was published on Thursday the second of December; but how it is liked or disliked, I know not. Whether it succeeds or not is no fault of the public, against whom I can have no complaint. But I am much more indebted to the tale than I can ever be to the most partial reader; as it wrung my thoughts from reality to imagination—from selfish regrets to vivid recollections—and recalled me to a country replete with the *brightest* and *darkest*, but always most *lively* colours of my memory.[135]

It is true that from the publication of *The Bride of Abydos*, Byron was crying all the way to the bank, but it was never about the money, and there is no reason to suspect that Byron's misgivings about catching the Turkish current were anything but sincere.

Byron was the prisoner of his own authenticity, having gone over the edge of the Christian world and returned to tell the tale. Not only did he convince the London literati that he knew as least as much about the Muslim world and the Turkish language as the diplomats and scholars, but his infectious confidence left its trace even in far-away Albania. Just as he was composing the first of his Turkish Tales, the celebrated traveller Dr. Henry Holland (1788–1873) brought Byron a letter from his old friend Ali Paşa. Byron loved telling the story to Lady Melbourne (Caroline Lamb's mother-in-law):

> A letter from A[nnabella]—from you—& from Ali Pacha by Dr. Holland just arrived in which that amiable potentate styles me his "most excellent & dearest friend."—What do you think was "dearest friend's" last exploit?— Forty two years ago the inhabitants of a hostile city seized his mother & 2 sisters & treated them as Miss Cunegonde was used by the Bulgarian cavalry. Well—this year he at last becomes master of the aforesaid city—selects all the persons living in the remotest degree akin to this outrage (in *Turkey* these are affronts) their children grand children—cousins &c. to the amount of 600—& has them put to death in his presence.—I don't wonder at it—but the interval of 42 years is rather singular.—this H[ollan]d tells me occurred in the present spring.—He writes to me to get him a gun made—& assures me of his tender remembrance & profound respect.[136]

Byron was proud to be on corresponding terms with an Albanian mass murderer since it gave him greater authority as an interpreter of that distant culture, and helped to absolve him from filling the prescriptions of London's readers. 'If the public will read things written in that debauched measure—that is their own fault,' he protested, 'and if they begin in the present instance—to dislike it—I shall be more happy in curing them— than in adding one to their Philistine Idols.'[137]

IX

Lord Byron married Anne Isabella Milbanke ('Annabella') on 2 January 1815, and their daughter Augusta Ada was born on 10 December, only four months before the couple signed a Deed of Separation (21 April 1816).[138] All around them, the world was changing rapidly. Napoleon had abdicated on 11 April 1814, and the Congress of Vienna began to sit in September. Escaping from his exile on the island of Elba, Napoleon landed in France on 1 March 1815 and began his 'Hundred Days' of renewed power, which came crashing down at the Battle of Waterloo on 18 June. Four days later, Napoleon abdicated for a second and final time.

Europe was safe again, thrown wide open for someone like Byron, who was desperate to leave England and make the Continental Grand Tour that had eluded him seven years before. On 25 April 1816, he sailed for the Low Countries, and never saw his homeland again. Within no time at all, he and his physician friend John William Polidori (1795–1821) were galloping over the fields of Waterloo, with Byron singing 'Turkish or Arnaout riding-tunes'.[139] That summer they settled at the Villa Diodati by Lake Geneva, and there became great friends with Percy Bysshe Shelley (1792–1822) and his wife-to-be Mary Godwin (1797–1851). Byron knew about Mary, since her stepsister Claire Clairmont (1798–1879) was one of the many women that Byron had slept with in London. As it happened, to Byron's chagrin she turned up pregnant, giving birth in January to his second daughter Allegra (1817–1822). Famously, in June 1816, over five days of rain, the party competed at writing horror stories. Mary Shelley wrote *Frankenstein*, and Polidori wrote *The Vampyre*, and earned themselves each a place in the literary canon. In November 1816, Byron went to Venice. He visited the Mekhitarist Order on Saint Lazarus Island and learned about Armenians and their language from the local Fr. H. Avgerian. Byron collaborated on two Armenian grammars and an Armenian dictionary and devoted himself with considerable energy to this new Eastern scholarly subject.[140] Not that he was done with Turkey: in

1820, from Ravenna, Byron wrote that he 'meant to have gone to Turkey and am not sure that I shall not finish with it'.[141]

While all this was going on, however, what Byron thought could never happen was starting to take form: the Greeks (or at least the diaspora Greeks) were beginning to organize a movement for national independence. About 1814, a 'Friendly Society' had been founded by three Greeks living in Odessa, the 'Philiké Hetairia' dedicated to the construction of a Greek state successor to the Byzantine Empire which had fallen to the Turks over 350 years before. Oddly enough, Byron's old friend Ali Paşa finally had his moment, and really did play a major role on the world stage. In February 1820, Ali Paşa was called to Istanbul to answer charges of various kinds. This time, he refused to play the role of troublesome yet loyal subject, and was consequently stripped of his titles and declared a rebel as Ottoman troops were sent to bring him to heel. Ali Paşa was soon holed up on Nissí Island on Lake Pamvotida (Lake Ioannina). Two years later, on 24 January 1822, the great Ali Paşa was killed on the island in the guesthouse of the Monastery of St Panteleimon, shot through the floor by Ottoman soldiers in the passageway below.[142] His body was supposedly buried at the Monastery of Hagion Anargyron in Ioannina, but his head was definitely sent on to Istanbul, where it was put on public display outside the palace. The heads of his four sons joined their father's soon afterwards.

Ali Paşa's two-year rebellion was a time- and energy-consuming distraction for the Ottoman authorities, one which was put to good use by the burgeoning movement for Greek independence.[143] In March 1821, there was an ineffectual military revolt in the Turkish Danubian Principalities of Wallachia and Moldavia, led by Prince Alexander Hypsilantes (1792–1828), an officer in the Russian army but of Greek heritage, who crossed the Pruth River with a small force of expatriate Greeks in the hope of raising the local Christians. They disappointed him, and Hypsilantes was forced to flee to Austria, where he was promptly imprisoned. Despite his spectacular failure, the Turks recognized Hypsilantes' revolt for what it was, and on 22 April 1821 the Greek Orthodox patriarch of Constantinople was hanged from a tree outside his church. Three days later, his body was dragged through the streets and thrown into the sea. Since that time, the main gate of the Patriarchate has remained sealed, as a reminder of those terrible scenes. Meanwhile, on the Greek mainland, during that spring of 1821, the Turks of Greece began to disappear, tens of thousands being murdered within a few weeks.[144]

Prince Alexander's brother Demetrius Hypsilantes (1793–1832), also an officer in the Russian army, was appointed by the Friendly Society to lead the Greek revolution, and landed at Hydra Island with fifteen supporters just as the revolt in the Danube was collapsing. One of his associates there was Alexandros Mavrokordatos, a scion of an old Istanbul family which had governed the Danubian Principalities in the eighteenth century. Indeed, Mavrokordatos looked more like a governor than a fighter, being a rather fat man with glasses whose French was better than his Greek, so in January 1822 the diaspora Greeks appointed him the first president of their virtual independent country. Mavrokordatos would become Byron's friend, and it was to him that Shelley dedicated his poem in praise of 'Hellas'.[145]

About two hundred foreign volunteers arrived in Greece during that first summer of 1821, although many went back home when they saw that the Greek revolt was more a concept than a military reality. In England, Dr John Lemprière (1765–1824), the author of a dictionary of classical antiquities, began to campaign for a subscription to help the Greek war effort, which was not going well. A few hundred Greeks from the island of Samos invaded Chios in March 1822, proclaiming independence and destroying a few mosques. The Turks retired to their citadel and called for reinforcements, who massacred the invading Greeks and others, taking survivors to Istanbul as slaves or worse. Delacroix's moving painting of the debacle only served to rally more Europeans to the cause.[146]

The London Greek Committee was founded on 3 March 1823, and for the next two years was the most important philhellenic organization in the world, picking up and collecting what was left of support for the Greek cause. The key figure here was Edward Blaquiere (1779–1832), an Irish journalist who had served with the British navy in the Mediterranean. But there were other more impressive people among the original twenty-six members, who were mostly members of parliament. There was John Bowring (1792–1872), who would later go on to a distinguished career.[147] The most prominent member was the celebrated philosopher Jeremy Bentham (1748–1832), who saw Greece as a very useful place to test his brand of liberalism, according to which public opinion was the most efficient way to identify and adopt the best policies, bolstered by a well-conceived written constitution. The London Greek Committee became a centre of Benthamite liberalism, no matter how divorced it might have been from the situation over there.

From our point of view, the most important figure among the original twenty-six was Lord Byron's 'oldest—indeed—ye. only friend', John Cam Hobhouse, who gave Blaquiere a letter of introduction to the famous poet, now in Geneva.[148] Byron was not against helping the noble cause of Greek independence, on condition that Blaquiere's accounts of the situation could be confirmed. Blaquiere leaked Byron's letters to the press without the poet's approval, putting Byron on the path that would end with his death at Missolonghi. Byron was bored in Italy, and here was an adventure too wonderful to be missed, one which brought him back to scenes of his youth which in some ways had been the high point of his active life. Byron left Genoa in the middle of July 1823 on board a chartered ship loaded with horses, cannon, equipment and the obligatory Romantic black servant among his personal staff, the whole thing paid for out of his own pocket. When they docked in the Ionian Islands at Cephalonia, however, Byron discovered that Blaquiere had not even bothered to wait for him, but instead had dashed back to London to spread the news that Lord Byron had picked up his sword and was girded for action. Byron figured out immediately that his role was to be ornamental rather than military, and that in essence he had been tricked into coming out to Greece.

But he was there, with all of his horses, cannon and equipment, so Byron advertised for fellow officers, and about fifty actually came out to join up (and be paid by him), although some of his volunteers were journalists rather than experienced fighters. Even Edgar Allan Poe (1809–1849) put out the story that 'I ran away from home without a dollar on a quixotic expedition to join the Greeks, then struggling for liberty.'[149] Actually, Poe never made it further than Boston, but his yarn shows how important a turn in the Greek revolution could be for an aspiring Romantic writer.

Following the pattern he established during his Eastern Grand Tour, Byron lodged with the British resident in Cephalonia, Charles James Napier (1782–1853), a hero of Victorian imperialism who would even merit a statute in Trafalgar Square. Although the European philhellenes let him down, Byron was entranced by the presence on the island of many Souliote fighters who had found refuge in Cephalonia in 1822 after being exiled from Albania as punishment for having supported the Mavrokordatos failed Epirus expedition in that year. These were the same sort of wonderful and colourful warriors with whom Byron had spent those inspiring days as Ali Paşa's guest and protégé. The Souliotes were keen to join Byron's private army, as long as he was paying, and soon other mercenary Albanians joined in, Souliotes or not.

It was in November 1823 at Cephalonia that Byron met Leicester FitzGerald Charles Stanhope (1784–1862) who was en route from Italy to Greece as the representative of the London Greek Committee. Stanhope was the eldest son of the earl of Harrington (and himself became the 5th Earl of Harrington), but meanwhile was serving as a lieutenant-colonel in the British army. He was also a fanatic Benthamite, obsessed with the virtues and practical effects of a free press, convinced that this was the key to whipping up local Greek enthusiasm for their own freedom. By the end of December 1823, Stanhope was at Missolonghi, encamped in the middle of a mosquito-infested swamp in a place without any classical associations whatsoever. Byron and Hobhouse had spent three days there fourteen years previously, and it had not improved. But there were no longer any Turks living at Missolonghi, all having been murdered by the Greeks in 1821, who then defended themselves against a Turkish siege in the winter of the following year. Now, along with Stanhope, Missolonghi was host to Thomas Gordon (1788–1841) of Cairness, a rich Scot who had been a British army officer, spoke Greek and Turkish and knew the area, and who like Byron had sailed to Greece (in 1821) with his own ship and weapons, working with Hypsilantes at Tripolitsa.[150] Gordon became ill and left soon afterwards, but his was the only expedition that the London Greek Committee actually sent to Greece, sparking yet another wave of volunteers, with London at the centre.

Byron arrived at Missolonghi on 5 January 1824 to a spectacular reception, joining forces with President Mavrokordatos. The next month, a supply ship arrived from the London Greek Committee, under the command of William Parry (fl. 1825), a rather vulgar artisan, who became great friends with Byron for some reason. In part due to Byron's very active participation in their efforts, it was just at that moment in February 1824 that the first loan in the name of the London Greek Committee was floated on the London Stock Exchange, to very great success.

Byron himself, however, was not doing very well. He had an epileptic fit on 15 February 1824, and early the following April caught a heavy cold, which became a fever, and eventually led to kidney failure. Lord Byron died on 19 April 1824, his famous last words being 'Poor Greece'. When Edward Blaquiere finally returned to the scene, to Zante six days later, it was aboard the English merchant vessel *Florida*, loaded with 30,000 English gold sovereigns and 50,000 Spanish silver dollars, being the first instalment of the loan that had been raised on the strength of Byron's name. The *Florida* turned around and carried Byron's body back to England. Over the two days of 10–11 July 1824, the public had the opportunity of attending Byron's lying-in-state before he was buried on 16 July 1824 in the Church of St Mary Magdalene, Hucknall, Nottingham. Byron lived on in death for the London Greek Committee, as Blaquiere, Parry and Stanhope all produced instant books about Greece that exploited Byron's name.[151]

The rest of the story of Greek independence is well-known and briefly told. In 1824, the sultan requested help in fighting the Greek rebellion from Mehmet Ali Paşa (1769–1849), ironically himself born of an Albanian father, in Kavala. Mehmet's son Ibrahim (1789–1848) landed in southern Greece in February 1825, leading an Egyptian army. In order to prevent a rout and protect their own interests, Britain, France and Russia clubbed together in defence of the Greeks, and on 4 April 1826, an Anglo-Russian protocol on the Greek situation was signed in St Petersburg. Less than a fortnight later, on 22 April 1826, Missolonghi itself was captured by the Turks, and some Europeans were killed in the process. But the Ottomans had failed to grasp that, thanks to Byron, Missolonghi had become the symbol of the Greek war of independence, and the loss of that insignificant town sparked a resurgence of philhellenism in Europe, illustrated so well by Delacroix's huge painting, 'Greece Expiring on the Ruins of Missolonghi'. In the Treaty of London (6 July 1827), Britain, France and Russia called on Greece and the Ottoman Empire to cease hostilities and agree on an independent Greece. Naturally, the Turks refused.

In June 1826, Sultan Mahmud II exterminated the Janissaries, and began to build up a new European-style army as the Egyptians had done. But it was no good. On 20 October 1827 at Navarino, the entire Egyptian navy was sunk by the European Allied fleet (Britain, France, Russia), under command of Admiral Edward Codrington (1770–1851), being the last great battle of the sailing ship era, even though it was really only a skirmish that had got out of hand. The Russians were pleased with this turn of events, since they could once again declare war on Turkey and invade the Balkans. Mehmet Ali, for his part, demanded Syria from the sultan in compensation for his naval losses, and when his request was refused, rebuilt his fleet and army himself, and prepared for his own rebellion against the Ottomans, which ended only in 1840, when Mehmet Ali was given hereditary rule of Egypt in return for withdrawing his troops from Ottoman lands.

Back in Greece, the rebellion was drawing to a successful conclusion. The Battle of Petra (26–28 July 1829) was the last real battle in the Greek War of Independence. In May 1832, Britain, France and Russia sitting in London by themselves agreed that there should be an independent Greece and that it should be a monarchy, and without consulting the Greeks, offered the job to a Bavarian prince named Otto. The Treaty of Constantinople establishing the borders of the new Greek state was signed on 21 July 1832, concluded by Byron's old friend, Stratford Canning. The following year, 1833, John Murray published Byron's complete works in seventeen duodecimo volumes, the literary equivalent of a massive statue in the public square.

X

For a young man of a certain class and education, the Grand Tour was an opportunity to celebrate the Western cultural tradition that made Europe the centre of his known universe. At the beginning of the nineteenth century, Napoleon was making his own Grand Tour of Europe, in homage to the emperors of the classical world. This was at first an inconvenience for the twenty-one-year-old Lord Byron, who was forced to deviate from the trodden path through European capitals and make a southern detour out of Napoleon's progress. In every possible sense, Greece was a liminal area, the fountainhead of Western civilization, but part of the Ottoman Empire, the archetypical symbol of the East. It may be that the Orient was at first 'a textual universe', as Edward Said insisted, 'less a place than a *topos*, a set of references, a congeries of characteristics, that seems to have its origin in a quotation, or a fragment of a text, or a citation from someone's work on the Orient, or some bit of previous imagining, or an amalgam of all these'.[152] But unlike many other travellers—to the Near East, to the Far East, to the New World, and elsewhere—Byron was actually able to take in what he saw, and what he saw in Greece he definitely did not like. Byron had been brought up on tales of the classical world, but the Greeks he met in Greece were nothing like their ancestors. Byron's position as Grand Tourist altered immeasurably as soon as he 'adventured on a shore unknown,/Which all admire, but many dread to view'.

Instead of paying homage to a Greece that no longer existed, Byron was now on a search for authenticity and universal values. Like the early anthropologists who combed Bedouin culture for representations of the immortal nomads, Byron saw in the Albanians a people whose daily life was admirably authentic. Alexis de Tocqueville (1805–1859) and others like him found among the American Indians the universal aristocratic values that had seemed to disappear from Europe. For Byron, even a man like the vicious dictator Ali Paşa was someone from his own social class, ruling a hierarchical feudal-like society that reminded him of his childhood homeland of Scotland. For those who need to connect everything literary to nineteenth-century imperialism, Byron was in a sense a representative from one burgeoning Western imperial power to a functionary of a centuries-old Eastern imperial power. Byron and Ali Paşa had a lot to talk about, and almost a common language. Byron refused to see the Orient as a primitive place at an earlier stage of universal human development, but rather as a different place on an alternate historical path. He also refused to accept the idea that the supposed moral failings of the Turks gave the West a justification for the conquest and occupation of the Ottoman Empire, the sort of argument that seemed so persuasive to the English during the period of North American colonialization. 'I see not much difference between ourselves & the Turks', he wrote, and he meant it.[153]

When Byron went on his Eastern Grand Tour in 1809, Greek independence was a hopeless cause, a utopian quest. But Byron refused to proclaim a Free Greece, even if it was a politically safe flag to unfurl. For Byron the Greeks 'have as small a chance of redemption from the Turks, as the Jews have from mankind in general'.[154] Jews and Greeks: two peoples living in the Ottoman Empire who were defined entirely by their religion, and in 1809 without a prayer of national sovereignty. 'Hebraism and Hellenism', as Matthew Arnold (1822–1888) would note later, 'between these two points of influence moves our world.'[155]

'He often spoke of a mysterious necessity for his return to the East,' recalled Byron's sometime wife Annabella,

> and vindicated the Turks with a spirit of Nationality, admiring above all their complete predestinarianism. He would say, 'The East—ah, there it is', ...and he has two or three times intimated to me that he abjured his religion there. In the autumn in London, he said with a shudder of conscious remembrance, 'I was very near becoming a Mussulman.' He preferred the Turkish opinions, manners and dress in all respects to ours.[156]

Byron was eventually tricked into supporting a cause in which he did not believe and (like Jewish national sovereignty) turned out to be not so hopeless. That he died without firing a shot for Greek independence had absolutely no effect on his evolution towards being the symbol of the cause, albeit dressed in the costume of the Muslim Albanian upper class with which he actually did have affinity. Overexposure in the Murray guide books made his Byronic heroism seem not only a cliché but actually comical, the subject of ridicule. Byron had a feeling that would happen, and in his last work lamented that 'every fool describes in these bright days/ His wonderous journey to some foreign court,/And spawns his quarto, and demands your praise—/Death to his publisher, to him 'tis sport'.[157] The 'Turkish Tales' which had capitalized on the fame of Childe Harold caused him not a little embarrassment as he metamorphosed in his last fictional character of 'Don Juan', cynical and humorous. The one place where his true loyalty to Turkey and to Muslim Albania was not forgotten was in Tepedelen, the Tepelenë of Communist Albania, where children at the age of sixteen studied the second canto of *Childe Harold's Pilgrimage*. On the wall of Ali Paşa's palace there was until recently a plaque with a quotation from Enver Hoxha (1908–1985), Albania's modern 'Mahometan Buonaparte': 'I like Byron, not that I am a Romantic, but for the fact that he sincerely loved my people.'[158] One can only be glad that Lord Byron never had the chance to meet Mr Hoxha: he might have recalled for Byron those pleasant days with Ali Paşa, amiably chatting about 'war & travelling, politics & England'.[159]

NOTES

1. See Terence Spencer, *Fair Greece, Sad Relic: Literary Philhellinism from Shakespeare to Byron* (London, 1954) regarding European writings about Greece. Cf. Timothy Webb, *English Romantic Hellenism* (Manchester, 1982); and his 'Romantic Hellenism', in *The Cambridge Companion to British Romanticism*, ed. Stuart Curran (Cambridge, 1993), pp. 148–76.
2. Specifically on Bryon and the 'Grand Tour', see William A. Borst, *Lord Byron's First Pilgrimage* (New Haven, 1948); James Buzard, 'The Uses of Romanticism: Byron and the Victorian Continental Tour', *Vict. Stud.*, 35 (1991), 29–49; Nigel Leask, 'Byron and the Eastern Mediterranean: *Childe Harold* II and the "polemic of Ottoman Greece"', in *The Cambridge Companion to Byron*, ed. Drummond Bone (Cambridge, 2004), pp. 99–117.
3. Byron to Lady Melbourne, 24 May 1813: Byron, *Letters and Journals*, ed. Leslie A. Marchand (London, 1973–82), hereafter

BLJ. This reference, BLJ iii. 51. The other standard editions are *Lord Byron: The Complete Poetical Works*, ed. Jerome J. McGann and Barry Weller (Oxford, 1980–93); *Lord Byron: The Complete Miscellaneous Prose*, ed. Andrew Nicholson (Oxford, 1991). See also *Byron's Bulldog: the Letters of John Cam Hobhouse to Lord Byron*, ed. Peter W. Graham (Columbus, OH, 1984) and Robert E. Zegger, *John Cam Hobhouse: A Political Life 1819–1852* (Columbia, MO, 1973); Peter Cochran, *Byron and Hobby-O: Lord Byron's Relationship with John Cam Hobhouse* (Newcastle, 2010).

4. Byron to Francis Hodgson, 5 May 1810, on board the *Salsette* frigate, in the Dardanelles off Abydos: BLJ, i. 241.

5. J.C. Hobhouse, *A Journey through Albania, and other Provinces of Turkey in Europe and Asia, to Constantinople, during the years 1809 and 1810* (Philadelphia, 1817), 2 vols: 1st edn (London, 1813).

6. J.C. Hobhouse's (mostly autograph) diaries (1809–65) were purchased by the British Library on 3 Apr. 1971, and are now shelfmark Brit. Lib. Addl. MSS. 56527–56568 (Supplementary Broughton Papers). His time in Albania is recorded in Addl. MS. 56527; their visit to Smyrna and Istanbul in Addl. MS. 56529. Peter Cochran made a transcription from some of the diaries, available online at https://petercochran.wordpress.com: hereafter, Hobhouse, 'Diary'.

7. Reinhold Schiffer, *Oriental Panorama: British Travellers in 19th Century Turkey* (Amsterdam, 1999); Philip Mansel, 'The Grand Tour in the Ottoman Empire, 1699–1826', in *Unfolding the Orient: Travellers in Egypt and the Near East*, ed. Paul & Janet Starkey (Reading, 2001).

8. Byron to Francis Hodgson, 5 May 1810, *Salsette* frigate, in the Dardanelles off Abydos, Byron, *Letters and Journals*, ed. Marchand, i. 240–1.

9. Generally, see K.E. Fleming, *The Muslim Bonaparte: Diplomacy and Orientalism in Ali Pasha's Greece* (Princeton, 1999); Dennis N. Skiotis, 'From Bandit to Pasha: First Steps in the Rise to Power of Ali of Tepelen, 1750–1784', *IJMES*, 2 (1971), 219–44; Peter Cochran, 'Byron and Ali Pacha', online at https://petercochran.wordpress.com. Older sources include William Plomer, *The Diamond of Jannina: Ali Pasha 1741–1822* (London, 1970), a reissue of his *Ali the Lion* (1936); Alphonse Beauchamp, *The Life of Ali Pacha, of Janina, Vizier of Epirus* (London, 1822); Richard Alfred Davenport, *The Life of Ali Pasha* (London, 1837).

10. *Childe Harold's Pilgrimage* [hereafter, CHP], ii. 43.
11. Edward Gibbon, *The History of the Decline and Fall of the Roman Empire*, ed. David Womersley (Penguin edn, London, 1994), ii. 750, n.25 (Chap. 43).
12. CHP, ii. 38.
13. 'The Souliot Women' (1827).
14. David Richard Morier was also the author of a triple-decker novel, *Photo the Suliote: A Tale of Modern Greece* (1857).
15. F.C.H.L. Pouqueville, *Voyage en Morée, a Constantinople et en Albanie* (Paris, 1805) = 3 vols, with Eng. trans. (London, 1806); idem, *Travels in Albania* (London, 1820); idem, *Travels in Greece and Turkey* (2nd edn, London, 1820).
16. His works would become important sources: *Researches in Greece* (London, 1814); *Journal of a Tour in Asia Minor* (London, 1824); *Travels in the Morea* (London, 1830); *Travels in Northern Greece* (London, 1835).
17. CHP, ii. 38.
18. Hobhouse, *Journey*, i. 51. This fabulous plane tree still stood in 2009, and probably does so still.
19. Hobhouse, *Journey* i. 68, with a footnote to 'History of the Turks, p. 205'. The reference is to Richard Knolles (late 1540s–1610), whose first Turkish history in English was brought up to date by Paul Rycaut (1629–1700) and printed in London in 1687.
20. Edward Said, *Orientalism* (London, 1978): (Penguin edn, Harmondsworth, 1985), p. 52.
21. It will come as no surprise that the site of that house is located in today's Ioannina on Vyronis Street.
22. According to Hobhouse (*Travels*, i. 67), Spiridion Colovo was captured by the Turks in 1820 while in Corfu on a mission to procure ammunition for Ali Paşa's rebellion, and was subsequently tortured to death.
23. Hobhouse, *Journey*, i. 57.
24. Hobhouse, 'Diary'. Byron was later painted in (apparently) this costume by Thomas Phillips.
25. On the site of Ali Paşa's palace in Ioannina is the town's Byzantine Museum, constructed in 1958 on its foundations.
26. Hobhouse, *Journey*, i. 60.
27. Two years later, Leake visted Byron in London: 'I had a visit lately from Major (Capt.) Leake "en passant" he talks of returning to Ali

Pacha...he is grown less taciturn, better dressed, & more like an (English) man of this world than he was at Yanina.': Byron to John Cam Hobhouse, 20 Sept. 1811, from Newstead Abbey: BLJ, ii. 102.

28. Hobhouse, *Journey*, i. 70–1.
29. CHP, ii. 38, notes.
30. Hobhouse, *Journey*, i. 80.
31. CHP, ii. 48–52.
32. CHP, ii. 48, notes.
33. Byron to his mother, 12 Nov. 1809: BLJ, i. 227.
34. CHP, ii. 55–66.
35. Hobhouse, *Journey*, i. 97.
36. *Don Juan*, xiii.47.
37. Hobhouse, *Journey*, i. 101–103: 1st meeting recorded by H in diary, BL Add MSS 56527, f.59r. Cf. Peter Oluf Brøndsted, *Interviews with Ali Pacha of Joanina in the autumn of 1812; with some particulars of Epirus, and the Albanians of the present day*, ed. Jacob Isager (Aarhus, 1999); Tessa de Loo, *In Byron's Footsteps* (London, 2010).
38. BLJ, i. 227–8.
39. Byron to his mother, 12 Nov. 1809: BLJ, i. 228.
40. Hobhouse, *Journey*, i. 103–104.
41. Ibid., i. 104–5.
42. Ibid., i. 112–113.
43. Ibid., i. 128–129.
44. Byron to his mother, 12 Nov. 1809, BLJ, i. 228–9.
45. Hobhouse, *Journey*, i. 158. Cf. Byron's disparaging remarks about their 'discovery' of an amphitheatre three hours' ride from Ioannina: Byron to Rev. Dr. Valpy, 19 Nov. 1811, from 8 St James's St: BLJ, ii. 134.
46. Hobhouse, *Journey*, i. 159–160.
47. Hobhouse, 'Diary'.
48. CHP, ii. 74, notes.
49. Hobhouse, 'Diary'.
50. Hobhouse, *Journey*, i. 160–161.
51. Hobhouse, 'Diary'.
52. CHP, ii.
53. CHP, ii. 70.
54. Hobhouse, *Journey*, i. 169–170. Cf. Gustav Meyer, 'Die Albanischen Tanzlieder in Byron's Childe Harold', *Anglia*, 15 (1893), 1–8.

55. Hobhouse, 'Diary'.
56. Allan Cunningham, *Anglo-Ottoman Encounters in the Age of Revolution* (London, 1993), i. 138.
57. 'Tomorrow, or this evening I sail for Constantinople in the Salsette 36 gun frigate, she returns to England with our Ambassador whom she is going on purpose to receive': Byron to his mother, from Smyrna, 10 Apr. 1810: BLJ, i. 235.
58. Hobhouse, 'Diary'.
59. *Don Juan*, iv. 91.
60. It was only when Heinrich Schliemann (1822–90) began to excavate at Hisarlık in 1871 that the actual location was revealed.
61. Jacob Bryant, *Observations upon a Treatise, entitled A Description of the Plain of Troy, by Monsieur le Chevalier* (Eton, 1795); idem, *A dissertation concerning the war of Troy, and the expedition of the Grecians, as described by Homer; shewing that no such expedition was ever undertaken, and that no such city of Phrygia existed* (London, 1796).
62. Ravenna journal for 11 January 1821: BLJ VIII 21–2. Cf. similar sentiments expressed in *Don Juan*, iv. 76.
63. *Don Juan*, iv. 78.
64. The other famous bridge of boats in the general area was that made by Xerxes' father Darius the Great, across the Bosphorus at the place now occupied by the Rumeli Hisarı. Boat bridges were apparently some sort of family tradition.
65. Hobhouse, 'Diary'.
66. Byron to Henry Drury, 3 May 1810, from the *Salsette*, in the Dardanelles off Abydos: BLJ: i.237.
67. Hobhouse, 'Diary'. In the meantime, Byron was feeling more energetic: 'Lord Byron up to breakfast, first time since coming out', wrote Hobhouse in his diary entry for 26 April 1810.
68. Hobhouse, *Journey*, ii. 219–20.
69. Hobhouse, 'Diary'.
70. Ov., Ep.18. 131–2.
71. Hobhouse, 'Diary'.
72. *Don Juan*, ii. 105, 7–8.
73. Byron to Henry Drury, 3 May 1810, from the *Salsette*, in the Dardanelles off Abydos: BLJ: i.237; cf. Byron to Henry Drury, 17 June 1810, from Istanbul: BLJ, i.246.
74. Byron to Francis Hodgson, 5 May 1810, from the *Salsette*, in the Dardanelles off Abydos: BLJ: i.240–1; Byron to his mother, 18 May 1810, from Istanbul: BLJ, i.242–3.

75. Byron to John Hanson, 23 May 1810, from Istanbul: BLJ, i. 243.
76. Byron to Robert Charles Dallas, 23 June 1810, from Istanbul: BLJ, i. 247–8; Byron to Edward Ellice, 4 July 1810, from Istanbul: 'I must beg leave to mention to you as a feat that I have swum from Sestos to Abydos': BLJ, i. 254–5.
77. Byron to his mother, 24 May 1810, from Istanbul: BLJ, i. 243–4. And again: Byron to his mother, 28 June 1810: BLJ, i. 250. Eight months later, he repeated the same joke to his mother about possibly forgetting to tell her about the swim: Byron to his mother, 14 Jan. 1811, from Athens: BLJ, ii. 34.
78. Byron to Francis Hodgson, 4 July 1810, from Istanbul: BLJ, 253.
79. Byron to Henry Drury, 3 May 1810, from the *Salsette*, in the Dardanelles off Abydos: BLJ: i.237–9. Similarly, to Robert Charles Dallas, 23 June 1810: ' We have, moreover, been very high up into Albania, the wildest province in Europe, where very few Englishmen have ever been': BLJ, i. 247–8.
80. Hobhouse, *Journey*, ii. 229.
81. Ibid., ii. 239. Their inn was located at the corner at which stands the Galatasaray Lisesi.
82. Ibid., ii. 242. Their lodgings seem to have been located on today's İstiklal Caddesi at what is now Odakule.
83. Hobhouse, 'Diary'.
84. Hobhouse, 'Diary'.
85. The [lost] memoirs of Stratford Canning, quoted in Stanley Lane-Poole, *The Life of the Right Honourable Stratford Canning* (London, 1888), i. 84.
86. Hobhouse, 'Diary'.
87. Ibid., for 19 May 1810.
88. Ibid., for 21 May 1810.
89. Hobhouse, *Journey*, ii.356.
90. Byron to Henry Drury, 3 May 1810, from the *Salsette*, in the Dardanelles off Abydos: BLJ: i.238.
91. Byron to Robert Charles Dallas, 23 June 1810, from Istanbul: BLJ, i. 247–8.
92. The [lost] memoirs of Stratford Canning, quoted in Lane-Poole, *Canning*, i. 85 6. Cf. Byron to Adair, 4 July 1810, from Pera: BLJ, i. 256.
93. Hobhouse, 'Diary'.
94. Ibid.
95. Ibid.

96. Hobhouse, *Journey*, ii. 407.
97. Lane-Poole, *Canning*, i. 90.
98. Hobhouse, *Journey*, ii. 374–5.
99. Ibid., ii. 376.
100. Ibid., ii.232–3.
101. Ibid., ii. 377.
102. Byron to his mother, 28 June 1810, from Istanbul: BLJ, i. 251.
103. Byron to John Murray, 23 Aug. 1811, from Newstead Abbey: BLJ, ii. 78.
104. Byron to Robert Charles Dallas, 11 Oct. 1811, from Newstead Abbey: BLJ, ii. 111.
105. Byron to Hobhouse, 2 Nov. 1811, from 8 St. James's St: BLJ, ii. 123–4; same to same, 3 Nov. 1811, from same: BLJ, ii. 124–7.
106. Byron to Hobhouse, 3 Dec. 1811, from 8 St. James's St: BLJ, ii. 135.
107. Thomas Moore, *Life, Letters and Journals of Lord Byron* (London, 1839), p. 159: 1st edn. 1830. In 1819 in Venice, Byron gave Moore the manuscript of his memoirs and allowed him to sell them to John Murray for posthumous publication. The memoirs were burned after Byron died, despite Moore's objections: BLJ, ii. 285. BLJ, xii: "The letters to Thomas Moore, first published by him in his *Letters and Journals of Lord Byron* (1830), were printed with many omissions and the manuscripts have since disappeared. Moore generally indicated omissions by asterisks, here reproduced as in his text. The same is true of the Journal of 1813–1814, the manuscript of which was no longer extant when Prothero published it from Moore." See the review by Thomas B. Macaulay, 'Moore's Life of Lord Byron', *Complete Works* (London, 1898–1906), vii. 528–69, orig. pub. *Edinburgh Rev.* (June 1830). See also Jeffery Vail, *The Literary Relationship of Lord Byron and Thomas Moore* (Baltimore, 2001); *The Letters of Thomas Moore*, ed. Wilfred S. Dowden (Oxford, 1964).
108. Quoted in Marchand, *Byron*, p. 121.
109. CHP, ii. 38, notes.
110. III. 24. Another writer who compared Albania with Scotland was Byron's friend and biographer John Galt (1779–1839), *Voyages and Travels* (London, 1812) and *Letters from the Levant* (London, 1813), and cf. his *Life of Lord Byron* (London, 1830). Generally, see

Massimiliano Demata, 'From Caledonia to Albania: Byron, Galt, and the Progress of the Eastern Savage', *Scot.Stud.Rev.*, 2 (2001), 61–76.

111. CHP, ii. 38, notes.

112. CHP, ii. 73 begins with the words: 'Fair Greece! sad relic of departed worth!/Immortal, though no more; though fallen, great!/Who now shall lead thy scatter'd children forth,/And long accustom'd bondage uncreate?', to which Byron notes: 'Some thoughts on this subject will be found in the subjoined papers', three in number. The above quotation is from the first paper.

113. These quotations are from the second paper, dated 'Franciscan Convent, Athens, January 23, 1811'.

114. 'Corrosive sublimate', *sülümen* in Turkish, mercuric chloride, was widely used for the treatment of syphilis.

115. These quotations are from the second paper, dated 'Franciscan Convent, Athens, January 23, 1811'. The third paper, dated from 'Athens, Franciscan Convent, March 17, 1811' is a response to article in the 31st number of the *Edinburgh Review*, demonstrating further erudition regarding Greek language, literature, and history.

116. 'Additional note on the Turks'.

117. For Byron's Orientalist knowledge, see generally Harold S.L. Wiener, 'Byron and the East: Literary Sources of the "Turkish Tales"', in *Nineteenth-Century Studies*, ed. Herbert Davis et al. (Ithaca, NY, 1940), pp. 89–129; Bernard Blackstone, 'Byron and Islam: The Triple Eros', *Jnl. European Stud.*, 4 (1974), 325–63; Abdur Raheem Kidwai, *Orientalism in Lord Byron's Turkish Tales* (Lewiston, NY & Lampeter, 1995); A.R. Kidwai, 'A Bibliography of Byron's Oriental Reading', *Notes & Queries*, 39 (1992), 167–8; Massimiliano Demata, 'A Bibliography of Byron's Oriental Reading: Addenda and Corrections', *Notes & Queries*, 46 (1999), 39–41; Naji B. Oueijan, *A Compendium of Eastern Elements in Byron's Oriental Tales* (New York, 1999); Wallace Cable Brown, 'Byron and English Interest in the Near East', *Stud. Philology*, 34 (1937), 55–64.

118. Thomas Moore, *The Works of Lord Byron, with his Letters and Journals, and his Life*, ed. J. Wright (London: Murray, 1832–3), 17 vols = augmented edn of the 1830 *Life, Letters and Journals*. Byron's reading list is i. 140–148, esp. p. 140, with Oriental vols. on p. 143. This quotation, i.140. The 1807 Reading List is published in *Lord*

Byron: the Complete Miscellaneous Prose, ed. Andrew Nicholson (Oxford, 1991), pp. 1–7.

119. Moore, Works, i. 141 (1832 edn).
120. Ibid., i. 146.
121. Thomas Moore, *Life of Lord Byron, With His Letters and Journals* (London, 1851), p. 119n.
122. Ibid., p. 119n., quoting 'Count Gamba's Narrative".
123. Byron to John Murray, 3 Dec. 1813: BLJ, iii. 190–191.
124. Byron to John Murray, 3–4 Dec. 1813?: BLJ, iii. 191.
125. Byron to Thomas Moore, 28 Aug. 1813: BLJ, iii.101. Moore would soon publish his own Eastern bestseller, *Lalla Rookh, An Oriental Romance* (London: Longman, 1817). Cf. *The Poetical Works of Thomas Moore* (London: Longman, 1855).
126. Byron to Annabella Milbanke, 10 Nov. 1813: BLJ iii. 160.
127. *Oxford English Dictionary*, 2nd online edition (1989), 'Giaour'.
128. 'The Giour', note to line 1328. Cf. note to *Don Juan*, v.92, where he writes that it was possible 'To find our way to Marmora without boats,/Stich'd up in sacks – a mode of navigation/A good deal practised here upon occasion.'
129. Fleming, *Muslim Bonaparte*, pp. 167–70. The Aslan Paşa Camii is now the Municipal Museum of Ioannina, and the medrese is now the Fotis Rapakousis Museum at the same site.
130. Byron to William Gifford, 12 Nov. 1813: BLJ iii. 162.
131. Moore's transcription of Byron's journal: 16 November 1813: BLJ, iii. 208.
132. Byron to Lord Holland, 17 Nov. 1813: BLJ, iii. 168.
133. Byron to Lord Holland, 17 Nov. 1813: BLJ, iii. 168.
134. Byron to Thomas Moore, 8 Dec. 1813: BLJ, iii.194.
135. Moore's transcription of Byron's journal: 5 December 1813: BLJ, iii. 230–231.
136. Byron to Lady Melbourne, 7 Sept. 1813: BLJ, iii. 110–111. He told the same story in another letter to Thomas Moore: Byron to Thomas Moore, 8 Sept. 1813: BLJ, iii. 111–112.
137. Byron to Lord Holland, 17 Nov. 1813: BLJ, iii. 168.
138. Ada Lovelace (1815–52) became a famous mathematician, and her own daughter Anne (1837–1917) married Wilfrid Scawen Blunt (1840–1922), who played an important role in Middle Eastern affairs.

139. Polidori to Hobhouse, 11 May 1816: John William Polidori, *The Diary of John William Polidori*, ed. William Michael Rossetti (London, 1911), p. 213.

140. *Lord Byron's Armenian Exercises and Poetry* (Venice, 1870). See generally, Anahit Bekaryan, 'Byron and Armenia: A Case of Mirrored Affinities', in *The Reception of Byron in Europe*, ed. Richard A. Cardwell (London, 2004), ii. 386–405.

141. Richard Milbanke Lovelace, *Astarte: A Fragment of Truth Concerning George Gordon Byron, Sixth Lord Byron* (new edn, New York, 1921), p. 112.

142. The bullet holes – or perhaps they are purpose-made drill holes – can still be seen in the room, now a modestly-popular tourist attraction.

143. Cf. the reports home (1819–22) from William Meyer (fl. 1835), British consul-general at Ioannina from 1819–35: *Epirus, Ali Pasha and the Greek Revolution: Consular Reports of William Meyer from Preveza*, ed. E. Prevelakēs & K. Kalliatakē Mertikopoulou (Athens, 1996).

144. See generally William St Clair, *That Greece Might Still Be Free: the Philhellenes in the War of Independence* (London, 1972); C.M. Woodhouse, *The Philhellenes* (London, 1969); Roderick Beaton, *Byron's War: Romantic Rebellion, Greek Revolution* (Cambridge, 2013); Suzanne L. Marchand, *Down From Olympus: Archaeology and Philhellenism in Germany, 1750–1970* (Princeton, 1996); Stathis Gourgouris, *Dream Nation: Enlightenment, Colonization, and the Institution of Modern Greece* (Stanford, 1996); T.J.W. Spencer, *Fair Greece, Sad Relic: Literary Philhellenism from Shakespeare to Byron* (London, 1954); idem, *Byron and the Greek Tradition* (Nottingham, 1960); Fani-Maria Tsigakou, *The Rediscovery of Greece: Travellers and Painters of the Romantic Era* (London, 1981).

145. See Stephen Minta, 'Lord Byron and Mavrokordatos', *Romanticism*, 12 (2006), 126–42; idem, *On A Voiceless Shore: Byron in Greece* (London, 1998).

146. Lee Johnson, 'Delacroix and *The Bride of Abydos*', *Burlington Mag.*, 114 (1972), 579–85; Paul Joannides, 'Colin, Delacroix, Byron and the Greek War of Independence', *Burlington Mag.*, 125 (1983), 495–500.

147. See John Bowring, *Autobiographical Recollections of Sir John Bowring*, ed. L.B. Bowring (London, 1877).

148. Byron to Lady Melbourne, 24 May 1813: BLJ iii. 51.

149. Edgar Allan Poe, 'Memorandum', MS accompanying a letter from Poe to Rufus W. Griswold (29 May 1841): *Collected Letters*, edited by J. W. Ostrom, B. R. Pollin & J. A. Savoye (Cambridge, USA, 1948 and New York, 1966 & 2008) i. 273 (notes to letter #112 and illustration #24); and Edgar Allan Poe, *Complete Works*, ed. James A. Harrison (New York, 1902), i. 344–6.

150. Thomas Gordon, *History of the Greek Revolution* (Edinburgh, 1832); Margaret Chapman, 'Thomas Gordon of Cairness: The Struggle for Greek Independence', *Aberdeen Univ. Rev.*, 47 (1978), 238–48.

151. Edward Blaquiere, *The Greek Revolution* (London, 1824); idem, *Narrative of a Second Visit to Greece* (London, 1825); William Parry, *The Last Days of Lord Byron* (London, 1825); Leicester Stanhope, *Greece, in 1823 and 1824* (London, 1824). Cf. Peter Gamba, *A Narrative of Lord Byron's Last Journey to Greece* (London, 1825). A more modern version is Harold Nicolson, *Byron: The Last Journey, April 1823–April 1824* (London, 1934).

152. Edward Said, *Orientalism* (London, 1978): (Penguin edn, Harmondsworth, 1985), p. 177. Scholars who have applied Said's paradigm to Byron include Saree Makdisi, *Romantic Imperialism* (Cambridge, 1998), esp. Chap. 6; Mohammed Sharafuddin, *Islam and Romantic Orientalism: Literary Encounters with the Orient* (London, 1994); Seyed Mohammad Marandi, 'The Oriental World of Lord Byron and the Orientalism of Literary Scholars', *Critique*, 15 (2006), 317–37; G.K. Rishmawi, 'The Muslim East in Byron's *Don Juan*', *Papers on Lang. & Lit.*, 35 (1999), 227–43; Shahin Kuli Khan Khattak, *Islam and the Victorians: Nineteenth-Century Perceptions of Muslim Practices and Beliefs* (London, 2008).

153. Byron to Henry Drury, 3 May 1810, from the *Salsette*, in the Dardanelles off Abydos: BLJ: i.237–9.

154. The second paper, dated 'Franciscan Convent, Athens, January 23, 1811'.

155. 'Hebraism and Hellenism', Chap. 4 of Matthew Arnold, *Culture and Anarchy* (London, 1869).

156. Blackstone, 'Byron and Islam', p. 356, from Malcolm Elwin, *Lord Byron's Wife* (London, 1962), pp. 270–1.
157. *Don Juan*, v. 52.
158. Paul Simpson-Housley, 'Tepelene, Land of Albania', *The Byron Journal*, 20 (1992), 92–5.
159. Byron to his mother, 12 Nov. 1809: BLJ, i. 228.

CHAPTER 4

Disraeli's Eastern Career, 1830–1880

Anyone with a modicum of political awareness in Victorian England knew that Benjamin Disraeli (1804–1881) was also speaking of his own life when he made a character in one of his novels proclaim that 'The East is a career'.[1] In some ways, the very personification of nineteenth-century Britain, Disraeli was also a permanent outsider, and not only because of his Jewish roots, which were impervious even to the holy water of his Anglican baptism while still a twelve-year-old child.

Disraeli's obsession with all things Eastern, and his belief that he and his family were members of a superior Semitic-Jewish-Arabian-Oriental race in a world where race was all that mattered, had an enormous influence on foreign affairs. For Disraeli, the Ottoman Empire was more than a convenient behemoth that lay astride the border between Russian and British possessions in India. He was pro-Turkish in a very deep sense, drawn to everything Turkish and a keen supporter of the Ottoman Empire throughout his long career. Those in British politics who rejected Disraeli also opposed the Ottoman Empire, the Turks, and much else with which Disraeli was associated, including Judaism and even the possibility that empires could cheat the inevitability of eventual decline. With Benjamin Disraeli, the East was not just a career; it was a lifetime.

© The Author(s) 2016   127
D.S. Katz, *The Shaping of Turkey in the British Imagination, 1776–1923*,
DOI 10.1007/978-3-319-41060-9_4

I

'But the question is, what is the Eastern question?'[2] Thus asks one of Disraeli's fictional personae, but it was a good metaquery nonetheless. As we have already seen, during Disraeli's early years informed opinion was far from unanimous regarding Turkey, and even the independence of Greece was a controversial subject. The legacy of Lord Byron, it is true, had already been hijacked for Greece. With more justification, Percy Bysshe Shelley (1792–1822) was another young martyr whose pleas for Greece echoed in the hearts of fashionable literary young people throughout early nineteenth-century Britain. 'We are all Greeks', Shelley announced in 1821. As for the modern Greeks themselves, the 'descendants of those glorious beings whom the imagination almost refuses to figure to itself as belonging to our kind', they were revolting against their Turkish masters, asserting their European-ness in the face of Oriental despotism: 'Greece, which is dead, is arisen!'[3] Indeed, Shelley posited,

> the Turkish Empire is in its last stages of ruin, and it cannot be doubted but that the time is approaching when the deserts of Asia Minor and of Greece will be colonized by the overflowing populations of countries less enslaved and debased, and that the climate and the scenery which was the birthplace of all that is wise and beautiful will not remain forever the spoil of wild beasts and unlettered Tartars.[4]

Percy Bysshe Shelley! For many young Englishmen in the 1820s, to see the Eastern Question in any other way was first and foremost a regrettable lapse of taste.

Benjamin Disraeli, on the other hand, was soon ready for the East. His father Isaac d'Israeli (1766–1848) was a well-known Jewish minor man of letters with many and varied London literary connections among writers, publishers, and antiquaries. He had his eldest son Benjamin baptized an Anglican before his thirteenth birthday, and by the time the boy was eighteen, the apostrophe in d'Israeli went as well.[5] Plans were soon afoot for a Grand Tour, Abroad. Disraeli had already visited Italy, Switzerland and Germany and the point was to do something new and bold. It had to be the East, and more specifically, along the path that Lord Byron had taken. Isaac d'Israeli was less than thrilled about his eldest son traipsing about the Mediterranean, barely recovered (if at all) from a very serious bout of depression. But Benjamin was not a boy anymore; he was now a Christian gentleman in his mid-twenties who had already published a few pot-boilers which could finance an Eastern project without his father's financial blessing. Disraeli began working on an Eastern adventure story, the germ of which would become *Alroy* (1833), but he put it aside in the winter of 1829–1830 to write another trashy crowd-pleaser, *The Young Duke*, for which he was paid £500 before the appearance of the book in 1831.

Travelling alone was a bore, and even Lord Byron for all his Childe Harold solo mystique had his straight-man sidekick John Cam Hobhouse as he sailed the Mediterranean. Disraeli's companion was William Meredith (1803–1831), engaged to his sister Sarah. In fact, they had been engaged for quite some time, and it was not a question of money, as William not only had an income but was the sole heir of a rich uncle. But Sarah d'Israeli was a Jewess, and the said uncle only withdrew his opposition to the match as Meredith prepared to set sail. William Meredith was an old friend of the family, and like Byron's Hobhouse did not have a sense of humour that he was aware of, although Disraeli found him to be unintentionally amusing.

And so they went to the East. The two young gentlemen departed from London on Friday, 28 May 1830, sailing to Falmouth in very bad weather.[6] By mid-June 1830, Disraeli and Meredith were at Gibraltar, having stopped there on the way to Malta. It ended up being a two-month stay in Gibraltar and in southern Spain. Disraeli thought that the 'rock is a wonderful place with a population infinitely diversified—Moors with costume radiant as a rainbow or an Easter melodrame Jews with gaberdines and scull caps' and many others.[7] The summer Mediterranean also gave Disraeli the locale for his usual flamboyant japes. 'I have also the fame of being the first who ever passed the Straits with two canes, a morning and an evening cane,' he boasted. 'I change my cane as the gun fires, and hope to carry them both on to Cairo. It is wonderful the effect these magical wands produce. I owe to them even more attention than to be the supposed author of—what is it—I forget.'[8]

They arrived in Malta on 19 August 1830, and as per regulations were quarantined a week in the Lazaretto, cholera being the main fear. The Lazaretto was a bore, but they were soon 'quartered in a capital hotel', and best of all, they met an old acquaintance:

> To our surprise we find James Clay here, immensely improved and quite a hero. He has been here a month, and has already beat the whole Garrison at Rackets and billiards and other wicked games, given lessons to their Prima Donna, and seccaturad the primo tenore. Really he has turned out a most agreeable personage … I had no need of letters of introduction here and have already "troops of friends".[9]

James Clay (1804–1873), as Disraeli's letter implies, was a character. He had been at Winchester with Disraeli's brother Ralph, and then had gone on to Balliol, where he took a gentleman's third in classics. Meredith had been a contemporary at Brasenose but had stayed clear of his raffish and fun-loving fellow student. Clay went on to become a rebellious Liberal MP who privately colluded with his Conservative friend Disraeli, but made his mark as England's best whist player and the author of an authoritative book on the subject.[10] In the meantime, Clay was naughty and fun while Meredith was not. 'To govern men you must either excel them in their accomplishments—or despise them,' Disraeli told his father. 'Clay does one: I do the other, and we are equally popular. Affectation tells here even better than wit.'[11]

Benjamin Disraeli quickly rivaled Clay in becoming the life of the party. The governor of Malta was Sir Frederick Ponsonby (1783–1837), a career soldier with an impressive combat record. His sister was Lady Caroline Lamb (1785–1828), for a brief moment in 1812 Byron's lover, who famously described him as 'mad, bad, and dangerous to know'. This was all too perfect. 'Yesterday I called on Ponsonby, He was fortunately at home,' Disraeli reported:

> I flatter myself that he passed through the most extraordinary quarter of an hour of his existence—I gave him no quarter, and at last made our nonchalant Governor roll on the sofa from his rissible convulsions. Then I jumped up, remembering that I must be sadly breaking into his morning and was off: making it a rule always to leave with a good impression. He pressed me not to go—I told him I had so much to do![12]

But eventually it was time to leave, and somehow a new plan had been hatched. 'A week ago I knew not what I [woul]d do,' Disraeli confessed to his brother Ralph:

> All is now settled. On Wednesday [m]orning I quit this place where on the [wh]ole I have spent very agre[e]able hours in [the] [y]acht which Clay has hired and in which [he] intends to turn pirate. The original [pl]an was to have taken it together, but [as] Meredith was averse to the plan, we [have] become his passengers at a fair [rate] and he drops us whenever and wherever [we] like.

The yacht itself, he reported, is 'an excellent size for these seas, with a crew of 7 men. She is a very strong sea boat and bears the unpoetical name of

Susan, which is a bore, but as we can't alter it we have painted it out.' Meredith was never very keen on Clay and his lifestyle, but Disraeli tried to allay his family's fears: 'Clay is immensely improved, and [a] very agreeable companion indeed, with [su]ch a valet! Giovanni by name, Byron [d]ied in his arms, and his mustachios touch [t]he earth. Withal mild as a lamb, tho' [he has two] daggers always about his perso[n].'[13]

The presence on board of Giovanni Battista ('Tita') Falcieri (1798–1874) was a powerful incentive for joining up with Clay. Tita was a Venetian gondolier, son of a gondolier, from a family of hereditary gondoliers to the Mocenigi family, whose palazzo had been rented by Lord Byron in May 1818. Tita stayed with Byron when he left town in December 1819, and from time to time became part of the household of Percy Bysshe Shelley as well. In a letter to his wife Mary, Shelley described Tita as 'a fine fellow with a prodigious black beard, who has stabbed two or three people, & is the most goodnatured looking fellow I ever saw'.[14] Tita served Byron at Cephalonia in August 1823 and was with the great poet when he died at Missolonghi on 19 April 1824, then bringing his body back to England in the company of Byron's faithful valet William Fletcher. Byron's travelling companion John Cam Hobhouse fixed up a job for Tita with his father Sir Benjamin Hobhouse, but Tita longed for the Mediterranean and returned to Greece, visiting London at least once more during this period. But now it was September 1830, and somehow Tita was in the service of James Clay, which pleased Disraeli no end. He had once been rowed across Lake Geneva by Byron's boatman Maurice, and now he was on board a 55 ton yacht served by the man in whose arms Byron had expired.[15]

Disraeli, Meredith and Clay arrived in Corfu at the beginning of October 1830. The Ionian Islands, which figured so prominently in Byron's Eastern adventure, were then under British control and remained so until 1864 when the islands were finally ceded to Greece. Lord Blake, Disraeli's celebrated modern biographer, placed great stress on Disraeli's Eastern adventure and his especial affection for Turkey and the Islamic milieu acquired therein:

He had fallen in love, as many Englishmen were to do after him, with the alien yet curiously hypnotic civilization of the Muslim world. Every further stage in his journey consolidated this strange love affair. The experiences of the roué and dandy of 1830–1831 were to affect the attitude of the Prime Minister and statesman nearly half a century later at the Congress of Berlin.[16]

As we shall see, Blake was right.

Disraeli's Grand Tour was based loosely on the premise that he was following in the footsteps of the great Lord Byron. On 10 October 1830, he wrote to his father that he was 'disappointed in entering Albania, and visiting Yanina and the "monastic Zitza" for the whole country is in a state of insurrection'. Disraeli, however, was clearly on the Turkish side: 'I am glad to say the Porte every where triumphant', he asserted. What Disraeli wanted was to be able to present a letter from Sir Frederick Adam (1781–1853), Lord High Commissioner of the Ionian Islands, to the Grand Vizier of the Ottoman Empire, who was reported to be with the Turkish army at Preveza. This was Reşid Mehmed Paşa (1780–1839), the Ottoman general who had defeated Ali Paşa, Byron's anti-hero. For 'once in my life,' Disraeli sighed with pleasure, 'I am to be an ambassador'.[17]

Disraeli need not have been so pessimistic. He was soon reporting home with great excitement that

> I ment[ione]d in my letter to you that there was a possibility of our paying the Grand Vizier a visit at head quarters at Yanina, the Capital of Albania. What was then probable has since become certain. We sailed from Corfou to this place where we arrived on the eleventh Inst.

This place, at which Disraeli, Meredith and Clay arrived on 11 October 1830 was Preveza.[18]

This brings us to *Contarini Fleming: A Psychological Auto-Biography*, the book Disraeli published in 1832 after his return to London.[19] Strictly speaking, it was nothing of the kind, at least in that the hero depicted came from a family whose details were rather different than Disraeli's. But large swathes of text are taken directly from Disraeli's letters home during his trip to the East, so much so that it is difficult to determine which of the two versions of his narrative is more authentic, the letters or their novelization. Indeed, it might even be argued that rather than the novel being based on the 'original' letters, the letters were based on the 'original' text of the novel, which was being written en route, on the model of Byron's composition of *Childe Harold's Pilgrimage* during his odyssey to the East. The *Home Letters* then become a posted back-up in a pre-digital age, which also brought news and pleasure to his family back in England. Certainly, once *Contarini Fleming* was published, it was that narrative printed text which entered the public consciousness rather than Disraeli's private manuscript letters.

In Chap. 10 of *Contarini Fleming*, Disraeli gives a much fuller description of Preveza than in the letters. Unfortunately, Disraeli's literary skills were still far more evident in his letters than in his novels, which had not yet achieved even the high mediocre standard of a work like *Lothair* (1870). In the meantime, *Contarini Fleming* sported phrases such as 'Hark! the clang of the barbaric horn, and the wild clash of the cymbal.'[20] Either way, the story is the same. From Preveza the three lads sailed in the Ambracian Gulf to Salora, and in the morning of 14 October 1830 they travelled overland to Arta, guarded by six armed horsemen. At Arta, they found themselves expected, and accommodation was prepared in a house belonging to the British consulate. Arta, he found, was

> a town once as beautiful as its site, and famous for its gardens, but now a mass of ruins. The whole place was razed to the ground, the minaret of the principal mosque alone untouched, and I shall never forget the effect of the muezzin with his rich, and solemn, and sonorous voice, calling us to adore God in the midst of all this human havoc.

The next morning, they paid their respects to Kalio Bey, the governor of Arta, an Albanian noble who had remained faithful to his masters in Istanbul, even when many of his cohort had recently rebelled:

> I found the Bey of Arta keeping his state, which, notwithstanding the surrounding desolation, was not contemptible, in a tenement which was not much better than a large shed...I must confess that it was with some awe that for the first time in my life I entered the divan of a great Turk, and found myself sitting cross-legged on the right hand of a bey, smoking an amber-mouthed chiboque, sipping coffee, and paying him compliments through an interpreter[21]

This was just the sort of experience that Disraeli had sought, an Eastern moment behind the carpet curtain of the Ottoman Empire.

But the destination was Ioannina, just as it had been for Byron. Kalio Bey provided the Englishmen with an escort of twenty Albanians, 'armed to the teeth, with daggers, pistols, and guns, invariably richly ornamented, and sometimes entirely inlaid with silver, even the tassel'. They made their way north, with a letter of introduction from Kalio Bey to be provided to the 'young bey' in charge of a vast but dilapidated khan, as big as a Gothic castle, situated on a high range, and built, for the accommodation of travellers from the capital to the coast, by the great Ali Pacha, when his long, sagacious, and unmolested reign permitted him to develop, in a country which combines the excellences of Western Asia and Southern Europe, some of the intended purposes of a beneficent nature. This khan had now been converted into a military post.[22]

Disraeli found the young bey very pleasant, but unfortunately he was unable to understand Tita's Greek.

What happened next is a wonderful story, told identically in the letter home and in *Contarini Fleming*:

What was to be done? Proceed we could not, for there was not an inhabited place before Yanina; and here was I sitting before sunset on the same divan with my host, who had entered the place to receive me, and would not leave the room while I was there, without the power of communicating an idea. I was in despair, and also very hungry, and could not therefore, in the course of an hour or two, plead fatigue as an excuse for sleep, for I was ravenous, and anxious to know what prospect of food existed in this wild and desolate mansion. So we smoked. It is a great resource. But this wore out, and it was so ludicrous smoking and looking at each other, and dying to talk, and then exchanging pipes by way of compliment, and then pressing our hands to our hearts by way of thanks. At last it occurred to me that I had some brandy, and that I would offer my host a glass, which might serve as a hint for what should follow so vehement a schnaps. Mashallah! the effect was, indeed, miraculous. My mild friend smacked his lips, and instantly asked for another cup. We drank it in coffee-cups. A bottle of brandy was despatched in quicker time, and fairer proportions than had ever solemnized the decease of the same portion of Burgundy. We were extremely gay. The bimbashee ordered some dried figs, talking all the time, and indulging in graceful pantomime, examining my pistols, inquiring about percussion locks, which greatly surprised him, handing his own, more ornamented although less effective, weapons for my inspection, and finally making out Greek enough to misunderstand most ludicrously every observation communicated. But all was taken in good part, and I never met such a jolly fellow in the course of my life.

In the mean time I became painfully ravenous, for the dry, round, unsugary fig of Albania is a great whetter. At last I asked for bread. The bimbashee gravely bowed, and said, "Leave it to me, take no thought," and nothing more occurred. I prepared myself for hungry dreams, when to my great astonishment and delight, a capital supper was brought in, accompanied, to my equal horror, by wine. We ate with our fingers. It was the first time I had performed such an operation. You soon get used to it, and dash, but in turn, at the choice morsels with perfect coolness. One, with a basin and ewer, is in attendance, and the whole process is by no means so terrible as it would at first appear to European habits. For drinking—we really drank with a rapidity which, with me, was unprecedented. The wine was not bad, but, had it been poison, the forbidden juice was such a compliment from a Moslemin, that I must quaff it all. We quaffed it in rivers. The bimbashee called for brandy. Unfortunately there was another bottle. We drank it all. The room turned round, the wild attendants, who sat at our feet, seemed dancing in strange whirls, the bimbashee shook hands with me, he shouted Italian, I Turkish. "Buono, buono," he had caught up—"Pecche, pecche," was my rejoinder, which, let me inform the reader, although I do not even now know much more, is very good Turkish. He roared, he patted me on the back. I remember no more.

In the middle of the night I awoke. I found myself sleeping on the divan, rolled up in its sacred carpet. The bimbashee had wisely reeled to the fire. The thirst I felt was like that of Dives. All were sleeping except two, who kept up, during the night, the great wood-fire. I rose, lightly stepping over my sleeping companions, and the shining arms, that here and there informed me that the dark mass wrapped up in a capote was a human being. I found Abraham's bosom in a flagon of water. I think I must have drunk a gallon at a draught. I looked at the wood-fire, and thought of the blazing blocks in the hall of Jonsterna, asked myself whether I were indeed in the mountain fastness of a Turkish chief, and, shrugging my shoulders went to sleep, and woke without a headach.

The next morning, they were on the road again, Disraeli having given his pipe to the young bey 'as a memorial of having got tipsy together'.

The Englishmen continued their journey to the north, dismayed to find evidence of the recent insurrection all around them:

villages in ruins, and perfectly desolate—khans deserted, and fortresses razed to the ground—olive woods burnt up, and fruit trees cut down. So complete had been the work of destruction, that I often unexpectedly found my horse stumbling amid the foundation of a village, and what at first appeared the dry bed of a torrent, often turned out to be the backbone of the skeleton of a ravaged town.

Finally, they came upon the city of Ioannina, 'jutting into the beautiful lake that bears its name'. Once they entered the town, however, they discovered that it had been completely and totally demolished, mostly by the

Albanian rebels, 'who heard of the destruction of their chiefs by the grand vizier. They revenged themselves on tyranny by destroying civilization.'

Despite the razing of the town, however, the life of the people went on: 'a swarming population, arrayed in every possible and fanciful costume, buzzed and bustled in all directions'. Disraeli was thrilled to be, as he thought, in a place where 'a Frank had not penetrated for nine years': 'Every thing was so strange and splendid, that for a moment I forgot that this was an extraordinary scene even for the East, and gave up my fancy to full credulity in the now almost obsolete magnificence of oriental life.' Following this phrase in *Contarini Fleming* but not in his letter home, Disraeli added the sentence, 'I longed to write an Eastern tale.' Disraeli took in everything he saw: a dervish, a *deli*, a *paşa*, a sheikh, and a hundred camels parading at the end of the street, bearing corn for the Turkish troops. 'It seemed to me that my first day in a Turkish city brought before me all the popular characteristics of which I had read, and which I expected occasionally to observe during a prolonged residence.'[23]

They lodged at the home of a Greek physician and the next day made their way to the fortress of Ali Paşa. Disraeli and his two friends were conducted through the gates and the narrow streets to the palace, ever closer to the Grand Vizier, 'for among the orientals all depends upon one brain, and we, with our subdivisions of duty, and intelligent and responsible deputies, can form no idea of the labour of a Turkish premier'. Disraeli described his surroundings in detail, for in 'the whole course of my life I had never mingled in so picturesque an assembly'. Finally, they were

> summoned to the awful presence of the pillar of the Turkish Empire, the man who has the reputation of being the mainspring of the new system of regeneration, the renowned Redschid, an approved warrior, a consummate politician, unrivalled as a dissembler in a country where dissimulation is the principal portion of moral culture.

Reşid Mehmed Paşa himself turned out to be 'a little ferocious-looking, shrivelled, care-worn man, plainly dressed, with a brow covered with wrinkles, and a countenance clouded with anxiety and thought'.[24] In *Contarini Fleming*, Disraeli interpolated into the text of his letters home a wish expressed by his literary doppelgänger that he might join the Turkish army and fight the rebellious Albanians. Reşid Mehmed Paşa does not object, noting that 'as a Frank, I could hold no command. I told him that such was not my desire, but that, as I intended to proceed to Stamboul, it would be gratifying to me to feel that I had co-operated, however humbly, in the cause of a sovereign whom I greatly admired.'[25] Recalling his meeting with the Grand Vizier, perhaps this is what Disraeli wished he had said. Indeed, Contarini Fleming, unlike Benjamin Disraeli, fights at the Battle of Monastir under the command of 'Mehmet, Pasha of Lepanto, he who stabbed Ali Pasha', and finds that 'a battle was, after all, the most delightful pastime in the world'. When Disraeli in the imaginary universe of Contarini Fleming meets Reşid Mehmed Paşa at Ohrid (Macedonia) after their victory, he is given 'the pipe of honour from his own lips'. Well, Contarini Fleming reflects,

> So much for the battle of Bitoglia or Monastir, a very pretty fray, although not as much talked of as Austerlitz or Waterloo, and which probably would have remained unknown to the great mass of European readers, had not a young Frank gentleman mingled, from a silly fancy, in its lively business.[26]

Silly fancy it was for young Benjamin Disraeli, a sort of a daydream about the 'delightful pastime' of war.

The real Disraeli, however, carried on his rather more sedate progress through the provincial Ottoman court at Ioannina. Reşid Mehmed Paşa passed Disraeli and his friends on to his son Amin, paşa of the town, a polished and superficially Westernized playboy. They also had much opportunity to hear Turkish music, which although 'frightful ... peculiar and different from that of other Eastern nations' could also be quite beautiful: 'I have seldom listened to more simple and affecting melodies than those with which the boatmen are wont to soothe their labours.'[27] By the end of several days in Ioannina, Disraeli had truly fallen in love with Turkey. 'There is no character in the world higher bred than a Turk of rank,' he thought. 'Some of these men, too, I found extremely intelligent, deeply interested in the political amelioration of their country, and warm admirers of Peter the Great.'[28] Disraeli's life-long hopeful belief that the Ottoman Empire might reform itself and was therefore worth preserving was born here in Ioannina.

Disraeli, Meredith and Clay departed from Ioannina and travelled south, reaching Preveza by 25 October 1830. They boarded the *Susan* once again and sailed along the south-western coast of Greece. When Disraeli made his Grand Tour, Greece was still very much part of the Ottoman Empire, as yet unretreated to the fastnesses of Anatolia, and it seems that Disraeli was unmoved by the splendours of ancient Greece after having lolled on divans with Turkish beys. 'I am quite a Turk,' Disraeli boasted to his erstwhile travelling companion Benjamin Austen; 'wear a turban, smoke a pipe six feet long, and squat on a Divan. Mehemet Pacha told me that he did not think I was an Englishman because I walked *so slow*. In fact I find the habits of this calm and luxurious people entirely agree with my own preconceived opinions of propriety and enjoyment, and I detest the Greeks more than ever.' As if to make the point, Disraeli and his friends did not even stop at Missolonghi, the philhellene's holy ground where their posthumous champion Byron breathed his last. 'We were a week at the scene of Codrington's bloody blunder, Navarino', however, wrote Disraeli, unappreciative of the total defeat of the Ottoman Egyptian navy only three years earlier.[29]

Even the Parthenon failed to impress him and in comparison with other noble buildings 'could only rank as a church with a cathedral'.[30] In any case, Disraeli argued, in 'art, the Greeks were the children of the Egyptians. The day may come when we shall do justice to the high powers of that mysterious and imaginative people.'[31] Next stop: Istanbul. Disraeli and his friends sailed up through the Dardanelles, those 'sublime shores' which seemed to him a fitting division between continents: 'Asia and Europe look more kindly on each other, than Europe and her more sultry sister.' Briefly 'becalmed off Troy', they glided up the Straits, through the Sea of Marmara, and finally, 'we cast our anchor in the famous Golden Horn'. In his letter to his father, he expressed his feelings more personally than could be included even in a self-described psychological autobiography: 'It is near sunset and Const. is in full sight—it baffles all description, tho' so often described; an immense mass of buildings, cupolas, cypress, groves, and minarets. I feel an excitement, which I thought was dead.'[32]

Disraeli remained in Istanbul for about six weeks, arriving on 10 December 1830. He had been expecting to link up with his friend at the British Embassy, George Hamilton Seymour (1797–1880), only to find he had already gone two months earlier, to be minister in Florence. But Disraeli was a charmer, and soon conquered the British envoy extraordinary, Sir Robert Gordon (1791–1847), the younger brother of Lord Aberdeen (who had just ended his role as Foreign Secretary and would later be Prime Minister, 1852–1855). Gordon was not actually ambassador, since full diplomatic relations between Britain and the Ottoman Empire had been broken off after the Battle of Navarino and would not be completely restored until 1832. But it hardly made a difference, certainly not to Disraeli and his friends. Gordon was also Byron's first cousin, and at the same time rather pro-Turkish and anti-Greek, just like Disraeli. By an odd twist of fate, when Gordon retired he acquired the lease of a shooting lodge in Scotland called Balmoral, which passed on his death in 1847 to his brother, who sold it to Prince Albert, the rest, of course, being history. Anyway, Gordon gave Disraeli, Meredith and Clay the run of the British Embassy, inviting them to dine there with him whenever they wished; 'we only send to the Palace in the morning'. The boys took lodgings in the European Pera district and Gordon was very pleased to have them as visitors, introducing them to all the ambassadors, and inviting them 'to every picnic, here a favourite expedition'.[33]

Apparently all this was too much fun for dour William Meredith, who ditched them around Christmas 1830. 'Meredith quitted us to our great regret,' Disraeli told his father, 'as he had always intended, and is now wandering among the Bithynian mountains, which are remarkable for being more devoid of interest than any hills in existence. We anticipate meeting him at Smyrna, and if so, may probably find him not disinclined to renounce his ambitious intentions of being a discoverer.'[34] Disraeli and Clay, meanwhile, surrendered themselves to the seductive beauties of Istanbul. 'Description is an acknowledged bore,' he wrote to his father. 'I dread it myself, and therefore sympathise with your already murmured fears. So I leave Constantinople to your imagination.'[35] But describe he did, not only in his letters home but in their polished version in *Contarini Fleming*. 'The two most wonderful things at Constantinople are the Bosphorus and the bazaar,' he thought, although the 'most wonderful thing here are the burial-grounds', and could not resist indulging himself in a bit of impressionistic narrative. He noted that the Jews wore 'a black hat wreathed with a white handkerchief' but otherwise took no especial interest in his former co-religionists. 'I have been inside a Mosque— Sulumania,' he noted proudly, 'which is nearly as large and far more beautiful than Sophia.'[36]

Unlike his creation Contarini Fleming, Benjamin Disraeli did not rate an audience with Sultan Mahmud II (r. 1808–1839), although he did manage to catch a glimpse of him several times. 'He affects all the affable activity of a European Prince,' Disraeli noticed, 'mixes with his subjects, interferes in all their pursuits and taxes them most unmercifully. He dresses like a European and all the young men have adopted the fashion.'[37] Disraeli also got a good look at the young men in uniform who composed the officer class of the Ottoman army and 'would not disgrace one of our crack cavalry regiments':

It is on the rising generation that the Sultan depends, and if one may form an opinion, not in vain. After all his defeats, he has now Sixty thousand regular infantry excellently appointed and well disciplined. They are certainly not to be compared to the French or English line—but they would as certainly beat the Spanish or the Dutch, and many think with fair play, the Russians.[38]

Disraeli by the time *Contarini Fleming* was published in 1832 had already fashioned himself into an expert on Ottoman affairs, if not because he had had in-depth discussions with the sultan but because he had been able to travel to the East, 'wear a turban, smoke a pipe six feet long, and squat on a Divan'.[39] The views and opinions that Disraeli formed in 1830–1831 as a vigorous young man in his mid-twenties stayed with him and gave him the confidence and even the authority to be aggressively pro-Turkish forty years later when it really mattered.

Contarini Fleming spent 'four or five months at Stamboul', while the real Disraeli could only spare six packed weeks.[40] The 'Ambassador has received me with a kindness which I shall always remember with gratitude,' he reported home. 'It is almost impossible for him to have done more, whatever ties existed between us.'[41] Shortly after 11 January 1831, the *Susan* sailed out of Istanbul with Benjamin Disraeli and James Clay aboard, 'Meredith having already departed for his exploration of Asia Minor, respecting which he was very mad, altho' I believe it to be a country equally unsatisfactory to the topographer, the antiquarian, and the man of taste'.[42] It was difficult to leave town, Disraeli reported, 'and were literally unable to make our escape from our friend Sir Robert, who at last in his desperation, offered us rooms in the Palace, when we complained of our lodgings, and finally, when all was in vain, parted from us in a pet'. They hitched on to 'a dashing breeze down the Dardanelles', but were becalmed for three days between the islands of Lesbos and Chios. 'You cannot conceive anything more lovely than the scenery of the Gulf of Smyrna,' Disraeli enthused, 'which is vaster and more beautiful than the Ambracian.' Disraeli and Clay had intended merely to pick up Meredith and leave, but it was winter, and a bad storm kept them in town for ten days:

Here, howr. we found Meredith in a very decent bivouack, so having much to say to each o[the]r, we got over the affair better than might have been expected. This is the only winter we have had, tho' this season at

Constantinople is usually more severe. I ascribe to this continuance of fine weather and to smoking the continued improvement in my health, which is most satisfactory.[43]

The original tentative plan was to arrive in Egypt about 21 January 1831, and return from there to Malta and then to Naples.[44] In theory, that should have meshed well with the travel plans of Disraeli's intended brother-in-law. 'At Smyrna I found that Mer[edith] began to indicate a wish to see Egypt,' Disraeli told his sister:

> The fact is, he had got hold of some books there, Hamilton's Egyptiaca etc., which had opened his mind upon the subject. The thing is, as I then discovered, he knew no more about Egypt than a child, and was quite surprised to learn that there were more remains there on one spot, than in all the rest of the globe united. I did the impossible to induce him to rejoin us, but he co[ul]d not make up his mind to give up an intended trip to the unseen relics of some unhea[r]d of cock and a bull city, and so we again parted.[45]

Disraeli must have realized that Meredith just did not fancy being the third wheel on a careening carnival vehicle and preferred to be on his own. Anyway, appearances were preserved, at least for the sake of his beloved sister Sarah.

For Disraeli and Clay, it was back on board the *Susan*. Unhelpful winds kept them from landing at Rhodes, even though they spent two days trying to wait it out. (Contarini Fleming, however, managed a visit.)[46] They made land at Cyprus, staying only a day, and there got a pilot to take them to Jaffa. Egypt would have to wait. Next destination: the Holy Land.

Landing at Jaffa, Disraeli and Clay departed the next day on the Jerusalem road, 'a party of six, well mounted and armed'. They spent the night at Ramla in the Hospice of St Nicodemus and St Joseph of Arimathea, which had been Napoleon's headquarters in 1799. On the morrow they completed their journey to Jerusalem, a vision well told both in a letter to his sister and in *Contarini Fleming*, although the view he describes could not have been his first towards the Jaffa Gate but rather was the much more dramatic sight from the Mount of Olives. 'I was thunderstruck,' he wrote to Sarah. 'I saw before me apparently a gorgeous city.' Indeed, he wrote, 'Athens and Jerusalem in their glory must have been the finest representations of the beautiful and the sublime. Jerusalem in its present state, wo[ul]d make a wonderful subject for Martin and a picture from him co[ul]d alone give you an idea of it.' Disraeli and Clay sought lodgings at the monastery of St Salvador, the Franciscan centre in Jerusalem, also known as 'Custodia Terra Sancta' in recognition of its special role at the Church of the Holy Sepulchre. They were given what Disraeli thought to be one of 'the best houses in Jerusalem, belong'd to the convent, and servants were allotted to us. They sent us provisions daily.'[47]

'Never more delighted in my life', wrote Disraeli from Jerusalem, and perhaps that is why he lacked the time to write letters about his experiences at great length.[48] He made up for this to some extent in *Contarini Fleming*, but here too much is left untold. 'There is only one way to travel in the East with ease,' he advised, 'and that is with an appearance of pomp. The Turks are much influenced by the exterior, and although they are not mercenary, a well-dressed and well-attended infidel will command respect.'[49] Disraeli did not seem to have much, if any, contact with Jews while visiting Jerusalem, although he does introduce a local Jewish character into *Contarini Fleming*: 'Besso, a rich Hebrew merchant', who lived near the Zion Gate.

By the middle of March 1831, Disraeli and Clay were off to Egypt and reached Alexandria. It was a 'wretched passage from Jafa,' he wrote, but was glad to find that Meredith had preceded them, 'just arrived as I understand in a Turkish ship—after a horrid passage'.[50] Disraeli's next (and last letter) home was to his sister Sarah, from Cairo, dated 28 May 1831. Much had happened during that time, and by then he was 'only waiting here for a ship to convey me to Malta' and then to London. The big news was that Meredith had finally got fed up and left, although Disraeli tried to be diplomatic.[51] Disraeli was hardly indolent, however, and told his sister a wonderful story about a trip from Alexandria to Rosetta, twelve hours across the desert, surrounded by a mirage, and rewarded with a first view of the Nile. He climbed the Great Pyramid, and then voyaged three weeks up to Thebes, surviving a sudden and violent sandstorm.[52]

Another three-week voyage, and they were back in Cairo, which, 'in spite of its dinginess is a luxurious and pleasant place'. 'The more I see of Oriental life,' he mused, 'the more I like.' Best of all, with all of his fantasizing, for once Disraeli really did have the chance of emulating his imaginary double Contarini Fleming by actually meeting the great Mehmet Ali Paşa (1769–1849), the vali of Egypt and Sudan:

> I have seen the Pacha in a very extraordinary manner. Wandering in the gardens of his palace at Shubra, I suddenly came upon him one afternoon surrounded by his Court, a very brilliant circle, in most gorgeous dresses,

particularly the black eunuchs in scarlet and gold, and who ride white horses. I was about to retire, but one of his principal attendants took me by the arm and led me to the circle. The Pacha is exceed[ing]ly fond of the English. His H[ighne]ss was playing chess with his fool, and I witnessed a very curious scene. I stayed about a quarter of an hour, and had I waited till his game was finished, I am informed that he wo[ul]d have spoken to me, but as I had no interpreter with me, and am pretty sure that he was in the same state, I thought it best to make my bow. My presentation has been delayed on account of Clay's illness, but it has been offered to me several times. I look forward to it rather as a bore than not—as he receives you quite alone and X [cross-] examines you to a death.[53]

Disraeli eventually was presented to Mehmet Ali, which he described a few years later, referring to himself in the third person:

Our countryman received the summons, which all instantly obey, and imme-diately repaired to the Divan of the citadel. He found the pacha surrounded by his courtiers, his engineers, his colonels, and his eunuchs. At length his Highness clapped his hands and the chamber was cleared, with the exception of a favourite minister and a faithful dragoman. The surprise of our country-man, when he received the communication of the pacha, was not inconsid-erable; but he was one of those, who had seen sufficient of the world never to be astonished, not altogether untinctured with political knowledge, and gifted with that philosophical exemption from prejudice, which is one of the most certain and the most valuable results of extensive travel. Our country-man communicated to the Egyptian ruler with calmness and with precision the immediate difficulties that occurred to him, explained to the successor of the Pharaohs and the Ptolemies that the political institutions of England had been the gradual growth of ages, and that there is no political function which demands a finer discipline, or a more regulated preparation, than the exercise of popular suffrage. The pacha listened in silence, nodding his head in occasional approbation: then calling for coffee, instead of looking at his watch like an European sovereign, delicately terminated the interview.

But there was more to the story, although with only Disraeli for a witness, it is hard to know how seriously to take his narrative:

Some short time afterwards the young Englishman repaired, as was his occa-sional custom, to the levee of the Egyptian ruler. When the pacha perceived him, he welcomed him with a favouring smile, and beckoned to him to advance to the contiguous divan.

"God is great!" said Mehemet Ali to the traveller; "you are a wise man — Allah! kerim, but you spit pearls. Nevertheless I will have a parliament, and

I will have as many parliaments as the King of England himself. See here!" So saying, his Highness produced two lists of names, containing those of the most wealthy and influential personages of every town and district in his dominions. "See here!" said he, "here are my parliaments; but I have made up my mind, to prevent inconvenience, to elect them myself."

Behold, my Lord, a splendid instance of representation without election! In pursuance of this resolution of Mehemet Ali, two chambers met at Cairo: called in the jargon of the Levant, the *alto Parliamento*, and the *basso Parliamento*. The first consisted of the pachas and chief officers of the capital: the second really of the most respectable of the provincial population. Who can doubt that the *basso Parliamento* of Cairo, if the invasion of Syria had not diverted the attention of Mehemet Ali from domestic politics, might have proved a very faithful and efficient national council, and afforded the governor of the country very important information as to the resources, necessities, and grievances of his subjects? Who can hesitate in believing that there was a much greater chance of its efficiency and duration when appointed by the pacha himself, than when elected by his subjects in their present condition? Who does not recognise in such an assembly the healthy seeds of a popular government? I for one should have much more confidence in the utility and duration of the Parliament of Cairo, than in that of Naples or Madrid; especially as, it is but candid to confess, Mehemet Ali had further secured a practical term of political initiation for his future legislators by two capital rules; first, that the *basso Parliamento* should only petition and not debate; and secondly, that the *alto Parliamento* should only debate, and not vote![54]

Disraeli may have improved the tale, but it is enormously significant that as a young man he had a chat with the famous Mehmet Ali, and then went on to become the prime minister of Great Britain during a crucial phase of the Eastern Question. Disraeli was a Romantic, and impressions upon his heart, especially at that stage of his life, were critical.

Disraeli's letters home end here, as did his Grand Tour, and rather abruptly. William Meredith, Disraeli's intended brother-in-law, returned from Thebes in late June, and the plan was for the three young men to return to England via Malta, Naples, Rome and Venice, and then overland to Calais. Clay went on ahead to Alexandria to organize the trip, leaving Disraeli and Meredith in Cairo. It was there that Meredith suddenly contracted smallpox and died on 19 July 1831, after what had seemed to have been only a mild case. Clay stuck to the original itinerary, but Disraeli hurried home to his distraught sister, that is to say, he made for Malta, sat out a month of quarantine there, and arrived in England in late October 1831.

II

'I confess to you that my Turkish prejudices are very much confirmed by my residence in Turkey,' Disraeli wrote to a friend:

The life of this people greatly accords with my taste, which is naturally somewhat indolent and melancholy, and I do not think would disgust you. To repose on voluptuous ottomans, and smoke superb pipes, daily to indulge in the luxuries of a bath which requires half a dozen attendants for its perfection, to court the air in a carved caique by shores which are a continual scene and to find no exertion greater than a canter on a barb, is I think a far more sensible life than all the bustle of clubs, all the boring of saloons—all this without any coloring and exaggeration is the life which may be here commanded accompanied by a thousand sources of calm enjoyment and a thousand modes of mellowed pleasure, which it wo[ul]d weary you to relate, and which I leave to your own lively imagination.[55]

These 'Turkish prejudices' were indeed to be life-long. As it happened, he had plenty of time to enhance them. Between the years 1853 and 1874, Disraeli's Conservative Party was out of office for more than sixteen years. The years of Disraeli's physical prime from the age of about 47 to almost 70 were mostly spent in the political wilderness, and he had the unwanted luxury of developing his ideas without the necessity of trimming his thoughts to fit the political exigencies of a ruling government.

After several unsuccessful tries, Disraeli first got into the House of Commons in 1837, sitting for Maidstone. His maiden speech (7 December 1837) was a disaster, and his Jewish origins made him an easy target for racist jibes. But the other Tory MP for Maidstone was Wyndham Lewis (1780–1838), who died the following March, almost bequeathing his widow Mary Anne (1792–1872) to Disraeli, who married her after a decent interval of seventeen months. In 1841, Disraeli was elected MP for Shrewsbury, and in 1847 made his final parliamentary migration to Buckinghamshire, which he represented until he went to the House of Lords in 1876, almost thirty years later.

Disraeli began to mark out his place as an Eastern novelist with *Contarini Fleming*, published in 1832. Although it was a transparently autobiographical work, the persistence of his affection for these themes became quite apparent with the publication of *Alroy* (1833) and *The Rise of Iskander* (1834).[56] But the detailed presentation of Disraeli's views on the philosophical and cultural aspects of the Eastern Question really began with his three 'Young England' novels (1844–1847). Disraeli began writing the first of the trilogy in September 1843: *Coningsby, or, the New Generation*. Set in the 1830s, the plot of the novel revolves around a certain Henry Coningsby, the orphaned grandson of an English marquess who eventually disinherits the boy when he falls in love with the daughter of a rich cotton merchant whose brother had been a pal of his at Eton. All turns out well in the end: Coningsby becomes a barrister and an MP and gets the girl as well.

In *Coningsby* we meet the somewhat mysterious and very rich Jewish banker named Sidonia, a sort of Rothschild Nathan the Wise. Sidonia introduces Coningsby (and the reader) to a full-blown racialist interpretation of history, and identifies the Jews as the most pure of the 'Caucasian races':

> The fact is, you cannot destroy a pure race of the Caucasian organisation. It is a physiological fact; a simple law of nature, which has baffled Egyptian and Assyrian Kings, Roman Emperors, and Christian Inquisitors. No penal laws, no physical tortures, can effect that a superior race should be absorbed in an inferior, or be destroyed by it. The mixed persecuting races disappear; the pure persecuted race remains. And at this moment, in spite of centuries, of tens of centuries, of degradation, the Jewish mind exercises a vast influence on the affairs of Europe. I speak not of their laws, which you still obey; of their literature, with which your minds are saturated; but of the living Hebrew intellect.[57]

What one needs to conquer the world is vision, of the religious variety:

> Such a temperament, though rare, is peculiar to the East. It inspired the founders of the great monarchies of antiquity, the prophets that the Desert has sent forth, the Tartar chiefs who have overrun the world; it might be observed in the great Corsican, who, like most of the inhabitants of the Mediterranean isles, had probably Arab blood in his veins. It is a temperament that befits conquerors and legislators[58]

The grandest visionary of recent memory was Napoleon; he must therefore be of Eastern stock, 'probably Arab'.

George Eliot, like many other of Disraeli's readers, was not convinced, and noted contemptuously that

> As to his theory of 'races' it has not a leg to stand on, and can only be buoyed up by such windy eloquence as 'You chitty-faced squabby-nosed

Europeans owe your commerce, your arts, your religion to the Hebrews—
nay the Hebrews lead your armies –' ... The fellowship of race, to which
D'Israeli exultingly refers the munificence of Sidonia, is so evidently an inferior impulse which must ultimately be superseded that I wonder even he,
Jew as he is, dares to boast of it. My Gentile nature kicks most resolutely
against any assumption of superiority in the Jews

Not everyone was so enamoured with race as the defining principle of
human existence. But George Eliot did have something nice to say after
all: 'On one point I heartily agree with D'Israeli as to the superiority of
the Oriental races—their clothes are beautiful and ours are execrable.'[59]

Disraeli pursued racialist theories with even greater vigour in the third
and last of his 'Young England' novels, *Tancred, or, the New Crusade*
(1847). It is our old friend Coningsby, in a cameo appearance towards
the beginning of the book, who predicts that Tancred may never return
to London from his planned visit to Jerusalem: 'The East is a career'.[60]
Sidonia is here too, and notes correctly that what Tancred wants to do 'is
to penetrate the great Asian mystery'.[61] The great lesson to be learned,
according to Sidonia, can be summed up in one sentence: 'All is race;
there is no other truth.'[62] Sidonia, admittedly, is only a character in a
novel, but the omniscient nineteenth-century narrator himself expresses
similar views.[63] For Disraeli, everyone was the same south of Anatolia:
'The Arabs are only Jews upon horseback.'[64] The Semitic race was one,
and included within its bosom Arabs, Bedouin and Jews. Disraeli used
those terms almost as interchangeably as one might call a person British or
English. 'Let men doubt of unicorns,' a character says, 'but of one thing
there can be no doubt, that God never spoke except to an Arab.'[65]

These Arabs, Jews and Semites were no slouchers, and their 'Emirs and
Sheikhs, some of whom are proprietors to a very great extent, and many of
whom, in point of race and antiquity of established family, are superior to
the aristocracy of Europe'.[66] These dwellers of the East could easily hold
their heads up against 'Europe, that quarter of the globe to which God
has never spoken'.[67] The proud English, on the other hand, are 'sprung
from a horde of Baltic pirates, who never were heard of during the greater
annals of the world'.[68]

Novels are a problematic source for an author's true views, even if quotations are lifted from the narrative voice. But Disraeli also spoke on his
own steam on these very issues, especially in his political biography of
his patron Lord George Bentinck, published in 1852. The tenth chapter

is entitled 'The Jews', a topic whose only connection with the subject (a younger son of the Duke of Portland) is his support of Jewish emancipation. Disraeli sung the praises of 'the Bedoueen race that, under the name of Jews, is found in every country in Europe', for indeed 'the only medium of communication between the Creator and themselves is the Jewish race' so therefore 'no existing race is so much entitled to the esteem and gratitude of society as the Hebrew'. The 'degradation of the Jewish race is alone a striking evidence of its excellence, for none but one of the great races could have survived the trials which it has endured'. If there is one thing history teaches us, it is that 'it is impossible to destroy the Jews' due to 'the inexorable law of nature, which has decreed that a superior race shall never be destroyed or absorbed by an inferior'.

Since Western Civilization is founded on both biblical and classical principles and traditions, Disraeli takes a moment to clarify what he means:

> the two most dishonoured races in Europe were the Attic and the Hebrew, and they were the two races that had done most for mankind. Their fortunes had some similarity: their countries were the two smallest in the world, equally barren and equally famous; they both divided themselves into tribes: both built a most famous temple on an acropolis; and both produced a literature which all European nations have accepted with reverence and admiration.

As opposed to the Greeks, Disraeli wrote,

> The Jews represent the Semitic principle; all that is spiritual in our nature. They are the trustees of tradition and the conservators of the religious element. They are a living and the most striking evidence of the falsity of that pernicious doctrine of modern times–the natural equality of man.

Disraeli may have supported parliamentary reform, but he was no believer in the family of man.

Benjamin Disraeli had already been prime minister when after returning to the Opposition he published his penultimate novel, *Lothair* (1870), in many ways his best. Like so many of his other books, it is the study of a naïve but well-bred young man who learns the ways of the world with the help of older men and women. Here too he puts racialist principles into the mouth of a literary character, 'the Syrian':

> by the various families of nations the designs of the Creator are accomplished. God works by races, and one was appointed in due season and after many developments to reveal and expound in this land the spiritual

nature of man. The Aryan and the Semite are of the same blood and origin, but when they quitted their central land they were ordained to follow opposite courses. Each division of the great race has developed one portion of the double nature of humanity, till, after all their wanderings, they met again, and, represented by their two choicest families, the Hellenes and the Hebrews, brought together the treasures of their accumulated wisdom, and secured the civilization of man.[69]

That, in a nutshell, was the history of Western culture.

There is another character in the book, a pompous, self-important artist named Mr. Phoebus, who goes on interminably about the differences between the Aryans and the Semites, until even gullible Lothair finds it quite unbearable:

> "Aryan principles," said Mr. Phoebus; "not merely the study of Nature, but of beautiful Nature; the art of design in a country inhabited by a first-rate race, and where the laws, the manners, the customs, are calculated to maintain the health and beauty of a first-rate race. In a greater or less degree, these conditions obtained from the age of Pericles to the age of Hadrian in pure Aryan communities, but Semitism began then to prevail, and ultimately triumphed. Semitism has destroyed art; it taught man to despise his own body, and the essence of art is to honor the human frame."[70]

Phoebus has much to say about how 'Semitism gave them subjects, but the Renaissance gave them Aryan art, and it gave that art to a purely Aryan race. But Semitism rallied in the shape of the Reformation, and swept all away', leaving us to conclude that 'nothing can be done until the Aryan races are extricated from Semitism'.

Phoebus is funny, not only in his own right, but because everyone in 1870 would have instantly recognized him as a parody of that great Victorian critic and poet Matthew Arnold (1822–1888), whose recent book *Culture and Anarchy* (1869) included as Chap. 4 an extended discussion of 'Hebraism and Hellenism'.[71] Disraeli was much more extreme than Arnold on the Hellene/Aryan—Hebrew/Semite question. When Disraeli posited that all is race, he meant it, and was not using the word as a metaphor for culture, or tradition, or common heritage. There was something in the blood, immutable tendencies and innate abilities. Matthew Arnold extracted the race from tendencies and abilities and emphasized the performative elements of the Hellene/Hebrew trope. Disraeli was adamant about the essentialist and racialist basis of culture. Unlike Arnold, Disraeli did not believe that a person or a nation could simply choose to be either

Hellene or Hebrew, Aryan or Semite. These were qualities that you were born with, a fate that could not be changed no matter how hard you tried.

For Disraeli, there was a religious element as well. Neither his Judaism nor his Anglicanism were normative, but he was a man of faith, even if his beliefs had more in common with European Romanticism than with biblical devotion. Somewhere behind the divisions of mankind was divine authority. 'God never spoke except to an Arab', —a Semite, a Jew— and Disraeli saw himself as all of those. Disraeli's obsession with racial terminology and his analysis of English culture as a philosophical struggle between Aryans and Semites was extraordinarily important. Benjamin Disraeli was not just an influential Victorian political figure, but also a highly successful novelist. When Matthew Arnold picked up the idea and made it into the centerpiece of his own work for a while, its success was assured. Whether Arnold was inspired by Heine (as he claimed) or was merely responding to Disraeli is unimportant. What was crucial was that it was now a commonplace of conventional wisdom to posit that English culture was comprised of two distinct elements, one Western and the other Eastern. Arnold promoted his idea of Hellenism over Hebraism. Disraeli dragged the Greeks back into the Ottoman Empire and insisted that all good things came from the Orient and that by rights the English owed a huge debt to the East, and to their own Conservative parliamentarian who in his person represented exactly that tradition.

III

Benjamin Disraeli's enthusiasm for all things Eastern and for the lands of the Ottoman Empire in particular was put to the test by contemporary events. His moment of truth was not the Crimean War (1853–1856), since after all Turkey and Britain (and even France) were on the same side, battling the common Russian enemy.[72] The key moment when Disraeli's romantic attachment to the East had genuine practical effect came twenty years later, when he was already prime minister and faced in 1876 with the crisis over the so-called 'Bulgarian Horrors' and the Russo-Turkish War of 1877–1878.[73] As A.J.P. Taylor put it, the Bulgarian Horrors 'aroused the greatest storm over foreign policy in our history', for it was 'the political crime of the century.'[74]

In February 1874, the Conservative Party came into office having won over 350 seats, which gave them a decisive majority. Benjamin Disraeli spent the next six years as prime minister, enjoying a close personal relationship with Queen Victoria. He was now sixty-nine years old, and for the last fourteen months a widower. Troubles in the Balkans began in July 1875 in Hercegovina when a small group of Christians who had recently been in Montenegro encouraged local people in the area of Mostar to revolt against their Turkish overlords. The reasons for this unrest are still unclear. Tax farmers and Muslim landowners were perennially unpopular, and Serbian or Slavic nationalism there was, but the revolt was fundamentally a Christian phenomenon, even if many of the so-called Turkish overlords came from families that had converted to Islam relatively recently, partly or even largely in order to preserve and ensure their land, wealth, and social position.

Whatever the causes, the disturbances spread and by August 1875, Bosnia was also arisen. The Great Powers were thus inevitably drawn into what was ostensibly a local Turkish matter, as the Turks tried to convince the relevant European governments to send their consuls to the centre of the rebellions in order to warn the insurgents that international help would not be forthcoming and that the only course was to come to some kind of agreement with Istanbul. With all of these disturbances in the Balkans, it was unfortunate timing that just then, on 6 October 1875, the Turkish government announced that it was unable to repay its foreign debt in timely fashion. Many British investors had put money down in the belief that not only was Turkey an important ally against Russia and a key component in Britain's imperial interest, but that the Ottomans had made significant reforms in government and administration so that investment in Turkey was a good financial bet. By the time the British government gave its first public official reaction to the Balkan revolt, it did so against the background of widespread public and press outrage about having just learned that the Turks did not intend to meet their financial obligations.

The combined effect of the Balkan insurrections and the restructuring of the Turkish debt gave Benjamin Disraeli pause: 'the Eastern question, that has haunted Europe for a century, and which I thought the Crimean War had adjourned for half another, will fall to my lot to encounter—dare I say, to settle?'[75] Disraeli's first move was to begin negotiations with Khedive Ismail of Egypt for the purchase of his 44 % stake in Suez Canal shares, which were rumoured to be coming on the market in Paris. The Rothschilds famously advanced Disraeli the four million in Sterling needed for the transaction, and by 25 November 1875, Great Britain held a huge chunk of the Suez Canal; never a majority of shares, but enough to make all the difference, especially given the fact that most of the ships that went through it were British. The sea route to India was now secured, and Britain could well afford to take a more aggressive line in foreign policy. Many people believed that recent events demonstrated that it was time to abandon Britain's long-standing support of Ottoman integrity.

The Balkan insurrection showed no sign of abating. Lacking sufficient regular troops and the money to pay them, the Ottoman authorities tended to rely increasingly on irregulars, the infamous *başıbozuk* ('broken-head') fighters, most often simply local Muslims (or emigrants from the Caucasus) who were happy to plunder and murder any Christian who crossed their path. The presence of irregulars in the fighting was seen to be particularly objectionable by Victorian Englishmen and women, who preferred soldiers to be properly dressed when killing people.

European help was largely in the form of highly demonstrative naval performances. Great Power ships were sent to loiter close to the conflict and not far from Istanbul itself. By the end of May 1876, the British already had ten ironclads in the eastern part of the Mediterranean, mostly at Beşik Bay. With all of these European warships floating about so close to the Dardanelles, Disraeli thought it best to have the British Cabinet remind everyone on 1 June 1876 that despite all that had happened it was still necessary to observe the Straits Treaties of 1841 and 1856, according to which foreign warships were not to enter the Dardanelles while the Ottoman Empire was at peace.

Sadly, things were about to get much worse, and it would be a very long time before one might describe Turkey as peaceful. *Punch* translated current events into a political cartoon published on 7 June 1876 entitled 'The Dogs of War'. The Serbian government declared war on Turkey on 30 June 1876, one day before Montenegro. 'We undertook, undoubtedly, twenty years ago, to guarantee the sick man against murder,' Foreign Secretary Lord Derby (1826–1893) explained, 'but we never undertook to guarantee him against suicide or sudden death.'[76] Although Derby still hoped that the Turks could sort out their Balkan problems by themselves, the parameters of the entire Eastern Question were being changed before their eyes by the publication of an article in the *Daily News* (23 June 1876) detailing alleged Turkish atrocities in Bulgaria.[77]

Many observers were surprised that the Bulgarians should be joining in the Balkan unrest. Although a Bulgarian Revolutionary Central Committee had been established in Bucharest in 1870, the Bulgarians won from the Ottomans the right to an independent Orthodox church in 1872, even over the vehement objection of the Greek Patriarch, which reduced the intensity of political grievances. There were about three million Bulgarians, but most were peasants and not politically active. Still, there were those who wanted their independence from the Ottoman Empire. A rather haphazard Bulgarian revolt broke out at the beginning of May 1876, and was mostly suppressed within a fortnight.[78] Lacking a sufficient number of Ottoman regular troops in the area, the Turkish authorities were once again forced to organize and arm the local Turks and Circassians, who enthusiastically set about killing Christian Bulgarians and burning down their villages.

As it happened, there were a fair number of Western travellers, journalists and even scholars in the area, and their reportage fanned the flames of outrage against the Turkish government, which had been profoundly unpopular at least since the defaulting on their financial obligations the previous year. Arthur Evans (1851–1941), the future excavator at Knossos on Crete, had been in Bosnia when the original rising erupted, wrote an instant book on what he had witnessed, and then became correspondent for the *Manchester Guardian*, based at Ragusa (Dubrovnik).[79] Also headquartered there was William James Stillman (1828–1901), an American who had been the *Times* correspondent at the Cretan uprising in 1866: he also produced a book.[80]

Once the disturbances moved to Bulgaria, reports of Turkish-sponsored enormities found an even more efficient channel. Robert College was established in 1863 a short distance from the heart of Istanbul up the Bosphorus, and as an American missionary institution its students were limited to Christians and (to some extent) to Jews.[81] There were many Bulgarian students at Robert College, and they passed on accounts from home to their teachers, especially Dr. Albert Long (1832–1901), who had been a missionary in Bulgaria for fifteen years, and Dr. George Washburn (1877–1903), the director of the College. Long and Washburn wrote up this information and gave it to Sir Henry Elliot (1817–1907), the British ambassador, in the mistaken belief that he might pass it on to his superiors in London. Elliot received independent confirmation that things were going badly wrong as early as the beginning of May 1876, in the form of reports from Joseph Hutton Dupuis (1827–1903), the British consul at Edirne (Adrianople), who estimated that many thousands of Bulgarians had been raped and massacred and their villages destroyed. For some reason, Elliot decided to put a lid on the entire nasty business.[82]

Not to be deterred, Washburn and Long turned to the press. The regular correspondent of the *Daily News* was Edwin Pears (1835–1919), whose day job was attorney at the Constantinople bar.[83] Antonio Gallenga (1810–1895) was the *Times* correspondent in Istanbul. Both men were given copies of the Robert College memorandum on 16 June 1876. For some reason, the *Times* decided not to publish Gallenga's report, so the *Daily News* had the scoop, in the article published on 23 June 1876.

The *Daily News* was admittedly an organ of the Liberal Party and was hostile to Disraeli's Conservative government in power. Nevertheless the article published by Edwin Pears had a wide impact, appearing under the stark headline, 'Moslem Atrocities in Bulgaria'. Pears dated the article 16 June 1876 from Constantinople, and his point was that not only were cruelties 'being revealed which place those committed in Herzegovina and Bosnia altogether in the background', but that these acts were the work of *başıbozuk* thugs in Ottoman employ. These were 'the dregs of the Turkish and Circassian population, with gipsies and gaol birds let out for the purpose', that is, 'to put down the insurrection in their own fashion'. Pears gave the number killed at between 18,000 and 30,000, and posited the destruction of something like a hundred villages.

This article in the *Daily News* was only the beginning. Questions were asked in the House (Commons and Lords) three days later. Derby in the House of Lords suggested that despite what one read in the papers, 'in the absence of any such official confirmation, I think we should be slow to believe those statements'.[84] Disraeli in the House of Commons took the same line and even suggested that it might have been the Turkish settlers in Bulgaria who had been attacked and forced to defend themselves.[85]

Behind the scenes, the Foreign Office showed more concern. Two days after denying that there was a problem, Derby sent a copy of the article from the *Daily News* to Elliot in Istanbul asking if the allegations were true.[86] Derby believed that the story Pears told in his article was unreliable, but having been asked in Parliament, the subject needed to be pursued.[87] Elliot in his reply confirmed that the Turks employed 'irregulars', but they really had little choice if the rebellion was to be put down: 'the Turks will retaliate with every instrument within their reach'. Derby admitted that there was probably little alternative.[88] Be that as it may, the country was outraged at the idea of armed Turkish Muslims prowling the Bulgarian countryside pillaging and raping Christians and then burning their homes. Queen Victoria's private secretary, Henry Ponsonby (1825–1895) was deeply worried. 'Whatever sympathy existed in this country for the Turkish government is becoming weaker daily,' he warned Derby, 'and the atrocities reported in Bulgaria will go far to obliterate all feelings on behalf of the Turks.'[89] Ponsonby advised the queen that many people in England 'believe that the collapse of the Turkish empire is inevitable and imminent, and that it will be damaging to the prestige of England if we are put forward as the protectors of Turkey and it falls to pieces'.[90]

Back in Istanbul, the Robert College professors were still on the case, working closely with Edwin Pears (the *Daily News*) and Antonio Gallenga (the *Times*). One can only speculate why Sir Philip Francis, the British consul-general at Istanbul, gave these journalists a copy of the original report from 23 June 1876 in which Dupuis detailed the thousands of Bulgarians who were murdered and their villages destroyed. It must have come as no surprise when the *Daily News* and the *Times* printed the information on 8 July 1876. 'The Moslem Atrocities in Bulgaria' was once again the title given to the article written by Edwin Pears.[91]

It was too late to ignore the Bulgarian Horrors. In the House of Commons, Disraeli was asked on 10 July 1876 for his reaction to the news from the East, especially reports of Christian girls being sold as slaves and many other Bulgarians being tortured in prison. 'That there have been proceedings of an atrocious character in Bulgaria I have never for a moment doubted. Wars of insurrection are always atrocious.' But then he continued, with a bad joke that would be taken out of context and constantly used against him:

> I cannot doubt that atrocities have been committed in Bulgaria; but that girls were sold into slavery, or that more than 10,000 persons have been imprisoned, I doubt. In fact, I doubt whether there is prison accommodation for so many, or that torture has been practised on a great scale among an Oriental people who seldom, I believe, resort to torture, but generally terminate their connection with culprits in a more expeditious manner.

Yet Disraeli concluded on a more serious and humane note, and said that he had 'no doubt there may be much to deplore in what has been done, and we may even become convinced that scenes have occurred which must bring to everyone feelings of the deepest regret'.[92]

Whatever the Government was doing to help the Christians of Bulgaria it could never be enough. Queen Victoria sent one of her habitual telegrams to Disraeli after reading the *Daily News*: 'It is too awful,' she lamented. 'It will turn everyone against Turkey.'[93] Certainly, religion and a Victorian ethical arrogance lay behind much of the anti-Turkish agitation. A 'League in Aid of Christians in Turkey' was organized, Lord Shaftesbury (1801–1885) presiding. In his opening speech on 27 July 1876, he declared to a cheering audience that surely 'it is high time for the kingdoms of Europe to interfere and declare that Turkey is a spectacle disgusting to humanity and wholly unfit to exercise rule and authority'. Disraeli's flip comments in the Lords did nothing to hold down the parliamentary indignation, and the Bulgarian Horrors were debated three more times in the Commons in rapid succession (31 July; 7 and 11 August 1876). Gladstone intervened on 31 July 1876 as the only politically active former minister responsible for Britain's role in the Crimean War, arguing that 'the greatest of all the results' of that conflict was the creation of a 'European Concert', indeed, 'a European conscience'.[94]

With Disraeli and his supporters in the Conservative government trying to minimize the scale of the Horrors and thereby to protect the Ottomans, already deeply unpopular for having defaulted on their debts, and with Gladstone and the Liberal opposition taking the high moral ground of conscience and Christianity, it became ever more important to find out what actually happened. The answers were probably to be found in Philippopolis (Plovdiv), but although the Austrians, the Russians and even the Greeks had consuls there, the British did not. Edwin Pears was still the chief source of British information and the Liberal *Daily News* the main conduit of its dissemination. For some reason, Pears took on an associate, and suggested to his paper that this other man actually be sent out in his place. He was Januarius A. MacGahan (1844–1878), an Irish-American journalist who was already famous for having crossed the desert at speed to overtake the army of General Kauffmann on its way to Khiva.[95] Robert College's George Washburn pressed for the involvement in the mission of the less flamboyant Eugene Schuyler (1840–1890), the American consul-general in Istanbul. Washburn himself went to Horace Maynard (1814–1890), the American minister in Istanbul (1875–1880) and 'begged him' to make it happen. MacGahan and Schuyler left Istanbul on 23 July 1876, taking along a Bulgarian student from Robert College who spoke Turkish and English as well.[96]

As the British Foreign Office obviously could not rely on the impartiality of the Americans, there had to be a mission of its own. Sir Henry Elliot, the British ambassador, sent out Walter Baring (1844–1915), a second secretary, but without an interpreter so everything he learned would have to be filtered through the Turks, which was the whole point.[97] Derby really wanted to get at the truth, and had the good idea of simply getting

Dupuis at Edirne (Adrianople) to go directly to Philippopolis, and by 21 July 1876 Dupuis had already telegraphed to London confirming his earlier report that although about 15,000 Bulgarians had been killed in the area and about sixty villages burnt, no women or children had been sold as slaves. In any case, these 'great atrocities have been committed by Turkish irregulars', the dreaded *başıbozuk*s.[98]

The American and British missions were enormously influential in determining public opinion regarding the Ottoman Empire. Baring's first stop on arriving in Philippopolis on 20 July 1876 was to visit the Turkish provincial governor. He then talked to various local people and sent a report to London two days later giving the figure of 12,000 Bulgarians massacred, which was exactly the number that Dupuis had supplied back in June.[99] Baring left Philippopolis on 23 July 1876 and heard more tales of plunder and murder by Turks, Circassians and Pomaks. At various times, he met up with Dupuis and they visited villages together. Dupuis returned to his post at Edirne by 7 August 1876 and immediately filed his report.[100] Baring was back in Istanbul on 22 August 1876 and finished his statement nine days later, sticking with his estimate of 12,000 Bulgarians killed.[101]

Although the English and the Americans had two fact-finding missions working in the same area and at the same time, they were not merely rivals with prescribed agendas. It is true that the American Eugene Schuyler was accompanied by a Russian embassy official at times, and Januarius A. MacGahan was famously pro-Russian, being married to a Russian woman whom he had met at Yalta. But Schuyler also travelled sometimes with Baring, and it would be wrong to see him merely as a parrot of Bulgarian pro-Russian and anti-Turkish sentiments. Schuyler's account of what he saw in Bulgaria was given to Elliot by the American ambassador at Constantinople, and Elliot duly forwarded it to the Foreign Office.[102]

The problem was Januarius A. MacGahan, Edwin Pears's successor, who was determined to make the Bulgarian horror show a reprise of his Persian desert ride, and painted the most lurid possible picture for readers of the *Daily News*. MacGahan did not spare Baring from pre-emptive aspersions, and peppered his accounts with ceaseless praise for the noble Bulgarians. 'I have always heard them spoken of as mere savages, who were in reality not much more civilized than the American Indians;' he claimed, but 'the percentage of people who can read and write is as great in Bulgaria as in England and France.'[103]

One of the centres of *başıbozuk* activity was the village of Batak, southwest of Philipopolis, and both the British and American investigators reported on the horrible scenes which they viewed and which were described to them by local people. But it was MacGahan's eye-witness description published in the 7 August 1876 issue of the *Daily News* that provoked the politicians into action.[104] A debate on the Bulgarian crisis ensued in the House of Commons within hours, and Disraeli's bad joke the previous month was bandied about as evidence for the Conservative government's callousness and indifference to Christian suffering. When Disraeli finally rose to reply, he began by criticizing the previous Liberal government for having reduced the number of British vice-consuls in the Ottoman Empire who could have alerted the Foreign Office before being overtaken by events:

> But those who suppose that England ever would uphold, or at this moment particularly is upholding, Turkey from blind superstition and from a want of sympathy with the highest aspirations of humanity are deceived. What our duty is at this critical moment is to maintain the Empire of England, Nor [*sic*] will we ever agree to any step, though it may obtain for a moment comparative quiet and a false prosperity, that hazards the existence of that Empire.[105]

The summer madness about the Bulgarians was beyond the Government's control, and perhaps Disraeli's reference to 'blind superstition' was an ironic nod to his racial theories, as opposed to Victorian Christianity, 'the highest aspirations of humanity'. As it happens, this speech was Disraeli's last in the House of Commons. The following day, 12 August 1876, he entered the House of Lords as the Earl of Beaconsfield.

The *Daily News*, meanwhile, kept publishing further letters from their own correspondent Januarius A. MacGahan throughout August 1876. By the end of the month, the tide of public protests throughout the country had increased considerably. Lord Russell (1792–1878), who had twice been prime minister (1846–1852; 1865–1866) was the first Liberal politician who called for real action, in a letter to the *Times*, advocating sending in the British fleet to sort things out in Bulgaria, even by allying with the Russians.[106] Even more useful was William Thomas Stead (1849–1912), the vigorous editor of the Darlington *Northern Echo*, who would ultimately meet his Maker on board the *Titanic*. Stead promoted atrocity meetings in the north and elsewhere, and on 25 August 1876 at Darlington he called on Gladstone to join the struggle.[107]

Edward Augustus Freeman (1823–1892) was the real villain of the piece, not only because he was a respected historian and came with substantial academic credentials, but because he was so vicious and mean-spirited. Freeman was also openly, even flamboyantly, antisemitic. Disraeli was for him an 'ever lying Jew', and thusly described him to Lord Bryce.[108] Freeman was so antisemitic and Turkophobic that he could be sympathetic even to Russia, 'a nation in the freshness of a new life, burning to go on the noblest of crusades and our loathsome Jew wants to stop them'.[109] Even Gladstone was not above citing Disraeli's Jewish origins in order to explain his pro-Turkish proclivities, telling his friend the Duke of Argyll 'that Dizzy's crypto-Judaism has had to do with his policy'.[110] Gladstone suggested to Halifax that the origin of Disraeli's foreign policy 'was his judaism'.[111] But this was nothing compared to Freeman, whose public appearances and writings were littered with vulgar antisemitism.

In any case, Gladstone was a political animal despite his trumpeted moralism, and grasped the fact that now, with Parliament in recess and Britain in this summer of 1876 all aflutter about atrocities in Bulgaria, it was time for a pamphlet. On 6 September 1876, John Murray printed Gladstone's thirty-two page pamphlet, entitled *Bulgarian Horrors and the Question of the East*.[112] It was a huge success, selling 40,000 copies within days and perhaps ultimately at least 200,000 in total.[113] More than anything else, it signalled Gladstone's political return after having been decisively rejected by the people two and a half years previously. On a more personal and emotional level, perhaps, it allowed him to atone publicly for having been such a keen supporter of Britain's alliance with Turkey in the Crimean War thirty years earlier, which may have been history for most people, but for a man in his mid-sixties, was a tragic waste still within his living memory.

Gladstone's *Bulgarian Horrors* is an extraordinarily powerful blast of moral indignation and demagoguery. 'Gladstone has had the impudence to send me his pamphlet, tho he accuses me of several crimes', Disraeli wrote to his friend Lord Derby.[114] Disraeli claimed to have been unimpressed and always believed that 'Gladstone, like Richelieu, can't write. Nothing can be more unmusical, more involved or more uncouth than all his scribblement'.[115] It was a 'vindictive and ill-written' pamphlet.[116] As to his supposedly taking the high moral ground on this issue, 'Posterity will do justice to that unprincipled maniac Gladstone—extraordinary mixture of envy, vindictiveness, hypocrisy and superstition—whether Prime Minister or Leader of Opposition—whether preaching, praying, speechifying or scribbling—never a gentleman!'[117]

The publication of *Bulgarian Horrors* was undeniably a political act, even an exploitation of current events, but Disraeli the writer was deaf to the power of Gladstone's words. It became a text mined for its most stirring phrases, brought to bear to testify to Gladstone's reincarnation as the Liberal prophet of rectitude and moral justice. Certainly, Gladstone knew well how to play that role, beating his breast that 'we have been involved, in some amount, at least, of moral complicity with the basest and blackest outrages upon record within the present century, if not within the memory of man'.[118] Gladstone took exaggeration to an entirely new plane: 'There is not a criminal in an European gaol, there is not a cannibal in the South Sea Islands, whose indignation would not rise and overboil at the recital of that which has been done'.[119]

But the pamphlet as a whole is not just rhetoric. A good portion is given over to narrating the history of the Bulgarian Horrors and describing the steps by means of which they came to light in Britain, from the moment of the 'first alarm … that sounded in the "Daily News," on the 23rd of June' by Edwin Pears, 'the gentleman who has fought this battle—for a battle it has been—with such courage, intelligence, and conscientious care'.[120] Even more interesting were Gladstone's specific policy recommendations regarding the Ottoman Empire. 'Indignation is froth, except as it leads to action,' he insisted.[121] 'Do not let us ask for, do not let us accept, Jonahs or scapegoats, either English or Turkish. It is not a change of men that we want, but a change of measures. New Sultans or ministers among Turks, new consuls or new ambassadors in Turkey, would only in my opinion divert us, at this moment, from the great practical aims in view.'[122] Chief among these, he still believed, was 'the territorial integrity of Turkey'.[123] We should 'avail ourselves of that happy approach to unanimity which prevails among the Powers' and thereby to postpone or even avert 'the wholesale scramble, which is too likely to follow upon any premature abandonment of the principle of territorial integrity for Turkey'.[124] To those who would argue that 'the integrity of Turkey should mean immunity for her unbounded savagery, her unbridled and bestial lust', Gladstone pointed to the example of Rumania, which for twenty years 'while paying tribute to the Porte and acknowledging its supremacy, enjoyed an entire autonomy or self-government'.[125] Rumania was the best model for the political organization of Bulgaria, Bosnia and Hercegovina. Disraeli's government, however, while also working to keep the territorial integrity of the Ottoman Empire, resists the notion of change:

Now the territorial integrity means the retention of a titular supremacy, which serves the purpose of warding off foreign aggression. The *status quo* means the maintenance of Turkish administrative authority in Bosnia, Herzegovina, and Bulgaria. Territorial integrity shuts out the foreign state; the *status quo* shuts out the inhabitants of the country, and keeps (I fear) everything to the Turk, with his airy promises, his disembodied reforms, his ferocious passions, and his daily gross and incurable misgovernment. This, then, is the latest present indication of British policy, the re-establishment of the *status quo*.[126]

Oddly enough, Gladstone even had some good things to say about the Turkish government in Istanbul, which 'has acquired, and traditionally transmits, a good deal of the modes of European speech and thought'. The problem lay lower down in the system, at the provincial level 'and the subordinate agents, who share little or none' of those Western virtues, and everything is seen to 'habitually and miserably break down'. Gladstone admitted that the 'promises of a Turkish Ministry given simply to Europe are generally good' and he knew 'of no case in which Turkey has refused to accede to the counsel of United Europe—nay, even of less than United Europe, if Europe was not in actual schism with itself'.[127]

But all was not sweetness and light in Gladstone's pamphlet despite his rather moderate programme for maintaining Turkish territorial integrity and giving the Balkans autonomy within the Ottoman Empire. As might be expected, there were a number of digs directed at Disraeli, especially his 'cynical remarks, such as that the allegations of lingering inflictions hardly could be true, since the Turkish taste was known to incline towards dispatch'.[128] Gladstone also cited Disraeli's belief that atrocities were 'inevitable, when wars are carried on in certain countries, *and between certain races*', underlining these four words so as to throw the Prime Minister's famous racial theories back in his own face.[129] Gladstone ridiculed people like Disraeli, who 'found themselves on notions drawn from their own fancy, or from what they call having been in the East, much more than on the recorded lessons of political and diplomatic experience'.[130]

Ultimately, however, Gladstone's *Bulgarian Horrors* was remembered not for its moderate political programme nor for its jibes against Disraeli, but for its stirring and violent condemnation of the Ottoman Empire, Turkey, and the Turks, which sometimes sat uncomfortably with other calmer parts of the text. 'Mahometan, it must be remembered, does not mean the same as Turk':[131]

Let me endeavour very briefly to sketch, in the rudest outline, what the Turkish race was and what it is. It is not a question of Mahometanism simply, but of Mahometanism compounded with the peculiar character of a race. They are not the mild Mahometans of India, nor the chivalrous Saladins of Syria, nor the cultured Moors of Spain. They were, upon the whole, from the black day when they first entered Europe, the one great anti-human specimen of humanity. Wherever they went, a broad line of blood marked the track behind them; and, as far as their dominion reached, civilisation disappeared from view. They represented everywhere government by force, as opposed to government by law. For the guide of this life they had a relentless fatalism: for its reward hereafter, a sensual paradise.[132]

Gladstone heaped scorn on the recent Turkish adoption of the Geneva Convention of 1864: 'They might just as well adopt the Vatican Council, or the British Constitution. All these things are not even the oysters before the dinner.'[133]

Gladstone saved his best for last—on the penultimate page of his pamphlet, the paragraph that contained a phrase that would forever be associated with the Ottoman Empire:

Let the Turks now carry away their abuses in the only possible manner, namely by carrying off themselves. Their Zaptiehs and their Mudirs, their Bimbashis and their Yuzbachis, their Kaimakams and their Pashas, one and all, bag and baggage, shall, I hope, clear out from the province they have desolated and profaned. This thorough riddance, this most blessed deliverance, is the only reparation we can make to the memory of those heaps on heaps of dead; to the violated purity alike of matron, of maiden, and of child; to the civilisation which has been affronted and shamed; to the laws of God or, if you like, of Allah; to the moral sense of mankind at large.[134]

The bit about 'bag and baggage' was not Gladstone's invention but Stratford Canning's, first used in a private letter over half a century earlier.[135] But Gladstone actually dedicated his pamphlet to Canning (now Viscount Stratford de Redcliffe), in tribute to 'a friendship of more than forty years', so presumably the 'bag and baggage' phrase was a gift, one that now might be engraved on Gladstone's political calling cards. The fact that Stratford Canning was a well-known Turkophile only gave *Bulgarian Horrors* greater authority.[136]

Gladstone had very much come back. On 9 September 1876, riding the wave of his pamphlet published three days previously, he gave a grand

oration at Blackheath to his Greenwich constituents, 10,000 people standing in the rain.[137] Turkey was now unmistakably the steed on which he had
chosen to ride back to national leadership and power. Derby, ever behind
the curve, was still mystified by the public hysteria about alleged British
complicity in the Bulgarian Horrors. 'Considering we never heard of them
until after they had occurred,' he tried to explain, 'I am quite unable to
understand what is the practical meaning of that charge.' Furthermore,

> There are a great many people in England under the impression that Lord
> Beaconsfield is the Sultan, and that I am the Grand Vizier. We have exactly
> the same right, and the same power of interference ... that is possessed by
> every other power. I do not know whether in France, Germany, Italy, and
> other countries people are crying out as they do here and denounce their
> government as being accomplices in these atrocities.

Despite the prevailing orthodoxy of humane hatred for Turkey, there were
some prominent figures who thought that Derby had it exactly right. The
celebrated historian J.A. Froude (1818–1894) was one.[138] Another was
Lord Stanley of Alderley (1827–1903), an eccentric ex-diplomat and
Oriental scholar who had even converted to Islam, and was thus the first
Muslim to sit in the House of Lords. He expressed his condolences to
Lord Salisbury (1830–1903) that he and his 'colleagues are the victims
of such factious hypocrisy', with Gladstone's determined efforts 'to get
up an agitation for party purposes and accuse you all of complicity in
massacres'.[139]

When the weather began to cool in October 1876 and the serious business of normal life began again, so too did the Bulgarian Horrors show
lose its intensity as fewer and fewer atrocity meetings were held.[140] But
it hardly mattered, for the point had been achieved. As Disraeli himself
admitted, they had 'changed the bent of opinion in England as regards
Turkey and which are worked out not merely by enthusiasts, but of course
by the Opposition and by Russia's agents, though the Government have
no more to do with the "atrocities" than the man in the moon'.[141] Like it
or not, his Conservative government had to make some concession to the
will of the people without making it look as if they were caving in to mass
hysteria and Gladstone's manipulations, and without needlessly insulting
their Turkish allies. After all, noted Lord Lyons (1817–1887), 'one can
hardly tell them to their faces that they are a set of savages, who must
not expect to be treated as if they were really members of the civilized

community of European nations'.[142] But indeed it was just this moralizing tone that Gladstone and his supporters had dragged into international politics, despite Disraeli's efforts to keep it at the level of pseudo-scientific racial prejudice if not simple *Realpolitik*.

Even more extreme in this regard than Gladstone was the Puseyite Canon Henry Liddon (1829–1890), who preached at St Paul's at the height of the hysteria that it 'may fairly be pleaded for the Power which has perpetrated these acts that it knows not the name of Christ, and that its proceedings are not to be judged by the standard of a European and Christian civilisation'.[143] A civilization could never truly be European without Christianity. Liddon thereupon went to Belgrade to see the effects of knowing not the name of Christ, accompanied by the Rev. Malcolm MacColl (c.1838–1907). Their claim to have seen an impaled man on the Turkish Bosnian shore became the subject of much controversy and derision.[144]

While Britain was gripped by Bulgarian Horrors, the war between Serbia, Montenegro and Turkey continued unabated, and Disraeli was becoming concerned that Russia would imagine his Government too weakened by the public debate to defend the Ottoman Empire. On 31 October 1876, the Russians actually presented an ultimatum to Turkey to stop the fighting, so the British had to do what they did best, call for an international conference, to be held in Istanbul. Lord Salisbury was to represent Britain, but he was not very optimistic: 'In the course of my travels I have not succeeded in finding the friend of the Turk,' he warned Derby. 'He does not exist. Most believe his hour is come. Some few think it may be postponed. No one has even suggested the idea that he can be upheld for any length of time.'[145] Salisbury made a slow two-week journey to Istanbul, arriving on 5 December 1876 and staying at the Hotel Royal in Pera. On the way, he had managed to meet nearly everyone of note in Europe, from heads of state and nobility to key diplomats, speaking to them in good French.[146]

Disraeli was still worried about the possible need to send ships and troops to Istanbul if the conference failed, and was especially irritated by the Germans. Bismarck claimed to be completely uninterested in Turkey, joking in an after-dinner speech in Berlin on 1 December 1876 that if asked what Germany wanted in the Eastern Question, he would give the same answer he gave his wife when she inquired as to what he wanted for Christmas: '*Es fiele ihm nichts ein*' ['He could not think of anything']. A few days later in the Reichstag, he promised that they would take no part in the Eastern Question, 'so long as I can see in the whole affair no interest for Germany which would be worth the healthy bones of a single Pomeranian musketeer'.[147] Disraeli was happy enough with that, but complained to Salisbury that at the same time he was 'surprised that Bismarck should go on harping about Egypt. Its occupation by us would embitter France, and I don't see it would at all benefit us, if Russia possessed Constantinople. I would sooner we had Asia Minor than Egypt.'[148]

The international conference began in preliminary session on 11 December 1876 at the Russian Embassy, chaired by the Russian ambassador to Constantinople, Count Nicholas Ignatiev (1832–1908). The Russians remained remarkably well-informed about British intentions through their ambassador in London, Count Pyotr Shuvalov (1827–1889), whose extraordinarily close personal relationship with Lady Derby made him privy to just about everything that transpired in the British Cabinet. The Turks understood that much was at stake, and rushed in a new Grand Vizier, Midhat Paşa (1822–1884).[149] Not without a sense of drama, the Turks had an even bigger surprise planned for the formal opening session of the conference on 23 December 1876 at the Admiralty building on the Golden Horn. Ottoman representative Mehmed Esat Safvet Paşa (1814–1883)—'a sleepy old man who can scarcely talk intelligible French', Salisbury told Victoria[150]—rose to welcome the delegates, but his speech was constantly interrupted by cannon fire nearby. Sultan Abdülhamid II (r. 1876–1909), apparently, had just promulgated a new constitution which included a proper European-style parliament, and the firing of cannon was part of the event.[151] The delegates were unimpressed, and after '*un profond silence*' of several minutes, carried on with their meeting.[152] Elliot himself was hardly involved in the conference, having been completely sidelined by Salisbury, so he finally decided to resign as British ambassador to Constantinople, sending a telegram to Derby just before the first full session opened.[153] Disraeli was happy to see him go, and be replaced by Austen Henry Layard (1817–1894), but this would not happen overnight.[154]

The conference itself was not moving very far forward, however.[155] Salisbury gave a hint to the Turks about British support by moving the British fleet from Beşik Bay all the way to Athens. Midhat Paşa and Salisbury never got along, and after meeting Sultan Abdülhamid himself, Salisbury was convinced that this 'poor weak creature' was completely in the hands of his new Grand Vizier.[156] Among the few people who had hopes for this conference was the elderly Moses Montefiore (1784–1885), who went with a delegation of British Jews to Lord Derby asking for Jewish equality in Serbia and Rumania to be put on the table as well. Derby instructed Salisbury to 'take such steps as you may think advisable in dealing with this matter'.[157] By 20 January 1877, the conference was over, the Turks having rejected all the proposals put forward by the Europeans, even the compromises.[158] 'Convincing the Turks is as easy as making a donkey canter,' said Salisbury in disgust.[159]

Diplomatic efforts having so demonstratively failed, Russia would declare war on the Ottoman Empire three months later. One factor in the Russian decision to risk armed conflict was probably the perception that now more than ever, the British people were not prepared to lift a finger in support of Turkey. Certainly, there was even more of a general sense that the Turks had missed their last opportunity and the Ottoman Empire was doomed to disintegrate. Count Andrássy (1823–1890), the Austro-Hungarian Foreign Minister (1871–1879), put it very nicely:

> It is like the case of baldness. When does it begin? When does it end? An Empire does not dissolve in a day. How then to define the degree of decomposition at which dissolution takes place? One person might consider it effective at the *first*, another at the *last* blow directed against the *status quo*.[160]

Undoubtedly one of the blows against the status quo was the inauguration of the ticket-only 'National Convention on the Eastern Question' held on 8 December 1876 at St James's Hall, Piccadilly. The impressive group of organizers included Lord Bryce, J.A. Froude, and of course, E.A. Freeman. Others who joined up among the conveners were Lord Acton, Robert Browning, Charles Darwin, Herbert Spencer, J.R. Green, William Lecky, Thorold Rogers, G.O. Trevelyan, Mark Pattison, Anthony Trollope, John Ruskin, William Morris (treasurer), W.T. Stead, and Goldwin Smith (who would rival Freeman in antisemitic abuse). The Duke of Westminster and Lord Shaftesbury chaired the sessions. A letter from Thomas Carlyle was read out. Gladstone spoke as well, of course.[161]

When E.A. Freeman took the podium, he ridiculed Disraeli's claim that the British Empire in some way depended on the territorial integrity of the Ottoman Empire: 'Look at the map: the path to India does not lie by Constantinople.'[162] Freeman concluded by noting that whether 'we are a majority I cannot tell; but I am sure we are a large enough part of the English people to make even the Jew in his drunken insolence think twice before he goes to war in our teeth'.[163] Freeman could never resist an antisemitic outburst when he had the opportunity.

In a very real sense, Gladstone and his distinguished body of supporters were pounding on an open door. Things had changed so much since
the beginning of the Balkan troubles in May 1876 that cultural history
was already being rewritten. 'I doubt if any real feeling of friendship ever
existed in this country for Turkey,' mused Henry Ponsonby,

> Some persons supported what they believed to be an oppressed national-
> ity—some had material interest … some believed that the friendship of the
> Sultan, the Caliph of the faithful all over the world strengthened our position
> in India and some were moved by the attitude of rivalry between ourselves
> and Russia—the object of wh. is believed to be the possession of Const ple.
> Besides wh. statesmen recoiled from encountering the inevitable difficulties
> which must arise on the dissolution of the Turkish Empire in Europe.[164]

Whether British foreign policy was ultimately based on 'real feeling' or
mere practicality, even after popular protests had been domesticated by
being incorporated into Liberal Party policy, it was clear that the Turks
were sliding towards a military abyss.

Abdülhamid sacked the new Grand Vizier Midhat Paşa on 5 February
1877 and had him deported to Brindisi, leaving him free to tour Europe
and even visit London before being condemned to death, reprieved,
and sent to Arabia where he was mysteriously strangled in 1884. On 19
March 1877, Sultan Abdülhamid opened the new Ottoman Parliament
in person, generally assisted by Ibrahim Edhem Paşa (1819–1893), the
even newer Grand Vizier. As it happened, Queen Victoria opened her
British Parliament only a few weeks before, proclaiming that her 'object
throughout has been to maintain the peace of Europe and bring about
the better government of the disturbed provinces, without infringing
upon the independence and integrity of the Ottoman Empire'. Victoria
read the words, but the thoughts belonged to Prime Minister Benjamin
Disraeli.[165]

While Gladstone was publishing another work entitled *Lessons in
Massacre*, a transparent attempt to keep the fire of indignation alight,
Disraeli's government was trying to save the Ottoman Empire from a war
that might be its ruin.[166] Disraeli reminded the House of Lords that

> the Empire of Constantinople, being now limited to its matchless city and
> to what in modern diplomatic language is called "a cabbage garden," was
> invested and fell. And it did not occur to us that if there were a chain of
> autonomous States and the possessors of Constantinople were again limited
> to "a cabbage garden," probably the same result might occur

but Russia would this time enjoy the role the Turks played four centuries previously.[167] The Turks were given one last chance, in the form of the London Protocol, signed by the Six Powers on 31 March 1877. Salisbury noted sardonically that 'English policy is to float lazily downstream, occasionally putting out a diplomatic boat-hook to avoid collisions'.[168] Regrettably, the Turks rejected the London Protocol the following week, taking the gamble that Russia would find war to be a financial impossibility.

It was just then, on 20 April 1877, that Austen Henry Layard arrived in Istanbul as Britain's new ambassador. Indeed, he was the only Great Power ambassador in town, since the others had not returned since being withdrawn after the failure of the Constantinople Conference. Layard made the rounds in the service of peace, calling on Ibrahim Edhem Paşa (the Grand Vizier), Safvet Paşa, and Abdühamid himself. While speaking with the sultan, a telegram arrived from the Ottoman ambassador in St Petersburg announcing the receipt of a Russian declaration of war, effective 24 April 1877.[169]

Disraeli saw the Russian move as signalling the disintegration of the Ottoman Empire, but he was not about to lose Istanbul without a fight. The road to India may not have run through Constantinople, but he was too heavily invested in Turkey in every possible way to see it become an outpost of the Czar's own empire. He proposed to the Cabinet that Britain occupy Gallipoli immediately, promising to return it to Turkey after the war. Salisbury objected, arguing that 'such a course would be in effect an alliance with Turkey', which of course was precisely the point.[170] Officially, the British declared themselves neutral on 30 April 1877, but warned Russia against three actions that would bring them into the war: a blockade of the Dardanelles, the occupation of Istanbul, or an attack on Egypt. On 6 May 1877, the British Cabinet added to this list three other demands: keeping the Suez Canal open, no change to the present international regulation of the Bosphorus, and the protection of the Persian Gulf.[171] According to the modern historian R.W. Seton-Watson, this last note in Derby's name 'may fairly be regarded as a turning-point in Anglo-Russian relations, and as time passed, it became the rallying ground of "centre" opinion in England'.[172]

Gladstone spoke in the House of Commons, which spent five days beginning 7 May 1877 discussing British policy towards Turkey. For him, 'the cause of the revolted subjects of Turkey against their oppressors is as holy a cause as ever animated the breast, or as ever stirred the hand of man'.[173] No doubt, argued the Conservatives, but is not the conduct of 'the White Man to the Red Man in America' as atrocious as anything that happened in Bulgaria? 'And are we going in our crusade of humanity to address the Government of Washington and say—"Your conduct now to the Red Man is such as we humane people cannot possibly in any way permit; we intend to go to war with you because you have been inhuman?"'[174] Gladstone, however, was very pleased with how things went in Parliament, and crowed about his perceived victory over Disraeli in a letter to a friend:

> I have watched very closely his strange & at first sight inexplicable proceedings on this Eastern Question: and I believe their fountainhead to be race antipathy, that aversion which the Jews, with a few honourable exceptions, are showing so vindictively towards the Eastern Christians. Though he has been baptized, his Jew feelings are the most radical & the most real, & so far respectable, portion of his profoundly falsified nature.[175]

But the ground underneath the Eastern Question was shifting beneath Gladstone's feet. Now that the Czar had declared war on Turkey and had begun a march towards Istanbul, the old British antagonism towards the Russians came bobbing to the surface, leaving even the Bulgarian Horrors down below. It was inconceivable that England could let the Russians have Constantinople.

Britain was represented in Istanbul by Austen Henry Layard who, if possible, was even more pro-Turkish than his predecessor, Henry Elliot. Lord Granville (1815–1891), the leader of the Liberal Party in the House of Lords, who had worked with Layard, assured Gladstone that Layard 'was a philo-Turk, but he is a very strong man with orientals, and I think he will be faithful to instructions, if the latter are of the right sort'.[176] But Layard was not a Foreign Office hack or an ambassador appointed because of his pedigree. He was the discoverer of Nineveh, who received an honorary degree from Oxford and the freedom of the City of London in grateful acknowledgement.[177] Layard was Stratford Canning's former go-to man in diplomatic missions and liaison with the British press. He had sat in Parliament as a Liberal MP and served as British minister in Madrid. But his aunt, Mrs. Austen, had been one of the young Disraeli's closest confidantes, and that made all the difference.

Layard was therefore a very different sort of British ambassador, and he knew it. 'I fancy that no ambassador has ever had such a conversation with a Sultan as I had with H.M.,' he reported to Derby after his second audience with Abdülhamid, and it was 'unprecedented' that he was allowed to bring his wife along as well.[178] In August 1877, Layard and his wife were invited 'to dine in a quiet way' with Abdülhamid, a complete 'departure from Imperial and Mussulman etiquette', so that 'our influence here is now re-established beyond what I could possibly have hoped'.[179] Layard kept Abdülhamid fully and frankly informed about the real progress of the war with the Russians when it came, and was not afraid to criticize to the Sultan Turkish officers and officials who were not up to the job. The net effect may have been to convince Abdülhamid that Britain was secretly more supportive of the Turks than it could admit in public, and he may have been right, especially in light of Layard's secret correspondence with Disraeli during this period.[180]

The Russian attack on the Ottoman Empire was going more slowly than expected.[181] Ardahan fell in the east, but with that the Russian advance was halted by weather and terrain. In the Balkans, the Turks were forced to defend the whole length of the Danube, but on 27–28 June 1877, the Russians made the crossing at Sistova. The British Cabinet, in a bit of a panic although the Danube crossing must have come as no surprise, sent the fleet back to Beşik Bay to await further orders. According to Layard, the word in the Istanbul street was that the so-called 'neutral' British merely wanted to be on hand when the Ottoman Empire was carved up.[182] In any case, the Russians soon captured Nicopolis (Nikopol),[183] and on 17 July they crossed the Shipka Pass into Rumelia.[184] Still at a loss about what to do, the British Cabinet considered moving the fleet with Abdülhamid's approval from Beşik Bay to Istanbul itself, which would have taken about twelve hours under good conditions, but it was feared that without controlling Gallipoli, the ships could be trapped between the Sea of Marmara and the Black Sea.[185] Against all odds, however, a reprieve came, in the form of the heroic Turkish resistance at Plevna, under the command of Osman Paşa (1832–1900), who defeated the Russians twice there, on 20 and 30 July 1877. For a while, the Russian advance was halted.[186] They tried again to take Plevna on 10–12 September 1877 and were halted once more.

'Opinion is getting more pro-Turkish every day,' noted Disraeli with satisfaction on 1 September 1877, the news from Bulgaria affirming Turkey's right to 'remain among the sovereign Powers of the world' with 'no clear evidence that a better Government than the Ottoman can be established in the regions in question'.[187] At the annual Lord Mayor's Guildhall banquet at the beginning of November 1877, attended by nearly every member of

Disraeli's cabinet, the diners listened to a speech by Kostaki Musurus Paşa (1807–1891), the Turkish ambassador, who announced that his country was now following the English model in promulgating 'a complete liberal constitution, based on free representation of all its peoples'. Disraeli was not slow to respond:

> For some years it has been a dogma of diplomacy that Turkey was a phrase and not a fact—that its Government was a phantom, that its people was effete. ... The independence of Turkey was a subject of ridicule a year ago ... the independence of Turkey is not doubted now.[188]

As the *Daily Telegraph* reported, 'Turkey must feel animated by such powerful praise.'[189]

All of this rejoicing was sadly premature. In eastern Anatolia, Kars fell to the Russians on 11 November 1877, the news reaching London a week later.[190] Even worse intelligence was soon to come. The gallant Osman Paşa attempted to break out of Plevna, but was forced back into the city, surrendering to the Russians on the following day (10 December 1877). About 30,000 Turkish soldiers were taken prisoner and forcibly marched towards Russia, without any plan for food, clothing, shelter or medical attention. Those who survived barely made it to Bucharest by the time the fighting stopped at the end of January.[191]

The road to Istanbul, via Edirne, was now almost open. Even Serbia declared war on the Ottoman Empire (14 December 1877) four days after the surrender of Plevna, which only made them look slightly ridiculous. The Turks tried to negotiate an armistice, and the British dithered, much to Layard's disgust:

> It is the most monstrous piece of folly that we should be ready to sacrifice the most vital interests of our country, India, our position as a first-class Power, the influence that we have hitherto exercised in the cause of human liberty and civilisation, rather than stand shoulder to shoulder with the Turks, because some Bashibazuks have murdered some worthless and unfortunate Bulgarians![192]

Layard was beginning to sound more like Elliot all the time.

The Russians, meanwhile, saw no reason to quit just because they were winning. Sofia fell in the first week of the new year 1878; the Shipka Pass through the Balkan Mountains was forced at the beginning of 9 January 1878, and the *Daily News* correspondent Archibald Forbes (1838–1900) rode to the Czar's headquarters to bring him an eyewitness report.[193] Philippopolis (where all the trouble started in 1876) fell by the middle of January 1878. Abdülhamid, meanwhile, was weighing the possibility of getting his friend Layard to provide a ship for a quick escape to England, his only refuge.[194] Queen Victoria, was almost out of control, protesting to Disraeli that

> She feels she cannot, as she said before, remain the Sovereign of a country that is letting itself down to kiss the feet of the great barbarians, the retarders of all liberty and civilization that exists. Her son feels more strongly than herself even. She is utterly ashamed of the Cabinet ... Oh, if the Queen were a man, she would like to go and give those Russians, whose word one cannot believe, such a beating! We shall never be friends again till we have it out. This the Queen feels sure of.[195]

Derby could not take the strain and had some kind of collapse, spending even more time in the country. Disraeli was trying to get the Cabinet to agree to sending the British fleet to the Dardanelles and landing men to hold Gallipoli against the Russians, pending permission from Abdülhamid.[196]

In the end, Disraeli convinced most of his colleagues to go one better, and on 23 January 1878, orders were sent to Admiral Geoffrey Hornby (1825–1895) with the Mediterranean fleet at Smyrna to keep the Straits open, 'and in the event of tumult at Constantinople you are to protect life and property of British subjects'. The hapless Lord Derby resigned (although Disraeli was persuaded to take him back). Derby's wife, naturally, conveyed to the Russian ambassador the Cabinet decision to send the fleet to Istanbul, as Disraeli knew she would.[197]

The British fleet never entered the Straits. Suddenly, a telegram arrived from Layard with the news that the Turks were about to sign an armistice with the Russians, who had reached Edirne (Adrianople) on 20 January 1878 and were now going through the motions of invading the city, which had been the Ottoman capital before the Turkish conquest of Constantinople. Hornby got the telegram sending him instead to Beşik Bay at the last possible moment. With the Russians practically in view of Istanbul, the war was over, and on 31 January 1878 an armistice was signed at Edirne.[198] Bulgaria and Bosnia-Hercegovina were to become autonomous; Montenegro, Serbia and Rumania would become independent states. In the east, Turkey would cede Erzurum to Russia.[199] As

Layard noted ruefully, 'It is scarcely necessary to say this amounts to the destruction of the Turkish Empire in Europe.'[200]

This was exactly what 'Bag and baggage Billy [Gladstone] and his long-eared crew' had worked for, but a Russian occupation of Istanbul had not been part of the plan.[201] Nevertheless, popular agitation and public meetings conspicuously revived, but now with a different emphasis in light of current events. On 16 January 1878, as Russian troops trudged through the snow to Edirne, a 'Committee in Favour of the Free Navigation of the Straits' came into being, formed by Canon Liddon, Auberon Herbert, Humphry Sandwith, C. Maurice and (of course) E.A. Freeman.[202] Carlyle, Browning, Froude and John Morley gave the new organization their blessing as well.[203] There was now less unanimity about whether Britain should back up the principle of free navigation of the Straits by actually going to war, but the intensity of expression was just as fierce as ever. Freeman even sneered at Queen Victoria for dining with Disraeli, going 'ostentatiously to eat with him in his Ghetto'.[204] The historian Froude denounced Disraeli as 'a Mountebank from the beginning'.[205] Even Lord Derby, his (former?) friend, said that Disraeli 'believes thoroughly in "prestige"—as all foreigners do'.[206] Disraeli denounced the lot of them as a bunch of 'priests and professors', but his erstwhile colleague Derby was neither.[207]

In the middle of January, *Punch* printed Tenniel's cartoon 'The Ass in the Lion's Skin' and a little poem about Disraeli that ran on 2 February 1878, a few days after the armistice:

> I am a wholehog Turcophil,
> Hold History and its teachings *nil*:
> Downtrodden tribes that won't keep still
> I'd stifle.

The reference to hogs was lost on no one.[208] But Disraeli's government sought to reply to all of this scurrility with facts, and published a huge Blue Book containing hundreds of documents, which appeared as *Turkey No. I* (1878).

Back in Istanbul, the situation was becoming even more dire. As the Russian troops had advanced through Bulgaria, they pushed before them a tidal wave of thousands of Muslims all the way to Istanbul (and Varna), where they huddled in hope of deliverance. Despite signing an armistice on 31 January 1878 which was supposed to end the conflict, the Russian army kept advancing as if in a trance towards Istanbul, coming to a halt the following week (6 February 1878) at Çatalca.[209] Layard reminded London that there were about 3,000 British nationals in the Istanbul area, and their lives and property needed to be protected.[210] Some British newspapers even reported the Fall of Constantinople, unable to resist a scoop.[211]

Once again, the Cabinet gave orders (8 February 1878) to send the British fleet to Istanbul, and Parliament approved the money, Gladstone dissenting but many Liberals in favour, hating Russia more than Turkey. 'I admit that the rule of the Porte in the past has combined every evil that can be covered by civil government,' explained one Liberal MP in the House of Commons, but 'it is only right to add that the Government of Turkey is no worse than that of other Asiatic and African states with whom we hold close if not cordial relations.' In fact, the government of 'Egypt, which is propped up by English capitalists, is worse'. As for human rights, it 'is true that the Christians in Turkey have been denied any participation in the civil administration, just as the Catholics and Jews were in this country till recently, and as our Hindoo and Mohamedan fellow-subjects are in India today'. Recall 'the ferocity' of British rule in Ireland, he said, and then 'manifest some moderation in our denunciation of the Turks'.[212]

Unfortunately, the British had not fully taken into account the Turkish reaction to the prospect of the British fleet sailing into Istanbul, its sailors making rude gestures at the half-frozen Russian soldiers sheltering on the shores of the Sea of Marmara. Admiral Hornby duly presented his fleet at the entrance to the Dardanelles, but the Turks denied him formal permission to proceed, so he turned everyone around and returned to Beşik Bay from whence he came. The Turks (and Layard himself) thought that the presence of the British ships in the waters of Istanbul would provoke the Russians into occupying the city itself. They too could protect Christian lives and property as well as the English.[213] 'We are in an awkward position just now,' Ponsonby reflected, 'with our fleet at the entrance of the Dardanelles sniffing like a dog at a hole hesitating for fear he may find a badger instead of a rabbit inside.'[214]

This time, it was really too ridiculous to stand down, even if sailing into Istanbul might result in another Fall of Constantinople. In that case, the Ottoman Empire would have to pay the price for British pride. The Cabinet gave Admiral Hornby further orders 'to sail up the Straits at daylight on Wednesday morning', 13 February 1878: 'Princes Island Anchorage suggested'.[215] Hornby this time ignored the Turkish protest when he and his six ironclads entered the Dardanelles, in the middle of a snowstorm, which caused one of his ships to run aground and the

DISRAELI'S EASTERN CAREER, 1830–1880   175

others to anchor overnight nearby. The rest of the ironclads made it to the Princes' Isles the next morning, and everyone waited to see if the Russians would blink first.[216]

The British fleet was still in the Sea of Marmara, and by not advancing into the Bosphorus might be seen as coming in peace. The Russians were not impressed and revitalized their threat to occupy Istanbul, so Hornby and Layard without asking permission from London on 15 February 1878 moved the British fleet a little further away, to Mudanya, on the Asiatic shore.[217] Abdülhamid was graciously offered free passage in the event of his having to flee from the collapse of the Ottoman Empire.[218]

But neither the Russians nor the British wanted to fight each other, especially now that Turkey was ready for plucking. The commander of the Russian forces, Grand Duke Nicholas (1831–1891), seeing that the British had moved about seventeen kilometres further away from Istanbul, on 24 February 1878 himself moved to a new position only about ten kilometres from the city walls, to San Stefano (today's Yeşilköy). War was still in the air, as was the threat of a Russian occupation, when the Turks turned the armistice of 31 January 1878 into a proper Treaty of San Stefano, signed at virtual gunpoint between the Russian and Ottoman Empires on 3 March 1878.

From both the Turkish and the British points of view, the Treaty was a nightmare. Some of its provisions had already been conceded in January: independence for Montenegro, Serbia, and Rumania; autonomy for Bulgaria. The big problem was the border adjustments for these places. Rumania got bigger and Montenegro nearly doubled in size. Russia received the southern part of Bessarabia (which she had lost to Turkey in 1856 after losing the Crimean War) and also got to keep parts of eastern Anatolia, including Ardahan, Kars, Beyazit and Batum. But the greatest shock was the invention of a monster Bulgaria stretching all the way down to the Aegean and including the city of Salonika. Numerous other clauses dealt with the Holy Mountain of Athos, razing the Danubian fortresses, and Russian pilgrims to Palestine. The Russians, however, ducked the question of the Straits by leaving them open in peacetime.

Clearly, this would not do. Apart from British objections, Austria-Hungary had no desire to see Bulgaria stretch from the Aegean to the Black Sea. Layard was working hard behind the scenes, including a private dinner with Abdülhamid right after the signing of San Stefano.[219] Two weeks later, Layard and his wife had another intimate chat with the Sultan in the garden of his Yıldız Palace.[220] *Punch* produced a cartoon (2 March

1878) which showed Layard as the 'Nineveh bull in the Stambul china-shop'. The result was a strong British demand that a proper international congress be called to settle the Balkan conflict, not some hastily cobbled-together treaty between two unequal partners at the point of a gun. On 27 March 1878, the Cabinet did not object to Disraeli's plan to call up the reserves, including Indian troops. Lord Derby was not prepared to gamble on a war with the Russians and resigned his post as Foreign Secretary immediately after the meeting ended, although he did support the calling of an international conference to revise the Treaty of San Stefano.[221] Lord Salisbury replaced Derby at the Foreign Office, and with some other min-isters shifted around, the Cabinet was now united behind Disraeli.

On 1 April 1878, the statement of British policy that became known as the 'Salisbury Circular' was submitted to the Cabinet, in which the new Foreign Secretary openly condemned the Russians for making a separate peace, in violation of what had been agreed back in the London Conference of 1871. British objections were carefully delineated. The document was brought to Parliament and leaked to the British and European press.[222] Russian ambassador Shuvalov was out of the loop this time, now that Lady Derby no longer was privy to Cabinet secrets. Layard was informed that as a result, 'Schouvaloff has made an attempt on the virtue of Lady Cairns, by attempting to persuade her that he wanted her assistance and instruction in reading the Bible. "Car je suis un peu Bibliste aussi" was his expression. But my Lord Chancellor [Cairns (1819–1885)] heard of it and stopped his biblical education.'[223] Salisbury and Layard established very good relations, and with Lady Derby out of the way, Layard could send his letters directly to the Foreign Secretary. 'No foreigner has seen so much of a Sultan as I have of the present sovereign,' he boasted. 'I con-stantly dine or breakfast with him or meet him in his garden.'[224]

Feelings in Britain continued to run high as the country waited to find out if the Russians would agree to an international conference that would probably take away much that they had gained, or if the Russians would march into Istanbul and precipitate a war. Radical John Bright (1811–1889), speaking on 30 April 1878 at a Liberal Party delegation meeting at Manchester, condemned the arrogance of Prime Minister Disraeli who was willing to shed English blood while he himself had 'not a single drop of English blood in his veins'.[225]

The Russians were still playing at brinksmanship. On 16 May 1878, they inched even closer to the walls of Istanbul, making some excuse about improved sanitation. Admiral Hornby and Layard were spooked, yet their request to the Cabinet to return the fleet to the Princes' Isles was denied.[226] But the diplomats were at work as well, and a Russian proposition for an international conference was already being drafted. On 24 May 1878, the Cabinet sent a telegram to Layard to suggest a defensive alliance to Abdülhamid, collateral being continued Russian presence in Armenia and British occupation of Cyprus. Salisbury collected from Cabinet members the draft copies of the Russian proposal that he had distributed to them, and burnt the papers in the fireplace.[227] Lady Derby was gone, but her spirit remained: the *Globe* on 30 May 1878 published an accurate summary of the final Anglo-Russian agreement, which it had bought from a temporary copying clerk at the Foreign Office.[228] In any case, Parliament was informed officially on 3 June 1878 that a Congress of Berlin would take place and begin its deliberations ten days hence.[229]

Come what may, Disraeli knew, Cyprus would now be under British control and was located perfectly in the eastern Mediterranean between Egypt and Turkey. Talk about Cyprus had been in the air for a long time, as a sort of finder's fee for the British to ensure that Disraeli would have a tangible gain to show the country no matter what happened at Berlin.[230] Layard received his Cabinet telegram on 25 May 1878, and as instructed went straight over to Abdülhamid to lean on his sultanic friend to turn over Cyprus as the price for British support at Berlin. Layard found Abdülhamid in a rather distracted state. As it happened, only the previous day, while the British Cabinet was deciding that they wanted Cyprus, a former teacher at Galatasaray School named Ali Suavi Efendi (1838–1878) stormed the Çırağan Palace with several hundred followers and tried to kidnap ex-Sultan Murad V and restore him to power. Ali Suavi and many others were shot and killed by the guards, but the whole business had clearly put Abdülhamid in a rather paranoiac mood. Layard began to outline British demands, but Abdülhamid had other things on his mind, and directed Layard to carry on his discussions with Safvet Paşa and the other ministers. The Ottoman leaders recognized that they had no choice but to cede Cyprus to the British, and the following evening (26 May 1878), Abdülhamid gave his final agreement, although the Cyprus Convention was formalized only on 4 June 1878. Queen Victoria, finally pleased at something, instructed Salisbury to offer Layard the Grand Cross of the Bath for having successfully bullied the Turks.

News of a congress rather than a war was welcome indeed and by the first days of June no longer unexpected. The big surprise was that Disraeli intended to make the voyage to Berlin and represent Britain himself.

Foreign Secretary Salisbury and British ambassador to Russia Odo Russell (1829–1884) were to be there as well, but why Disraeli? Not only was he almost seventy-four years old, but he was crippled by gout, rather deaf, and had trouble breathing. Parliament would have been less surprised by his resignation as prime minister for reasons of health. Worst of all, not only did he not understand German but he could not even speak French, which rendered him dumb and even more deaf as well as lame. Bismarck (whose health was also problematic), naturally would speak for Germany, with Shuvalov for the Russians and Andrássy representing Austria-Hungary.[231] Even Italy was represented, for the first time as a nearly Great Power.

Disraeli left London on 8 June 1878, destination Berlin. Even Salisbury was not so keen on the Prime Minister's participation, as he wrote to his wife once the meetings were underway: 'What with deafness, ignorance of French and Bismarck's extraordinary mode of speech, Beaconsfield has the dimmest idea of what is going on, understands everything crossways and imagines a perpetual conspiracy.'[232] Others picked up on Disraeli's undiplomatic lack of foreign languages. E.A. Freeman deplored the fact that 'the Jew is going, in full cap and bells, to represent England on the Berlin stage', and doubted whether he knew 'any tongue beside the dialect of his own novels'.[233] Punch (22 June 1878) mocked Disraeli's 'facility lingual, if not quite linguistic'. Perhaps this was also the inspiration for Odo Russell's brilliant suggestion that instead of Disraeli mangling a prepared French text, that the Congress of Berlin be treated to an address from 'the greatest living master of English oratory'.[234] No matter that most delegates did not understand him; they knew what he was going to say.

Bismarck had been elected President of the Congress of Berlin at the outset, upon a motion of Andrássy, and their task was defined as 'to submit the work of San Stefano to the free discussion of the signatories of the Treaties of 1856 and 1871'.[235] Bismarck was an eccentric mediator, rude to the Turks, bullying to the Rumanians over improving Jewish rights, and pandering to Disraeli, who always felt a bit left out.[236] Serbia and Montenegro would get their independence from the Ottoman Empire, but not at the size envisioned at San Stefano. Rumania would also become an independent state. Bosnia and Hercegovina remained under Turkish sovereignty, but autonomous, administered by Austria-Hungary (which supposedly had been neutral in the recent war). Turkey retained Macedonia, and it was supposed to give the Greeks Epirus to the west, but that huge area remained under Turkish rule until 1913. Most crucially, however, autonomous Bulgaria shrunk back to a third of its bloated San

Stefano size, and lost her outlet to the Aegean. 'There is again a Turkey-in-Europe,' Bismarck said to Disraeli, and everyone seemed to be able to live with that.[237]

Benjamin Disraeli on his return to London coined the arresting slogan, 'Peace with Honour'. Disraeli and Salisbury enjoyed a hero's welcome, and when Victoria offered the Prime Minister the Garter, Disraeli accepted on condition that Salisbury get one too. Victoria tried to get Disraeli to take a dukedom or a marquisate, and since he was childless even threw in peerages for his brother and nephew, so that his glory would not terminate with his own passing. Disraeli declined these further honours, explaining rather biblically that her confidence in him was 'more precious than rubies'.[238]

Disraeli's appearance in the House of Lords on 18 July 1878 allowed him to bask in glory. Europe had reached 'the unanimous conclusion that the best chance for the tranquility and order of the world is to retain the Sultan as part of the acknowledged political system of Europe'. The Ottoman Empire, though reduced in size, was still very much intact: 'a Sovereign who has not yet forfeited his capital, whose capital has not yet been occupied by his enemy—and that capital one of the strongest in the world—who has Armies and Fleets at his disposal, and still rules over 20,000,000 of inhabitants, cannot be described as a Power whose Dominions have been partitioned.' Without going to war, Britain had played a crucial role in determining that 'Turkey in Europe once more exists'. Yes, the Greeks were still unhappy, but it was 'impossible to give satisfaction to a State which coveted Constantinople for its capital, and which talked of accepting large Provinces and a powerful Island [Crete] as only an instalment [sic] of its claims for the moment'. Disraeli reminded the Lords 'that our connection with the East is not merely an affair of sentiment and tradition'; Britain had 'urgent and substantial and enormous interests which we must guard and keep'. As for taking Cyprus, Disraeli explained, 'the movement is not Mediterranean; it is Indian'. Britain had come out of the Congress of Berlin with enhanced prestige, for 'in the Eastern nations there is confidence in this country, and that, while they know we can enforce our policy, at the same time they know our Empire is an Empire of liberty, of truth, and of justice'.[239]

The following week (22 July 1878), Disraeli took the opportunity of a Tory banquet held in honour of the two heroes to praise Abdülhamid as 'apparently a man whose every impulse is good', for he is 'not a tyrant, not dissolute, not a bigot or corrupt'. Gladstone, on the other hand, was 'a sophisticated rhetorician, inebriated with the exuberance of his own verbosity, and gifted with an egotistical imagination that can at all times command an interminable and inconsistent series of arguments to malign an opponent and to glorify himself'.[240] At yet another victory banquet, held at Guildhall a fortnight later (3 August 1878), Salisbury expressed the 'hope we are opening a gentler period of contemporary politics':

> For good or for evil, I hope we have done with the Eastern Question in English politics. I never remember a question which has so deeply excited the English people, moved their passions so thoroughly and produced such profound divisions and such rancorous animosity[241]

Sadly, Salisbury was often wrong when predicting the future.

Gladstone was not active in many of these conversations, among other reasons being that the key players from the Congress of Berlin were all members of the House of Lords and he was not. His time came during the great debate in the House of Commons between 29 July and 3 August 1878. History would show, he fulminated, 'that it is from the councils of statesmen that on this occasion there has proceeded the most extraordinary crop of wild and speculative ideas which were ever grown in the hottest of all the hothouses of politics'.[242] Privately, Layard agreed with Gladstone, updating his predecessor Elliot that as 'for settling the Turkish or Eastern Question, it will unsettle everything. We are calling into life new nationalities and dangerous ambitions.'[243]

Disraeli believed himself to be at the height of his political power, so as 'Peace with Honour' still rang in his ears, on 8 March 1880 he called a General Election. But twenty months is an eternity in politics, and as one travelled north in Britain, the Eastern Question became correspondingly more uninteresting. On 5 April 1880, the Liberal Party won a sweeping victory at the polls, and Gladstone was prime minister once again. 'It is a great impediment to public business that Mr. Gladstone cannot be made to understand a joke,' Disraeli once said, but now the joke was on him.[244] Gladstone, for his part, judged that 'Disraeli is a man who is never beaten. Every reverse, every defeat is to him only an admonition to wait and catch his opportunity of retrieving, and more than retrieving, his position.'[245]

Lord Salisbury would later famously claim that 'we put all our money upon the wrong horse' in the Eastern Question.[246] But at the same time, he noted that when Gladstone and the Liberal Party came to office, they neglected to maximize the gains that Disraeli had won for them in terms of British influence in Istanbul: 'They have just thrown it away into the sea, without getting anything whatever in exchange.'[247] The Turks, having lost Britain, had no choice but to turn to Bismarck and Germany, with well-known disastrous consequences.

Disraeli gave his last major speech in the House of Lords in March 1881. He died a month later, on 19 April 1881. Although Disraeli is often presented as an Orientalist villain, many people forget that it was his moralistic rival Gladstone who bombarded Alexandria, and occupied Cairo on 15 September 1882. Egypt was still officially part of the Ottoman Empire. Disraeli constantly repeated when he was alive that despite what Bismarck and others urged him to do, he did not want to possess any mainland Ottoman territory. Disraeli when dead would have cringed to see British rule in Egypt.

IV

Gladstone gained Egypt but lost Turkey and thought that he had done well out of the bargain. But Gladstone and the Liberals in his train were incapable of seeing the Ottoman Empire from a distance, gazing at Turkey through a fog of other issues. Firstly, educated people were convinced that history showed us that empires both rose and fell. Gibbon taught them that, and so did other writers about empire, especially the comte de Volney (1757–1820), whose popular *Les ruines, ou Méditations sur les révolutions des empires* was published in Paris in 1791 and soon translated into English.[248] Second of all, the British attitude towards imperialism was changing, and the questionable acquisition of Cyprus and the shares in the Suez Canal made people realize that the road to India might be worth having for its own sake and not merely to secure transportation.

Disraeli's youthful Turkish adventures and Jewish racist philosophy were at the base of his foreign policy and support of Istanbul, but his foreign policy was not irrational, and fitted very well with traditional British fears of Russian imperialism in the Balkans and further east towards India. Yet it was ideological as well, and Disraeli's opponents responded with their own version of racism, injecting antisemitism into British political culture where it had not been emphasized before. The Jews 'are essentially Tories', claimed Disraeli's creation Sidonia, and by drawing the fire of people like E.A. Freeman and his protector William Gladstone, Disraeli made sure that art would imitate life, as Jewish MPs and the Jews they represented migrated to the Conservative Party.[249] In a sense, the Ottoman Empire never recovered from Disraeli's love, and submitting to the German embrace made the Turks easy prey for the British propagandists and political strategists who tried to seal their fate in the First World War.

NOTES

1. Benjamin Disraeli, *Tancred: or, The New Crusade* (London, 1847), Chap. 20.
2. Ibid., Chap. 48.
3. *Hellas* (1821), l. 1059.
4. Shelley, 'A Philosophical View of Reform' (1820), often said to be his greatest political statement.
5. Robert Blake, *Disraeli* (London, 1966); B.R. Jerman, *The Young Disraeli* (Princeton, 1960); Donald Sultana, *Benjamin Disraeli in Spain, Malta and Albania 1830–1832* (London, 1976); Robert Blake, *Disraeli's Grand Tour: Benjamin Disraeli and the Holy Land, 1830–1831* (Oxford, 1982).
6. BD to SD, 1 June 1830, from Royal Hotel, Falmouth: Benjamin Disraeli, *Letters*, ed. J.A.W. Gunn et al. (Toronto, 1982–), Letter 89 (i. 126–8), esp. i. 126–7. This letter (and many others are) reprinted (with very many mistakes) in *Home Letters*, ed. Ralph Disraeli (London, 1885), Letter I.
7. BD to ID, 1 July 1830, from Gibraltar: Disraeli, *Letters*, Letter 90 (i. 128–31), esp. i. 128–9.
8. BD to ID, 1 July 1830, from Gibraltar: ibid., Letter 91 (i. 131–3), esp. i. 133.
9. BD to ID, 25 Aug. 1830, from the Lazaretto, Malta: ibid., Letter 97 (i. 150–6), esp. i. 154–5.
10. M.C. Curthoys, 'Clay, James', *Oxford Dict. Nat. Biog.* (2004–12).
11. BD to ID, 25 Aug. 1830, from the Lazaretto, Malta: Disraeli, *Letters*, Letter 97 (i. 150–6), esp. i. 155.
12. BD to ID, 25 Aug. 1830, from the Lazaretto, Malta: ibid., Letter 97 (i. 150–6), esp. i. 155–6.
13. BD to Ralph Disraeli, n.d. [17 Sept. 1830?], from Malta: ibid., Letter 99 (i. 160–3), esp. i. 161–3.
14. *The Letters of Percy Bysshe Shelley*, ed. Frederick L. Jones (Oxford, 1964), ii. 324, no. 651.

15. Ralph Lloyd-Jones, 'Falcieri, Giovanni Battista', *Oxford Dict. Nat. Biog.*
16. Blake, *Disraeli*, p. 31.
17. BD to ID, 10 Oct. 1830, from Corfu: Disraeli, *Letters*, Letter 100 (i. 163–5), esp. i. 164.
18. BD to ID, 25 Oct. 1830, from Preveza: ibid., Letter 101 (i. 165–72), esp. i. 165. Cf. George W. Gawrych, *The Crescent and the Eagle: Ottoman Rule, Islam and the Albanians, 1874–1913* (London, 2006).
19. The various editions of the book exhibit small differences. I have used that published in New York: D. Appleton & Company, 1870, part of the 'Uniform Edition of Disraeli's Novels'.
20. *Contarini Fleming*, V.x.
21. *Contarini Fleming*, V.x; cf. BD to ID, 25 Oct. 1830, from Preveza: Disraeli, *Letters*, Letter 101 (i. 165–72).
22. *Contarini Fleming*, V.x; cf. BD to ID, 25 Oct. 1830, from Preveza: Disraeli, *Letters*, Letter 101 (i. 165–72).
23. *Contarini Fleming*, V.xii; BD to ID, 25 Oct. 1830, from Preveza: Disraeli, *Letters*, Letter 101 (i. 165–72).
24. *Contarini Fleming*, V.xiii; BD to ID, 25 Oct. 1830, from Preveza: Disraeli, *Letters*, Letter 101 (i. 165–72).
25. *Contarini Fleming*, V.xiii.
26. *Contarini Fleming*, V.xv.
27. *Contarini Fleming*, V.xiii–xiv; cf. BD to ID, 25 Oct. 1830, from Preveza: Disraeli, *Letters*, Letter 101 (i. 165–72).
28. *Contarini Fleming*, V.xiv; cf. BD to ID, 25 Oct. 1830, from Preveza: Disraeli, *Letters*, Letter 101 (i. 165–72).
29. BD to Benjamin Austen, 18 Nov. 1830, from [Nauplia, Greece]: Disraeli, *Letters*, Letter 103 (i. 172–4), esp. i. 173–4. The notion of the East as operating on an entirely different time scale is explored by Johannes Fabian, *Time and Other: How Anthropology Makes its Object* (New York, 1983), which has been employed by many scholars when discussing Orientalism, including Saree Makdisi, *Romantic Imperialism: Universal Empire and the Culture of Modernity* (Cambridge, 1998).
30. *Contarini Fleming*, V.xix.
31. Ibid.
32. BD to ID, 30 Nov. 1830, from Athens and Constantinople: Disraeli, *Letters*, Letter 104 (i. 174–7), esp. i. 176; *Contarini Fleming*, V.xxii.

33. BD to ID, 11 Jan. 1831, from Istanbul: Disraeli, *Letters*, Letter 109 (i. 182–5), esp. i. 183.

34. BD to ID, 11 Jan. 1831, from Istanbul: ibid., Letter 109 (i. 182–5), esp. i. 182–3.

35. BD to ID, 11 Jan. 1831, from Istanbul: ibid., Letter 109 (i. 182–5), esp. i. 183.

36. *Contarini Fleming*, V.xxiii; cf. BD to Id, 11 Jan. 1831, from Istanbul: cf. BD to ID, 11 Jan. 1831, from Istanbul: Disraeli, *Letters*, Letter 109 (i. 182–5).

37. BD to ID, 11 Jan. 1831, from Istanbul: ibid., Letter 109 (i. 182–5), esp. i. 184.

38. BD to ID, 11 Jan. 1831, from Istanbul: ibid., Letter 109 (i. 182–5), esp. i. 184.

39. BD to Benjamin Austen, 18 Nov. 1830, from [Nauplia, Greece]: ibid., Letter 103 (i. 172–4), esp. i. 173–4.

40. *Contarini Fleming*, V.xxv.

41. BD to ID, [23? Dec. 1830, from Istanbul]: Disraeli, *Letters*, Letter 105 (i. 177).

42. BD to Sarah Disraeli, 20 Mar. 1831, from Alexandria: ibid., Letter 110 (i. 185–9), esp. i. 185.

43. BD to Sarah Disraeli, 20 Mar. 1831, from Alexandria: ibid., Letter 110 (i. 185–9), esp. i. 186.

44. 'I expect in ten days to be in Egypt as the wind is most favourable. From that country I shall return to Malta and then to Naples—at least these are my plans which may probably not be executed': BD to ID, 11 Jan. 1831, from Istanbul: ibid., Letter 109 (i. 182–5), i. 184.

45. BD to Sarah Disraeli, 20 Mar. 1831, from Alexandria: ibid., Letter 110 (i. 185–9), esp. i. 186; cf. *Home Letters*, Letter XIII. The book in question is William [Richard] Hamilton (1777–1859), *Ægyptiaca: or, some Account of the Antient and Modern State of Egypt* (London, 1809).

46. BD to Sarah Disraeli, 20 Mar. 1831, from Alexandria: Disraeli, *Letters*, Letter 110 (i. 185–9), esp. i. 186; *Contarini Fleming*, VI. ii.

47. BD to Sarah Disraeli, 20 Mar. 1831, from Alexandria: Disraeli, *Letters*, Letter 110 (i. 185–9), esp. i. 187–8; *Contarini Fleming*, VI. iv–vi. Disraeli's reference is to John Martin (1789–1854), the great Victorian apocalyptic painter.

48. BD to Sarah Disraeli, 20 Mar. 1831, from Alexandria: Disraeli, *Letters*, Letter 110 (i. 185–9), esp. i. 188.
49. *Contarini Fleming*, VI. v.
50. BD to Sarah Disraeli, 20 Mar. 1831, from Alexandria: Disraeli, *Letters*, Letter 110 (i. 185–9), esp. i. 188–9.
51. BD to Sarah Disraeli, 28 May 1831, [from Cairo]: ibid., Letter 111 (i. 189–95), esp. i. 190.
52. BD to Sarah Disraeli, 28 May 1831, [from Cairo]: ibid., Letter 111 (i. 189–95), esp. i. 193–5.
53. BD to Sarah Disraeli, 28 May 1831, [from Cairo]: ibid., Letter 111 (i. 189–95), esp. i. 195.
54. [Benjamin] Disraeli the Younger, *Vindication of the English Constitution in a Letter to a Noble and Learned Lord* (London, 1835), pp. 102–6. The Lord in question was Lyndhurst (1772–1863), three times Lord Chancellor.
55. BD to Edward Bulwer, 27 Dec. 1830, from Istanbul: Disraeli, *Letters*, Letter 107 (i. 107–8).
56. See generally, Patrick Bratlinger, 'Nations and Novels: Disraeli, George Eliot, and Orientalism', *Vict.Stud.*, 35 (1992), 255–75; idem, 'Disraeli and Orientalism', in *The Self-Fashioning of Disraeli 1818–1851*, ed. Charles Richmond & Paul Smith (Cambridge, 1998), pp. 99–105; Ivan Davidson Kalmer, 'Benjamin Disraeli, Romantic Orientalist', *Comp.Stud.Soc.Hist.*, xx (2005), 348–71; Mark F. Proudman, 'Disraeli as an "Orientalist": The Polemical Errors of Edward Said', *Jnl.Hist.Soc.*, 5 (2005), 547–568.
57. *Coningsby*, Chap. 15.
58. Ibid., Chap. 10.
59. George Eliot to John Sibree, Jr., [11 Feb. 1848]: George Eliot, *Letters*, ed. Gordon S. Haight (London & New Haven, 1954–1978), i. 245–8.
60. *Tancred*, Chap. 20. Edward Said used this line as one of the two colophons of his famous *Orientalism* (London, 1978), although it might be argued that it appears there out of context and with a distorted meaning.
61. *Tancred.*, Chap. 17.
62. Ibid., Chap. 20.
63. Ibid., Chap. 29.
64. Ibid., Chap. 32.
65. Ibid., Chap. 33.

66. Ibid., Chap. 42.

67. Ibid., Chap. 38.

68. Ibid, Chap. 53.

69. *Lothair*, Chap. 77.

70. Ibid, Chap. 29.

71. Arnold claimed to have borrowed the idea from Heinrich Heine, which appears in his *Ludwig Börne. Eine Denkschrift* (1840): see Matthew Arnold, *The Complete Prose Works*, ed. R.H. Super (Ann Arbor, 1960–1977), v. 435–6.

72. The historical literature about the Crimean War is so vast that it would be redundant to chart the effects of this war on British perceptions of Turkey. Among recent studies of the Crimean War are: Trevor Royle, *Crimea: The Great Crimean War 1854–1856* (London, 2000); Clive Ponting, *The Crimean War* (London, 2004); Orlando Figes, *The Crimean War* (London, 2010); Andrew Lambert, *The Crimean War: British Grand Strategy Against Russia, 1853–1856* (2nd edn, Farnham, 2011).

73. See generally, Richard Millman, *Britain and the Eastern Question 1875–1878* (Oxford, 1979); R.W. Seton-Watson, *Disraeli, Gladstone and the Eastern Question: A Study in Diplomacy and Party Politics* (London, 1935); R.T. Shannon, *Gladstone and the Bulgarian Agitation 1876* (London, 1963); Barbara Jelavich, *The Ottoman Empire, the Great Powers, and the Straits Question 1870–1887* (Bloomington, IN, 1973). Even more generally, see M.S. Anderson, *The Eastern Question 1774–1923: A Study in International Relations* (London, 1966).

74. A.J.P. Taylor, *The Troublemakers: Dissent over Foreign Policy, 1792–1939* (London, 1957), p. 74.

75. Disraeli to Lady Bradford, 3 Nov. 1875: W.F. Monypenny & G.E. Buckle, *The Life of Benjamin Disraeli, Earl of Beaconsfield* (London, 1910–1920), vi. 14: quoted in Seton-Watson, p. 26.

76. *Speeches and Addresses of Edward Henry XVth Earl of Derby*, ed. T.H. Sanderson & E.S. Roscoe (London, 1894), i. 289: speech of 14 July 1876. This collection includes a 'prefatory memoir' by W.E.H. Lecky.

77. Some might cite three articles, published on 8, 23, and 30 June 1876.

78. Harold Temperley, 'The Bulgarian and other Atrocities, 1875–1878, in Light of Historical Criticism', *Proc.Brit.Acad.*, 17 (1931),

105–46, esp. pp. 124–5; Richard Millman, 'The Bulgarian Massacres Reconsidered', *Slav. & E.Eur. Rev.*, 58 (1980), 218–31; Mark Rathbone, 'Gladstone, Disraeli and the Bulgarian Horrors', *Hist. Rev.* (Dec. 2004), 3–7; Millman, *Eastern Question*, p. 161.

79. Arthur J. Evans, *Through Bosnia and the Herzegóvina on Foot During the Insurrection, August and September 1875* (London, 1876).

80. W.J. Stillman, *Herzegovina and the Late Uprising* (London, 1877). Cf. idem, *The Autobiography of a Journalist* (London, 1901).

81. See Keith M. Greenwood, *Robert College: the American Founders* (Istanbul, 2003); John Freely, *A History of Robert College* (Istanbul, 2000). See also Justin McCarthy, 'Missionaries and the American Image of the Turks', in *Turkish-American Relations*, ed. Mustafa Aydın & Çağrı Erhan (London, 2004), pp. 26–48; idem, *The Turk in America* (Salt Lake City, 2010); Joseph L. Grabil, *Protestant Diplomacy and the Near East: Missionary Influence on American Policy 1810–1927* (Minneapolis, 1971); David H. Finnie, *Pioneers East: The Early American Experience in the Middle East* (Cambridge USA, 1967); Lealand James Gordon, *American Relations with Turkey 1830–1930: An Economic Interpretation* (Philadelphia, 1932). Other Americans who wrote general books include Samuel S. Cox 'late American minister to Turkey', *Diversions of a Diplomat in Turkey* (New York, 1887); E.D.G. Prime, *Forty Years in the Turkish Empire* (New York, 1876); and a book by Prime's father-in-law William Goodell, *Forty Years in the Turkish Empire* (New York, 1883) and works by Goodell's associate Horatio Southgate, *The Cross Above the Crescent* (Philadelphia, 1878) and his earlier *Narrative of a Tour Through Armenia, Kurdistan, Persia and Mesopotamia* (New York, 1840).

82. For Dupuis's letter of 23 June 1876 and speculation about Elliot's motives, see W.N. Medlicott, 'Vice Consul Dupuis "Missing" Dispatch of June 23, 1876', *Jnl Mod. Hist.*, 4 (1932), 33–48. Cf. idem, 'The Near Eastern Crisis of 1875–1878 Reconsidered', *Middle Eastern Stud.*, 17 (1971), 105–9.

83. Edwin Pears, *Forty Years in Constantinople* (London, 1910) gives his version of these events as remembered in old age, followed by his *Turkey and Its People* (London, 1911) with a second edition the following year. Cf. idem, *The Destruction of the Greek Empire and the Story of the Capture of Constantinople by the Turks* (London, 1903?8?). He also did a *Life of Abdul Hamid* (London, 1917), in

the series 'Makers of the Nineteenth Century', ed. Basil Williams. Pears also wrote for the *Cambridge Medieval History* and was knighted in 1909.

84. *Hansard*, HL Deb 26 June 1876, vol. 230, cc. 385–8.
85. *Hansard*, HC Deb 26 June 1876, vol. 230, cc. 424–6. The Duke of Argyll was, after Gladstone himself, the principal survivor from the Crimean Cabinet: cf. his *The Eastern Question ... 1836 to ... 1878* (London, 1879), 2 vols.
86. Derby to Elliot, 28 June 1876, PRO FO 424/42, no. 2 (also numbered 425): quoted in Millman, *Eastern Question*, p. 131.
87. Derby to Ponsonby, 3 July 1876, QVL, ii. 467; Millman, *Eastern Question*, pp. 131–2.
88. Elliot to White, 29 June 1876, White Pap., PRO FO 364/7; same to same, 4 July 1876, ibid.: Millman, *Eastern Question*, p. 131. Cf. H. Sutherland Edwards, *Sir William White. His Life and Correspondence* (London, 1902), pp. 100–1; Colin L. Smith, *The Embassy of Sir William White at Constantinople, 1886–1891* (Oxford, 1957).
89. Ponsonby to Derby, 8 July 1876: QVL, ii. 470–1; quoted in Millman, *Eastern Question*, p. 132.
90. Ponsonby to Victoria, 8 July 1876: Windsor, Royal Archives, H8/127: quoted in Millman, *Eastern Question*, p. 511.
91. David Harris, *Britain and the Bulgarian Horrors of 1876* (Chicago, 1939), p. 47; Millman, *Eastern Question*, p. 133. Francis died on 19 Aug. 1876 on board the *Antelope* between Beşik and Smyrna.
92. *Hansard*, HC Deb 10 July 1876, vol. 230, cc. 1180–6.
93. Victoria to Disraeli, telegramme, 13 July 1876: quoted in Millman, *Eastern Question*, p. 137.
94. Seton-Watson, *Disraeli*, pp. 54–5; Monypenny & Buckle, *Disraeli*, vi. 45.
95. He wrote a book about his adventures: J.A. MacGahan, *Campaigning on the Oxus and the Fall of Khiva* (London, 1874). MacGahan would contract typhus and die in Istanbul in 1878. The MacGahan American Bulgarian Foundation was established on the centenary of his death in his hometown of New Lexington, Ohio. See Januarius Aloysius MacGahan, *The Turkish Atrocities in Bulgaria. Letters ... with ... Mr. Schuyler's Preliminary Report* (London, 1876). Cf. Archibald Forbes, *The War Correspondence of the Daily News 1877: With a Connecting Narrative Forming a Continuous History of the*

War Between Russia and Turkey (London, 1878). Cf. idem, *Czar and Sultan: The Adventures of a British Lad in the Russo-Turkish War of 1877–1878* (New York, 1894).

96. George Washburn, *Fifty Years in Constantinople and Recollections of Robert College* (New York, 1909), pp. 109–10; Eugene Schuyler, *Selected Essays* (New York, 1901), pp. 61–3.

97. Seton-Watson, *Disraeli*, p. 57; Millman, *Eastern Question*, p. 144.

98. Seton Watson, *Disraeli*, p. 57, Millman, *Eastern Question*, p. 144.

99. Baring to Elliot, 22 July 1876, from Philippopolis: PRO FO 424/43, no. 27 (rec'd FO, 4 Aug. 1876); Millman, *Eastern Question*, pp. 148–9.

100. Dupuis to Derby, 7 Aug. 1876, from Adrianople: PRO FO 424/43, no. 239. Cf. his supplementary report, 19 Aug. 1876, ibid., no. 337: Millman, *Eastern Question*, pp. 150–4.

101. Baring's report of 1 Sept. 1876 was enclosed in a letter from Elliot to Derby, 5 Sept. 1876: PRO FO 424/43, no. 602. It was received at the FO on 14 Sept. 1876: Millman, *Eastern Question*, pp. 150–5.

102. Schuyler to Maynard, 10 Aug. 1876, from Philippopolis: enclosed in Elliot to Derby, 5 Sept. 1876: PRO FO 424/43, no. 602.

103. J.A. MacGahan collected his *Daily News* reports in his *The Turkish Atrocities in Bulgaria* (London, 1876). See especially his articles of 28 July 1876 and 2 Aug. 1876. This quotation from ibid., pp. 24–5. Cf. Robert Jasper More, *Under the Balkans. Notes of a Visit to the District of Philippopolis in 1876* (London, 1877).

104. The article is dated 2 Aug. 1876: MacGahan, *Turkish Atrocities*, pp. 18–33.

105. *Hansard*, HC Deb 11 Aug. 1876, vol. 231, cc 1078–1147.

106. Seton-Watson, *Disraeli*, p. 73.

107. See esp. R.T. Shannon, *Gladstone and the Bulgarian Agitation, 1876* (London, 1963). Generally, see also Paul Auchterlonie, 'From the Eastern Question to the Death of General Goron: Representations of the Middle East in the Victorian Periodical Press, 1876–1885', *Brit.Jnl.Middle Eastern Stud.*, 28 (2001), 5–24. Cf. idem, 'A Turk of the West: Sir Edgar Vincent's Career in Egypt and the Ottoman Empire', *Brit.Jnl.Middle Eastern Stud.*, 27 (2000), 49–67. See also James J. Sack, 'The British Conservative Press and Its Involvement in Antisemitic and Racial Discourse, Circa 1830–1895', *Jnl.Hist. Soc.*, 8 (2008), 567–583.

108. Freeman to Bryce, 27 Aug. 1876: Bodl. Lib., Bryce Papers: quoted in Millman, *Eastern Question*, p. 181.

109. Freeman to Bryce, 23 Nov. 1876: Bodl. Lib., Bryce Papers: quoted in ibid., p. 524.
110. Morley, *Life*, ii. 552; Seton-Watson, *Disraeli*, p. 78. Gladstone also wrote to Argyll regarding Disraeli: 'He is not quite such a Turk as I had thought: what he hates is Christian liberty and reconstruction': Morley, *Life*, ii. 550; Seton-Watson, *Disraeli*, p. 78.
111. Halifax to Grey, 11 Oct. 1876: Hickleton Papers, Garrowby: quoted in Shannon, *Gladstone*, p. 524.
112. W.E. Gladstone, *Bulgarian Horrors and the Question of the East* (London, 1876).
113. Millman, *Eastern Question*, p. 183.
114. Disraeli to Derby, 8 Sept. 1876: Monypenny & Buckle, *Disraeli*, vi. 60; Seton-Watson, *Disraeli*. p. 80.
115. Monypenny & Buckle, *Disraeli*, vi. 181; Seton-Watson, *Disraeli*, p. 79.
116. Disraeli to Derby, 8 Sept. 1876: Monypenny & Buckle, *Disraeli*, vi. 60; Seton-Watson, *Disraeli*, p. 80.
117. Disraeli to Derby: Monypenny & Buckle, *Disraeli*, vi. 67; Seton-Watson, *Disraeli*, pp. 78–9.
118. Gladstone, *Bulgarian Horrors*, p. 8
119. Ibid., p. 31.
120. Ibid., p. 13 and n.
121. Ibid., p. 29.
122. Ibid., p. 25.
123. Ibid., p. 26.
124. Ibid., p. 27.
125. Ibid., pp. 27, 28.
126. Ibid., p. 28.
127. Ibid., p. 30.
128. Ibid., p. 12.
129. Ibid., p. 14. Nevertheless, Gladstone himself used racial terminology here, not only about the Turks (pp. 9, 10), but also in distinction to 'our race' (pp. 10, 31). Alas, even the great historian R.W. Seton-Watson (1879–1951) permitted his pen to write that 'Disraeli possessed the oriental imagination and resource of his ancient race ... The Jew knew how to infect his royal mistress and his aristocratic followers with enthusiasm for a programme of self-interest seductively decked out in imperial trappings.' (Seton-Watson, *Disraeli*, p. 561).

130. Gladstone, *Bulgarian Horrors*, p. 30.

131. Ibid., p. 31.

132. Ibid., p. 9.

133. Ibid., p. 24.

134. Ibid., p. 31. Gladstone clarified his position in a letter to the *Times* (9 Sept. 1876), explaining that his call for expulsion was 'strictly limited to military and official Turks' and that Muslims in general had the same rights as Christians: Seton-Watson, *Disraeli*, p. 77.

135. Stratford Canning to his cousin George Canning, 29 Sept. 1821: 'as a matter of humanity I wish will all my soul that the Greeks were put in possession of their whole patrimony and that the Sultan were driven, bag and baggage, into the heart of Asia, or as a provisional measure that the divided empire which existed four centuries ago could be restored.': Stanley Lane Poole, *Life of ... Stratford Canning Viscount Stratford de Redcliffe* (London, 1888), i. 307.

136. Stratford Canning to Gladstone, 10 Sept. 1876: 'My feelings naturally go with yours on the subject of Turkish misrule. Whatever shades of difference appear in our opinions may be traced to your having made Bulgaria the main object of your appeal, whereas the whole Eastern Question was my theme, and the Bulgarian atrocities, execrable as they were, only a part of it.': Seton-Watson, *Disraeli*, pp. 76–7; John Morley, *The Life of William Ewart Gladstone* (London, 1903), ii. 555. Canning also wrote a letter to the *Times* in support of Gladstone (9 Sept. 1876): Seton-Watson, *Disraeli*, p. 77.

137. Shannon, *Gladstone*, pp. 113–14; Millman, *Eastern Question*, p. 185. The speech is repr. in W.E. Gladstone, *Bulgarian Horrors and Russia in Turkistan* (Leipzig, 1876).

138. Millman, *Eastern Question*, p. 186. Froude wrote to Lady Derby (19 Sept. 1876) saying how much he liked her husband's response and wrote to her again in the same vein three days later: Herbert Paul, *The Life of Froude* (London, 1905), pp. 279–80.

139. Stanley of Alderley to Salisbury, 21 Sept. 1876: Salisbury Papers, E: quoted in Millman, *Eastern Question*, p. 526.

140. PRO FO 78/2551-6 are six volumes with letters and notices of atrocity meetings, including resolutions passed there, which were sent to the FO, from the beginning of Sept. 1876 to the end of Dec. 1876. These were used extensively by Shannon, *Gladstone*, who counted almost 500 atrocity meetings in the six-week period with Sept. 1876 in the middle: Millman, *Eastern Question*, pp. 241, 527.

141. Disraeli to Lady Bradford, 1 Sept. 1876, from Hughendon Manor: *The Letters of Disraeli to Lady Chesterfield and Lady Bradford*, ed. Marquis of Zetland (New York, 1929), ii. 84.
142. Lyons to Derby, 7 Sept. 1876: Derby Papers; Millman, *Eastern Question*, p. 190. Richard Lyons had served as British ambassador in Constantinople (1865–1867), being replaced by Elliot. Lyons was now ambassador at Paris.
143. Quoted in Seton-Watson, *Disraeli*, p. 84.
144. Cf. Malcolm MacColl, *The Eastern Question: Its Facts and Fallacies* (London, 1877); idem, *Three Years of the Eastern Question* (London, 1878); and *The Sultan and the Powers* (London, 1896).
145. Salisbury to Derby, 30 Nov. 1876, from Rome: Lady Gwendolen Cecil, *Life of Robert Marquis of Salisbury* (London, 1921–1932), ii. 107.
146. Ibid., ii. 107–8.
147. Seton-Watson, *Disraeli*, pp. 120–1, where he notes that it is usually translated as 'grenadier' but 'Musketier' was the word used (p. 121n.)
148. Disraeli to Salisbury, 29 Nov. & 1 Dec. 1876: quoted in Seton-Watson, *Disraeli*, p. 109.
149. Cf. his article 'The Past, Present, and Future of Turkey' in the *Nineteenth Century*, 3 (18) (June 1878), 981–993, repr. as *La Turquie, son passé, son avenir* (Paris, 1878). See the *Vanity Fair* caricature entitled 'The Turkish Constitution', 30 June 1877.
150. Salisbury to Victoria, 23 Dec. 1876: QVL, ii. 505–7; Millman, *Eastern Question*, p. 221.
151. Articles 3 and 4 stated: 'the Exalted Ottoman Sultanate possesses the Great Islamic Caliphate, which is held by the eldest member of the Ottoman Dynasty in accordance with ancient practice. ... His Imperial Majesty, The Padişah, by virtue of the Caliphate, is the protector of the religion of Islam and the Ruler and Emperor of all Ottoman subjects.'
152. Charles de Moüy, *Souvenirs et causeries d'un diplomate* (Paris, 1909), p. 51.
153. Elliot to Derby, 23 Dec. 1876, telegram: PRO FO 424/46, no. 406; Millman, *Eastern Question*, p. 220.
154. Millman, *Eastern Question*, pp. 220–1. Elliot left Istanbul only after the Conference closed, and even then at the last possible moment

after the Great Powers recalled their ambassadors: Seton-Watson, *Disraeli*, p. 135.

155. Seton-Watson (pp. 129–30) and others have emphasized the damaging presence in Istanbul at this time of Henry Alexander Munro Butler-Johnstone (1837–1902), a very pro-Turkish Conservative MP for Canterbury, who pretended to be an intimate confidant of Disraeli. Butler-Johnstone stayed on in Istanbul until July 1877, working with Admiral Selwyn and British engineers in surveying the Bosphorus. See his *The Eastern Question* (Oxford, 1875), from the *Pall Mall Gazette*, and his *Bulgarian Horrors, and the Question of the East* (London, 1876) and *The Turks* (Oxford, 1876).

156. Salisbury to Derby, 26 Dec. 1876, telegram: PRO FO 424/37, no. 93; Millman, *Eastern Question*, pp. 222, 224–5.

157. Derby to Salisbury, 28 Dec. 1876: *Turkey. No. 2 (1877): Correspondence Respecting the Conference at Constantinople and the Affairs of Turkey: 1876–1877* (London, 1877), p. 66.

158. Ibid., pp. 228–9.

159. Ibid., p. 225.

160. 28 Feb. 1877: Seton-Watson, *Disraeli*, p. 144.

161. The chief organizer was A.J. Mundella, MP for Sheffield.

162. Seton-Watson, *Disraeli*, p. 113.

163. W. T. Stead, *The M.P. for Russia Reminiscences & Correspondence of Madame Olga Novikoff* (London, 1909), i. 265.

164. Ponsonby to Prince Leopold, 25 Aug. 1876: Royal Archives, Windsor, Add. MS A12/316; Millman, *Eastern Question*, p 240.

165. Seton-Watson, *Disraeli*, p. 148.

166. W.E. Gladstone, *Lessons in Massacre* (London, 1877): published March. 1877.

167. *Hansard*, 232, pp. 713, 718, 721–2, 725; Seton-Watson, *Disraeli*, p. 155.

168. Salisbury to Lord Lytton, 9 Mar. 1877: Cecil, *Life of Salisbury*, ii.130.

169. Millman, *Eastern Question*, pp. 264–5, 274, 548–9.

170. Salisbury to Carnavon, 18 Apr. 1877; Cecil, *Salisbury*, ii. 139–40.

171. Millman, *Eastern Question*, pp. 279–81.

172. Seton-Watson, *Disraeli*, p. 173.

173. *Hansard*, HC Deb 7 May 1877, vol. 234, c437.

174. J.A. Roebuck, HC Deb 8 May 1877, vol. 234, c.558–9.

175. Gladstone to Arthur Gordon, 16 May 1877: Millman, *Eastern Question*, p. 291. So even Gladstone admitted that there was something sincere about Disraeli's proclaimed views about something: for a more nuanced argument of this sort, see J.P. Parry, 'Disraeli and England', *Hist.Jnl.*, 43 (2000), 699–728. Wilfrid Scawen Blunt (1840–1922) also thought that Disraeli's '*Semitic* politics of course were genuine enough': *My Diaries Being a Personal Narrative of Events 1888–1914* (London, 1922), ii. 72.

176. Granville to Gladstone, 20 Mar. 1877: Gladstone Papers; Seton-Watson, *Disraeli*, p. 207.

177. Lady Palmerston famously responded that 'We are grateful to Mr. Layard for bringing Nineveh to light, but not at all to Nineveh for bringing Mr. Layard to light': Seton-Watson, *Disraeli*, p. 203.

178. Layard to Derby, 18 May 1877: Layard Papers; ibid., p. 207.

179. Layard to Derby, 29 Aug. 1877: ibid., p. 229.

180. Millman, *Eastern Question*, pp. 293–4, 302.

181. Disraeli thought that 'a Turk as a soldier is worth 20 Spaniards': Disraeli to Derby, 13 Sept. 1877: Monypenny & Buckle, *Disraeli*, vi. 178–9. Cf. the *Punch* cartoon, 'Disturbed Dreamers', 23 June 1877.

182. Millman, *Eastern Question*, p. 305.

183. There is a painting (1883) by Nikolai Dmitriev-Orenburgsky (1838–1898) of this event in St Petersburg at the Central Military Historical Museum of Artillery, Engineers and Signal Corps. See also his painting (1885), in the same museum, of the very brief capture of the Grivitsa redoubt by the Russians before it was retaken by the Turks, finally falling to the Rumanians (30 August 1877).

184. This is depicted in a painting by Vasily Vereshchagin (1842–1904), 'Battlefield at the Shipka Pass' (1878), now in the Tretyakov Gallery (Moscow).

185. Millman, *Eastern Question*, p. 309.

186. See Captain Frederick William von Herbert, *The Defence of Plevna, 1877 Written by One Who Took Part in It* (London, 1911): 1st edn, 1895; John Sandes, *Under the Red Crescent: Adventures of an English Surgeon with the Turkish Army at Plevna and Erzeoum 1877–1878* (London, 1897); Richard Graf Von Pfeil, *Experiences of a Prussian Officer in the Russian Service During the Turkish War of 1877–1878* (London, 1893); Henry O. Dwight, *Turkish Life in War Time*

(New York, 1881); F[rederick] Maurice, *The Russo-Turkish War 1877* (London, 1905).
187. Disraeli to Derby, 1 Sept. 1877: Monypenny & Buckle, *Disraeli*, vi. 177–8.
188. Thompson, *Public Opinion*, ii. 262–3; Monypenny & Buckle, *Disraeli*, vi. 192. *Vanity Fair* published a caricature of Musurus Paşa on 8 Feb. 1871. Seton-Watson, *Disraeli*, p. 238 gives the date of the banquet as 6 Nov. 1877; Millman, *Eastern Question*, pp. 328–9 gives 9 Nov. 1877.
189. Seton-Watson, *Disraeli*, p. 238.
190. Ibid., p. 240; Millman, *Eastern Question*, p. 330.
191. Anderson, *Balkan*, pp. 106–13; Millman, *Eastern Question*, pp. 335–6.
192. Layard to Lytton, 2 Jan. 1878: Lytton Papers; Seton-Watson, *Disraeli*, p. 244.
193. Ibid., p. 263.
194. Layard to Derby, 23 & 30 Jan. 1877: Derby Papers, and telegram of 19 Jan. 1877; ibid., p. 263.
195. Monypenny & Buckle, *Disraeli*, vi. 217.
196. Millman, *Eastern Question*, pp. 357–8.
197. Ibid., pp. 366–7.
198. Ibid., pp. 368–9; Seton-Watson, *Disraeli*, pp. 297–9.
199. Seton-Watson, *Disraeli*, p. 311.
200. *Turkey No. III* (1878): *Affairs of Turkey*, no. 40; Seton-Watson, *Disraeli*, p. 311.
201. Stephen Gwynn & Gertrude M. Tuckwell, *The Life of ... Sir Charles W. Dilke* (London, 1917), i. 216.
202. Cf. Edward Freeman, 'Neutrality Real or Pretended', *Contemp. Rev.* (Oct. 1877).
203. Seton-Watson, *Disraeli*, pp. 272–3; Millman, *Eastern Question*, p. 362. Others who condemned Disraeli's policy towards Turkey at that time were Church, Dale, Spurgeon, Kinglake, J.R. Green, Stubbs, Bryce, Goldwin Smith, George Cox, and Thorold Rogers: Seton-Watson, *Disraeli*, p. 281. For more on the agitation, see Roman Golicz, 'The Russians Shall Not Have Constantinople', *Hist. Today* (Sept. 2003), 39–45.
204. Stead, *M.P. For Russia*, i. 419.
205. Ibid., i. 508.
206. Derby to Salisbury, 23 Dec. 1877: Cecil, *Salisbury*, ii. 170–1.

207. Seton-Watson, *Disraeli*, p. 281.
208. Cf. Anthony S. Wohl, '"Ben JuJu": Representations of Disraeli's Jewishness in the Victorian Political Cartoon', *Jew.Hist.*, 10 (1996), 89–134; and idem, '"Dizzi-Ben-Dizzi": Disraeli as Alien', *Jnl.Brit. Stud.*, 34 (1995), 375–411.
209. Millman, *Eastern Question*, p. 381; Seton-Watson, *Disraeli*, p. 311.
210. Layard to Derby, 31 Jan. 1878, telegram: PRO FO 424/67, no. 11; Millman, *Eastern Question*, p. 376.
211. The *Morning Advertiser* and the *Morning Post*: ibid., p. 379.
212. Joseph Cowen, a Liberal MP from Tyneside: *Hansard*, 11 Feb. 1878, 3rd ser. 237, 1421–54; Millman, *Eastern Question*, pp. 385–6.
213. Ibid., pp. 387–8. Cf. J.C. Hurewitz, 'Russia and the Turkish Straits: A Revaluation of the Origins of the Problem', *World Politics*, 14 (1962), 605–632.
214. Ponsonby to Paget, 11 Feb. 1878: Paget Papers, Add. MS 51205; Millman, *Eastern Question*, p. 388.
215. Derby to Loftus, 11 Feb. 1878, telegram: PRO FO 424/67, no. 438; Millman, *Eastern Question*, pp. 388–9.
216. Ibid., p. 390.
217. Ibid., p. 394.
218. Seton-Watson, *Disraeli*, p. 321.
219. Ibid., p. 352. Layard also wrote to Sir William White (1824–1891), then diplomatic agent at Belgrade and eventually ambassador at Istanbul, concerning San Stefano, and also telling him to advise young diplomats to study Turkish rather than Slavic languages if they wanted to get on: Layard to White, 1 Feb. 1878, from Istanbul; same to same, 1 Mar. 1878, from Istanbul: Edwards, *White*, pp. 127–9.
220. Seton-Watson, *Disraeli*, p. 353.
221. Millman, *Eastern Question*, p. 413.
222. Thompson, *Balkan*, ii. 408–9; Salisbury to H.M. Embassies, 1 Apr. 1878: PRO FO 146/2027, no. 243; Millman, *Eastern Question*, pp. 416–17, 592n.21.
223. Reeve to Layard, 5 Apr. 1878: Layard Papers, Add. MS. 39019, lxxxix: Millman, *Eastern Question*, p. 417.
224. Layard to Salisbury, 3 Apr. 1878 (his first to Salisbury as Foreign Secretary): Layard Papers; Seton-Watson, *Disraeli*, p. 406.
225. Millman, *Eastern Question*, p. 430.
226. Ibid., pp. 434–5.

227. Ibid., p. 437.
228. Ibid., p. 444.
229. *Hansard*, HL Deb 3 June 1878, vol. 240, cc.1055–6.
230. See generally Dwight E. Lee, *Great Britain and the Cyprus Convention Policy of 1878* (Cambridge USA, 1934); C.J. Lowe, *The Reluctant Imperialists: British Foreign Policy, 1878–1902* (London, 1967); Robert Holland & Diana Markides, *The British and the Hellenes: Struggles for Mastery in the Eastern Mediterranean, 1850–1960* (Oxford, 2006).
231. See the painting of the Congress of Berlin by Anton von Werner (1843–1915), which shows Bismarck offering his hand to Shuvalov as Andrássy and Disraeli supervise.
232. Salisbury to Lady Salisbury, 23 June 1878: Cecil, *Salisbury*, ii. 287.
233. Freeman to Madame Novikoff, June 1878: Stead, *M.P. For Russia*, i. 503.
234. Seton-Watson, *Disraeli*, p. 437.
235. Seton-Watson, *Disraeli*, p. 446.
236. Mary Neuburger, 'The Russo-Turkish War and the "Eastern Jewish Question"': Encounters Between Victims and Victors in Ottoman Bulgaria, 1877–1878', *East European Jewish Affairs*, 26 (1996), 53–66. See also her *The Orient Within: Muslim Minorities and the Negotiation of Nationhood in Modern Bulgaria* (Ithaca, 2004). Cf. Eliyahu Feldman, 'The Question of Jewish Emancipation in the Ottoman Empire and the Danubian Principalities after the Crimean War', *Jew.Soc.Stud.*, 41 (1979), 41–74. Generally see K.E. Fleming, '*Orientalism*, the Balkans, and Balkan Historiography', *Amer.Hist. Rev.*, 105 (2000), 1218–1233.
237. Seton-Watson, *Disraeli*, p. 450.
238. Disraeli to Victoria, 17 July 1878: Monypenny & Buckle, *Disraeli*, vi. 346–7.
239. *Hansard*, HL Deb 18 July 1878, vol. 241, cc. 1753–1774.
240. Seton-Watson, *Disraeli*, pp. 502–3.
241. Ibid., p. 504.
242. Ibid., pp. 507–8.
243. Layard to Elliot, 5 July 1878: Layard Papers, Add. MSS. 39,138, vol. ccviii; Seton-Watson, *Disraeli*, p. 510. Cf. same to same, 26 July 1878: Layard Papers; Seton-Watson, *Disraeli*, p. 510.
244. Ibid., p. 548.
245. Ibid., p. 569.

246. *Hansard*, HL Deb 19 Jan. 1897, vol. 45, c29.
247. Cecil, *Salisbury*, ii. 326.
248. Volney from 1782 spent three years in Egypt, Lebanon and Palestine, studying and learning Arabic. He then published *Voyage en Syrie et en Égypte* (Paris, 1787) and *Considérations sur la guerre actuelle des Turcs* (London, 1788).
249. *Coningsby*, Chap. 15. See generally Michael Clark, *Albion and Jerusalem: The Anglo-Jewish Community in the Post-Emancipation Era, 1858–1887* (Oxford, 2009).

Greenmantle at the Ministry of Information: John Buchan, the First World War and the Turks

At the beginning of December 1914, just as the Great War was beginning to explode, John Buchan sent the manuscript of a novel to his London publisher. It was dedicated to his old friend Tommy Nelson, whom he had known at Oxford and who was now his business partner. 'My Dear Tommy,' he began,

> You and I have long cherished an affection for that elemental type of tale which Americans call the 'dime novel' and which we know as the 'shocker'— the romance where the incidents defy the probabilities, and march just inside the borders of the possible. During an illness last winter I exhausted my store of those aids to cheerfulness, and was driven to write one for myself … in the days when the wildest fictions are so much less improbable than the facts.

The story was entitled *The Thirty-Nine Steps*, published in book form in October 1915. It was the first of five novels starring the daring Richard Hannay, and is John Buchan's most famous book, filmed three times, the first in a classic film by Alfred Hitchcock. We find Hannay on the eve of the First World War, hot on the trail of a sinister group of German spies who go by the name of the 'Black Stone'. The following year, Buchan in another novel put Hannay in danger yet again, this time in a desperate attempt to prevent the unscrupulous Germans from fomenting a Muslim rebellion in the East under the leadership of a holy man they called 'Greenmantle'.

© The Author(s) 2016
D.S. Katz, *The Shaping of Turkey in the British Imagination, 1776–1923*,
DOI 10.1007/978-3-319-41060-9_5

This time, however, Buchan's book of that name was more than a shilling shocker, for he was already a key player in Britain's propaganda war. His hugely successful novel called *Greenmantle* ultimately painted a rather favourable view of Turkey and its people, based in part on Buchan's visit to Istanbul only five years earlier and, along with his popular historical writing, helped detach Turkey in British public opinion from its alliance with the German enemy in the First World War.

I

The most important fact about John Buchan (1875–1940) is that he was from Scotland.[1] He was born on 26 August 1875 in Perth, where his clergyman father had his first job at the Knox Free Church. It was during those years that Buchan acquired the deep scar on his left forehead which gave him a very distinctive look—the result of having fallen out of a carriage aged five, fracturing his skull when the carriage ran over his head.

Buchan went up to Glasgow University in 1892, at the age of seventeen. 'As a student I was wholly obscure,' Buchan confessed, but 'I was fortunate to find in Gilbert Murray a great teacher. He was then a young man in his middle twenties and was known only by his Oxford reputation. ... Gilbert Murray was the principal influence in shaping my interests.'[2] Murray (1866–1957) was then only twenty-six years old, and in 1908 would be appointed Regius Professor of Greek at Oxford.[3] If young Buchan found Murray to be an inspiring mentor, the young classicist was equally impressed with this 'very brilliant student': 'It was John Buchan, who at the age, I think, of seventeen was doing an Everyman edition of Bacon's Essays.'[4]

Buchan's first novel appeared in October 1895. By that time he had already published his first professional article, in the *Gentleman's Magazine* in August 1893. More importantly, Buchan had secured a scholarship at Brasenose College, for by now it 'became clear that I must somehow contrive to go to Oxford'. Buchan was among the poorest students in the college, and during his first two years could not even afford to dine in Hall.[5] 'I can't quite make up my mind whether I like it or not,' Buchan wrote to Gilbert Murray. 'The men appear to be a curious mixture of overgrown schoolboys and would-be men of the world.'[6] Buchan could hardly complain about 'men of the world': he published a collection of essays in September 1896, before coming up for his second year, under the title *Scholar Gipsies*. While fame was undoubtedly a motivator, so too was the need for additional funds a powerful factor in turning to writing. By the time he entered his third year, Buchan was satisfied that 'what with scholarships, prizes and considerable emoluments from books and articles, I became rather rich for an undergraduate'.[7]

The Oxford method of cultivating effortless superiority entailed a good deal of careful work behind the scenes, and apparently Buchan's literary output came at a price. To his disgrace, he took a Second in his second-year Mods examination, but it was 'a very near shave' below a First. Ironically, at the same time, in June 1897, he won the Stanhope History Prize with an essay on Sir Walter Raleigh, reciting part of it at Encaenia before a distinguished audience that included the Prime Minister of Canada. Nevertheless, despite these ups and downs, Buchan's life was looking up, because he had not only more money, but more friends as well. He was already acquainted with some of the young men who would be important in his life, such as Alfred Zimmern (1879–1957), then an undergraduate at New College, along with Stair Gillon (1877–1954), a fellow Scot from Edinburgh. There was Tommy Nelson (1877–1917), also a Scot, at University College. Among his more colourful undergraduate companions was Aubrey Herbert (1880–1923) at Balliol, who came up in 1898 from Eton, the second son of the Earl of Carnarvon, and was apparently the model for a central character in Buchan's novels: Sandy Arbuthnot. In March 1898, Buchan was elected Librarian of the Oxford Union, and President the following January. He also won the Newdigate Prize for poetry in 1898 (on his third attempt), with a piece entitled 'The Pilgrim Fathers', and published a commissioned history of Brasenose College. It was a grand career that won him an entry in the 1898 edition of *Who's Who*. He listed his occupation as 'undergraduate'.

'My whole mind just now is filled with my future career,' he wrote to a friend in November 1897. 'I want to ... travel in E. Asia Minor next year doing some historical work and writing letters to the *Chronicle* on the political aspect of the country.'[8] While Buchan was swotting for Mods, exciting things were happening in Asia Minor and it was much in the news. Greek soldiers landed in Crete at the end of January 1897, following a local rebellion to liberate the island from Ottoman rule. The European powers were not pleased with this plan to enlarge Greek territory, and declared Crete to be an international protectorate. The Greeks, undaunted, tried to take over more of Thrace as well, and in April 1897 crossed the Macedonian border. This Greco-Turkish War of 1897, the 'Thirty Days' War', was a blunder, and by the middle of May 1897, the

Greeks were in final retreat. When the European-brokered peace treaty was signed on 20 September 1897, Turkey received a large amount of money for their trouble, and a small amount of land, being the only conflict between the two countries during the nineteenth century in which Greece was forced to cede territory to Turkey. Buchan decided to put off his trip, but it is telling that the notion of being a man on the spot in Turkey for an English newspaper was articulated as early as his undergraduate years. In any case, there was the Oxford degree to finish. Although he did manage to produce yet another book—a collection of stories and poems that appeared in March 1899—Buchan finally took his coveted First that spring.[9]

What to do next? A young man, a published novelist and essayist, sometime president of the Oxford Union, and best still, romantically Scots: the world was his proverbial oyster. In fact, the decision to become a lawyer had more or less been made two years previously, when Buchan entered his name at the Middle Temple in March 1897 and began to eat his statutory dinners there.[10] Buchan at this time was a hybrid figure, at the same time a working lawyer and an active writer, publishing both fiction and nonfiction. Apart from the *Spectator*, he also wrote for *Blackwood's, Magazine*, and his first stories appeared just as Joseph Conrad's *Heart of Darkness* and *Lord Jim* were being serialized in the same periodical. 'Looking back, that time seems to me unbelievably secure and self-satisfied,' he remembered. 'Its strength was its steadiness of nerve, its foible its complacence—both soon to be rudely shattered.'[11]

II

On 7 August 1901, John Buchan was summoned to the Colonial Office to meet with Lord Alfred Milner (1854–1925), High Commissioner for South Africa, Governor of the Transvaal and Orange River Colony. A few months previously, Buchan had run into his old Oxford friend Leo Amery (1873–1955), then *Times* correspondent in South Africa, and later himself Colonial Secretary among many other posts in a distinguished political career. Milner wanted Amery to join his 'Kindergarten', the band of young men who were helping him in South Africa. Amery was previously engaged at the *Times*, so he suggested John Buchan. Milner was impressed, and appointed Buchan as his Political Private Secretary on a two-year contract at £1,200 per annum. Less than six weeks later, Buchan set sail for Cape Town to help Milner reorganize the two former Boer republics into British colonies.[12] 'I had never been out of Britain—indeed I had never wanted to,' Buchan admitted. 'In London I had slipped into a sort of spiritual middle-age. Now, at the age of twenty-five, youth came back to me like a spring tide, and every day on the voyage to the Cape saw me growing younger.'[13]

At any rate, South Africa was a good place for post-graduate training, not least because of the people he met, beginning with Douglas Haig (1861–1928), then only a captain and not yet a field marshal. Buchan also met Edmund Ironside (1880–1959), a career soldier who later served controversially in Persia, and may have been one of the inspirations for the character of Richard Hannay. In the end, Buchan did not make South Africa his life's career, and despite his important work there, never pretended to have been among Milner's most devoted young men. Indeed, he liked to say that he was never a member of the famous Kindergarten, only the Creche.[14]

Historians are prone to see the years between 1903 and 1914 as 'the germinal period of the Great War', Buchan complained, 'but to some of those who lived through them they seemed rather an empty patch'. He returned to London at the very end of the summer of 1903 and immediately found himself back in his old rooms, working as a lawyer and writing for the *Spectator*, as if nothing had happened. But in 1907, just 'before my marriage I changed my profession,' Buchan explained, 'and at the invitation of my Oxford friend, Thomas Arthur Nelson, became a partner in his publishing firm, one of the oldest in Britain'.[15] Although he had no experience in publishing, Buchan had already produced a good many books, and he had some creative ideas.

'In business I found that I had a reasonable amount of leisure,' Buchan admitted. 'I had opportunities for European travel, and, when our children were young, my wife and I visited the Balkans and Constantinople,' riding the Orient Express in the Spring of 1910.[16] Buchan loved Istanbul. 'Constantinople is pure Arabian Nights,' he wrote in a letter home on 30 April 1910. 'My experiences varied from lunching in state with the Sultan's brother and dining at Embassies to chaffering with Kurds for carpets in a sort of underground Bazaar. I don't know any place where one feels history more vividly.'[17] In Istanbul, the Buchans joined an old friend on his yacht for a month's cruise in the Aegean, visiting Athens, Salamis, Delphi and Parnassus, returning to London from Venice. Just as his time in South Africa provided Buchan with local colour and personal knowledge for his book *Prester John*, so too did these trips on the eve of the First World War give him some insight into places about which he would write.

What this boy needed was a good war, and one was coming. Eventually, on 4 August 1914, Britain declared war on Germany. Buchan and his wife Susan spent the pre-war summer of 1914 on holiday on the Kentish coast. They were close to his wife's cousins, who were living in a house with thirty-nine steps tunnelled through the cliff down to a private beach. The talk was of war and the distinct danger of a German invasion by sea, a popular subject of 'invasion literature' for at least forty years.[18] Buchan worked on *The Thirty-Nine Steps* that summer, and it was serialized in *Blackwood's Magazine* in three parts between July and September 1915, appearing in book form the following month, October 1915. 'It's like a penny novelette,' muses Sir William Bullivant, the fictional top chap in British intelligence about the plot of the book in which he is created.[19] Perhaps, but on the other hand, maybe the innkeeper who shelters the hero Richard Hannay on the run is nearer the mark when he reacts to the story in progress: '"By God!" he whispered, drawing his breath in sharply. "it is all pure Rider Haggard and Conan Doyle."'[20]

III

As much as *The Thirty-Nine Steps* may have resembled a 'penny novelette', it was also part of the war effort, and even the pure and very much real Sir Arthur Conan Doyle (1859–1930) was also heavily engaged in transforming shockers into shock troops. Wartime propaganda was as yet very much an amateur effort cobbled together by well-meaning non-professionals. The first of these to have a go at putting Britain's case forward under the shadow of war was C.F.G. Masterman (1874–1927), a Liberal Party politician and journalist. David Lloyd George (1863–1945), then Chancellor of the Exchequer, felt the need to address this issue, and during a Sunday lunch in August 1914 turned to Masterman and asked, 'Will you look into it, Charlie, and see what can be done?'[21] On 31 August 1914, the propaganda question was brought to the Cabinet, where 'Mr. Lloyd George urged the importance of setting on foot an organization to inform and influence public opinion abroad and to confute German mis-statements and sophistries.'[22]

Lloyd George's charge came at a good time for Masterman. His appointment in 1903 as literary editor of the *Daily Chronicle* had put him into contact with a number of important British writers. Masterman was elected to Parliament in 1906, and shortly before the war was created Chancellor of the Duchy of Lancaster, a largely honorific post that meant a seat in the Cabinet. The practice then current was for new Cabinet ministers to resign and then stand again for re-election, but Masterman was unable to hold on to his seat and thereby lost the prize. As consolation, he was appointed head of the National Insurance Commission, with headquarters in a block of flats in Buckingham Gate known as Wellington House.

Masterman was convinced from the outset that the British people would never stand for overt propaganda but needed to be approached with greater subtlety. Being a man deeply entrenched in London's literary world, Masterman began with the intellectual capital he knew best, the very authors he had been courting for the past decade, calling them to a most extraordinary secret meeting held on 2 September 1914 in the conference room at Wellington House.

Everyone who was anyone was there, even writers who many people today assume had died long before the Great War broke out. Some of those present enjoyed reputations that have not kept their names alive in the public mind. Others remain safely ensconced in the British literary canon, including Arthur Conan Doyle, Thomas Hardy, John Masefield, G.K. Chesterton, John Galsworthy, J.M. Barrie and H.G. Wells. Also attending were Arnold Bennett, Israel Zangwill, George Trevelyan, Robert Bridges and Buchan's old mentor, Professor Gilbert Murray. Rudyard Kipling and Arthur Quiller Couch were unable to make the meeting but sent their encouragement and offers of help. The very idea of so much literary talent sitting together in one room at the beginning of the Great War is absolutely breathtaking.[23]

Most of this activity was completely unknown to the general public.[24] Even Parliament was in the dark, creating the ironic situation that the more successful Masterman was at his job, the more he came under criticism for apparently doing very little. Even lecturers who were dispatched from his office were ordered not to reveal that they were working for the British government.[25] Further information came out as the Second World War approached, and the government began to look into how things were done before, producing a short history of British propaganda.[26] It emerged that Masterman's men got commercial publishing houses to print their material, and paid up to five guineas for the privilege. Even more astonishing, it transpired that some authors were actually receiving royalties for books that were published and distributed free by Wellington

House, which in turn guaranteed a minimum number of copies at an agreed price.[27]

Masterman and his people had an abiding faith in the power of the pamphlet, a kind of throw-back to Victorian tractarianism in what was already the early age of cinema. These pamphlets were meant to be serious and even academic in tone, presenting a factually correct and carefully reasoned case that enabled the reader to reach his own correct anti-German conclusions. Once written and published, the Wellington House pamphlets were casually scattered around railway stations, doctors' surgeries, barber shops, any place where people were so desperate to find something to read that they might just pick up a sonorous examination of the Belgian border question.

Masterman was very proud of his efforts in this area, which he emphasized in his first annual report of the work done at Wellington House, filed in June 1915. His records showed that in less than ten months, they had produced about 2.5 million copies of pamphlets, books and other texts in seventeen different languages.[28] By the following February 1916, that number rose to 7 million copies. Unlike the wasteful Germans, who ran off huge quantities of single-sheets, the people at Wellington House only produced bound propaganda, and they were proud to point this out in the report.[29] Eventually, Wellington House would also move into pictorial propaganda, printing images on postcards, cigarette cards, maps and posters.[30] The most famous, or notorious, of the other texts was the *Report on Alleged German Outrages* by Lord Bryce (1838–1922), the respected former British ambassador to the United States. Although it was presented in the format and style of a legal brief, Bryce's report included a mass of unsubstantiated material gleaned from Belgian refugees who were pouring into Britain.[31]

Masterman's most deft stroke was to place the Canadian novelist and MP Sir Gilbert Parker (1862–1932) in charge of welding together his beloved pamphlet campaign and the requirement to put the pamphlets into the hands of Americans. Parker invented the technique of mass mailings, compiling a list of 13,000 names of important and influential people, academics, businessmen, doctors, lawyers and others. Their British counterparts were encouraged to write personal notes to barely-remembered colleagues, encouraging them to have a look at the enclosed. Ambassadors and consuls became distribution agents, spreading the pamphlets in the usual railroad waiting rooms and the other way-stations of boredom.[32]

Although John Buchan would eventually run the propaganda operation at Wellington House, replacing Masterman, he was as yet on the outside, anxious to be a part of the British war effort, but unsure how his literary and academic talents could be of much use. He took the first obvious step by trying to join the army, but was rejected on grounds of age and health. Failing in making war, Buchan had the idea of recording it, in the hope that this second-hand heroism would encourage the others. He approached Sir Arthur Conan Doyle to produce a history of the war as it happened, but was turned down, not least because Conan Doyle was busy with Masterman's secret official war propaganda work. Buchan decided to do the job himself, putting together *Nelson's History of the War* at great and consistent speed and under his own name as author, the first part coming out in February 1915.

The idea was to produce fortnightly parts with the 'Story of the War told in a readable narrative', that is to say, 50,000 words at a shot, all written by Buchan. The intervals became monthly, but as Buchan later confessed, it was also 'designed to keep my work-people in employment, and its wide circulation induced the authorities to advise its continuance'. All profits from this work, including Buchan's royalties, went to the families of Nelson employees who had enlisted in the forces, with the remainder going to war-related charities.[33] In the end, Buchan produced well over a million words, which were published in twenty-four volumes from 1915 to 1919, with an abridged version appearing in 1922.

The 'authorities', as Buchan described them, were very pleased indeed with *Nelson's History of the War*, which was further promoted by a number of public lectures that Buchan gave for war charities. Three talks in London in April 1915 were chaired respectively by Foreign Secretary Sir Edward Grey (1862–1933), General Sir Francis Lloyd (1853–1926), and A.J. Balfour (1848–1930), who in May would become First Lord of the Admiralty. They were so sufficiently impressed that the *Times* invited Buchan in May 1915 to serve as their special correspondent to what would be known as the second Battle of Ypres. Buchan was thus one of the five journalists embedded in the British army there, after pressure had been put on the government by Reuters. In October 1915 he was back in France, this time properly in uniform as a lieutenant in the Intelligence Corps, reporting on the Battle of Loos. This was just as his *Thirty-Nine Steps* appeared in book form, becoming an instant best-seller, with 25,000 copies bought between October 1915 and the end of the year alone. Now his ever-popular and frequent public lectures were described as being given by John Buchan, 'the famous novelist and war correspondent'.[34]

Buchan had definitely become an on-the-spot team player, popular with both the War Office and the Foreign Office. In February 1916, Buchan took a Russian delegation up to Scapa Flow and gave them a lecture about the Russian army, emphasizing the recent Russian capture of Erzurum. Buchan's chief responsibility was to do what he did best: produce summaries of the fighting as it progressed that could be used both by the press and by Masterman's propaganda people.[35] There was hardly any time to rest. Prime Minister H.H. Asquith (1852–1928) was forced out of office on 5 December 1916, and two days later, David Lloyd George replaced him. The new prime minister had recognized the importance of propaganda from the beginning of the war, when he had asked Charles Masterman to put something together, but now had come to feel that that something was not enough. Masterman had to be replaced. One of Lloyd George's new cabinet ministers was Lord Milner, who thought that his former Political Private Secretary John Buchan was the man for the job, even if the prime minister had his doubts. Lloyd George took Milner's advice, and now asked Buchan to submit a proposal for organizing a completely new Department of Information, which was approved by a Cabinet minute of 9 February 1917. At the same time, Buchan was appointed Director, at a salary of £1,000 and the rank of lieutenant-colonel, responsible directly to the prime minister.[36]

Despite everyone's obvious enthusiasm, things got off to a slow start. Buchan's recurring gastric problem turned out to be a duodenal ulcer (which he soon gave to one of his fictional characters, the American hero in *Greenmantle*). Back in England at the beginning of 1917, he underwent a dangerous operation, conveniently performed at his own home in Portland Place. It kept him away from his new job for six weeks, but when he finally got down to business he approached his task with enthusiasm and characteristic optimism. Buchan's own view regarding propaganda was that its 'aim is to state honestly and fully the different aspects of Britain's achievement in the war, to circulate in the popular mind the main principles of Allied policy and its justification, and to inform the world accurately of the atrocities and claims of our opponents'.[37]

IV

All the while that Buchan held official positions in the British propaganda effort, he was producing *Nelson's History of the War*. 'This was a hard job in France,' he admitted, 'but it was easier in London—indeed, my difficulty was that I now knew too much and was often perplexed as to what I could print.'[38] His own firm, Nelson, was already putting out Masterman's clandestine propaganda publications, and Buchan now knew this. In retrospect, Buchan's little tour for the Russian officers to Scapa Flow in February 1916 had been a key moment for solving this personal dilemma about how much he was able to reveal, and its solution would have a great effect on the British public's perception of Turkey and the war in the East. The previous month, Buchan had already contracted for another Richard Hannay book, following on the phenomenal success of *The Thirty-Nine Steps*. He received an advance of £750, but as he wrote the novel between February and June 1916 it became the story of the Russian capture of Erzurum and the role of the Ottoman Empire in the Great War.

While Buchan had been concentrating on European trench warfare, an entirely different kind of battle was shaping up at the eastern end of the conflict. Placing himself in personal command of the Ottoman Third Army, and ignoring the advice of his German advisors, Enver Paşa (1881–1922) prepared to take about 100,000 poorly equipped men to the east in the dead of winter. Crossing the mountains into Russian territory reduced the Turkish force, as it succumbed to frostbite, hypothermia and the temptation to desert. The Russians had about 60,000 men at their command in the area. Between 29 December 1914 and 3 January 1915, Enver's forces made their appearance at Sarıkamış, deep in eastern Anatolia. Although the Turks had some initial successes, the Russians quickly recovered and trounced the Ottoman army, which withdrew on 4 January 1915 in complete disarray, back through the mountains to where they had started, all the while suffering appalling winter conditions. The number of Turkish casualties is still unclear, the best estimate being 33,000 dead, 10,000 wounded, and 7,000 prisoners. It was in any case the worst single defeat for the Turkish army in World War I, and Enver relinquished his field command, even though as many as 50,000 soldiers were still standing.

The Russian offensive in eastern Anatolia began on 11 January 1916 when its army secretly left winter quarters and marched towards the Ottoman fort of Erzurum, the Turkish staging point. Oddly enough, the Erzurum forts had been built by the British at the end of the Russo-Turkish war (1877–1878), and finished before German military advisors came in to replace them after the Gladstonian reorientation of foreign policy. This perimeter covered only about 180° of the arc, leaving a gap. The Turks assumed that this gap was naturally protected by the 'inaccessible' high rocky ridge of Kargapazar, on which there were neither tracks nor paths, made worse by winter snow and cold. The Russians soon discovered that this gap was undefended, and that this was their path to victory.

Even after the Russians initiated some minor incursions from that area, the Turkish forces still did not understand what was happening, preferring to hunker down on the western slopes of the Kargapazar, suffering from the extreme cold and praying that they would not die of hypothermia. The rest of the soldiers took refuge in the Erzurum forts. The Ottoman officers were sure that the Russians would not be so foolhardy as to launch a major attack in these conditions, but would wait until the spring thaw, by which time the Ottoman troops from Gallipoli would have made the long and difficult journey across Anatolia to reinforce their comrades in the east. The Russians were soon to prove them wrong. At about 1400 hours on 11 February 1916, Russian heavy artillery fire began to rain on the forts. On 16 February 1916, at about 0700 hours, a Cossack regiment entered Erzurum to find it deserted.

V

The Fall of Erzurum was a grand story with a happy end in an exotic location, which was just waiting to be fictionalized. Buchan was well-informed about the conflict between the Russians and the Turks, being chained to his history of the war in its relentless intervals. It was just a matter of adding the dialogue, fleshing out the characters, and adding something magically else, to create 'romance where the incidents defy the probabilities, and march just inside the borders of the possible'. That was *Greenmantle*, published in book form in November 1916, a novel about historical events only nine months in the past, which not only entertained but also helped educate its readers through the most subtle form of propaganda, novelized instant history.

Greenmantle opens on 17 November 1915, when Major Richard Hannay is summoned out of convalescence to the Foreign Office to meet with Sir Walter Bullivant, the British intelligence man from *The Thirty-Nine Steps*. Bullivant gives Hannay a quick summary of the situation in the East as understood by experts in British intelligence (like Buchan):

> You are an intelligent fellow, and you will ask how a Polish adventurer, meaning Enver, and a collection of Jews and gipsies should have got control of a proud race. The ordinary man will tell you that it was German organization backed up with German money and German arms. You will inquire again how, since Turkey is primarily a religious power, Islam has played so small a part in it all. The Sheikh-ul-Islam is neglected, and though

the Kaiser proclaims a Holy War and calls himself Hadji Mohammed Guilliamo, and says the Hohenzollerns are descended from the Prophet, that seems to have fallen pretty flat. The ordinary man again will answer that Islam in Turkey is becoming a back number, and that Krupp guns are the new gods. Yet—I don't know. I do not quite believe in Islam becoming a back number.

Bullivant is not finished:

'Look at it in another way,' he went on. 'If it were Enver and Germany alone dragging Turkey into a European war for purposes that no Turk cared a rush about, we might expect to find the regular army obedient, and Constantinople. But in the provinces, where Islam is strong, there would be trouble. Many of us counted on that. But we have been disappointed. ... There is a dry wind blowing through the East, and the parched grasses wait the spark. And that wind is blowing towards the Indian border. Whence comes that wind, think you?'

'It looks as if Islam had a bigger hand in the thing than we thought,' Hannay tells Bullivant. 'I fancy religion is the only thing to knit up such a scattered empire.' Indeed, Bullivant reveals, there 'is a jehad preparing' and the Germans were behind it. According to credible information vouchsafed to British intelligence, the 'East is waiting for a revelation. It has been promised one. Some star—man, prophecy, or trinket—is coming out of the West. The Germans know, and that is the card with which they are going to astonish the world.' Hannay's 'crazy and impossible mission' is to find out what is going on. 'Beyond Persia, remember, lies India,' Bullivant warns him, as if he didn't know already.[39] Bullivant is convinced that the key to the Islamic mystery was to be found in Constantinople and that Hannay was not being entrusted with saving a sideshow for Britain: 'The war must be won or lost in Europe. Yes; but if the East blazes up, our effort will be distracted from Europe and the great *coup* may fail. The stakes are no less than victory and defeat, Hannay.'[40] Hannay naturally agrees to save the British Empire from the Islamic Jihad, and enlists his old friend Sandy Arbuthnot, ex-Eton and New College, Oxford, possessed of 'a pair of brown eyes like a pretty girl's'. Sandy knew all the requisite Eastern languages and could pass undetected in unaccented linguistic perfection. Bullivant adds to the mix an American named John Scantlebury Blenkiron with a painful Buchan-like ulcer that wreaks havoc with his digestion.[41]

Before setting out, Sandy, Blenkiron and Richard Hannay try to work out what might set the East on fire. Sandy was not surprised that something was on the horizon, but was sure that this something was not a prophecy, or a flag, or a jewel, but a man: 'To capture all Islam ... the man must be of the Koreish, the tribe of the Prophet himself.' After many adventures avoiding capture by Germans, on 16 January 1916 Richard Hannay arrives in Istanbul. Our heroes now reunited on the appointed day, they put their heads together and pool what they have learned. Sandy, of course, has discovered the most and reports that Sir Walter Bullivant had been right in Chap. 1:

> 'There's a great stirring in Islam, something moving on the face of the waters. ... Those religious revivals come in cycles, and one was due about now. ... A seer has arisen of the blood of the Prophet, who will restore the Khalifate to its old glories and Islam to its old purity. His sayings are everywhere in the Moslem world. All the orthodox believers have them by heart. That is why they are enduring grinding poverty and preposterous taxation, and that is why their young men are rolling up to the armies and dying without complaint in Gallipoli and Transcaucasia. They believe they are on the eve of a great deliverance.' ...

'I know,' I said; 'he is called Greenmantle.'

Blenkiron then went on to explain the Turkish political arena, arguing that the Young Turks lacked genuine support in their country, and that the alliance with Germany was made out of desperate necessity:

> 'It is no sort of a happy family. But the Young Turks know that without the German boost they'll be strung up like Haman, and the Germans can't afford to neglect an ally. Consider what would happen if Turkey got sick of the game and made a separate peace. The road would be open for Russia to the Aegean... Things would look pretty black for that control of the Near East on which Germany has banked her winnings. Kaiser says that's got to be prevented at all costs'

The entire edifice was about to collapse, and Germany's last trump card is to be played by a mysterious old man called Greenmantle.

When Sandy turns up later, he announces that he has been able to find Greenmantle himself, dying of cancer. No prophet, no crusade; which was a shame in a way, since Sandy found much to admire in Islam:

It isn't inhuman. It's the humanity of one part of the human race. It isn't ours, it isn't as good as ours, but it's jolly good all the same. There are times when it grips me so hard that I'm inclined to forswear the gods of my fathers! ... Well, Greenmantle is the prophet ... He speaks straight to the heart of Islam, and it's an honourable message. But for our sins it's been twisted into part of that damned German propaganda. His unworldliness has been used for a cunning political move, and his creed ... for the further-ance of the last word in human degeneracy. My God, Dick, it's like seeing St Francis run by Messalina.'

There is room for only one villain in Buchan's simple plots, and that vil-lain is Germany, Turkey having been kidnapped for Germany's evil plans. When Blenkiron arrives, it is to deliver more news about the Turkish mili-tary predicament: they

were shepherded in from north and east and south, and now the Muscovite is sitting down outside the forts of Erzerum. I can tell you they're pretty miserable about the situation in the highest quarters... Enver is sweating blood to get fresh divisions to Erzerum from Gally-poly, but it's a long road and it looks as if they would be too late for the fair

Naturally, it is Sandy who gets it: 'We're going to Erzerum,' he shouts. 'Don't you see that the Germans are playing their big card? They're send-ing Greenmantle to the point of danger in the hope that his coming will rally the Turkish defence.'[42]

Two days later, our heroes are already getting off the train at Ankara on the way to Erzurum, along with masses of Turkish soldiers being moved from Gallipoli to the east. 'I must say I took a fancy to the Turkish fight-ing man', Hannay confessed, 'I remembered the testimonial our fellows gave him as a clean fighter, and I felt very bitter that Germany should have lugged him into this dirty business.' Sandy turns up, his head shaved, wearing a long linen tunic and a green turban, bringing the news that Greenmantle has died, and a successor has been chosen. 'Why do I wear these clothes?' he explained, 'Because I am Greenmantle ... for all Islam. In three days' time I will reveal myself to my people and wear on my breast the green ephod of the prophet.'[43] Hannay, Blenkiron and Sandy meanwhile make a mad dash for the hills of Erzurum, aided by Sandy, who reveals himself in all his green glory, but on the *Russian* side, before whom all of the Turkish soldiers abandon their German masters, enabling the Russians to occupy the town: 'Then I knew that the prophecy had been true, and that their prophet had not failed them. The long-looked for revelation had come. Greenmantle had appeared at last to an awaiting people', saving Turkey from German domination.

VI

What an extraordinary tale! But it was more than an adventure story, for this Richard Hannay book was written while its author was engaged in active government propaganda work, apart from the production of *Nelson's History of the War*. As we have seen, in March 1917, four months after the publication of *Greenmantle* in book form, John Buchan found himself Director of the Department of Information set up by the War Cabinet and based in the Foreign Office, with the rank of lieutenant-colonel. A year later, in March 1918, when the Ministry of Information was officially formed under Lord Beaverbrook (1879–1964), reporting directly to the prime minister, John Buchan became Director of the Intelligence Department.[44] Indeed, after Beaverbrook's resignation on the grounds of ill-health in October 1918, it was Buchan who was asked the following month to disband the Ministry by the end of the year, now that the war was finally over.[45] Whatever its literary merits, *Greenmantle* was a work of subtle persuasion from the pen of a professional wartime propagandist.[46]

The gobbit which opens up the entire text of *Greenmantle* is Sandy's speech in Chap. 12: 'There's a great stirring in Islam ... A seer has arisen of the blood of the Prophet, who will restore the Khalifate to its old glories and Islam to its old purity.' 'Khalifate' was the Islamic buzz-word for intelligence wallahs like John Buchan, a compelling combination of academic erudition, orientalist enthusiasm and invented tradition that helped drive British foreign policy with regard to the Ottoman Empire and Central Asia.

When Abdülhamid II ascended the throne as sultan on 31 August 1876, he also assumed quite automatically the title of 'caliph'. The Ottoman constitution, promulgated on 23 December 1876, in Articles 3 and 4 stated quite clearly that 'the Exalted Ottoman Sultanate possesses the Great Islamic Caliphate, which is held by the eldest member of the Ottoman Dynasty in accordance with ancient practice. ... His Imperial Majesty, The Padişah, by virtue of the Caliphate, is the protector of the religion of Islam and the Ruler and Emperor of all Ottoman subjects.' Abdülhamid introduced no new claims in assuming the caliphate, and it was not a controversial move when he took the title. The only possible objection was a doubtful *hadith* (prophetic tradition), according to which 'the Caliphs (Imams) are from the Quraysh', the tribe to which the Prophet belonged. Later on, this *hadith* would be quoted to support transferring the caliphate to an Arab ruler. The Ottomans, however, noted a further *hadith* which quoted the Prophet as affirming that 'the Caliphate after me will endure for thirty years; then will come the rule of kings'. It was on this basis that the Mamluk sultans assumed the additional title of 'caliph', and when the Ottomans conquered Syria and Egypt from the Mamluks, they took over that title as well. Sultan Selim I (r. 1512–1520) was the first Ottoman ruler to call himself 'caliph', and also 'Servitor of the Two Holy Sanctuaries', Mecca and Medina. When Selim brought the holy relics and the keys to the Kaaba from Mecca to Istanbul, his status was sealed. Even better, a widely accepted story began to circulate in the eighteenth century that when the Abbasid Caliph al-Mutawakkil III was overthrown by Selim in 1517, he transferred to the Ottoman sultan and his heirs all rights and privileges connected with the caliphate.[47] By the time Abdülhamid II came to the throne in 1876, his position as caliph was virtually unassailable. The Ottoman Empire was the only large Islamic empire which had preserved its independence, and Muslims in India and throughout the world had come to accept that there was no serious pretender to the assertion of the sultan in Istanbul that he was the caliph and he alone.

A number of retired British civil servants who had served in India were not convinced and made their views known. First among many into the field was Sir George Campbell (1824–1892), a Scottish Liberal MP, and Lieutenant-Governor of Bengal from 1871 to 1874. Campbell's position was very clear:

> I do assert in the most unqualified manner that the idea of any direct religious connection between the Sultan of Turkey and the Indian Mahommedans, that he is, or ever has been, in any sense whatever the religious head of any one of them, is absolutely and entirely untrue. It would be quite as correct to say that the Emperor of Russia is the religious head of the English and French Christians. The only difference is, that while we do know a good deal of the Emperor of Russia, the Indian Mahommedans are more separated from and know and care far less about the Sultan of Turkey. ... To suppose that ... Mahommedan subjects owed any religious allegiance to the Sultan of Turkey is a downright absurdity. As a matter of fact, I again

assert that there never has been any such connection, and that every Indian Mahommedan perfectly knows this to be the case. ... The present Osmanlee dynasty seems to have assumed the title of khalif when they conquered the khalifs of Egypt, themselves quite a local and sectarian dynasty, on the same principle, I suppose, on which a New Zealander claims land because he has eaten the last possessor.[48]

This view was reinforced by George Birdwood (1832–1917), a Bombay-born statistician at the India Office with numerous scientific, scholarly, and journalistic credits. Birdwood asserted in a letter to the *Times* published on 12 June 1877 that it 'is a great pity that we do not get the Mahomedans of India to look up to the Sheerif of Mecca as the Caliph of Islam for he lives by the side of our road to India, and would be as completely in our power as the Suez Canal'. In another letter to the *Times* published on 10 October 1877, Birdwood proclaimed: 'Let the Sultans of Turkey drop their spiritual office, relegate it to the Sheerif of Mecca, and become the husbands, each, of one wife at a time, and the Eastern Question will be on the road to a solution.' Other articles appeared as well, stressing the importance of the office of caliph to Islam and denying that the Turkish Sultan had a right to that office at all. Abdülhamid was an avid reader of the European press, and he was not amused: 'England's aim is to transfer the Great Caliphate from Istanbul to Jidda in Arabia or to a place in Egypt,' he told a journalist, 'and by keeping the Caliphate under her control to manage all the Muslims as she wishes'.[49]

The debate was far from over. Rushing to the sultan's rescue came none other than Sir James Redhouse (1811–1892), the most celebrated Turkologist of his day, and one of the greatest of all time.[50] Redhouse took the trouble to publish a pamphlet in which he argued that these objections to the Ottoman caliphate were 'erroneous, futile, and impolitic'. The caliphate of the Ottoman sultan was 'accepted and adopted by the whole orthodox world of Islam', he claimed.[51] George Birdwood for his part refused to concede, and thrice replied to Redhouse in the *Times*, with characteristic arrogance.[52] Coming in on the Redhouse side was Arabic scholar George Percy Badger (1815–1888). After lengthy etymological discussion of the terms 'caliphate' and 'imamate', Badger came to the conclusion that 'the Ottoman Sultan has as much right to the dignity as any other pretender; nay more, considering the large body of Muslims who acknowledge his claim'.[53]

Clearly, this was not a disinterested scholarly debate. It began just at the time when the bad news of massacres in Bulgaria was coming in, and Disraeli's pro-Turkish foreign policy was being attacked in Parliament and in the press. Both Redhouse and Badger consulted for the Foreign Office, and everyone knew that the discussion was really about India, and the loyalty of Indian Muslims to the British government and the British Empire. But it was a learned discussion nonetheless, and generated a good deal of interest among educated readers. Many people thought that the issue of the caliphate was an internal Islamic affair, and British interference, scholarly or otherwise, was too dangerous to contemplate, especially in light of the fact that there were some signs that Arab scholars were beginning to explore the possibility of returning the religious headship a bit closer to where it began. Ismail Paşa (1830–1895), the sometime khedive of Egypt (1863–1879) who had been deposed by Abdülhamid in June 1879 and was now living in Italy, also fostered a journalistic campaign to claim the title for himself. So too in England did the anti-Ottoman movement find support in Louis Sabunji (1838–1931), a former Catholic priest from Syria but living in England since 1874, who put out a newspaper in London that appeared in only three numbers in 1881, in which he denounced not only Abdülhamid's right to be caliph, but the entire institution itself.[54]

But the real problem was Wilfrid Scawen Blunt, who had served in the British Diplomatic Service, and then married Byron's grand-daughter. The couple travelled throughout the Middle East, and became very interested in Arabian horse-breeding and all things Oriental.[55] The Bedouin excited his imagination, and Blunt became very pro-Arab and anti-Turkish, agitating for an independent Syria, united with British Egypt against the Ottoman Empire.[56] When Gladstone became prime minister in April 1880, Blunt suddenly had an ally in Turkophobia, and even better, the old man's private secretary was Blunt's good friend Sir Edward Hamilton (1847–1908), who organized a meeting between the two men, and encouraged Blunt to write articles and memos promoting his views.[57] It was at this moment that Wilfrid Blunt discovered the caliphate:

I do not well remember whether it was from this Sabunji or from Malkum Khan that I first came to understand the historical aspect of the caliphal question and its modern aspects, but, opposed as I was to Ottoman rule, it struck me at once as one of high importance to the kind of reform I was beginning now to look for.[58]

His caliphate studies bore fruit in a 'Memoir by W.S. Blunt on the Position of the Ottoman Sultans Towards Islam', dated 24 July 1880. Blunt claimed that 'the question of the right of the House of Othman to the Caliphate has been once more in all men's mouths'. Perhaps an exaggeration, but possibly an accurate reflection of topics of discussion among the clubbable classes. After a learned survey of the entire caliphate issue, Blunt concluded that it was in Great Britain's interests that an Arab caliph be installed in Mecca under England's protection: 'This is probably the only solution which could assure India permanently to her'. Sir Edward Hamilton, at least, was convinced, and his influence with Gladstone was enormous.[59]

Blunt distilled his oriental experiences into a series of articles on the future of Islam which he published in the *Fortnightly Review* from July 1881 to January 1882 and then immediately in book form. Abdülhamid himself had a copy in his Yıldız Palace library, and he may even have read it.[60] By now, Blunt finally understood that the Ottoman sultan was universally recognized as the caliph, even if scholars may dispute the point: 'There must be a Caliph, and the Caliphate deserves respect; there is no other Caliph but Abd el Hamid; ergo, Abd el Hamid deserves respect.'[61] Nevertheless, Blunt wondered if there was a 'man of sufficient eminence and courage to proclaim himself caliph, in the event of Abd el-Hamid's political collapse or death'. Such a person would probably have to be a descendant of the Quraysh tribe. In that case, the caliphate would be spiritual rather than political, and other Muslim rulers would 'acknowledge the nominal sovereignty of a caliph who could not pretend to coerce them physically'. In any case, Blunt argued, the caliphate 'must be taken under British protection, and publicly guaranteed its political existence, undisputed by further aggression from Europe'. Furthermore,

> Established at Mecca, our duty of protecting the head of the Mussulman religion would be a comparatively simple one. The Hejaz for all military purposes is inaccessible by land for Europeans; and Mecca, were it necessary at any time to give the caliph a garrison of Mussulman troops, is within a night's march of the coast.[62]

A British puppet installed as caliph: what a wonderful idea.

As it happened, the Ottomans themselves were not oblivious to the importance of the caliphate issue, at least in regards to public relations.

After the disaster of the Russo-Ottoman War of 1877–1878, Sultan Abdülhamid emphasized more and more the Islamic foundations of the Ottoman Empire, a change of policy made more coherent by the fact that so many Christian provinces had been lost in the Balkans. He himself placed much greater emphasis on his role as caliph, in what was essentially an invented tradition. It was not only the British who were putting the caliphate issue 'once more in all men's mouths' (as Blunt put it), but the Ottomans themselves, as part of a propaganda war for the hearts and minds of Muslims everywhere, especially in British India.[63]

In 1906, when John Buchan was a writer at the *Spectator* and on the look-out for topics of contemporary interest, just then the caliphate issue came into public view once again. Prince Sabahaddin (1879–1948), a nephew of Abdülhamid who was then living in Europe, had written in defence of the sultan's claim to the title. These views were warmly recommended to readers of the *Times* by the celebrated Hungarian-Jewish Orientalist Arminius Vambery (1832–1913), who was duly rebuked by the Rev. Malcolm MacColl (c. 1838–1907), who himself had spent years in Muslim lands and saw himself as a bit of an expert.[64] Other views followed predictably, capped by a meeting in London in mid-November 1906 of the Central Asian Society to discuss the caliphate, attended by the foreign editor of the *Times* Valentine Chirol (1852–1929), the orientalist scholar Thomas Walker Arnold (1864–1930), General Thomas Gordon (1832–1914) and the Indian scholar Syed Ameer Ali (1849–1928).[65]

Even before the Great War began, then, the right of the Ottoman sultan to claim the caliphate was a subject of learned discussion both for Muslims and for British intellectuals and civil servants who fancied themselves wise in the ways of the Orient. The caliphate soon became a more intense subject of political interest as well. In February 1914, the emir of Mecca, Hussein bin Ali (1854–1931) made a declaration referring to 'the desire of the people of the Hijaz to cling to its ancient rights and to the conditions by which Sultan Selim I was confirmed in the caliphate'.[66] Hussein was not only the last of the Hashemite rulers over the Hejaz to be appointed by the Ottoman Empire (since 1908), but also held the title of '*sherif*', a descendant of the Prophet.

The caliphate was a compelling and irresistible subject for erudite Englishmen, just what Buchan needed to make *Greenmantle* not only thrilling but unaggressively educational. It was, in brief, a chestnut, a debate that might go on for years, with no regard to diminishing returns.

As it happened, in the end, long after *Greenmantle* had done its work and despite the learned arguments on whether the caliphate was indissolubly wedded to the sultanate, when the sultan went, soon followed the caliph. Sultan Mehmed V died on 3 July 1918, just as the First World War was coming to an end, and his brother succeeded him as Sultan Mehmed VI (Vahideddin). The last sultan was too clever and independent to survive the transition to the Turkish Republic, and on 1 November 1922 the sultanate was abolished entirely, Mehmed VI himself being spirited out of Constantinople sixteen days later aboard a British warship. The caliphate lasted a bit longer, transferred to the Crown Prince, cousin Abdülmecid II (1868–1944), who was elected caliph by the Turkish National Assembly on 19 November 1922. But the spiritual head could not survive without the political body, and sixteen months later, on 3 March 1924, the caliphate was abolished, and the caliph was deposed and expelled from Turkey along with the rest of the family of Osman. Four days later, Hussein the emir of Mecca declared himself to be the next caliph, but nobody paid the slightest bit of attention; the following year he went into exile in Cyprus, moving later to Transjordan, where his son Abdullah was king. Mehmed died on the Riviera in 1926 and was buried in Damascus; at the height of the next world war, in 1944, Abdülmecid died in Nazi-occupied Paris, and was laid to rest in Medina.

VII

John Buchan wrote both historical narratives, such as *The Thirty-Nine Steps* and *Greenmantle*, and narrative histories, especially *Nelson's History of the War*—twenty-four volumes of 50,000 words each, a total of 1.2 million words altogether, only 20% shorter than Gibbon's *Decline and Fall* and produced in four years, whereas Gibbon took three times as long to come to the end. Propaganda has been described as the art of persuading others of what one does not believe oneself. John Buchan's writings were not propaganda, but rather mobilized history. He served in an organization which had been charged by the British prime minister as early as the first month of the war 'to inform and influence public opinion abroad and to confute German mis-statements and sophistries'.[67] John Buchan's *Greenmantle* is not heavy-handed thought control, but an honest attempt to get it right, in full accordance with the position of his department that the British people would not tolerate overt governmental interference in their minds. The Turks come out surprisingly well in *Greenmantle*, victims simultaneously of forty years of British neglect and German aggression. Even the Germans were not uniformly presented as brutes; there were also kindly poor German widows to help a fellow creature in dire need, and the book includes a sympathetic portrait of the Kaiser himself.[68]

Buchan's *Nelson's History of the War* was also far from being propaganda, and this worried his superiors even as it was being written. Brigadier-General John Charteris (1877–1946), Haig's chief of military intelligence, was concerned that Buchan's work would become the official history, and insisted that 'critical words should not come from anyone who has access to such papers as we propose to show Buchan'. All chapters had to be submitted to Charteris before publication, and in any event could not describe events until five months had passed.[69] After the war, former prime minister Lloyd George excoriated 'Mr Buchan, in his "History of the War," lapsing into his fictional mood':

> When a brilliant novelist assumes the unaccustomed rôle of a historian it is inevitable that he should now and again forget that he is no longer writing fiction, but that he is engaged on a literary enterprise where narration is limited in its scope by the rigid bounds of fact. Had he taken the trouble to read the documents which were in the possession of the War Office and therefore available to him, he would have known ... Three fundamental inaccuracies in a single sentence are not a bad achievement even for a writer who has won fame by inventing his facts. The real explanation is that Mr. Buchan found it so much less trouble to repeat War Office gossip than to read War Office documents.[70]

Actually, the real explanation was that John Buchan did not think that his brief extended to lying and falsification.[71]

John Buchan wrote many books, perhaps 100 of them: novels, short stories, essays and non-fiction. Buchan also wrote biographies of Julius Caesar (1932), Augustus (1937), Montrose (1928), Oliver Cromwell (1934), Sir Walter Scott (1932), and even the 4th Earl of Minto (1924).[72] In his day, he was a famous author and very much a maker of British public opinion. Because his output consisted both of fiction and non-fiction, Buchan's views have often been misconstrued. He has often been accused of antisemitism, because the characters in his books, including Richard Hannay, often display the casual antipathy towards Jews that was socially acceptable before the Second World War.[73] Buchan himself, on the other hand, was an enthusiastic Zionist, even more vocally after the Nazis rose to power, serving as chairman of the Palestine Parliamentary Committee.

'I have been an enthusiast for the Zionist cause ever since twenty years ago when I talked it over with my old friend Lord Balfour,' Buchan declared at a public meeting in Shoreditch on 9 May 1934, as he was entered into the Jewish National Fund Golden Book. 'Zionism is a great act of justice and reparation for the centuries of cruelty and wrong.'[74] Richard Hannay is not Buchan, and anyone who overlooks the irony and the parody in these novels misses out on much of the fun.

Part of the problem is that there is nothing funny about Orientalism, and since the publication of Edward Said's book in 1978 we are meant to be sensitive to stereotypical representations of the East, to be seen as part of a Western conspiracy to objectify, define and rule.[75] It is no accident that Said's background was in literary criticism rather than in history, for in his approach to Orientalism he wields Deconstruction's axiom of unequal binary opposites on the principle that everything in human culture is a text, written or not. Buchan's wartime writing, simplistic as it may seem, is actually more complicated than that, as he tries to serve several masters: the Ministry of Information, Clio, and his own conscience. Buchan's *Greenmantle* is an adventure story which employs conventional images of Turkey, Islam and the East, hovering on the reader's 'horizon of expectations', but utilizing irony, parody and somewhat two-dimensional characterization in order to make some important points.[76]

Buchan's emphasis on the Muslim caliph was certainly in part due to a desire to give his books the whiff of erudition. But he also wanted to emphasize the role of religion in a time when many people were eulogizing its decline. *Greenmantle* was published only four years after Emile Durkheim's study of *Les formes élémentaires de la vie religieuse* (1912). While religion was not his chief delight, Buchan was the son of a clergyman, and understood its power.

Buchan's emphasis on the role of Islam as a unifying force also went against the growing British conceptualization of what the new East would look like. Their hope was that the former territories of the Ottoman Empire could be divided into distinct nation states, whose local patriotism would be nurtured under British protection. In this narrative, the British would not be expanding colonial domination of subject peoples, but rather enabling subject peoples to free themselves of Ottoman rule.[77] Oddly enough, Buchan played an important part in this narrative shift, since he it was who in December 1917 first put American journalist Lowell Thomas (1892–1981) on the track of T.E. Lawrence (1888–1935), having been approached for a lead about a dramatic war story. Buchan arranged through the War Office for Thomas to go to General Allenby's HQ, and it was Thomas's reporting and public lectures that created the myth of 'Lawrence of Arabia'.[78]

Nevertheless, Buchan's writing about the caliphate and his kind words about Islam came dangerously close to Pan-Islamism, which was not ever going to be the policy of the British government. Perhaps this political deafness is one reason that Buchan never really succeeded in the things that mattered to him. Although he was famous as a writer and as a war historian, he never was officially honoured for his work. Disappointed, he withdrew from London in 1919 and pretended to be an English country gentleman in Elsfield manor house outside Oxford, his most important post being member of the board of Reuters. Buchan did manage to get elected to Parliament in 1927, not to a real constituency, but as the Conservative member for the Scottish Universities, the representative of their alumni alone. Ceremonial honours were sometimes tossed his way, such as the post of Lord High Commissioner to the General Assembly of the Church of Scotland.

His public profile rose again in 1935, when Alfred Hitchcock's film adaptation of *The Thirty-Nine Steps* appeared in the cinemas. That was also the year that he left Britain, appointed Governor General of Canada, and created Baron Tweedsmuir of Elsfield after George V insisted on being represented by a peer, reaching true North American fame by being put on the cover of *Time* magazine for the 21 October 1935 issue. He was very active in his new post, lecturing in English and French, but his wife hated Canada and was often indisposed. Buchan perhaps dreamed that the Canadian job was just a stepping-stone to greater things, and that in the footsteps of his predecessors Lords Lansdowne, Minto and Willingdon he might follow up the Governor Generalship of Canada by being appointed Viceroy of India. It never happened. On 6 February 1940, he had a stroke while shaving and hurt himself badly in the fall, dying five days later in Montreal. He was cremated and his ashes sent back by destroyer to Elsfield churchyard.

John Buchan was sixty-five years old when he died, ultimately a very frustrated man. He was being more morose than modest when he wrote that 'I cannot believe that the external incidents of my life are important enough to be worth chronicling in detail.'[79] No doubt he contemplated the reasons for his failure. He was a Scot, not an Englishman, an outsider if not quite an Other.[80] His novels, lightweight in appearance, perhaps made him seem like a lightweight himself. On the other hand, comparison with Benjamin Disraeli suggests another factor. Disraeli, like Buchan, was an outsider, a baptized Jew, and like Buchan made no attempt to hide his difference, but instead revelled in his Otherness, even to the point of claiming that his essentiality was the upside of this particular binary opposition. Disraeli was also the author of numerous lightweight novels, some with Oriental themes, which like Buchan made him a household name and helped fund the lifestyle of a counterfeit English country gentleman. But Disraeli's life was a great success, while Buchan's was cloaked in failure and missed opportunity. Why?[81]

Perhaps the answer is that Buchan died too soon. Disraeli between the ages of forty-seven and almost seventy dwelled mostly in the political wilderness, when his Conservative Party was out of office, giving him the unwanted leisure to write his novels. Had Disraeli died aged sixty-five, his career would have looked very different. Had Buchan lived past age sixty-five, he probably would not have been given India, never having even been there. But having risen to the challenge in the First World War, he might have achieved greatness in the Second, doing what he did best—creating reliable fictional and non-fictional narratives for popular consumption. On the other hand, since Buchan and Churchill did not get along, he might never have been given the chance.

When Buchan arrived in North America in 1935, professional historians in the United States were in the midst of a great debate about what some of them under the influence of Leopold van Ranke (1795–1886) were calling the 'noble dream' of finding and writing objective truth. Many historians there believed this was a Germanic fantasy, including presidents of the American Historical Association like Carl Becker (1873–1945) and Charles A. Beard (1874–1948). Indeed, Becker in his presidential address in December 1931 went as far as to admonish historians that their proper function is not to repeat the past 'but to make use of it, to correct and rationalize for common use Mr. Everyman's mythological adaptation of what actually happened'.[82] Becker could almost have been paraphrasing John Buchan. 'As a reconstruction of the past,' Buchan insisted, history 'demands precisely the qualities that we look for in a novel or a play. It is primarily a story, and must have the swiftness and cohesion of good narrative.'[83]

Buchan introduced his tale of *Greenmantle* with a moving invocation:

Let no man or woman call its events improbable. The war has driven that word from our vocabulary, and melodrama has become the prosiest realism.

Things unimagined before happen daily to our friends by sea and land. The one chance in a thousand is habitually taken, and as often as not succeeds. Coincidence, like some new Briareus, stretches a hundred long arms hourly across the earth. Some day, when the full history is written—sober history with ample documents—the poor romancer will give up business and fall to reading Miss Austen in a hermitage.

In the meantime, Buchan could imagine what happened to his heroes at the conclusion of his tale:

> Sandy you know well. That great spirit was last heard of at Basra, where he occupies the post that once was Harry Bullivant's. Richard Hannay is where he longed to be, commanding his battalion on the ugliest bit of front in the West. Mr. John S. Blenkiron, full of honour and wholly cured of dyspepsia, has returned to the States.

Three more Richard Hannay novels were yet to come, the last published in 1936. The Turkey Buchan had actually visited and found so fascinating, and the religion of Islam that he respected, were shown in a positive light to his huge reading public. For Buchan, popular literature was the continuation of mobilized history by other means. The impact of historical narratives and narrative histories, best-selling fiction and mass-market non-fiction, in determining educated world views has not diminished, and Buchan was a pioneer in the art of subtle opinion-making.

NOTES

1. John Buchan wrote a very selective autobiography, entitled *Memory Hold-The-Door* (London, 1940), also pub. under the title *Pilgrim's Way*. The classic biography is Janet Adam Smith, *John Buchan* (Oxford, 1985), first pub. 1965. See also her *John Buchan and his World* (New York, 1979); and Andrew Lownie, *John Buchan: The Presbyterian Cavalier* (London, 1995).
2. Buchan, *Memory*, p. 34.
3. Gilbert Murray's daughter Rosalind married Arnold Toynbee: see below, p. 234.
4. Gilbert Murray, *An Unfinished Autobiography* (London, 1960), p. 97.
5. Buchan, *Memory*, p. 48.
6. Buchan to Murray, 14 Oct. 1895: NLS MS. 303: quoted in Lownie, *Buchan*, p. 40.

7. Buchan, *Memory*, p. 48.
8. Buchan to Charles Dick, NLS MS. 304: quoted in Lowie, *Buchan*, p. 47.
9. John Buchan, *Grey Weather* (London, 1899).
10. Smith, *Buchan*, p. 65.
11. Buchan, *Memory*, p. 94.
12. Smith, *Buchan*, pp. 106–8. Buchan used a South African setting for three books and three short stories.
13. Buchan, *Memory*, p. 96.
14. John Buchan, speech, 7 Dec. 1933, House of Commons Debate col. 1895: cited in Lownie, *Buchan*, p. 72.
15. Buchan, *Memory*, p. 137.
16. Ibid., p. 140.
17. Buchan to Charles Dick: NLS MSS 310: quoted in Lownie, *Buchan*, p. 116.
18. The first celebrated book in this genre was *The Battle of Dorking*, published by George Tomkyns Chesney (1830–95) in 1871. An estimated 400 invasion novels were published between 1870 and 1914, most of them depicting France as the invader until the villain shifted to Germany at the beginning of the century. Cf. *Before Armageddon: An Anthology of Victorian and Edwardian Imaginative Fiction Published Before 1914*, ed. Michael Moorcock (London, 1975); I.F. Clarke, *Voices Prophesying War, 1763–1914* (Oxford, 1966).
19. Chapter 4.
20. Chapter 3. The innkeeper also confesses to a desire to 'write things like Kipling and Conrad', and is proud to have managed to 'get some verses published in CHAMBERS'S JOURNAL'.
21. Lucy Masterman, *C.F.G. Masterman* (London, 1939), p. 272, quoted in Peter Buitenhuis, *The Great War of Words: British, American, and Canadian Propaganda and Fiction, 1914–1933* (Vancouver, 1987), p. 12.
22. Herbert Asquith to the King, 31 Aug. 1914: quoted in M.L. Sanders, 'Wellington House and British Propaganda During the First World War', *Hist. Jnl*, 18 (1975), 119–146, esp. p. 119.
23. Gilbert Murray would soon be joined by his son-in-law, Arnold Toynbee and fellow historian Lewis Namier.
24. The first serious examination of this war work came from James Duane Squires, *British Propaganda at Home and in the United States*

from 1914 to 1917 (Cambridge, USA, 1935). More recent works include M.L. Sanders and Philip M. Taylor, *British Propaganda During the First World War, 1914–18* (London, 1982); Gary S. Messinger, *British Propaganda and the State in the First World War* (Manchester, 1992).

25. Gilbert Murray was a favourite Wellington House lecturer. For more on Gilbert Murray's various roles during World War I, see below, pp. 234–5, 257. Cf. Sanders, 'Wellington House', p. 139.

26. PRO, Ministry of Information, Files 4/4a: a history of British propaganda by H.O. Lee; PRO, Ministry of Information, Files 4/11: parliamentary investigation into the activities at Wellington House: cited by Buitenhuis, *War of Words*, p. 15.

27. PRO, Ministry of Information, Files 4/11: parliamentary investigation into the activities at Wellington House: cited by Buitenhuis, *War of Words*, pp. 15–6. The Oxford Faculty of Modern History also organized historians to write propaganda pamphlets: Cate Haste, *Keep the Home Fires Burning* (London, 1977), p.94.

28. First report on Wellington House work, 7 June 1915: Public Record Office, Inf. 4/5 (Ministry of Information): cited in Sanders, 'Wellington House', p. 129.

29. Second report on Wellington House work, February 1916: Public Record Office, Inf. 4/5 (Ministry of Information): cited in Sanders, 'Wellington House', pp. 129–30. Sanders reprints (p. 144) the complete staff list of Wellington House from the second report, including L.B. Namier ('Journalist') as 'Reader & Reporter Austrian papers—adviser Polish & Austrian affairs' and A.J. Toynbee ('Oxford Don') as 'Asst. director U.S.A. propaganda general duties—pamphlet compiler'.

30. Sanders, 'Wellington House', p. 135.

31. H.C. Peterson, *Propaganda for War: the Campaign Against American Neutrality* (Norman, 1939), p. 58 calls the Bryce Report 'one of the worst atrocities of the war': cited by Buitenhuis, *War of Words*, p. 27.

32. Wellington House even had a go at producing its own picture newspapers, printed on the very presses of the *Illustrated London News*, which they were meant to resemble. These papers appeared in various languages, including a version of its *Al Hakitat* in Turkish: Sanders, 'Wellington House', pp. 130, 134.

33. Smith, *Buchan*, p. 194.

34. Ibid., pp. 194–7.

35. Quoted in ibid., p. 197.
36. Ibid., pp. 199–200. Buchan's proposal is printed in Sanders, 'Wellington House', p. 145. The Cabinet approved Buchan's plan on 20 Feb. 1917: PRO, CAB 23/1, 75 (13): Sanders and Taylor, *Propaganda*, p. 65.
37. John Buchan, memorandum, 1 Dec. 1917: FO 395/235, quoted in ibid., p. 252.
38. Buchan, *Memory*, p. 167.
39. John Buchan, *Greenmantle* (London, 1916), Chap. 1.
40. Ibid.
41. Ibid., Chap. 2.
42. Ibid., Chap. 15.
43. Ibid., Chap. 19.
44. Among those who refused to work under Beaverbrook were Arnold Toynbee and Lewis Namier. They continued to work under the Foreign Office as an intelligence bureau. Lloyd George himself thought that the appointment of Beaverbrook was a good thing, 'on the ground of Buchan's ineffectiveness': *The Political Diaries of C.P. Scott, 1911–28*, ed. T. Wilson (London, 1970), entry for 4 Mar. 1918: quoted in Sanders and Taylor, *Propaganda*, p. 95.
45. There is a comic element to this task in that Buchan had been under constant attack from Lord Northcliffe's newspapers immediately on his appointment as head of the Department of Information in Feb. 1917, on the grounds that he was too close to the Foreign Office. After the very critical second Donald report, Buchan was effectively replaced by Beaverbrook and Fleet Street, those who had attacked Buchan and his work.
46. Note that a separate department was established on 13 February 1918 at Crewe House under Lord Northcliffe to deal with British propaganda against the enemy, now that victory was assured. Northcliffe was responsible directly to the Prime Minister, not to Beaverbrook. Northcliffe resigned in November 1918, after increased tension with Lloyd George.
47. See Ş. Tufan Buzpınar, 'Opposition to the Ottoman Caliphate in the Early Years of Abdülhamid II: 1877–1882', *Die Welt des Islams*, 36 (1996), 59–89.
48. Sir George Campbell, *A Handy Book on the Eastern Question Being a Very Recent View of Turkey* (2nd edn, London, 1876), pp. 41–4. Misquoted in Sir James Redhouse, *A Vindication of the Ottoman*

Sultan's Title of Caliph (London, 1877), p. 1 as saying that the Ottoman sultan was 'no more the head of the Muslims than the Tsar of Muscovy was the head of the Roman Catholics and the Protestants of England'; misquotation continued by Buzpınar, 'Opposition', p. 65.

49. A. Cetin & R. Yıldız, *Sultan ikinci Abdülhamid Han: Devlet ve Memleket Görüşlerim* (Istanbul, 1976), p. 302; Buzpınar, 'Opposition', p. 64.

50. See esp. Carter V. Findley, 'Sir James W. Redhouse (1811–1892): The Making of a Perfect Orientalist?', *Jnl Amer. Oriental Soc.*, 99 (1979), 573–600.

51. Sir James Redhouse, *A Vindication of the Ottoman Sultan's Title of Caliph* (London, 1877).

52. *The Times*, 9 July 1877, 10 Oct. 1877, and 15 Oct. 1877.

53. G.P. Badger, 'The Precedents and Usages Regulating the Muslim Caliphate', *Nineteenth Century*, 2 (Sept. 1877), 274–82; and article in the *Times*, 12 Oct. 1877; Buzpınar, 'Opposition', p. 67.

54. L. Zolondek, "Sabunji in England 1876–91: His Role in Arabic Journalism," *Middle Eastern Studies* 15 (1978): 102–15; Martin Kramer, 'Pen and Purse: Sabunji and Blunt', in *The Islamic World From Classical to Modern Times: Essays in Honor of Bernard Lewis*, ed. C.E. Bosworth et al. (Princeton, 1989), pp. 771–80.

55. Elizabeth Longford, *A Pilgrimage of Reason: The Life of Wilfrid Scawen Blunt* (London, 1979); Albert Hourani, 'Wilfrid Scawen Blunt and the Revival of the East', in his *Europe and the Middle East* (Berkeley, 1980), pp. 87–103, 205–6.

56. Blunt even met with Foreign Secretary Salisbury, who rejected the idea. Blunt also promoted the idea of a Turkish Arabia under the command of an Englishman appointed for life and holding the title of 'emir': Brit. Lib. Add. MSS 54077 (Blunt Papers, diaries): quoted in Buzpınar, 'Opposition', pp. 80–2.

57. *The Diary of Sir Edward Walter Hamilton*, ed. Dudley W.R. Bahlman (Oxford, 1972–80), i. 28.

58. Wilfrid Scawen Blunt, *Secret History of the English Occupation of Egypt* (New York, 1922), p. 66. Martin Kramer notes that Malkolm Khan does not mention the caliphate, so therefore 'John L. Sabunji...seems the more likely source of Blunt's enlightenment on questions of the Muslim Caliphate': Martin Kramer, *Islam Assembled: The Advent of the Muslim Congresses* (New York, 1986), pp. 11–12.

59. W.S. Blunt, 'Memoir by W.S. Blunt on the Position of the Ottoman Sultans Towards Islam', 24 July 1880: FO 539/18, No. 19: quoted in Buzpınar, 'Opposition', pp. 83–5.

60. Abdülhamid's copy is now at Istanbul University Library, 297/141.

61. W.S. Blunt, *The Future of Islam* (London, 1882), p. 92. See also the work of the Protestant missionary and orientalist Sir William Muir (1819–1905), *The Caliphate: Its Rise, Decline and Fall (from Original Sources)* (3rd edn, London, 1899).

62. Blunt, *Islam*, pp. Cf. Abd al-Rahman al-Kawakibi (1849–1903), *Umm al-Qura* (Cairo, 1902), who was inspired by Blunt's work to promote the idea of an Arab caliphate based at Mecca.

63. Selim Deringil, 'The Invention of Tradition as Public Image in the Late Ottoman Empire', *Comp. Stud. Soc. Hist.*, 35 (1993), 3–29.

64. Letters to the *Times* from Malcolm MacColl, from the Residence, Ripon (18 Aug. 1906, 7 Sept. 1906); and from Vambery (28 Aug. 1906, 15 Sept. 1906); Caesar E. Farah, 'Great Britain, Germany and the Ottoman Caliphate', *Der Islam*, 66 (1989), 264–88, esp. pp. 265–6. Cf. Azmi Özcan, 'The Press and Anglo-Ottoman Relations, 1876–1909', *Middle Eastern Stud.*, 29 (1993), 111–117. See also Linda B. Fritzinger, *Diplomat Without Portfolio: Valentine Chirol His Life and The Times* (London, 2006). Chirol was knighted in 1912. For more on MacColl during the Bulgarian Horrors controversy, see above, p. 164.

65. Reported in the *Times* (16 Nov. 1906), p. 3; Farah, 'Caliphate', pp. 274–5. Cf. Thomas Walker Arnold, *The Caliphate* (Oxford, 1924), and in a new edn (London, 1965) with an additional chapter by Sylvia G. Haim, 'The Abolition of the Caliphate and its Aftermath', pp. 205–244. For Arnold, see now Katherine Watt, 'Thomas Walker Arnold and the Re-Evaluation of Islam, 1864–1930', *Modern Asian Studies*, 36 (2002), 1–98.

66. C. Ernest Dawn, 'The Amir of Mecca Al-Husayn ibn-'Ali and the Origin of the Arab Revolt', *Proc. Amer. Philosophical Soc.*, 104 (1960), 11–34, esp. p. 18.

67. Herbert Asquith to the King, 31 Aug. 1914: quoted in Sanders, 'Wellington House', p. 119.

68. See Lisa Hopkins, 'The Irish and the Germans in the Fiction of John Buchan and Erskine Childers', *Irish Stud. Rev.*, 9 (2001), 69–80; Colin Storer, '"The German of Caricature, the Real German, the Fellow We Were Up Against": German Stereotypes in John Buchan's *Greenmantle*', *Jnl of European Stud.*, 39 (2009), 36–57.

69. Hew Strachan, 'John Buchan and the First World War: Fact into Fiction', *War in History*, 16 (2009), 298–324, esp. p. 306.
70. D. Lloyd George, *War Memoirs* (new edn, London, [1938]), i. 886–7.
71. In that he was similar to Arnold Toynbee at the Foreign Office's Political Intelligence Department who tried to be as accurate as possible even when producing one-sided documents about *The Treatment of the Armenians in the Ottoman Empire, 1915–1916* (London, 1916).
72. Gilbert John Elliot-Murray-Kynynmound, the 4th earl of Minto (1845–1914), among other positions, served as Governor General of Canada (1898–1904) and then Viceroy of India (1905–10), and thereby embodied the full career trajectory that eluded Buchan. Minto also served with the Turkish army during the Russo-Turkish War of 1877–8.
73. Famously by Gertrude Himmelfarb, 'John Buchan: The Last Victorian', *Encounter* (Sept. 1960), repr. in her *Victorian Minds* (New York, 1968), Chap. 9. See also Paul Nicholls, 'John Buchan and the Dictators', *Quadrant* (Nov. 2011), 48–52.
74. 'Zionism "great Act of Justice," Buchan Says to London Jews', *Jewish Telegraphic Agency*, 20 May 1934.
75. Said posits 'Orientalism as a Western style for dominating, restructuring, and having authority over the Orient.' 'From the outset, then, Orientalism carried forward two traits: (1) a newly found scientific self-consciousness based on the linguistic importance of the Orient to Europe, and (2) a proclivity to divide, subdivide, and redivide its subject matter without ever changing its mind about the Orient as being always the same, unchanging, uniform, and radically peculiar object.': Edward Said, *Orientalism* (Penguin edn, Harmondsworth, 1985), pp. 3, 98: first pub. 1978.
76. Said mentions Buchan only once in *Orientalism*, p. 251, quoting him about China, and that from a secondary source without giving the original citation, noting only that it was written in 1922. See also Ahmed Al-Rawi, 'Buchan the Orientalist: *Greenmantle* and Western Views of the East', *Jnl. of Colonialism and Colonial History*, 10 (2009).
77. See esp. James Renton, 'Changing Languages of Empire and the Orient: Britain and the Invention of the Middle East, 1917–1918', *Hist. Jnl*, 50 (2007), 645–667.
78. Buchan always remembered Lawrence fondly: Buchan, *Memory*, pp. 211–18.

79. Ibid., p. 8.
80. Cf. Christopher Harvie, 'Second Thoughts of a Scotsman on the Make: Politics, Nationalism and Myth in John Buchan', *Scottish Hist. Rev.*, 70 (1991), 31–54.
81. David Cannadine, 'John Buchan: A Life at the Margins', *Amer. Scholar*, 67 (1998), 85–93 ponders the same question.
82. Carl Becker, 'Everyman His Own Historian', *Amer.Hist.Rev.*, 37 (1932), pp. 221–236, esp. p. 235. The presidential address was delivered in Minneapolis on 29 December 1931.
83. An address to the Workers' Educational Association printed in *Blackwood's Magazine* (January 1914), and published as 'The Muse of History', in his *Homilies and Recreations* (London, 1926), pp. 91–108, esp. p. 101.

CHAPTER 6

Arnold Toynbee on the Quay at Smyrna, 1921–1922

The defeat of the Ottoman Empire and the subsequent occupation of Istanbul in November 1918 was an opportunity to alter the face of the Near East. Greek forces landed at Smyrna on 15 May 1919 armed with Allied permission, fighting to restore the Byzantine Empire as they propelled themselves towards central Anatolia. It took the Greeks more than three years to awaken from their dream, as the last of their troops fled from that same port of Smyrna by 9 September 1922, defeated by the Turks under the leadership of Mustafa Kemal [Atatürk] (1881–1938). The following year, on 29 October 1923, the Turkish Republic was established on the ruins of the Ottoman Empire.

This was a big 'story', and every newspaper baron knew it. Then, as now, there was nothing like having a man on the spot. The *Manchester Guardian* sent out Arnold J. Toynbee (1889–1975). The thirty-two-year-old Englishman arrived in Smyrna on 27 January 1921, and after eight months left for home from Istanbul (16 September 1921). Toynbee's assignment to Turkey would change his life. For it was on his way home, travelling on the *Orient Express* on 17 September 1921, that he had the idea of how to organize the books that would become his famous *A Study of History*, the dozen volumes published between 1934 and 1961 that would make him a household name throughout the English-speaking world and put him on the cover of *Time* magazine, crowned by the popular press as the greatest historian of his day.[1]

© The Author(s) 2016
D.S. Katz, *The Shaping of Turkey in the British Imagination, 1776–1923*,
DOI 10.1007/978-3-319-41060-9_6

I

Arnold Joseph Toynbee was born to rule.[2] Although his family was far from wealthy and his father spent the last thirty years of his life in and out of mental institutions, he was the nephew of another Arnold Toynbee (1852–1883), the famous social reformer. In October 1907, Toynbee went up to Balliol College, Oxford, and three years later fell in love with the daughter of Gilbert Murray, the Regius Professor of Greek, who was himself married to the eldest daughter of the Earl of Carlisle, installed in the family seat of Castle Howard.[3]

Toynbee and Rosalind Murray were married in 1913, but not before he had added other distinctions to his curriculum vitae. In May 1911, Toynbee accepted a post as tutor in Balliol College, for all intents and purposes a job for life. On 22 September 1911, however, he left England for a year-long solo journey through Italy and Greece, having won the Jenkins Prize at Oxford which bankrolled his trip. The voyage opened Toynbee's eyes to the real world of the eastern Mediterranean and disabused him of any romantic notions about the modern Greek peasants as recognizable incarnations of their ancient forebears.[4] Indeed, in his very frequent letters home to Mother, he referred to everyone he met there as a 'dago'.[5] Unfortunately, on 26 April 1912 Toynbee drank water flowing in a stream in the Peloponnese and contracted dysentery, which effectively ended his wanderings and brought him home early to London on 6 August 1912.

Considering his public school and Oxford background, one would have expected Toynbee to have joined up with the first wave of British soldiers, to fight and die in the trenches of the Great War, along with the other glorious dead of the lost generation. Yet when the guns of August began to roar, Toynbee suddenly remembered his bout of dysentery and managed to stay out of uniform entirely.

By the spring of 1915, Toynbee was finding it increasingly difficult to avoid the Great War completely. On the first of May, he began working in a government office he privately referred to as the 'Mendacity Bureau'. Their task was to place articles in the American press, to prepare a digest of those newspapers for the Cabinet, and to answer queries sent to the British government about foreign policy. Towards the end of October, however, Toynbee was given a more interesting and challenging assignment, as he wrote in a letter to his father-in-law, Gilbert Murray: 'They have turned over to me Bryce's evidence about the Armenians, to make up into a report,' he announced. 'It is quite beyond one's range—the horrors of it I mean ... There can't have been anything like it since Assyria.'[6] (Already, Toynbee was making challenging comparisons across time and space.)

The Armenian issue became a political tool in Britain only after 6 October 1915, when Lord Bryce gave a stirring speech in the House of Lords. James Bryce (1838–1922) was not only a statesman of the Liberal party, but a professor of law at Oxford, and had served as ambassador to the United States for six years right before the First World War (1907–1913). Lord Bryce was a formidable man, and at seventy-seven years of age and possessed of a patriarchal beard, he could look and sound like a prophet of doom.[7]

Bryce had received information from American missionaries in Turkey, where they had established schools and hospitals in accordance with the usual pattern of using orderly Western institutions to attract heathens to the gospel. As it happened, the local Muslims were not attracted, but the Americans found ready clients in the Armenians and other Christians who were glad to benefit from the philanthropy of their transatlantic almost co-religionists. When the Ottoman government decided to push Armenians away from the Russian border, the American missionaries were witnesses to what transpired. Until the United States entered the war in April 1917, the Americans resident in Anatolia were neutrals, and generally were not molested. Instead, they sent their reports to Lord Bryce.

Ever cynical, the Foreign Office was quick to see the political advantage that could be gleaned from Lord Bryce's well-meaning intervention on behalf of the Armenians. The Foreign Office was less concerned about Armenians than it was worried about American Jews, whose influence might keep the United States out of the war, since Jews in America were much more upset about pogroms in Russia (Britain's ally) than German territorial aggression in Belgium or France. By emphasizing outrages against Armenians, the British hoped to convey to American Jews and others that in tolerating such Turkish travesties, the Germans were choosing loyalty to a rogue ally rather than fealty to standards of humanity and common decency. According to the Foreign Office spin, as bad as the Russians were now, the Germans were potentially worse: it could be the Jews next time around, so the Germans should be defeated while we still had the chance. Lord Bryce himself had no idea why the government should suddenly be interested in the Armenians of eastern Anatolia, but he agreed to compile an official record of what happened. That is to say, Bryce hired Toynbee to do the actual work.

Even apart from the nature of the material, it was a difficult task. 'I don't half like the job,' Toynbee confessed to his father-in-law, 'but whether that is because I think it evil, or because it is at present without form and void, and I can't see what shape to put it into or what meaning to give to that great slough of vile facts, I don't in the least know.'[8] Arnold Toynbee was on the Armenian beat until the end of the war, and since he took all research subjects seriously, he was soon transformed into an expert on the Ottoman Empire in general, and the Armenian question in particular.[9]

In the light of Arnold Toynbee's later reputation as a sworn Turkophile, it might come as a surprise to learn that the early Toynbee built his career on Turkey-bashing. Despite the massive amount of written work that he produced, the book that is most easily obtained on the internet is that report he wrote for Lord Bryce, which in some quarters has almost achieved the status of a holy text. *The Treatment of the Armenians in the Ottoman Empire, 1915–1916*, published in London in 1916, was certainly wartime propaganda. On the other hand, the research involved in producing this report was exactly the kind of painstaking study that Toynbee loved, and he did try to be as accurate as possible. What was missing from his text was a consideration of why Armenians and Turks should have been so mutually antagonistic. In a sense, it was this question which would drive his massive 'study of history' in later life.

In the meantime, Arnold Toynbee followed up his Armenian report with a series of rather lurid propaganda pamphlets which may have served the British war interests in the short run, but brought him no credit as a dispassionate political observer. Two of them belaboured the theme of the Terrible Turk and his German masters, the first published as if written by Lord Bryce, and the second under his own name.[10] Toynbee proved to be so proficient at churning out these shilling shockers, duly translated into European languages, that he was asked to write some more about the nasty Germans in Belgium, France and Poland.[11] By this time, Toynbee had been assigned to a new 'Political Intelligence Department', known in the Foreign Office corridors as the 'Ministry of All the Talents'.[12] It was an apt name, since among its ranks served such luminaries as Lewis Namier (1888–1960), Alfred Zimmern (1879–1957), and Edwyn Bevan (1870–1943). James Headlam-Morley (1863–1929), who was to have a distinguished career at the Foreign Office, summed up the zeitgeist of the group rather well:

Because they knew so much, argued so well, and had few doubts about their own abilities to foresee the future, the Political Intelligence Department exerted considerable influence on British foreign policy during the last phases of the war, and some, including Toynbee, continued to serve as expert advisers at the Peace Conference.[13]

For Toynbee, being included in this team meant that he might have some power over the course of the war and its aftermath, and he knew it.

For the Foreign Office's Political Intelligence Department, young Arnold Toynbee was the resident expert about the Ottoman Empire, with an important sideline in the Muslims of Central Asia. As with all his work, Toynbee took the task seriously: he looked at things comparatively, and he thought big. Already at the end of the Great War, Toynbee grasped the fact that the British Empire was a declining power. Indeed, he saw many similarities with the nineteenth-century Habsburgs, who were helpless against the rise of eastern European nationalism, which ultimately ripped apart their empire. The problem for the British was not the Balkans, however, but Islam. Toynbee was convinced that once fully self-conscious, the nations of Islam would pose a huge threat for the British Empire, not only in the Ottoman lands, but also in India and Africa.

Arnold Toynbee submitted these important insights for the scrutiny of the Foreign Office as a 'Memorandum on the formula of "the Self-Determination of Peoples" and the Moslem World', dated 10 January 1918.[14] His argument was that the wartime policies of both Britain and Germany had created the menace of Islamic political self-determination. Britain backed the Arabs against the Turks, and Germany defended the Turks, but ultimately the unleashing of nationalist sentiments would cost the Great Powers dearly. Toynbee's operative suggestion was for the British to encourage the United States to serve as trustees of the Dardanelles, while at the same time making a determined effort to win the trust of the Islamic world.

Things were now moving very fast. The Armistice that ended the First World War was declared on 11 November 1918; the Peace Conference opened in Paris on 18 January 1919. President Woodrow Wilson was keen to attend, and Prime Minister David Lloyd George had no choice but to follow suit. Arnold Toynbee was still not thirty years old, but he had no doubts that his advice was crucial information, invaluable for the future of world peace. Not everyone agreed, certainly not Lloyd George, who never listened to experts.[15]

'The Middle Eastern Sections of both the British and American Delegations', wrote Toynbee in an official minute, 'hold the view that Smyrna and the surrounding district ought not to be separated from Turkey, but this view has, I believe, been overruled by the British and American plenipotentiaries.'[16] It was frustrating to leave diplomacy to the politicians. Toynbee then roped in a fellow Balliol man only three years older than he, but permanent Foreign Office: Harold Nicholson (1886–1968), whose published diaries would one day make him almost famous. They were in complete agreement that the terms of the treaty as regards the Ottomans were impossible to implement, especially the notion of giving the United States the League of Nations mandates for an independent Armenia and for Istanbul. All they could do was to fire off another official minute, this one entitled 'Future Frontiers of Turkey':

> Having carefully considered the above objections in all their bearings, we question whether peace would not in the end be better served by some less elaborate, if more drastic idea, that is, by cleaving Europe from Asia, and by giving Greece Constantinople and the European shores of the Straits and Sea of Marmora, and by leaving Turkey in Anatolia and on the southern and eastern side of the water.[17]

In retrospect, this was probably not such a very good idea, but no one was listening anyway. Nicolson made a note in his diary regarding the fate of what he called 'Toynbee's scheme': 'We put this down on paper; we sign it with our names; we send it in. It will not be considered.'[18]

Confident of his abilities as he was, even Arnold Toynbee realized by November 1918 that his days at the Foreign Office were numbered, not least because the war was over. Having foolishly resigned his Balliol fellowship in December 1915, however, there was no reason to go back to Oxford.[19] As luck would have it, just at the right moment a position came open. In July 1918, a new chair at the University of London was announced, dedicated to Byzantine and Modern Greek History. The endowment was contributed by the Greek diaspora in London, and it was expected that the successful candidate would be sympathetic to the Greek struggle against the Turks. Toynbee understood the politics, but his experience in the Foreign Office led him to take a much more even-handed approach. Indeed, he was already well on the way to Turkophilia, and made it clear to the appointments committee that in any case he did not see his brief as extending all the way to modern Greek literature. But

Toynbee was, after all, the author and editor of the famous compilation of Turkish enormities against the Armenians, and in due course a letter of appointment was issued for him as Koraes Professor of Modern Greek and Byzantine History, Language and Literature at King's College London. His appointment was for five years, renewable to retirement—that is to say, like his casually discarded Balliol position, essentially a job for life.[20]

The unwritten premise of Toynbee's appointment was that he would use the chair to promote Greek interests, just as he had done during the war by writing anti-Turkish propaganda. What the Greek philanthropists never understood, however, was that Toynbee never thought himself to be the slavish tool of political masters, churning out academic fluff on demand. His own view of the situation in Anatolia was rather more complicated, and his Foreign Office publications told only half the story. It is not much of an exaggeration to say that Toynbee spent the rest of his working life telling the other half.

In any case, Arnold Toynbee was no longer quite the same self-enclosed Balliol classicist that he had been before the war. During the summer of 1920, his wartime comrade-in-pens, the historian Lewis Namier, lent him a copy of *Der Untergang des Abendlandes*, the renowned study by Oswald Spengler (1880–1936) on the decline of the West, the first volume of which was published in 1918, as World War I dragged on to a close. Toynbee read German easily, and Spengler's analysis of world history and its civilizations made a deep impression.[21]

Another source of inspiration for Toynbee in 1920 was the work of Frederick J. Teggart (1870–1946), an Irishman who taught at Berkeley.[22] Teggart described his goal as trying 'to do for human history what biologists are engaged in doing for the history of the forms of life'. Indeed, he explained, 'the analytical study of history must be founded upon a comparison of the particular histories of all human groups', including non-Western civilizations. The 'human achievement is the outcome of the commingling of ideas through the contact of different groups' so that this connection may lead to 'the mental release of the members of a group or of a single individual from the authority of an established system of ideas'.[23]

Teggart in California and Spengler in Munich were both macrohistorians, looking at the progress of humankind through the largest possible lens, but each with a vision clouded by temperament. The optimistic Irish-American saw contact between strangers as a good thing, and as the impetus to wide-reaching change. The dour German, however, thought that civilizations were and ought to be separate. When civilizations collide and mix ideas, it is a symptom not of progress but of degeneration, and the end is nigh. Toynbee suspected that there might be some kind of cosmic truth in the writings of Spengler and Teggart which might explain both the similarities between ancient and modern civilizations, and the collision of East and West.[24] What that was as yet eluded him, and even if he was only thirty-one years old, he was troubled by it.

II

'The revolution of 1908 in Turkey had caught my attention at the time,' Toynbee remembered years later, 'and it had appealed to my imagination. In fact, it was the event that had led me to take an interest in current international affairs.'[25] There was a lot going on in Turkey to interest Toynbee.[26] The Armistice of Mudros (30 October 1918) signed by Turkey and the Allies, which signified the defeat of the Ottoman Empire in World War I, included as Article 7 the provision that the 'Allies have the right to occupy any strategic points in the event of any strategic situation arising that threatens the security of the Allies'.[27] The Ottoman authorities were duly informed that Allied troops were to be landed in Smyrna, and an Allied naval squadron left Istanbul under the command of the British High Commissioner, Admiral Sir Somerset Arthur Gough-Calthorpe (1865–1937). At the same time, the Allied control officers in Smyrna began to disarm the Turkish troops still in the city, in accordance with Articles 5 and 20 of the Armistice. At some point during this process, word got out that these so-called Allied troops to be landed in Smyrna were in fact Greeks.[28]

In the evening of 14 May 1919, an Allied plan had been agreed upon providing for the orderly disembarkation of the Greek troops, according to which they would land at opposite ends of the city and march around the outskirts to the middle of Smyrna, and enter together from the land side. Instead, the next day (15 May 1919), the Greeks landed smack in the middle of Smyrna and disembarked at the quay. They were rapturously greeted as liberators by the local Greek population, led by their Metropolitan Bishop. Orthodox prayers and traditional dances followed as the Greek troops marched along the quay to the Konak (government house), behind which were the Turkish barracks. When the Greek and Turkish soldiers were separated by only a hundred yards, someone fired a shot. The Greek soldiers panicked and fired into the crowd, killing a number of Turks and many others, and then took into custody the surviving Turkish troops. The British forces were under orders to give the Greeks a free hand, and merely observed the riot from their docked ships. Over the next two days, about two hundred Turks were murdered by Greek troops and armed civilians.[29] Furthermore, although the Allies had allowed for a Greek occupation of Smyrna, they neglected to define its area. The Greeks saw the opportunity to extend their territory into Anatolia, in a misguided application of the 'Megali Idea' of restoring the glories of the Byzantine Empire which had perished four and a half centuries earlier. The result was the Turkish War of Independence, and the beginning of the struggle that finally put the toothpaste back in the tube by driving the Greeks out of Anatolia via the same port of Smyrna in September 1922.

These were fateful times, and the significance of these events was not lost on Arnold Toynbee, sometime Ottoman expert at the Foreign Office. His duties as Koraes Professor of Modern Greek and Byzantine History, Language and Literature at King's College London allowed him plenty of free time to write numerous articles on what was happening in Anatolia, and to get them published in the leading journals for contemporary affairs. Stand-up teaching was never Toynbee's idea of a full life, certainly not after his wartime experience when he had had a clear view of the top table. In the summer of 1920, he applied for a sabbatical in order to see 'how Greece is handling her Moslem minority' in the newly conquered areas.[30] The University Senate granted him two terms' paid leave to travel to Greece, specifically in order to forge contacts 'with Professors, officials and publishers in order to strengthen the bonds between Greece and the Department of Modern Greek in the College'.[31] For Toynbee, however, this was not enough, and thanks to the patronage of C.P. Scott (1846–1932), the legendary proprietor of the *Manchester Guardian*, Toynbee found a way to increase his income, as he explains:

> Mr. Scott had commissioned me to serve, during my stay in the Levant, as the *Guardian*'s special correspondent. This commission had a double value for me; it was going to help finance my expedition to the Levant and it also promised to help me get an inside view of what was happening there. People would be readier to talk to the representative of a famous newspaper than they would have been to pay attention to a young don if he had been representing no one but himself.[32]

Better still, Toynbee made a deal with Scott to be paid £10 per week for travel, and 4 guineas per column for letters and telegrams. With that money, plus his regular salary from the University of London, Toynbee was even able to bring along his wife Rosalind, who was with him for much of the time.[33]

Fifty years later, Toynbee explained that he had been so horrified by his work on the Armenian Blue Book that he began to see the events in terms of 'the reality of Original Sin'. Rather than remaining content with the image of the brutal and dehumanized Turks that he himself had helped to exacerbate, even before the Great War was over, Toynbee resolved to learn Turkish so as to 'get to know live Turkish men and women individually'. 'So, as soon as I had a don's margin of leisure once again in the Koraïs Chair at the University of London,' Toynbee recalled, 'I enrolled myself as a student of Turkish at the London School of Oriental and African Studies.' His teacher in the language was Ali Riza Bey (1876–1945), the first lecturer in Turkish at SOAS, and head of the Turkish section of the BBC during the Second World War.[34] When Ali Riza learned that Professor Toynbee intended on being his pupil, he marched into the office of the Director of SOAS and protested against the presence of a man who had been so demonstrably hateful to Turkey only a few years before. Sir Denison Ross, the Director, prevailed upon Ali Riza to accept Toynbee, who claimed that 'this brought me my first Turkish friend', their 'work together resulting in a lasting friendship'.[35]

Toynbee left London on 7 January 1921, and went first to Greece, keenly interested in the new government of the restored King Constantine I (r. 1913–1917, 1920–1922), and interviewing the prime minister. He then proceeded to Smyrna, travelling as a guest of the Greek military. Toynbee liked the Greek officers, he wrote to his mother, but ultimately they were still 'dagos' for him, and he gradually warmed to the enemy: 'I am, of course,' he confessed, 'charmed, as everybody is, by the Turks.'[36]

Arnold Toynbee disembarked in Smyrna on 27 January 1921, and immediately set to work.[37] 'Of necessity,' he explained,

I had travelled under official auspices and was shown things from the official standpoint. I should also add that I have not had first-hand experience of the Turkish Nationalist administration. At the time when I was at Constantinople, Turkish resentment against the British Government's policy was so intense that it was impossible for a British subject to get a visa for travelling in Nationalist territory, and most of my information about conditions in the interior is derived from American relief-workers, missionaries, business-men, and journalists who were travelling freely between Constantinople and Angora by several routes from different Black Sea ports, and who thus saw between them a considerable part of the country.[38]

By March, Toynbee had made three forays into Anatolia to see for himself how the Greeks were dealing with the temptations of invasion and occupation.[39]

Not only were these very exciting times, but Toynbee himself was rather prone to excitement. He paid a visit to Ephesus on 11 February 1921, escorted by two Greek gendarmes, and a strange thing happened while espying the impressive theatre there from above:

> At the instant at which this historic panorama impinged on the spectator's eyes, the empty theatre peopled itself with a tumultuous throng as the breath came into the dead and they lived and stood upon their feet...These two dishevelled figures must be Gaius and Aristarchus; that ineffectual-looking creature must be Alexander. What is this rhythmic roar into which the babel of tongues is resolving itself? Will Gaius and Aristarchus escape with their lives? Thank Heaven for the intrepid town clerk's promptness and presence of mind. But at the moment when the cries of 'Great is Diana' are dying down and the clerk is beginning to reason tactfully with the crowd, the life flickers out of the scene as the spectator is carried up again instantaneously to the current surface of the Time-stream from an abyss, nineteen centuries deep into which the impact of the sight of the theatre at Ephesus had plunged him.[40]

Toynbee was prone throughout his life to such mystical experiences, 'a larger and a stranger' one occurring near Victoria Station, which he described years later in these words: 'the writer, once, one afternoon not long after the end of the First World War—he had failed to record the exact date—had found himself in communion, not just with this or that episode in History, but with all that had been, and was, and was to come. In that instant he was directly aware of the passage of History gently flowing through him in a mighty current, and of his own life welling like a wave in the flow of this vast tide.'[41] Whatever happened more strongly at Victoria Station first happened in Turkey, at Ephesus.

On 17 March 1921, Arnold Toynbee arrived in Istanbul. It was just in time. The following week, on 23 March 1921, the Greeks celebrated the beginning of springtime and better weather by launching a new offensive. By 30 March 1921 they had taken Afyonkarahisar and Eskişehir. The next day, however, İsmet Paşa (1884–1973) launched a counter-attack and within a week the Greeks had been driven out of both towns, even though they managed to strengthen their front line at a position to the west, at what would become much later in the war the fateful site of Dumlupınar. Although the

Greeks had only been stopped, not defeated, this important campaign went down in (Turkish) military lore as the Second Battle of İnönü.

For Toynbee, this was history in the making. In an article entitled 'The Battle of In Önu', written at Bursa on 5 April 1921, he described in stirring narrative and analysis what he had seen while travelling around the outskirts of the conflict. As always, Toynbee also looked for the deeper, even metaphysical, meaning of current events: 'that smoke rising above the hill to our left front as we dipped into the ravine was symbolic too,' he insisted:

> It marked the site of Söyüd, the first Anatolian village possessed by the ancestor of the Ottoman Dynasty, and now the Osmalis were fighting for their natural existence on the very spot where that existence had begun. Ertoghrul, the father of Osman, coming through the defile from the south, had founded an empire which in two centuries spread north-westward to the Danube. To-day, along that line of hills through which the defile made its way, the Greeks were fighting for a lodgment to the south-east which might eventually give them the empire of all Anatolia.[42]

Toynbee would always remain convinced that the Second Battle of İnönü 'proved to have been a turning-point in the Graeco-Turkish war of 1919–22'.[43]

The main problem Toynbee faced in Turkey was that he was already widely known as a British government apologist for the Armenians, a professor of Greek studies, and a protégé of the invaders. 'Worst of all,' Toynbee says,

> I was the representative of that Gladstonian English newspaper the *Manchester Guardian*. I had a number of unprofitable interviews with the director of the Istanbul Red Crescent, Hâmid Bey [Hasancan (1870–1943)] … One day, Hâmid Bey suddenly challenged me to board, that very evening, a Red Crescent ship that was going to Yalova, on the Marmara coast of Anatolia, to evacuate Turkish refugees. Yalova was under Greek military occupation, and there had been a massacre of the local Turkish population by local Greeks and Armenians.[44]

Arnold and Rosalind Toynbee landed at Yalova in the early afternoon of 24 May 1921. In many respects, the work they did there together on that day, and during the following few weeks, was Toynbee's most important contribution to humankind.

Toynbee worked out only much later what the Greeks were trying to accomplish by the wholesale massacre of Turkish civilians on the shore of the Sea of Marmara and inland. Yalova sits on the north shore of a peninsula that juts out into Sea of Marmara, the end of which is due south of Istanbul, even a little to the west. Having failed to make significant headway against the Turks earlier in the year, the Greeks made the decision to abandon the entire Yalova Peninsula and concentrate on the thrust towards Ankara. In order to ensure that their planned withdrawal would not be perceived as a sign of weakness, or perhaps simply out of revenge and cruelty, the Greek forces encouraged local bands of irregular fighters—*çetes*, as they are sometimes called—to rape and pillage the Muslim Turkish civilians left behind. By the time the Toynbees disembarked in the Yalova area, fourteen of the sixteen Turkish villages had been destroyed, and of the 7,000 Muslims who lived there before the hostilities, only 1,500 had survived.

Arnold Toynbee behaved exactly like a young Englishman of his class, born if not to wealth, then to the notion that he belonged to a privileged group of superior beings whose natural (if sometimes reluctant) task it was to lead and to rule, imposing British values on benighted natives. Toynbee dashed from ship to shore, remonstrating with the local Greek officers, making lists of terrified Turkish women, children and old men who wished to escape with their lives to Istanbul, leaping into the breach to unite families and pluck potential victims from the deadly grasp of the occupying power. In large part because of Toynbee's efforts, and the local Greek understanding that their entire enterprise depended on British military and political support, hundreds of lives were saved that day and the ones following. The Red Crescent evacuated 320 Turkish civilians, ferrying them across the short distance from Yalova to Istanbul.

Over the next fortnight, Arnold and Rosalind Toynbee accompanied two more Red Crescent ships as they evacuated Turkish refugees from the Sea of Marmara shore. Not only did Arnold write a full account of what happened for the *Manchester Guardian*, but Rosalind sent a detailed letter to her mother, the influential Countess of Carlisle, asking her to circulate it to anyone who might be able to help.[45]

Toynbee's next problem was to convince his readers to believe this narrative of events, but to do so, he first had to persuade his editor, the inestimable C.P. Scott, to publish his piece at all. Toynbee's fears notwithstanding, his employer backed him up, and more:

Some influential readers...now wrote (so I learnt later) to Mr. Scott, charging him with betraying their principles and his own in publishing dispatches that were sympathetic to 'the unspeakable Turk'; but these critics received an uncompromising answer. Mr. Scott told them that he had confidence in his correspondent; that he believed that he was reporting the truth; and that he was therefore going to continue to publish his correspondent's reports. Mr. Scott was as good as his word. He supported me in my reporting of facts that were unwelcome news, not only in British Liberal circles, but in the Western World as a whole, in which the traditional 'Christian' prejudice against Muslims had survived in many minds that had repudiated Christianity itself.[46]

Toynbee rightly took pride, he said, that 'I had been the only newspaper correspondent present, and my telegram to the *Guardian* was the first news of the battle to be published in any European or American newspaper'.[47]

So too was the Director of the Red Crescent in Istanbul impressed with Toynbee's achievement:

Hâmid Bey was surprised when I jumped at this opportunity of seeing things from the Turkish side; he was more surprised when, after returning to Istanbul, I showed him the text of the telegram, reporting what I had seen, that I had sent to the *Manchester Guardian*; he was most surprised of all when he received a copy of the issue of the *Guardian* in which my dispatch was printed. I can still see the scene in the Red Crescent's office: big Hâmid Bey with the English newspaper in his hands, and his colleagues crowding round, with radiant faces. Their case was being put in Britain at last.[48]

After Yalova, it was impossible to paint Toynbee as a pro-Greek propagandist in the pay and pocket of powerful supporters.

This was just as well, for the war was hotting up once more. On 9 June 1921, a Greek warship bombed the Black Sea port of İnebolu, the closest harbour to the Nationalists' HQ at Ankara. Between 25 and 30 June 1921, Greek forces finally withdrew from the Yalova Peninsula, having prepared the way, as we have seen, by widespread violence and the massacre of the Muslim Turkish population.

Yet again, Arnold and Rosalind Toynbee were there. 'On the 29th June 1921,' he solemnly reported, 'my wife and I personally witnessed Greek troops in uniform committing arson without provocation along the south coast of the Gulf of Ismid.' As at Yalova, Toynbee did not stop with outrage; he compiled lists of victims and criminals. Turkish villagers 'gave me the following names of chetté band leaders from Greek villages,' he recorded, and produced a list of the tormenters. These eye-witness reports, Toynbee testified, 'confirmed what we had seen for ourselves, that there had been no fighting during the retreat, and that the Turkish towns and villages had been burnt in cold blood, without provocation.' Furthermore, he thought, in 'these deportations, the Greek authorities adhered to their policy of striking at the Turkish upper class. No doubt they hoped to establish their ascendancy more rapidly over the peasantry if their natural leaders were bodily removed.' Toynbee was convinced that the Greek authorities 'were able to stop this sport at any moment if they chose to do so'.[49]

On 14 August 1921, the Greek army was on the march again, objective Ankara, in what would be their last offensive operation in Anatolia. 'Jaded by an unprofitable victory,' Toynbee wrote,

and with no further military prospect of terminating the war, the Greeks pushed forward through the northern gap towards the boundless hinterland of Central and Eastern Anatolia. It was a crazy enterprise, for every rational objective had disappeared. The annihilation of the enemy? Three times already that stroke had missed its aim. The occupation of his temporary capital? As if the loss of Angora would break a Turkish *moral* which had survived the loss of Constantinople, or would prevent the Great National Assembly from resuming its activities at Sivas or Kaisaria.[50]

The Turkish victory at the Battle of the Sakarya (23 August–13 September 1921) came at a deadly cost for both sides. The Greeks were now back at their starting position before the summer campaign, at Eskişehir, and at Afyonkarahisar. They would hold this line for nearly another year before their ignominious flight from Smyrna, but the Greek invasion of Turkey was permanently stalled, and the Nationalists looked well-placed to inherit the peace after the Ottomans had lost the war.

Arnold Toynbee was still in Turkey while all this was going on, arriving in Constantinople itself on 9 September 1921, and staying a week. It was clear to him and to everyone else that the next stage after Sakarya would be somewhat drawn out, as the Turks used their military victory to obtain diplomatic concessions. On 16 September 1921, Toynbee boarded the Orient Express from Sirkeci Station in the heart of Constantinople, to begin the long journey back to London.[51]

III

After eight months in Istanbul and environs, Arnold Toynbee had a lot to think about, and three clear days in which to do so. As it happened, it was a journey that changed Toynbee's life, since during its course he had the idea of writing *A Study of History*, the project that would occupy him over the next four decades and make him famous. Toynbee recalled years later how it happened:

> How did the plan of *A Study of History* take shape? The gist of it must have been in my mind by 1920, because I made my first deliberate attempt at writing it that summer. The first essay came to nothing...My second shot at planning the book was made on the 17th September, 1921, in the train between Adrianople and Nish, and this time I succeeded; for, by the end of that day, I had written down, on half a sheet of paper, a list of about a dozen headings; and these headings stand, with very little change, as the titles of the thirteen parts of the book, now published in ten volumes. This time I had not deliberately set myself to make the plan. I had spent the day looking out of the railway carriage window, and the plan that I had jotted down at the end of the day had seemed to come of itself[52]

It would be very satisfying to find that 'half a sheet of paper', but sadly the document seems not to have survived. There is something similar preserved at the Nihon University Library in Japan, but it is a twelve-page outline with many changes, written by Toynbee and headed at the top of the first page, 'Drafted in Orient Express, September 1921'. This heading, however, is not contemporary, but was added by Toynbee in 1971 when the document went on display at an exhibition in his honour. In any case, there are nine headings listed (not 'about a dozen'), none of which exactly matches the thirteen major divisions of *A Study of History*. Indeed, this document hardly resembles the finished work at all.

Yet, in spite of what has been said, there is one clause in the document, perhaps a quarter of a page out of the twelve, that seems to have some connection to the later books. A clause labelled '(iii) Comparison of Civilisations' deals with the stages of civilization, the concept that became Toynbee's stock-in-trade. In this Japanese document, he jots down the stations of birth, differentiation, expansion, breakdown, empire, universal religion, and interregnum—points of reference very similar indeed to the ideas developed over twelve volumes in *A Study of History*. In other words, Toynbee's story about the 'half a sheet of paper' stands, but only just.[53]

From the point of view of his personal development, Toynbee's experiences in Turkey provided him with the insight and the emotional depth to take in the notion of a rise and fall of civilizations. With his 'half a sheet of paper', his massive tomes were just beginning to take shape; for the genealogist of ideas, *A Study in History* itself becomes a mere epilogue. Yet there is another way of looking at Toynbee's legacy, especially in light of the tremendous chorus of derision that washed over Toynbee's *Study* almost at the appearance of the first volumes, becoming deafening after the Second World War, and drowning out nearly all other possible voices by the beginning of the twenty-first century. Intellectual that he was, Arnold Toynbee was unable to leave his impressions of Turkey at the level of mere action and the rescue of hundreds of living people. Nor was he willing to entrust his observations to the crumbling newsprint pages of the popular press. He had to have a book, and in many respects it was his greatest book, and the one that has been least remembered.[54]

On 22 March 1922, Arnold Toynbee completed the preface to the first edition of *The Western Question in Greece and Turkey: A Study in the Contact of Civilisations*. Apart from reprinting his *Guardian* pieces, Toynbee also confronted the deeper issues of the conflict between Greece and Turkey, prefiguring his later writing on the nature of civilizations. 'The shadow upon the rest of humanity is cast by Western civilisation,' Toynbee wrote, 'but it is difficult for either party to comprehend the whole situation.' Indeed, he thought, whenever 'one analyses a contemporary movement—political, economic, religious, or intellectual—in these societies, it nearly always turns out to be either a response to or a reaction against some Western stimulus'. Taking the long view, Toynbee saw during his time in Turkey 'the break-down of Middle Eastern civilisation' built on the ruins of ancient Egypt and Mesopotamia, and the crash of Near Eastern civilization, which grew up from the ruins of the ancient Hellenic, Greek-Roman civilization in Anatolia and Constantinople, each manifesting 'universal religions', Islam and Orthodox Christianity respectively.[55] Both of these great civilizations had been forced by international politics to organize themselves artificially along national lines, as Western states had done, and were now in the process of dissolution, owing to the superior power and attraction of the West, being demoralized by their inability to master the alien Western civilization to which they aspired. Therefore, the so-called 'Eastern Question' which had bedeviled international diplomacy since the late eighteenth century, is in reality a 'Western Question', the result of encounters among three different civilizations, and the disastrous subsequent breakdown of the two weaker Middle Eastern (Turkish) and Near Eastern (Greek) partners in the face of the West (Europe).

In the West, an idea grew up that a state should be constructed around speakers of a single vernacular, countries like Belgium and Switzerland surviving only as a result of European sanity and their own political moderation. But this method of political division was not of universal application: only in the West does this kind of linguistic division work. 'The introduction of the Western formula among these people has therefore resulted in massacre.' The war between the Greeks and the Turks, 'perhaps the first movement in this region produced by a conscious application of the Western national idea, occasioned massacres of Turks throughout the Morea and of Greeks at Aivali and in Khios'. Indeed, Toynbee wrote, 'Conflicts between civilisations are terrible, because civilisations are the most real and fundamental forms of human society.'[56]

Anyone who has read Toynbee's *A Study in History*, even in the abridged two-volume edition, or heard anything about his views, will recognize in this the first chapter of *The Western Question*, much more than the germ of his later, more mature, philosophy of history.[57] The notion of civilizations as the basic units of society; words like 'response', 'reaction', 'stimulus', 'universal religions'; these were the concepts that Toynbee manipulated unceasingly in a vain attempt to adjust his grotesquely complicated theory of history to all places at all times. That Toynbeeism was conceived against the backdrop of the Turkish War of Independence has never been recognized.

When Toynbee contemplated the events that he had witnessed, he took a very long view. 'The breakdown of Near and of Middle Eastern civilisation,' he insisted, 'the introduction of the Western idea of political nationality, the traditional rivalries of the Powers and the attraction of Greece and Turkey into the vicious circle, remote though they may have seemed, are the necessary prologue to the Anatolian drama.' If you looked at Anatolia, he pointed out, the idea of Greeks and Turks at polar extremes is rather unhistorical. 'This process of Turcification in East-Central Anatolia is one of the puzzles of history,' he thought. 'The mediaeval Greek population was not exterminated by the Saljuqs but converted. As they had once turned from Hittites and Phrygians into Greeks, so they turned again from Greeks into Turks, under the influence of a few nomad intruders.' Unlike, say, Anglo-Saxon culture which absorbed the Norman invaders, 'Near Eastern civilisation here, in spite of an imposing exterior, must have become a hollow crust which broke under the nomads' horse-hoofs.'[58]

The tragedies that accompanied the recent war between the Greeks and the Turks were beset by prejudices and propaganda, and Toynbee did not deny that he had been part of that machine during the First World War.[59] But, he pointed out,

> Persecuted minorities are not necessarily blameless because they suffer…the accusations of sedition brought against them by their persecutors are often partly true, though they are generally stultified by the disproportionate savagery of the repression.[60]

That being said, Toynbee thought,

> Greeks and Turks will not learn to treat each other as equals so long as the Western public, by vulgar insults and hardly less vulgar applause, encourages them to strut like fighting-cocks and stimulates all their feelings of hatred and scorn. Western sentiment about the Greeks and Turks is for the most part ill-informed, violently expressed and dangerously influential.[61]

Worst of all, this sentiment was not evenly balanced: 'Among the Western public,' Toynbee noticed,

> the names 'Greek' and 'Turk' are chiefly familiar as pegs on which people hang false antitheses—always to the Turks' disadvantage…the three false antitheses of Christianity and Islam, Europe and Asia, civilisation and barbarism. These are so deeply rooted in Western minds and so unfortunate in their effect upon the minds of Near and Middle Easterners that, at the risk of pedantry, I shall attempt to confute them.[62]

Pedantry was never a temptation that Toynbee could resist, and off he went, beginning with 'the last phase of the Ancient Hellenic or Graeco-Roman society'.

Much of what Toynbee writes is well-known to anyone who has taken an introductory course on the history of the Byzantine Empire, or the history and geography of the Middle East. Here too there is much that foreshadows his later more fully expressed opinions, such as his vocal support for Islam:

> The unconscious grievance of the West against Islam is not that Islam is incompatible with progress of any kind, for we are practically indifferent to progress or stagnation on Islamic lines. We really resent the fact that

Islam offers an alternative system of life to our own. Rightly or wrongly, we consider this alternative inferior, and we feel that if only it were not held before them, the peoples that at present cling to it might have caught us up at one stride and entered into full possession of the best that we have to offer them.[63]

If there was any single nail in the coffin of Toynbee's later public image, it was his BBC Reith Lectures of 1952, especially the second one, entitled 'Islam and the West', which developed this pro-Muslim theme before a bewildered and unsympathetic English audience.[64]

But what really riled Toynbee was the false antithesis between 'Europe' and 'Asia'. Not only was the entire notion of continents a geographer's fiction, but the Ottoman Empire itself 'found its destiny on the continent of Europe', and 'its transference to Anatolia was only faced by the Turkish nation after the Balkan War, and was not avowed till Mustafa Kemal Pasha summoned the Great National Assembly to Angora in 1920'. In fact, Toynbee insisted (as he would do throughout his life), the 'real entities of human geography' are civilizations: '"Europe" is, of course, a confusion between the fictitious continent and reality of Western civilisation. "Western" is what people mean when they talk of "European" in this connection.' This confusion has been especially pernicious in the Turkish context:

If the Allied states were right, and being 'radically alien to Western civilisation' is a valid reason for 'the expulsion from Europe of the Ottoman Empire,' many other non-Western European states, beginning with Greece herself, will have to pack their bags and remove their baggage. But 'Europe for Westerners only' is a monstrous and a most impolitic claim, for, if titles go by continents, what standing have we Westerners who have colonised the four quarters of the world, to our holdings in America, Africa, and Australia?

Indeed, Toynbee wrote, '"Europe" and "Asia" are conventions which are only possible on a small-scale two-colour map. The scientific physical geographer knows of no barrier between the two continents.'[65]

If Toynbee had learned one thing from his time at the Foreign Office, it was that politicians rarely listened to experts, unless it was for confirmation of a view already held. Yet Toynbee still hoped to make a difference, and he was most troubled by the Turkish predicament. 'The Turks are aware of the prejudice against them that exists in Western minds,' he wrote,

and are inclined to despair of the possibility of overcoming it...We have injured the Turks most by making them hopeless and embittered. Our scepticism has been so profound and our contempt so vehement, that they have almost ceased to regard it as possible to modify them by their own action.[66]

Toynbee's purpose in writing his study of *The Western Question in Greece and Turkey* was to try to change people's minds.

IV

The first edition of Toynbee's book appeared in early summer 1922; the preface to the second edition is dated 20 November 1922, the day the Lausanne Conference opened to make a final determination of Turkey's immediate future. Much had happened since Toynbee had returned home to London in September of the previous year. The Greek army had been utterly defeated, and driven from the coast of Anatolia by way of Smyrna, from whence it came. Mustafa Kemal entered the city on 10 September 1922, and the Greek invasion was over.

But Toynbee was back in London now, facing the Greek music.[67] He knew all along that his articles would get him into trouble, and having already resigned from a job for life at Balliol, in retrospect it certainly looks as if Toynbee had some kind of academic death-wish in regard to teaching posts. On 22 November 1921, exactly two months after returning to London from Constantinople, he gave a lecture at Chatham House which he had specifically arranged 'in order that I might have an opportunity of describing my experiences to the members of the Institute and of putting before them the case for the Turks'. Toynbee's task was not made any easier by a uncompromisingly pro-Greek introduction from the chairman of the meeting, the eminent archaeologist of Crete, Sir Arthur Evans (1851–1941).[68]

As if writing and speaking in public defending the Turks were not enough, Toynbee even tried to be an honest broker between the British government and the Turks. When Mustafa Kemal's representative (Ali) Fethi (Okyar) (1880–1943) came to London in August 1922, before the final Turkish military push, no one would see him, not Lloyd George, nor Foreign Secretary Lord Curzon (1859–1925):

At this critical moment, H.M.G. were inexcusably blind. Either their military intelligence was at fault, or they themselves were guilty of ignoring it. If they had appreciated the realities of the military situation in Anatolia at this date, they would have jumped at the chance, which the Turks were now offering to them, of negotiating for peace while the Greek armies, whose *moral* had already sunk low, were still physically intact.

As Toynbee saw himself to be 'one of a rather small number of people in Britain who were in sympathy with the Turkish nationalist movement', he and his wife invited Fethi Bey and his colleagues round to his flat to meet Conservative rebel Samuel Hoare (1880–1959) and T.E. Lawrence 'of Arabia' (1888–1935). Not much came of it, but it was the highest level meeting that the Turkish delegation had obtained.[69]

It was not as if Toynbee was unaware of the precariousness of his academic situation. In the preface to the second edition of *The Western Question*, he recognized that despite the fact that he held a chair endowed by the Greek diaspora,

> The actual circumstances, whatever personal unpleasantness they may entail for me and my Greek friends and acquaintances, at least preclude the suspicion that an endowment of learning in a British University has been used for propaganda on behalf of the country with which it is concerned. Such a contention, if it could be urged, would be serious; for academic study should have no political purpose, although, when its subject is history, its judgments upon the nature and causal connection of past events do occasionally and incidentally have some effect upon the present and the future.[70]

Indeed, already in May 1921, by the same Constantinople post that contained his first *Guardian* articles, Toynbee sent a letter to Ernest Barker (1874–1960), the Principal of King's College London, offering to resign his chair. Toynbee made the same suggestion in another letter to Barker the following year, on 6 May 1922. Not only did Barker refuse, but he helped Toynbee revise the preface to *The Western Question*. The first edition appeared in the early summer of 1922, just before the Greeks met total defeat in Anatolia, culminating in the burning of Smyrna. The Greeks of London were not amused, even less so after a second edition was published early in 1923, just as the exchange of populations was being organized, involving the destruction of communities centuries-old on both sides of the Greek-Turkish border.[71]

Principal Barker at first supported Toynbee, writing to him on 31 January 1923 that

> you can count on me absolutely to do whatever I can to maintain the freedom of teaching—a thing I value above most things, but which seems to me

to have been entirely sacrificed at the time of the foundation of the Chair which you hold. The position in which you and I consequently find ourselves is to me simply tragic[72]

Things rapidly became rather ugly, and the Greeks who made up the Subscribers' Committee held their first meeting of many on 24 January 1923, reviving a body which had never sat since Toynbee took up his position.[73] They and their supporters in the College, which included some other professors who held similar chairs supported by particular interest groups, attacked Toynbee not only for taking a public stance seemingly at odds with the purpose for which the chair had been endowed, but also for general incompetence. While no one doubted that Arnold Toynbee was a young man of great ability, it was clear that his heart was not in teaching, and his lectures sometimes attracted only two students. Even his devoted mother, with whom Toynbee maintained a frequent and lively correspondence throughout her life, wrote to tell him that for 'a long time now I have felt very strongly that the post was an impossible one for anyone, and most of all so for you with your strong Turkish sympathies'. His mother thought that the subscribers were probably right to think of him as less than an impartial observer, and she herself declared that 'I will not promise not to think that you may be a little obsessed with your Turks.'[74]

There is no doubt that Toynbee was more than a little obsessed, and as if to show it, just at the moment that his fate was being decided by the Greek Subscribers' Committee, Toynbee chose to take up a mini-assignment from his old friend C.P. Scott at the *Manchester Guardian* and go out to Turkey yet again in April 1923 to interview Mustafa Kemal at Ankara. Like so many others, Toynbee was very powerfully impressed by Mustafa Kemal. Toynbee wrote to his wife on 13 April 1923 that Kemal was 'undoubtedly a great man'. Indeed, Toynbee thought, 'You would swear that he was an Austrian or a German. He is sympathetic but not amiable ... a little like a leopard preparing to spring.'[75] Over forty years later, Toynbee still recalled 'the evening in the spring of 1923 on which I was Atatürk's guest for dinner at Ankara.' Toynbee had made a very general point about inter-personal relations which did not go down well:

When Atatürk disagreed with what someone had said, he intimidated the other person visually, before opening his mouth, with a frown that brought the whole of his forehead down, like a thunder-cloud, upon his brows; and I was confronted by this lowering face while he was telling me that I was entirely wrong.[76]

By now, Toynbee was so convinced of the importance of good relations between Great Britain and the Turkish Nationalists, that he was no longer willing to pay even lip service to Greek grievances. Furthermore, he was sure more than ever that British foreign policy gave insufficient attention to the needs of rising Muslim nationalism, as he wrote to his wife from Turkey: 'I have been seeing Afghans and Indians here as well as Turks, and there is no doubt that they are getting up momentum (momentum of will power to be our equals) and that the whole brunt is going to fall on the British Empire.'[77] This was all vintage *Manchester Guardian* Toynbee, but it was salt in Greek wounds.

Eventually, returning to London, even Toynbee saw that his position was untenable, and on 6 November 1923, he wrote to Principal Barker, confirming his offer to resign from the Koraes Chair, reserving his right to make a public statement explaining why he was going.[78] This he did, in the most public fashion possible, by sending a letter to the *Times*, which was duly printed on 3 January 1924.

Much of Toynbee's letter is concerned with the minutiae of his relations with the Chair's Subscribers' Committee, but he begins by taking the high moral ground:

> In the course of a visit to the Near East in 1921 I felt it my duty to comment publicly in a strongly unfavourable sense upon the conduct of the Greek authorities in the territories then occupied by Greece in Asia Minor; and since then I have taken every opportunity to study Graeco-Turkish relations from both sides and have given free public expression to my opinions as the situation has developed. This freedom I believe to be my right as a Professor in a British University; and personally I should not be willing to hold an academic Chair under other conditions. It was obvious, however, that in the present case such action, though taken on my own responsibility, might affect the interests of the College and University, and therefore, by the same mail by which I dispatched from Constantinople my first articles to the English Press which were unfavourable to Greece, I wrote to Dr Barker, the Principal of King's College, explaining what had happened and what action I was taking, and informing him that I should be ready thenceforth to resign at any time if the situation became too embarrassing for the College and the University.

Toynbee included along with his letter a testimonial written by Principal Barker eight days before, and printed in the *Times* with the writer's permission.[79]

As far as the general public was concerned, Toynbee came out ahead in this dispute with the local Greeks.[80] Most of the English press was with him, especially the prestigious *The Nation and Athenaeum* which on 12 January 1924 published a strongly worded leader about the injustice done to this 'historian and scholar of unusual brilliance'. The fact that it was written anonymously by Toynbee's father-in-law Professor Gilbert Murray was surely an irrelevance.[81] A number of Toynbee's colleagues, however, were against him, worried that in going in the face of his donors he put other chairs and projects in danger, for his actions might have a ripple effect throughout the university. R.W. Seton-Watson (1879–1951), for example, was the Masaryk Professor of Central European History, and it was the Czech government that paid half of the endowment, promising to pay for the entire chair for the 1924–1925 academic year.[82] Seton-Watson even wrote to Professor Murray, outraged that his son-in-law's behaviour was 'altogether scandalous and unjustifiable ... at the supreme crisis in the fate of the Greek nation—perhaps without exaggeration the most decisive since Xerxes ... [he had] plunged into a violent propagandist campaign in favour of the Turks'.[83]

On 26 March 1924, the University Senate put the final seal on the affair of the Koraes Chair, after many further meetings and much correspondence. Toynbee was well and truly out, effective 30 June 1924, when his current term expired. Oddly enough, the following month, there was a rumour going around that Toynbee had accepted a position at the University of Constantinople, and he published another letter in the *Times* on 16 April 1924 admitting that although he had indeed been approached, he had no intention of accepting the offer at this time.[84]

Toynbee was out of a job, but as luck would have it, a new position had already loomed up over the horizon. On 16 January 1924 he had a note from his wartime boss J.W. Headlam-Morley, asking him to lunch. Toynbee was offered a temporary appointment at the British (after 1926, Royal) Institute of International Affairs at Chatham House, which had been founded by veterans of the Paris Peace Conference who still believed that if people knew more about international affairs, then perhaps another war might be prevented. Toynbee's job was to write book-length surveys of these international affairs, beginning with the end of the Great War, and then annually. Toynbee remained as Director of Studies at Chatham House until he retired thirty years later, and thus finally retrieved the academic prize that he had so carelessly thrown away during the First World War, a job for life.[85] Even better, he began to work there with Veronica Boulter

(1894–1980), who would become his second wife in 1946, after Rosalind Murray left him and they divorced.[86] As Toynbee put it nearly half a century later, in characteristic overblown prose, 'the *culpa*, at whatever door it may have lain, turned out, for me, to have been *felix*'.[87] Equally *felix* was his journalistic fact-finding tour to Turkey in 1921, which gave the world an ultimately unconvincing, but complex and strangely fascinating theory to explain the crash of civilizations, and helped to reorient British public opinion towards Turkey in its War of Independence.

NOTES

1. Toynbee appeared on the cover of *Time* on 17 Mar. 1947.
2. Generally, see William H. McNeill, *Arnold J. Toynbee: A Life* (New York & Oxford, 1989); and his 'Arnold Joseph Toynbee', *Proc. Brit. Acad.*, 63 (1977), 441–69.
3. To be perfectly accurate, Gilbert Murray was a tutor at New College at the time: he did not become Regius Professor until 1908, remaining at this post until his retirement in 1936.
4. Oddly enough, in light of later developments, Toynbee was twice arrested during his journey as a Turkish spy, on 16 Nov. 1911 (by the Italians) and on 21 July 1922 (by the Greeks). He tells the story in his *A Study of History* (London, 1934–1961), x. 31 and n.
5. According to the *Oxford English Dictionary*, the word 'dago' is supposedly a corruption of 'Diego', and is a 'name originally given in the south-western section of the United States to a man of Spanish parentage; now extended to include Spaniards, Portuguese, and Italians in general, or as a disparaging term for any foreigner.' The *OED* gives its first appearance as a generic term in 1832.
6. Toynbee to Gilbert Murray, 25 Oct. 1915; McNeill, *Toynbee*, p. 73. Toynbee's papers are still uncatalogued, and are temporarily stored in 136 boxes and 1 archival envelope at the Bodleian Library, Oxford. Boxes 50–58 contain material mostly about the Turkish War of Independence. Box 50 contains many photographs, mostly taken by Toynbee, including a wonderful picture of Arnold and Rosalind Toynbee at Constantinople in 1921. Some of letters are original, some have been typed from originals, and sometimes both originals and typescripts survive. Box 51 includes Toynbee's draft ideas on how to solve the Turkish problem, and journals by Arnold and Rosalind Toynbee, mostly typescript produced by a certain William Hunt, The

Oxford Copying Office (opp. Balliol), 18 Broad Street. Box 52 contains material about the atrocities and refugees, including Toynbee's autograph MS., 'Antecedents of the Smyrna Fire of the 13th September 1922'. Box 54 includes reviews and letters concerning Toynbee's book, *The Western Question*.

7. Toynbee paid tribute to Bryce in his *Acquaintances* (London, 1967), Chap. 11 (pp. 149–60), and in his *A Study of History*, x. 234.

8. Toynbee to Gilbert Murray, 21 Sept. 1916: McNeill, *Toynbee*, p. 73.

9. Later on, Toynbee's view of the Armenian question rather softened: 'These were bad marks against the Nationalist Government, even allowing for the fact that they were omissions to repair the ill-doing of their predecessors and not positive misdeeds of their own': Toynbee, *Western Question*, p. 191.

10. Arnold J. Toynbee, *Armenian Atrocities: The Murder of a Nation* (London, 1915), with a preface based on a speech by Lord Bryce delivered at the House of Lords, 6 Oct. 1915; Arnold J. Toynbee, *The Murderous Tyranny of the Turks* (London, 1917), with a preface by Lord Bryce.

11. Arnold J. Toynbee, *The Destruction of Poland. A Study in German Efficiency* (London, [1916]); idem, *The Belgian Deportations* (London, [1917]), with a statement by Lord Bryce; idem, *The German Terror in Belgium* (London, 1917); idem, *The German Terror in France* (London, 1917).

12. Toynbee was appointed on 7 May 1917. See generally Stuart Wallace, *War and the Image of Germany: British Academics 1914–1918* (Edinburgh, 1988).

13. Sir James Headlam-Morley, *A Memoir of the Paris Peace Conference, 1919* (London, 1972), pp. xx–xxi.

14. PRO, FO, PID, 371.4353 Peace Series, cited in McNeill, *Toynbee*, pp. 76–7.

15. Toynbee met other experts and scholars at the Paris Peace Conference, such as W.L. Westermann (1873–1954), head of the Turkish section of the US delegation; and Albert H. Lybyer (1876–1949), Toynbee's 'opposite number' on the American side: Toynbee, *Acquaintances*, pp. 198–207, 208; and idem, *A Study of History*, x.234.

16. PRO, Peace Conference, Smyrna Files, 1919. Doc. F. 6102, cited in McNeill, *Toynbee*, 81.

17. PRO, Peace Conference, Future Frontiers of Turkey, Delegation Minute, Doc. F. 7335, cited in McNeill, *Toynbee*, pp. 81–2.

18. Harold Nicolson, *Peacemaking 1919* (rev. edn, London, 1943): entries for 14 & 16 Apr. 1919. Toynbee has a few cryptic remarks about working for the government in his *A Study of History*, x. 227.

19. Toynbee gives an indication of why he resigned in his *A Study of History*, x. 21–2n.

20. Among the uncatalogued Toynbee Papers at the Bodleian Library, Oxford, Box 46 includes correspondence and papers relating to the Koraes Chair. The definitive account of this episode is Richard Clogg, *Politics and the Academy: Arnold Toynbee and the Koraes Chair* (London, 1986), orig. pub. as a special issue of *Middle Eastern Studies*, 21, no. 4 (1985). Further research on the subject was published as 'The "Ingenious Enthusiasm" of Dr. Burrows and the "Unsatiated Hatred" of Professor Toynbee', Chap. 3 of his *Anglo-Greek Attitudes* (Oxford: Macmillan, 2000), pp. 36–59, 173–5, repr. from the *Modern Greek Studies Yearbook*, 9 (1993), 75–98. See also Chap. 1, 'Anglo-Greek Attitudes: an Introduction', pp. 4–18, 166–71, including material in his 'Beware the Greeks', *Times Lit. Supp.*, 17 Mar. 2000; and Chap. 2, 'The British School at Athens and the Modern History of Greece', esp. pp. 21–6 regarding Toynbee. See also Roderick Beaton, 'Koraes, Toynbee and the Modern Greek Heritage', *Byzantine and Modern Greek Studies*, 15 (1991), 1–18; and Robert Irwin, 'Toynbee and Ibn Khaldun', *Middle Eastern Studies*, 33 (1997), 461–79.

21. For Toynbee's views on Spengler, see Arnold J. Toynbee, *Civilization on Trial* (London, 1946), pp. 9–10. Toynbee also spent the summer holiday of 1920 writing a commentary on the second chorus of *Antigone* by Sophocles, 'The Mystery of Man': Nihon Univ. Library, Tokyo: 'Unsuccessful attempt at starting A Study of History, done at Yatscombe, in the cottage, summer, 1920', 38 pp.: McNeill, *Toynbee*, p. 99.

22. Toynbee, *A Study of History*, x. 232.

23. Frederick J. Teggart's works include: 'The Circumstance or the Substance of History', *Amer. Hist. Rev.*, 15 (1910), 709–19; *Prolegomena to History: The Relations of History to Literature, Philosophy, and Science* (Berkeley, 1916); *The Processes of History* (New Haven, 1918); *Theory of History* (New Haven, 1925): latter two reissued as *Theory and Processes of History* (Berkeley & LA, 1941); and *Rome and China: A Study of Correlations in Historical Events* (Berkeley, 1939; repr. 1969).

24. When Toynbee actually started working on *A Study of History*, another important influence was the South African statesman Jan Christiaan Smuts (1870–1950), whose book *Holism and Evolution* (New York, 1926) had just appeared. Toynbee read the book in the early summer of 1927: 'I was excited and encouraged to find that the goal at which I was aiming had already been reached along a quite different mental road'. Toynbee had done some work for Smuts at the Paris Peace Conference in 1919 and had been greatly impressed: 'Smuts was like one of the characters in Plutarch's *Lives*.': Arnold Toynbee, *Experiences* (London, 1969), pp. 108–9; Toynbee, *Acquaintances*, p. 170 and generally, pp. 169–77; Toynbee, *A Study of History*, x. 234–5.

25. Arnold Toynbee, *Acquaintances* (London, 1967), p. 241. In fact, Toynbee wrote elsewhere, 'The Turkish revolution of 1908 interested me so much that it turned me into the regular reader of *The Times* that I still am today.': Arnold Toynbee, *Experiences* (London, 1969), p.107, from an essay entitled 'Janus at Seventy-Five', written on 14 Apr. 1964.

26. Toynbee had also been interested in the First Balkan War: 'I sympathized whole-heartedly with the peoples of Greece, Bulgaria, Serbia, and Montenegro when, in 1912, they made war on Turkey in order to put an end to Turkish rule over the Ottoman Empire's surviving dominions in South-Eastern Europe in which the majority of the population was non-Turkish and non-Muslim': Toynbee, *Experiences*, pp. 208–9.

27. Arnold J. Toynbee, *The Western Question in Greece and Turkey: A Study in the Contact of Civilisations* (2nd edn, Boston & NY, 1923), p. 77.

28. Ibid., pp. 77–8.

29. Ibid., pp. 271–2. Cf. p. 183: 'If the Greek landing at Smyrna created the Turkish National Movement, the British support of the Sultan at Constantinople made its fortune.' Toynbee repeatedly called for the publication of the classified 'Bristol Report' on the events of those days, made by a commission of senior officers from the Allies and Associated Governments, under Admiral Mark L. Bristol (1868–1939), US High Commissioner in Turkey (1919–1927): ibid., pp. 78–9.

30. Toynbee to R.W. Seton-Watson (1879–1951), 21 Sept. 1920: quoted in Clogg, *Politics*, p. 53.

31. University of London Senate Minutes, 1920, 255: quoted in ibid., p. 53.

32. Toynbee, *Acquaintances*, p.229.
33. McNeill, *Toynbee*, pp. 104–5. Toynbee was a terrible penny-pincher throughout his life, and during his sojourn for the *Guardian* he kept a careful record of each shilling he spent. Altogether the trip cost him £259 1 s. 10½d., which was £30 17 s. 4½d. *less* than he was paid: i.e., Toynbee made a profit: McNeill, *Toynbee*, p. 105. While in Constantinople with Rosalind, they stayed at the American College for Girls at Arnavutköy (now the campus of Robert College): Toynbee, *Acquaintances*, p. 233.
34. See his obituary in the *Bulletin of the School of Oriental and African Studies*, 11 (1946), 912.
35. Toynbee, *Acquaintances*, pp. 243–4. The story is also told in his *A Study of History*, x. 22n.
36. Toynbee to his mother, 2 Apr. 1921: Toynbee Papers, Bodleian Library, Oxford; McNeill, *Toynbee*, p. 105.
37. Arnold Toynbee, 'Two Ruined Cities', written at Smyrna, 21 Feb. 1921: repr. in his *Western Question*, pp. 148–52; 'A Journey Through the Mountains', written at Smyrna, 21 Feb. 1921: repr. ibid., pp. 196–201; 'An Agricultural Experiment', written at Smyrna, 21 Feb. 1921: repr. ibid., pp. 201–4.
38. Toynbee, *Western Question*, p. 162.
39. In the first journey he visited Alaşehir, Uşak, Kula, Salıhlı and Sart (Sardis); in the second he visited Efes (Ephesus), Kirkince, Aydın, Tire and Torbalı; in the third he visited Manısa, Soma, Kinik, Bergama (Pergamum), Ayvalık and Dikeli.
40. Toynbee, *A Study of History*, x. 138–9 [volume pub. in 1954]; idem, *Western Question*, p. 161.
41. Toynbee described these mystical experiences, with exact dates and with absurdly purple prose, in his *A Study of History*, x. 107–44. Indeed, the constant, incessant recording of the exact dates of his life, even as he writes the book the reader is reading, is one of Toynbee's most annoying self-indulgences. Toynbee defended these excesses to Ved Mehta, *Fly and the Fly-Bottle: Encounters with British Intellectuals* (Boston & Toronto, 1962), pp. 147–8.
42. Arnold Toynbee, 'The Battle of In Önü', written at Bursa, 5 Apr. 1921: repr. in his *Western Question*, pp. 246–54: this quotation from pp. 247–8. See also his article, 'The Origin of a Legend', written at Constantinople, 15 Apr. 1921, repr. ibid., pp. 254–8. He incorporated the same historical connection in his *A Study of History*: 'The battlefield

of In Önü, on which the decisive action of the Graeco-Turkish war of 1919–1922 was fought, lies in that original patrimony which the last of the Saljuqs had assigned to the first of the 'Osmanlis six hundred years before. The wheel had come full circle.': Arnold J. Toynbee, *A Study of History: Abridgement of Volumes I–VI*, ed. D.C. Somervell (London, 1946), p. 120: from Vol. II in the original.

43. Toynbee, *Acquaintances*, p. 229, and similarly Toynbee, *Western Question*, p. 234.
44. Toynbee, *Acquaintances*, p. 245.
45. Arnold Toynbee, 'Yalova', written at Constantinople, 1 June 1921: repr. in his *Western Question*, pp. 299–311. Rosalind Toynbee's letter was dated 28 May 1921. See also *Reports on Atrocities in the Districts of Yalova and Guemlik and in the Ismid Peninsula* (London: HMSO, 1921) = 1. Cmd. 1478 = Turkey No. 1 (1921); and *Revue Internationale de la Croix Rouge* (3ᵐᵉ Année, No. 31, 15 July 1921: Geneva, 1921), cited in Toynbee, *Western Question*, p. 259.
46. Toynbee, *Acquaintances*, pp. 229–30.
47. Ibid., p. 245.
48. Ibid., p. 245.
49. Toynbee, *Western Question*, pp. 282n, 287–8, 291.
50. Ibid., pp. 237–8.
51. His wife Rosalind left Turkey by sea the previous month, on 15 August 1921: ibid., p. xxix.
52. Arnold Toynbee, 'A Study of History: What the Book is For: How the Book took Shape', repr. *Toynbee and History: Critical Essays and Reviews*, ed. M.F. Ashley Montagu (Boston, 1956), pp. 8–11, esp. pp. 8–9, saying that it is from a 'Pamphlet written by Professor Toynbee upon the completion of the last four volumes of *A Study of History*, and issued by the Oxford University Press.'
53. McNeill, *Toynbee*, pp. 110–12, 305.
54. Among the uncatalogued Toynbee Papers at the Bodleian Library, Oxford, Box 54 includes reviews and letters concerning *The Western Question*.
55. '...in this connection Greece and Turkey represent respectively the Near Eastern and the Middle Eastern worlds.': Toynbee, *Western Question*, p. 27.
56. Ibid., pp. 1, 5, 12, 15–17, 36.
57. Readers will also find the essence of what historian Elie Kedourie called 'The Chatham House Version', in his *The Chatham House Version and*

other Middle-Eastern Studies (London, 1970), pp. 351–94, 457–62 (Chap. 12 and notes), the idea that it was the introduction of Western nationalism to the Middle East that infected and destroyed local societies. Toynbee was Director of Studies at the Royal Institute of International Affairs (Chatham House) from 1924 to his retirement in 1955: 'During thirty years he was the dominant intellectual influence at Chatham House, and the Chatham House Version is very much his handiwork.' (p. 353). Although virulently critical of this version, Kedourie did describe Toynbee's *The Western Question* as 'substantial', 'perhaps the best book he has ever written': 'The book admirably shows Toynbee's virtues as a historian: the breadth of his learning, the fecundity of his imagination, his ability to connect the political, the economic, the social and the spiritual, and his topographical eye.' (pp. 356, 366).

58. Toynbee, *Western Question*, pp. 108, 111–13, 128, 148.
59. Ibid., p. 50.
60. Ibid., p. 326.
61. Ibid., p. 327.
62. Ibid., pp. 327–8. One is almost tempted to see Toynbee as a precursor of Derrida and deconstructionism, with his emphasis on false antitheses.
63. Ibid., p. 331.
64. Toynbee's BBC Reith Lectures (1952), including 2nd lecture, 'Islam and the West' were published as *The World and the West* (New York & London, 1953), and in Turkish as *Dünya, Batı ve İslam* (Istanbul, 2002). It was here that he developed most clearly his familiar theme of Western aggression and degradation, and laid out the unjustices inflicted on the Arabs. Of course, the corollary of Toynbee's pro-Islamic and pro-Arab views was a consistent hostility to Judaism, Zionism and to the State of Israel, which caused him not a small amount of controversy during his lifetime. He argued that the source of Western arrogance was the Judaic notion of a 'chosen people', and that Judaism itself is a 'fossil'. In the uncatalogued Toynbee papers is a letter he wrote on 9 October 1973 to Syrian Major-General Moustapha Tlass, in which he says, 'I send you my heartfelt wishes for an Arab victory'; McNeill, *Toynbee*, p. 248.
65. Toynbee, *Western Question*, p. 332–4.
66. Ibid., pp. 345, 353.
67. See, for example, the attack on Toynbee by [George] Georgios Mélas, *The Turk as He is. Answer to a Libel. Sidelights on Kemalism, Bolshevism*

and Pan-Germanism (London, [1922]). Cf. idem, Ex-King Constantine and the War (London, [1920]).

68. Toynbee, Acquaintances, pp. 247-9.

69. Ibid., pp. 184-5; cf. p. 239. See also Andrew Mango, Atatürk (London, 1999), pp. 337-8 for Fethi's visit, although without mention of Toynbee; and Fethi Okyar, Üç Devirde Bir Adam, ed. Cemal Kutay (Istanbul, 1980), pp. 308-9.

70. Toynbee, Western Question, p. xxxi.

71. Clogg, Politics, p. 57. Toynbee: 'One practical guarantee is created by the fact that, wherever the lines of demarcation between the national states of the Near and Middle East may finally be drawn, the respective hostages in the hands of each state will be comparable in number.': Toynbee, Western Question, p. 323 and similarly on next page as well.

72. Clogg, Politics, p. 60.

73. Ibid., p. 60.

74. Ibid., p. 68.

75. Toynbee to Rosalind Toynbee, 13 April 1923; McNeill, Toynbee, p. 117.

76. Toynbee, Acquaintances, p.249. Oddly enough, even before meeting him, Toynbee in 1922 felt compelled to note that "In regard to Mustafa Kemal Pasha, I have therefore only to say that he is not a Jew': Toynbee, Western Question, p. 178. Toynbee greatly admired Atatürk, referring to him even years later as 'a great man': Toynbee, Experiences, p. 73; cf. idem, Acquaintances, pp. 181, 235, 237-8.

77. Toynbee to Rosalind Toynbee, 13 April 1923; McNeill, Toynbee, p. 117.

78. Clogg, Politics, p. 75.

79. Toynbee's letter of 3 January 1924, including Barker's to Toynbee (26 Dec. 1923) repr. Clogg, Politics, pp. 116-17.

80. Toynbee's pro-Turkish sympathies became very widely known, especially after the letter to the Times was published. When E.M. Forster (1879-1970) foolishly involved Toynbee in a plan to translate into English the works of the Egyptian-Greek poet Constantine Cavafy (1863-1933), the project went cold: Peter Jeffreys, 'Cavafy, Forster, and the Eastern Question', Jnl of Mod. Greek Studies, 19 (2001), 61-87. For Forster's somewhat pro-Turkish views, see David Roessel, 'Live Orientals and Dead Greeks: Forster's Response to the Chanak Crisis', Twentieth Cent. Lit., 36 (1990), 43-60.

81. Clogg, *Politics*, pp. 84–5.

82. Ibid., p. 76.

83. Ibid., p. 91. Nevertheless, Toynbee paid a little tribute to Seton-Watson in his *A Study of History*, x. 225.

84. In Toynbee's papers, however, there is a draft letter to Youssouf Kemal, the Turkish minister in London, in which Toynbee offers his services as a lecturer at the University of Constantinople between May 1925 and the end of March 1926. Toynbee suggested a salary of £1200 tax free, plus travelling expences, which was twice as much as he made as Koraes Professor: Clogg, *Politics*, p. 102. For more on the Turkish reaction to the issue, see Cem Cakmak, 'Arnold Toynbee ve bir kürsünün hikayesi', *Mülkiyeliler Birliği Dergisi*, 116 (Feb. 1990), 19–23.

85. In fact, he would stay on the books at the University of London. While on his first visit to the United States in the summer of 1925, a Glasgow coal magnate named Sir Daniel Stevenson agreed to fund another chair for Toynbee at the University of London, on the understanding that he would divide his time between teaching international relations and working at Chatham House. He gave his inaugural lecture in 1926, but Toynbee never liked teaching, so in December 1928, his title at the University of London was changed to 'Research Professor', at a reduced salary, with most of the difference being made up by Chatham House: McNeill, *Toynbee*, pp. 128, 130–2.

86. Veronica Boulter Toynbee, *The Gentle Giant's Lady and Her Friend: Selected Letters of Veronica Boulter Toynbee, 1964–1980*, ed. Lois Wiegardt Whitaker (Dubuque, Iowa, 1997).

87. Toynbee, *Experiences*, p. 72; cf. p. 111. Toynbee's later calm and philosophical attitude towards the Koraes affair as 'ancient history' was oft-repeated.

CHAPTER 7

Conclusion: Turkey-in-Europe, Turkey-in-Asia, Turkey-in-Britain

'The cross descends, thy minarets arise' were the words that came to mind as Lord Byron recalled the moment when he first set foot in the Ottoman Empire. The contrasts are stark in this line from *Childe Harold's Pilgrimage*: cross *versus* minarets; descends *versus* arise, and behind it all, West *versus* East. His words were meant to evoke shivers of anxiety and fear as the poem's hero enters the territory of the archetypical Islamic Other. In fact, however, Childe Harold (like his creator) first penetrated the Ottoman Empire at Greece, and adding to the confusion, in the lands known at the time as Albania.

Byron, like Disraeli and Toynbee and many of their contemporaries, came to know and value Turkey after having been disappointed with Greece. They were the victims of 'reading blindness', a temporary condition that hindered them for a short time from seeing the images before their eyes. Educated English men and women set forth on their journeys with a horizon of expectations created by their reading. They were ready to find in Greece the familiar well-spring of their own European civilization and were shocked to discover that Greece was the East. Not only were modern Greeks unexpectedly distinct from the heroes of the classical world, but their landscape was thick with mosques and Muslims.

Four of the five writers whose lives and work have been discussed here actually travelled on to Istanbul and were entranced by a culture that was not only distinctly alien but was also perceived as authentic. The 'textual universe' in which Edward Said's Orient existed was so fragile for these

© The Author(s) 2016
D.S. Katz, *The Shaping of Turkey in the British Imagination, 1776–1923*,
DOI 10.1007/978-3-319-41060-9_7

men that it evaporated almost on contact. As each new writer came onto the stage, he inevitably built on the foundations laid by his predecessors, to the extent that it was almost as if they had all lived at the same time.

The first writer, Edward Gibbon, had few illusions about Greeks and none about their Byzantine successors, but was full of admiration for the 'rise and progress of the Ottomans'. Gibbon was read in Victorian England by those with a general education, and if his attacks on Christianity rendered him unsatisfactory for many a pious reader, his scholarship was undeniably deep and his writing was exceedingly brilliant. Even the hopelessly devout Cardinal Newman (1801–1890) had to admit that it 'is melancholy to say it, but the chief, perhaps the only English writer who has any claim to be considered an ecclesiastical historian, is the infidel Gibbon'.[1] The entire second half of Gibbon's great six-volume work gives a picture of the genesis, growth and genius of the Ottoman Empire that, even today after nearly two and a half centuries, remains compelling and still historically accurate in many of its interpretations and narrative details.

If Gibbon provided a universal scholarly foundation upon which every 'informed or at-home' English reader based his or her perception of Turkey and the Ottoman Empire, then Lord Byron added a more emotional response that quickened the hearts of thousands more. Byron became the symbol of the struggle of some Greeks to create an independent Orthodox polity, but this was a role not of his choosing. The Greeks he admired were Albanians, and in his writings he portrayed with respect and even love the culture and ambience of the Turkish empire. Byron's work was produced by the publishing firm of John Murray, which also put out guidebooks and eventually pocket editions of Byron's poetry that could be carried around while visiting the places described. Indeed, much of Byron's poetry came with footnotes, being a travel narrative as well as a lyric. The romance of the East that was Byron's legacy was as much about Turkey as Greece. Even readers who thought that Orthodox Christians who spoke Greek ought to be given their own state could not fail to be entranced by Byron's Turkish tale of a complex and exotic culture built on the ruins of Byzantium.

Benjamin Disraeli knew his Gibbon and his Byron, and his youthful Grand Tour largely followed Byron's route to Istanbul and included a man who had actually served the great poet. One thinks of Disraeli primarily as a politician, but he spent decades in the political wilderness, the years of his prime between the ages of forty-seven and sixty-nine. Throughout most of his life, and especially during those years, Disraeli was primarily a novelist, and he drew heavily on his Grand Tour and his Turkish experience. His visit to the East gave him the inspiration for his own remaking from being a baptized Jew barely tolerated by Anglican society towards a new heroic image as an aristocratic gentleman of the Middle East whose glorious heritage and breeding were superior even to that of the British nobles who snubbed him. Disraeli supported the integrity of the Ottoman Empire throughout his political career, and in this he was continuing traditional British foreign policy according to which the Turks served as a buffer between Russia and the West. As it happened, hostility to Disraeli had the effect of damaging British support for the Ottoman Empire itself. Disraeli's constant harping on the virtues of Jews, Arabs, Turks and everyone he conceived of as somehow Semitic or Eastern, in his novels and in his parliamentary speeches and political writings, presented an easy target for Gladstone and the Liberals, especially after the Bulgarian massacres of 1876. Nevertheless, his enormously popular novels presented Turkey in a very attractive light and, like Gibbon and Byron, Disraeli helped create a perception of the Ottoman Empire to counterbalance the effects of the shift in British foreign policy against the Turks that followed on Gladstone's resumption of power in April 1880.

The gradual enfolding of the Ottoman Empire into Germany's embrace was the result of Britain's turning her back on an old ally. When Turkey joined with the Germans in the First World War, many people thought that Gladstone had been right all along. But Germany was the villain of the piece, and in the war of propaganda, the standing order is to keep things simple. John Buchan, author of the celebrated thriller *The Thirty-Nine Steps* (1915) and serving as an officer in the Intelligence Corps, was keenly aware of the power of subtle persuasion. The sequel, *Greenmantle* (1916), novelized the recent Russian conquest of Erzurum in the middle of February 1916, when the combined German and Turkish force lost that fortified town. Buchan's image of the Turks retained an Orientalist quality, but the blame for having backed the wrong side in the Great War was placed squarely on Germany, portrayed as wickedly exploiting devout belief in Islam. *Greenmantle* was simultaneously mobilized popular history, pulp non-fiction, and a good read, a best-seller, which helped set public opinion. In Buchan's narrative, the Turks were not England's mortal enemies, but a religious people who had succumbed to German trickery, in part out of desperation after having been abandoned by the British who had been their supporters for so many years.

Arnold Toynbee worked in British propaganda as well, writing texts that were designed to put the Germans in the worst possible light, but in a more devious fashion. His wartime brief was to show the Turks as so ferocious that even the bloodthirsty Germans should have been ashamed of their alliance. The chief product of his labour was the report on the Armenian massacres, published under the name of Lord Bryce. After the war, Toynbee sought a more complex understanding of the problematic relations between Turkey and its minorities, part of his motivation for going out there in 1921 to cover the Turkish War of Independence. This was the basis of a life-long admiration for Turkey and its people, a stance which soon cost him his university post. It was also, however, the inspiration for his monumental twelve-volume *A Study of History* (1934–1961), which temporarily made his reputation as a world-class historian.

There were certainly many other writers in Britain who published about the Ottoman Empire and Turkey in the long nineteenth century. Even forgotten authors had an influence over decision makers whose opinions had a tangible effect on British foreign policy towards the Ottoman Empire as well as on actual events in Turkey during this period. But the five writers discussed in the chapters of this book were universal figures whose impact had a huge spread and rippled through contemporary cultural life. For anyone who was even mildly 'at home' with books, these five men lived cumulatively and simultaneously in the minds of their readers as the century moved on. There was a kind of a sedimentary effect at work, as each writer's books were added to the pile of volumes one might be expected to have read. Toynbee read Gibbon, and Disraeli knew his Byron. The attitude towards Turkey that is the almost inevitable result of reading these books is curious, respectful and generally positive.

At the end of this rather bright horizon of expectations sits an important political fact. On 29 October 1923, the Turkish Republic was established under the leadership of Mustafa Kemal (Atatürk). Perhaps the most important antecedent to this momentous event was the decision of the Allies, led by the British, to allow the Greeks to land their forces on the west coast of Turkey in 1919 in an ill-advised and doomed attempt to recapture some of the imagined glories of the Byzantine Empire which had been encircled and finally destroyed by the Turks almost five centuries earlier. Mustafa Kemal's victory over the Greeks sealed both the creation of the Turkish Republic and his own place in its history. British attitudes and prejudices regarding Turkey had a direct relevance to that moment in October 1923. An educated English observer on that date, reading in a newspaper about the metamorphosis of the Ottoman Empire into the Turkish Republic, might have marshalled what he or she knew about Turkey, remembered from things by Gibbon, Byron and Disraeli, from Buchan's novels and Toynbee's newspaper articles. These men furnished the minds of English readers with images of Turkey that compelled fascination and bolstered an attitude which kept Turkey-in-Europe without abandoning Turkey-in-Asia, the most Western part of the East, unmistakably the most Eastern country in the West.

NOTE

1. John Henry Newman, *An Essay on the Development of Christian Doctrine* (London, 1845), p. 5.

SUGGESTIONS FOR FURTHER READING

This work is called an 'essay' in the strictest sense of the word. The author is well aware of the limited means and powers with which he undertook so arduous a task; and even if he could view his research with greater confidence, he would not feel any more assured of the approval of the experts. To each eye the outlines of a given civilization probably present a different picture—the individual judgement and feeling of both writer and reader must come into play at every moment. On the vast ocean upon which we venture, the possible ways and directions are many; and the same studies that have served for this work might easily, in other hands, not only receive a wholly different treatment and interpretation, but might also lead to essentially different conclusions.

With these words, the great Jacob Burckhardt (1818–1897) began his 'essay' on *The Civilization of the Renaissance in Italy*, first published in 1860. In that spirit, what follows is a somewhat idiosyncratic list of the sources that I found most useful in writing this book. It is a supplement to the materials cited in the chapter footnotes, which have been severely truncated to meet limitations of space. In any case, the history of ideas covers such a large amount of ground that there is no substitute for reading primary sources and waiting until a pattern emerges that seems to make order among the chaos.

© The Author(s) 2016
D.S. Katz, *The Shaping of Turkey in the British Imagination, 1776–1923*,
DOI 10.1007/978-3-319-41060-9

GENERAL

Although this book is not a history of the nineteenth-century Ottoman Empire and its relations with the European powers, this is necessary background to recreating the mental world of the writers discussed here. There is an ever-growing mass of exciting work in both Turkish and European languages about this period, as new scholars face the arduous linguistic and paleographic challenge of joining the family of Ottoman historians. We read their work with admiration, beginning with the *Cambridge History of Turkey*, eds. Suraiya N. Faroqhi, Kate Fleet and Reşat Kasaba (Cambridge, 2006–13). These four volumes are a portal to detailed studies of the entire period, with articles by many of the key scholars in the field, culminating in comprehensive bibliographies that obviate the need to repeat those titles here.

CHAPTER 2. EDWARD GIBBON'S EASTERN QUESTION
(1776–1788)

Gibbon appears in a number of different editions, many of which truncate the entire second part of his work which is the subject of this chapter. The Penguin edition is mostly used nowadays: *The History of the Decline and Fall of the Roman Empire*, ed. David Womersley (London, 1994), although the various Everyman versions are still cited. The most monumental study of Gibbon in our time is J.G.A. Pocock, *Barbarism and Religion* (Cambridge, 1999–2015), in six volumes, although Pocock declined to write very much 'about the *Decline and Fall*'s second trilogy', saying (vi. 8) that 'I see myself as leaving this narrative to others; how they will see the later *Decline and Fall* is for them (if any there are) to tell their readers.' David Womersley, *Gibbon and the 'Watchmen of the Holy City'* (Oxford, 2002) is an important source. As always, and not only because of the Gibbonian style, one reads with profit Hugh Trevor-Roper, 'Dimitrie Cantemir's *Ottoman History* and its Reception in England', *Revue roumaine d'histoire*, 24 (1985), 51–66: repr. in his *History and the Enlightenment* (New Haven, 2010), Chap. 4 (pp. 54–70, 284–6). *Edward Gibbon and Empire*, ed. Rosamond McKitterick and Roland Quinault (Cambridge, 1997) has a number of interesting articles. Still useful are the pioneering works by Bernard Lewis, *The Emergence of Modern Turkey* (3rd edn, Oxford, 2002) [1st pub. 1961], and by M.S. Anderson, *The Eastern Question 1774–1923* (London, 1966). Generally, see *The Cambridge*

History of the Byzantine Empire c.500-1492, ed. Jonathan Shepard (Cambridge, 2008).

CHAPTER 3. LORD BYRON, TURKOPHILE, AND HIS GRAND TOUR TO THE EAST (1809–1811)

The best place to start is with Byron's own writings: *Lord Byron: The Complete Poetical Works,* ed. Jerome J. McGann and Barry Weller (Oxford, 1980–93); Byron, *Letters and Journals,* ed. Leslie A. Marchand (London, 1973–94); J.C. Hobhouse, *A Journey through Albania, and other Provinces of Turkey in Europe and Asia, to Constantinople, during the years 1809 and 1810* (Philadelphia, 1817), 2 vols: 1st edn (London, 1813). Generally, there is *The Cambridge Companion to Byron,* ed. Drummond Bone (Cambridge, 2004). Specifically on Tepedelenli Ali Paşa, see K.E. Fleming, *The Muslim Bonaparte: Diplomacy and Orientalism in Ali Pasha's Greece* (Princeton, 1999). There is a good deal to be read about the English and the Greek struggle for independence. Still useful is William St Clair, *That Greece Might Still Be Free: the Philhellenes in the War of Independence* (London, 1972); and C.M. Woodhouse, *The Philhellenes* (London, 1969). See now Roderick Beaton, *Byron's War: Romantic Rebellion, Greek Revolution* (Cambridge, 2013). Additional sources might include Suzanne L. Marchand, *Down From Olympus: Archaeology and Philhellenism in Germany, 1750–1970* (Princeton, 1996); Stathis Gourgouris, *Dream Nation: Enlightenment, Colonization, and the Institution of Modern Greece* (Stanford, 1996); T.J.W. Spencer, *Fair Greece, Sad Relic: Literary Philhellenism from Shakespeare to Byron* (London, 1954); idem, *Byron and the Greek Tradition* (Nottingham, 1960); and Fani-Maria Tsigakou, *The Rediscovery of Greece: Travellers and Painters of the Romantic Era* (London, 1981).

CHAPTER 4. DISRAELI'S EASTERN CAREER, 1830–1880

The place to begin, of course, is with Disraeli's *Letters,* ed. J.A.W. Gunn et al. (Toronto, 1982–), followed by his novels, beginning with *Contarini Fleming: A Psychological Auto-Biography* (London, 1832) and *Tancred, or, the New Crusade* (London, 1847), without neglecting *Lothair* (London, 1870), which is almost (but not quite) a page-turner. The best biography is still Robert Blake, *Disraeli* (London, 1966), followed by his *Disraeli's Grand Tour: Benjamin Disraeli and the Holy Land, 1830–1831* (Oxford,

1982). Also useful is *The Self-Fashioning of Disraeli 1818–1851*, ed. Charles Richmond and Paul Smith (Cambridge, 1998). For the diplomatic and political events relevant to Disraeli's attitude to the East, all of the following books are very important: R.W. Seton-Watson, *Disraeli, Gladstone and the Eastern Question: A Study in Diplomacy and Party Politics* (London, 1935); M.S. Anderson, *The Eastern Question 1774–1923: A Study in International Relations* (London, 1966); Richard Millman, *Britain and the Eastern Question 1875–1878* (Oxford, 1979). Specifically on the Bulgarian crisis, begin with the polemical W.E. Gladstone, *Bulgarian Horrors and the Question of the East* (London, 1876), followed by R.T. Shannon, *Gladstone and the Bulgarian Agitation 1876* (London, 1963). Other useful books include Barbara Jelavich, *The Ottoman Empire, the Great Powers, and the Straits Question 1870–1887* (Bloomington, 1973) and Robert Holland and Diana Markides, *The British and the Hellenes: Struggles for Mastery in the Eastern Mediterranean, 1850–1960* (Oxford, 2006). Fascinating in its own way is also Stanley Lane Poole, *Life of … Stratford Canning Viscount Stratford de Redcliffe* (London, 1888).

Chapter 5. Greenmantle at the Ministry of Information: John Buchan, the First World War and the Turks

John Buchan published an autobiography entitled *Memory Hold-The-Door* (London, 1940), which also appeared under the title *Pilgrim's Way*. The classic biography is Janet Adam Smith, *John Buchan* (Oxford, 1985), [1st pub. 1965]. See also her *John Buchan and his World* (New York, 1979); and Andrew Lownie, *John Buchan: The Presbyterian Cavalier* (London, 1995). For the context of Buchan's war work, see M.L. Sanders and Philip M. Taylor, *British Propaganda During the First World War, 1914–1918* (London, 1982); Peter Buitenhuis, *The Great War of Words: British, American, and Canadian Propaganda and Fiction, 1914–1933* (Vancouver, 1987), and Gary S. Messinger, *British Propaganda and the State in the First World War* (Manchester, 1992). There is also the pioneering book by James Duane Squires, *British Propaganda at Home and in the United States from 1914 to 1917* (Cambridge, USA, 1935). Important articles include: M.L. Sanders, 'Wellington House and British Propaganda During the First World War', *Historical Journal*, 18 (1975), 119–46; and Ş. Tufan Buzpınar, 'Opposition to the Ottoman Caliphate in the Early Years of Abdülhamid II: 1877–1882', *Die Welt des Islams,* 36 (1996), 59–89. Inevitable is also Gertrude Himmelfarb, 'John Buchan: The Last Victorian', *Encounter* (Sept. 1960), reprinted in her *Victorian Minds* (New York, 1968), Chap. 9. There has been a huge amount of new work in the anniversary period of the First World War, and more is to come, the latest being Eugene Rogan, *The Fall of the Ottomans: The Great War in the Middle East* (London, 2015).

CHAPTER 6. ARNOLD TOYNBEE ON THE QUAY AT SMYRNA, 1921–1922

The unsurpassed biography is by William H. McNeill, *Arnold J. Toynbee: A Life* (New York and Oxford, 1989); and his earlier 'Arnold Joseph Toynbee', *Proc. Brit. Acad.,* 63 (1977), 441–69. Toynbee himself produced several collections of essays which include a good deal of autobiographical material: *Acquaintances* (London, 1967); and *Experiences* (London, 1969). His most important book for us here is his under-rated study of *The Western Question in Greece and Turkey: A Study in the Contact of Civilisations* (2nd edn, Boston and New York, 1923). Toynbee's BBC Reith Lectures (1952), including 'Islam and the West', were published as *The World and the West* (New York and London, 1953). For the immediate results of his growing Ottomania, see the comprehensive study by Richard Clogg, *Politics and the Academy: Arnold Toynbee and the Koraes Chair* (London, 1986), originally published as a special issue of *Middle Eastern Studies,* 21, no. 4 (1985). For more personal reflections, see the interview with Toynbee in Ved Mehta, *Fly and the Fly-Bottle: Encounters with British Intellectuals* (Boston and Toronto, 1962), and also the book by his second wife, Veronica Boulter Toynbee, *The Gentle Giant's Lady and Her Friend,* ed. Lois Wiegardt Whitaker (Dubuque, Iowa, 1997). A useful collection of essays is *Toynbee and History: Critical Essays and Reviews,* ed. M.F. Ashley Montagu (Boston, 1956). Toynbee's world view was strongly attacked by Elie Kedourie, *The Chatham House Version and other Middle-Eastern Studies* (London, 1970). Work on the Armenian issue has gathered pace in recent years, including Toynbee's role in producing documentation, and will no doubt be continuing. Last, and least, is Arnold Joseph Toynbee, *A Study of History* (London, 1934–61), 12 vols, which is filled with irrelevant autobiographical asides, culminating in two bizarre sections, 'The Inspirations of Historians' (x. 130–44); and

'Acknowledgements and Thanks' (x. 213–42). For a fierce demolition of Toynbee's work, see the article by my teacher Hugh Trevor-Roper, 'Arnold Toynbee's Millennium', in his *Men and Events* (New York, 1958), Chap. 43, which originally appeared in *Encounter* (June 1957).

AND FINALLY...

When writing about British history, a most important source is the *Dictionary of National Biography*, originally a great Victorian printed monument, and now a continuously updated computerized website. While the internet version is more up to date, it lacks the humour and the wit of the original, which should also be consulted for its hidden minor treasures.

INDEX

© The Author(s) 2016
D.S. Katz, *The Shaping of Turkey in the British Imagination, 1776–1923*,
DOI 10.1007/978-3-319-41060-9

first English Lord to convert to, 163
future of, according to Blunt, 218
Germany's exploitation of, 269
history of, 13
identified by Toynbee as challenge
to British Empire, 237
Ockley's sympathetic view of, 13
prospect of being taught at
Oxford, 24
Sale's fascination with, 15
scholarly work on, 14
Toynbee's account of its encounter
with West, 249
Toynbee's vocal support, 251
Ismail Paşa (1830–95), 217
İsmet [İnönü] Paşa (1884–1973),
resists Greek troops in Turkey, 243
Istanbul
Ali Paşa's head sent to, 107
Allied occupation of, 1918–22, 233
Antoine Galland in, 14
bombarded by British, 1807, 67
British fleet and Russian troops
position themselves around
(February 1878), 172, 174–7
Buchan on, 203, 204
Byron and Hobhouse arrive at, 86,
88
Disraeli arrives at, 137, 138
Great Power ships close to, 1876,
152
to host international conference on
Turkey and the Eastern
Question, 1876, 164, 165
independent city under League of
Nations deemed impractical, 238
and leaves, 91, 140, 244, 246, 247
meets Red Crescent representative,
244, 246
mistaken European view of, 92
Ottoman treaty to establish
Septinsular Republic, 66
refuge for Muslims in Russian-
Turkish War, 1878, 173

Russian right to put up a church
there, 18
and tours, 89, 139
Toynbee visits, 1921, 233, 243
Istanbul Conference, 1876
request for Jewish equality in Serbia
and Rumania by Moses
Montefiore, 166
Turkish intransigence, 167

J

Janissaries, 33
eliminated by Sultan Mahmud II in
1826, 33, 111
Gibbon's admiration for, 39
as translator for Byron, 88
Jauss, Hans Robert (1921–97), 3
Jerusalem
Disraeli visits, 142
Selçuk rule in, 1076–1096, 27
Jews. *See also* antisemitism
in America supposedly affecting
foreign policy, 235
Bar Hebraeus possibly a, 52n22
casual antipathy towards them
socially acceptable before
WWII, 222
compared to Greeks by Byron, 97,
113
compared to Greeks by Disraeli, 148
conducts puppet show at Ionnina,
viewed by Byron, 78
Disraeli as baptized one, tolerated
by Anglican society, 269
for Disraeli, only medium of God in
the world, 148
Disraeli's superior race, 146
as irrevocably foreign, 176, 177
in Istanbul, according to
Hobhouse, 89
refuted by George Eliot, 147
representing Britain at Berlin
Congress, 178